D1535086

Power
and
Process

The Formulation and Limits
of Federal Educational Policy

Harry L. Summerfield

McCutchan Publishing Corporation
2526 Grove Street
Berkeley, California 94704

This work was developed under a grant from the U.S. Office
of Education, Department of Health, Education, and Welfare.
However, the opinions and other content do not necessarily
reflect the position or policy of the Agency, and no
official endorsement should be inferred.

This truth is a matter of context, and if we place ourselves outside it—as the man of science must do—what appeared as an experienced truth first becomes confused and finally disappears altogether.
—Claude Lévi-Strauss
from *The Savage Mind*

Contents

Note to the Reader

This book is a statement of the formulation and limits of federal educational policy. Part I by Harry L. Summerfield is a descriptive analysis of the structure and dynamics of the federal policy process for educational decision-making in the lobbies, the Congress, and the administration. The substantive material in chapters 2-4 is followed in chapter 5 by a more general conceptualization and theoretical perspective of the operations of the policy process. Chapter 6 concludes Part I by assessing the limits of the use of the federal policy process for making American education policy. Part II, entitled "Supplementary Essays," highlights three major aspects of the policy process that are not treated fully in Part I. In the first essay John McDermott examines the role of the federal judiciary in education policy-making. Everyone knows that the courts have played a major role in education policy matters, but, because of the concept of separation of powers, affairs of the court—the methods as well as the limits—proceed quite differently from the administrative or legislative process. In the spirit of chapter 6, but in the context of the court, McDermott offers arguments why the federal judiciary is limited in its education policy role. The second essay by James W. Guthrie examines the economics behind the appropriations process and the means by which federal dollars are annually allocated to education provisions that have been authorized by law. The reader should understand that the authorization of laws is separate from the annual appropriation of dollars for authorized programs. The appropriations process takes place separately and is a subject in itself. Finally, Jack H. Schuster provides a unique examination of the relation of electoral politics to the legislative life of Representative John Brademas, a congressman who has built a career on education affairs.

Guthrie, McDermott, and Schuster each produced their work independently of me and of each other. I am grateful to them for filling in my research and knowledge gaps. Each of them would disagree with some of my conclusions, and vice versa, but not with the goal of elucidating the structure and dynamics of federal involvement in education. Thus, it only remains for me to acquit them of any responsibility for the content and interpretations of Part I and particularly chapter 6. Their willingness to contribute essays where my own work was incomplete testifies to their generosity and tolerance, not their agreement or disagreement.

My autobiographical recollections of the evolution of this book go back to St. Paul, Minnesota. In spring 1969, I finished my doctoral work at the University of Minnesota and discovered that, far from having achieved an end, I had ended a beginning. The world appeared to be a great open corridor with innumerable closed doors. It seemed that my education would be greatly enhanced by looking behind the doors to compare the myths of men of power and the elusive operations of institutions with my personal view of their reality. It was one good reason to go to Washington.

Another reason had to do with an orientation developed from my political science background, which made power seem to be the organizing principle of society. And, like many people who came to political maturity at the time of John Kennedy, I believed that the federal level of government harbored the most important potentials for improving America, and specifically American education. The myth structure of liberalism vested federal decisions, federal decision-makers, and federal power with more importance than the vast, apparently diluted spread of state and local governments.

My belief was not held unequivocally, however. In 1968, while still a student, I lived in St. Paul, in the congressional district that launched Eugene McCarthy to Congress. The drama of unseating Lyndon Johnson that year was particularly magnified in our district (and, indeed, our neighborhood) because McCarthy soon directly challenged Minnesota's illustrious presidential candidate, Vice-President Hubert Humphrey (McCarthy had a complete triumph). Two branches from the same root of midwestern liberalism clashed in their, and my, native soil. McCarthy's vision of the presidency posed deep opposition to the executive and war powers of Lyndon Johnson. McCarthy's viewpoint tempered the ambition to help people—at home and abroad—with restraint based on the distrust of the arrogance that can accompany power. He believed in the system—and that one could be witty rather than mean toward it—but he was skeptical of power. He confronted Humphrey's less circumspect optimism about the humane potentials for the use of federal power. Between McCarthy and Humphrey I experienced one of the oldest American dilemmas, foreshadowed in the debates of Jefferson and Hamilton. I embraced McCarthy, but still believed that federal power held deep mysteries and potentials, and, indeed, that power was mysterious *because* of its potential. Not until the near completion of this book did I realize clearly that power is not the primary unifying force of society unless the society is in a state of collapse. In a viable society, culture, the collective and often unconscious myths, symbols, and structured relations, can be aided by power but not substituted or dominated by it. In retrospect, I went to Washington and wrote this book to discover not only how the government worked— and if it worked—but also when and where its power should be used, particularly in regard to education. Chapter 6 elaborates my conclusions.

To get inside Washington, one needs the right kind of job, and in the spring of 1969 I had no idea how to get one. My story about job procurement may help some reader who lacks established connections. One day, while I was sitting in my kitchen in St. Paul, my landlady walked in. (Her father, a clear-eyed and quick-minded man who I think was in his nineties, was the only man I ever met who had the complete works of Herbert Hoover on his shelf.) I told her of my desire to go to Washington, but that the only person I knew about who was remotely connected with education was a southern

Minnesota Republican congressman, Albert Quie. Her eyes lit. "Oh, Al. Al is a wonderful man." I learned a lot about him in the effusive minutes that followed, and Betty, with her natural generosity, went to phone her cousin in southern Minnesota who had been a campaign director. His one-paragraph introductory letter plus the name of an education lobbyist supplied by a political science professor launched me off to Washington in a Volkswagen, with a *Washington on $5 a Day* hotel name, a new suit, shoes, shirt, and naive confidence.

Mr. Quie welcomed me into his office. He eased my tensions, but knew of no jobs. He gave me an important resource, however—the use of his name as an entré to several places. One man he sent me to was the chairman of the Education and Labor Committee, Carl Perkins.

In his big office, taking all comers that morning, Mr. Perkins sat in his leather chair, a characteristic fixed but gentle smile on his face. Four men stood quietly against the wall. At first I resented the lack of privacy, but shortly got my first lesson in Capitol Hill life—the boss needs and uses his staff. The chairman leaned back in his chair and said in his Kentucky drawl, "You come for money? How much do you want?" Everyone laughed. Demurring, I tried to explain my goal. Looking to the wall and the four men, the chairman took an interest and said how much he would like to help Mr. Quie—and, by proxy, me—and one of his aides sprang off the wall saying that he knew how he might help me.

I was ushered out and guided to the office of Congressman John Brademas and introduced to his administrative assistant, Jack Schuster. "The chairman" had sent me, said my escort. Jack took time to find out my interests and qualifications and, after a forty-five-minute talk, discovered that we shared common concerns about education. He decided, for reasons never made entirely clear, that he wanted to help. He proved invaluable. As the top assistant to Representative Brademas, Jack could phone to offices of other members of the Education and Labor Committee. After many calls, and miles of my walking the corridors of the Rayburn House Office Building, a vacancy appeared for a legislative assistant to Representative James H. Scheuer, Democrat of the Bronx, New York. Endless interviews and other communications followed, until I found myself, after a week's delay, legislative assistant to the New York congressman (I had never been to the Bronx), a fellow of Washington Internships in Education, and a Washingtonian—a new life-style.

The events of the ensuing year are too long to record here, but one point is notable. The move from St. Paul to Washington served to disintegrate and reconstruct many of my assumptions about power, social relations, and myself. Ventures into strange and potent social structures, with unforeseeable impact on the personality and life chances, are both beneficial and costly, but not tranquil.

The year in Washington was followed by a move to Atlanta, Georgia, where I became assistant professor of education at Georgia State University. I gratefully acknowledge grants from the university and, later, from the U.S. Office of Education (later transferred to the National Institute of Education) which enabled me to return to Washington physically for short trips, and intellectually to gather more systematic data and put my thoughts and impressions into order.

A number of people were of help to me, and I want to thank them. Roy M. Hall, dean of the School of Education at Georgia State University, deserves special mention. Respecting research and writing, he facilitated my work with aid in obtaining financial support, organizational cooperation (and on occasion needed shelter), and friendship. He went far to make Georgia State a developmental place for me. Charles Thompson and especially Professor Edgar Gumbert of the university spent long hours talking with me philosophically, in the relative seclusion of Atlanta, about the meaning of federal power. Gumbert's critique of the relationships among government, schools, and corporate capitalism influenced my thinking in chapter 6 and I am grateful to his erudite conversation. William Ammentorp, Larry Gladieux, Barbara Heyns, H. Thomas James, Michael Kirst, Leon Lessinger, Michael O'Keefe, S. Francis Overlan, Jack Schuster, Grant Venn, Welford W. Wilms, and others read parts of the manuscript and offered many corrections and suggestions. Mary Allen Jolley, a Washington lobbyist with a deep and gentle Alabama drawl and an incisive and liberal mind, became an early friend and discussant in my Washington experience and she remained so afterward. My gratitude extends to many people in Washington—members of Congress, staff aides, federal officials, lobbyists, and all others presented in the book—for their willingness to talk frankly with me. For the most part, they remain anonymous; however, I hope I have represented them fairly in role and structure.

I wish also to thank Nevitt Sanford, who in 1973 invited me to make an intellectual home at the unique Wright Institute in Berkeley.

The manuscript was finished while I was visiting assistant professor of sociology at the University of California and visiting scholar at the Wright Institute. The ambiance at the Institute proved conducive to linking scholarly research with thought about its contribution to human action.

The findings and opinions in this book are not necessarily those of any of these people nor of my financial sponsors. Indeed, it is because some of them disagreed with me that I was able to come to the conclusions I did. I thank them all.

Harry L. Summerfield

The Wright Institute
Berkeley, California
1974

Contributors

Harry L. Summerfield received his M.A. degree in political science from Washington University, St. Louis, and his Ph.D. from the University of Minnesota. He has taught high school; and in 1969-70 he served as legislative assistant to a member of the U.S. House Education and Labor Committee and was briefly on the staff for educational planning in the Office of the Assistant Secretary for Planning and Evaluation, Department of Health, Education, and Welfare. He was also a fellow of Washington Internships in Education. He has been assistant professor of education, Georgia State University (Atlanta) and during the conclusion of this book was visiting assistant professor of sociology, University of California, and visiting scholar at the Wright Institute, Berkeley. His first book, *The Neighborhood-Based Politics of Education,* was published in 1971.

James W. Guthrie is associate professor of education, University of California, Berkeley. While a fellow of Washington Internships in

Education he served as special assistant in the Office of the Secretary, Department of Health, Education, and Welfare in the area of legislative liaison. He has been consultant to the U.S. Commissioner of Education and was deputy director of the New York State Fleischmann Commission. He is now director of a Ford Foundation study of school governance, and is conducting simulations of future federal aid to education formulas. Dr. Guthrie is author of *Schools and Inequality* and *New Models for American Education.*

John McDermott received his J.D. degree from Harvard Law School. He is a member of the California and federal bars and served as chief attorney for the plaintiffs in *Serrano v. Priest,* the California case challenging the federal and state constitutionality of the spending inequities in the California school finance system.

Jack H. Schuster received his degree in law from the Harvard Law School. He holds a master's in political science from Columbia University and is finishing his Ph.D. at the University of California, Berkeley, specializing in higher education. While a fellow of Washington Internships in Education, he served as legislative assistant to Congressman John Brademas, a subcommittee chairman of the House Education and Labor Committee, and subsequently as his administrative assistant. He is currently assistant to the chancellor of the University of California, Berkeley, and a lecturer in the department of political science.

PART I

THE FEDERAL
POLICY PROCESS
FOR DECISION-MAKING

1. Policy Process

Washington, D.C., is a company town. Its business is politics; the politics of virtually everything vital to American life. A small proportion of Washington political energy, among the vying demands of defense, welfare, highways, housing, and a myriad of other subjects, is devoted to education. The federal policy process for educational decision-making, a part of the federal government in general, is the subject of this book.

A policy process is a pattern of events leading to a governmental decision. A policy process exists wherever a decision is made. An examination raises such questions as: What are the origins of a policy proposal? Whose needs are represented? How does a proposal enter the system of political actors? Within the political system, which proposals are offered by what actors to which official decision-makers? Who has power? In a particular system, what constitutes power? How is power exercised by different participants? How do patterns of power finally congeal to promulgate a policy? Where are the points of conflict, and how are they resolved? that is, what are the problem-raising and problem-solving interactions among men and women whose assigned roles and interests cause them to differ? In reaching a compromise, how does a decision in one part of the system affect another? Examination of the policy process looks to political roles, structures, actions, interactions, myths, precedent, and, ultimately, to the use of power.

Each policy process is somewhat different from every other. A policy process can be very simple as, for example, in the case of a routine local school board decision to purchase chalk and erasers, or it can be incomprehensibly complex, as it is sometimes in the federal system, involving a number of autonomous but interlocking institutions. Within the same federal system the process can be relied on to change because the substantive content of decisions change, and with it comes a partially new constellation of actors and structures. Further, the process can change markedly over time on the same substantive area. A federal education decision made in 1965 in the Johnson years in parts barely reflects the same process during the Nixon tenure.

Washington politicos like to emphasize the lack of regularity in the federal policy process. One veteran, offended by the notion that another political scientist was again trying to make sense of the process, said, "How do things happen? I don't know; they just happen." His frustration in trying to rationalize the process is unquestionably warranted, but it is overly pessimistic. Lack of regularity in the policy process is not the whole story because continuities do abide in the federal system. This is in part the legacy of the founding fathers, who constructed the government on the basis of constitutional separation of powers requiring an institution called Congress and an institution called the executive to perform certain independent activities if a policy is to come into existence. Within these institutions and the lobbies, and among them, custom and procedural and normative regularities have developed that keep the decisional processes similar enough over time to permit participants—both government officials and petitioners from the public—to play by rules that preserve tranquillity and facilitate efficient operations of government.

The pillars of stability, the established organizational units, in the federal policy process should not be confused with its congenital fragmentation. At the federal level, many groups, bureaus, bureaucrats, committees, individuals, and other pieces each hold partial authority for decisions. The complexity of the process results from this fragmentation of structure of authority within government as well as in the representation of diverse, nongovernmental private and public interests who perpetually seek to exert influence. Each actor in the process—within and outside of government—receives and represents interests. Some actors are able to receive and represent more, and more diverse, interests than others. The sum of their interactions yields a complex network of messages, many of which conflict with each other. Conflicting voices outside government conflict with conflicting voices within Congress and the administration, and all can conflict with each other.

Fragmentation further characterizes the federal educational policy process because the founding fathers designed both a division and a separation of power. Division of power connotes distinct jurisdictional differences between the states and the federal government. In education matters, as opposed to defense or highway construction, the division is particularly crucial because, from the founding of the Union, delivery of education has been a function of the states. Thousands of state and local governmental units make localized educational policy outside the purview of the federal government. Every attempt at federal policy formulation meets this powerful extant condition of decentralization in educational government. The focus of this book is the political dynamics at the federal level, but ultimately our concern is with the manner by which federal policy affects state-local operation of the schoolhouse.

Conflict is not perpetual. The representation of diverse interests and the sparks generated among them lead toward compromise and decision. The reward for reaching a decision—that is, a formulation of government policy (or a decision to have no policy)—ultimately exceeds conflict. So, conflict periodically presses toward unity. The conflicting structures, roles, and actions, their characteristics and perpetual motion in the fragmented lobby, Congress, and administration and their movement toward decision are the foci of the first part of this book.

Methodology

While I was interviewing people as part of the research, one seasoned Washington veteran suggested that I finish the interviews and then return to my office and write a fiction about the federal policy process. He said that the fiction would be as good as the reality and probably more pleasant to read. He had a point. The nervous arrangement of fragmented units of Washington policy processes for education and the shifting issues make quantified research virtually impossible. A fiction would at least give the flavor of essential struggles and structures without the binding pretense of reflecting total reality.

But what is fiction except the discombobulating reality stripped to essential flashes of identifiable action; images cleaned of the impossibly complex set of perceptions that are beyond description or linear comprehension. Marcel Proust says:

> And once the novelist has brought us to that state, in which, as in all purely mental states, every emotion is multiplied tenfold, into which his book comes to disturb us as might a dream, but a dream more lucid, and of a more lasting impression than those which come to us in sleep; why, then, for the space of an hour he sets free within us all the joys and sorrows in the world, a few of which, only we should have to spend years of our actual life in getting to know, and the keenest, the most intense of which would never have been revealed to us because the slow course of their development stops our perception of them.[1]

Unfortunately, the descriptive prose of social science carries neither the luxury of revelation of emotion nor the grace of poetic imagery, but the best descriptive social science is perhaps more like fiction, not in the sense of relaying a conjured tale but in the Proustian sense of releasing the essence of reality from the shroud of its natural, infinite trappings. A fetish for comprehensiveness makes revelation of the crucial lines impossible. Precision about the essence is the proper expectation of the reader.

Chapters 2, 3, and 4 relay a series of facts and accounts about the federal policy process for educational decision-making. It is not the whole story, simply a compilation of extracts of important facets of the processes occurring in the educational lobby, the Congress, and the administration. Hopefully, it adds up to an image of the federal policy process for educational decision-making in which the gaps will be closely enough spaced to reveal a mosaic of the ongoing operation. Chapter 5 offers a theoretical framework that represents the process in an abstract, condensed form.

The method of this research includes: (1) a combination of carefully selected interviews with key participants in the federal education policy process; (2) participant observation both as a legislative assistant to a member of the House Education and Labor Committee and on the staff of the deputy assistant secretary for educational planning of Health, Education, and Welfare; and (3) document review. As much as possible, the data sources were used to immerse the author personally into the realities of the lives of the people who participated.

Selecting interview respondents was largely by design with a bit of good fortune. A basic pattern was followed. In each of the three areas—lobbies, Congress, and administration—principal roles were identified. During the second Johnson administration and the first Nixon administration, scores of men and women served in these vital positions affecting educational policy. All come for a while; some go, and some stay longer. The giant of one moment, like Senator Wayne Morse during the Johnson years, is a cattle rancher in Oregon in the Nixon years, while Harold Howe II, a Johnson commissioner of education, remains in the picture by becoming a vice-president in charge of educational affairs for the powerful Ford Foundation. The cast of characters changes over time, and sometimes the same man plays more than one role, but, since no one event represents the true picture of the federal policy process, it is fitting that different men and women who have seen different times and roles were interviewed for their versions of their activities in the total process.

With few exceptions, the policy makers or related personnel I sought to see were willing to accommodate me with at least an hour and often more of their time. Most of the respondents appeared to be open, frank, and willing to answer whatever questions I could generate. They rarely offered sensitive material, but, if asked, they responded. The quality of information I gained varied. Junior staff and lower ranking bureaucrats sometimes seemed less explicit than the top ranking officials. Perhaps institutional paranoia conditioned them to be imprecise and noncommittal, but it seemed more likely that on matters of policy decision they are often further removed from the policy process than they like to admit, and simply do not know much about what is going on. Sometimes, however, people who would appear to be low in rank actually are in the thick of the action and are the best informed. I collected information from sources high and low, gaining as many perspectives on the process as possible. Forty-eight tape-recorded interviews, which when transcribed amounted to over one thousand typewritten pages, were conducted; there were also scores of casual conversations with involved people. Some of the formal interviews and most of the casual conversations were "off the record" (tape recorder off), necessitating recall and later notation, as well as discretion, on my part.

As a staff member on Capitol Hill and in the Department of Health, Education, and Welfare, I participated in several episodes of the policy process and observed many other events from a distance. In a description of research methodology, there is little to say about the importance of such observations (some of which are recorded in detail in the following chapters) except that the act of doing offers a graphic, intimate understanding of the process as well as some myopic distortion. Hopefully the broadly ranging interviews, taken a year after my government service ended, gave a perspective to the whole process and offset any distortions that arose from being too close as a participant. The document review, which was in many ways the least important aspect of the research, relied on congressional records, the *Congressional Quarterly* weekly service news accounts, memoranda, and the few scholarly works on the subject.

Conclusion

The bulk of Part 1 of the book is descriptive. The descriptive chapters build somewhat on each other; thus, the chapter on the lobby is an incomplete outline that becomes fuller when the activities of the lobby are more fully discussed in the chapters on Congress and the administration. By the end of chapter 4, the reader will have touched on most of the vital points of the policy panorama.

The ensuing description of the federal policy process for educational decision-making may appear at times to approach the model of an introductory civics text, and I would be the last to deny it. Education policy emerges from the same Congress and administration as do policies on housing and highways. The issues and actors are different, and the paths have a different shape, but the rudiments are shared. Following federal decision-making in the vehicle of education is an interesting tour which in the areas of housing or highways would have different scenery but not essentially different concepts of locomotion. Unique here is the focus on education with the goal of elucidating the process to help assess the potential contributions of the federal government to the public schools.

Notes for Chapter 1

1. Marcel Proust, *Remembrance of Things Past* (New York: Random House Modern Library, 1934), vol. 1, *Swann's Way*, p. 64.

2. The Education Lobby

The Washington education lobby is a concatenation of hundreds of voices seeking to influence members of Congress and administration officials on the course of public policy. Some of the most influential groups, like the National Education Association (NEA) or the National School Boards Association (NSBA), would never call themselves "lobbies." They prefer to mark their identity as "professional organizations," although they maintain active governmental relations units. Many of the individuals who appear before congressional committees or consult with the administration define themselves as experts or education professionals and would also shun the title of lobbyist, although their influence would lead to one policy output rather than another. Similarly, foundations like Carnegie or Ford scrupulously eschew being branded as lobbies to protect their tax exempt status, yet they fund studies designed to affect the policy process. Unlike other policy areas such as agriculture or defense, most of the individuals and groups who seek to influence education policy renounce the appellation of "lobby," but this should not deter us from making a pragmatic judgment about their activities nor conceding to the convenience of the term.

The American Vocational Association (AVA) is the granddaddy of education lobbies. It has been based in Washington and active in federal legislation since the first vocational education measure, the Smith-Hughes Act, was passed in 1917. The AVA lobbyist says:

We are Washington-based, I guess, for one reason alone, and that is because this is the seat of the federal government, and it is a place of power; so, vocational education has to be represented here we think. That is our reason for being.

Since then numerous lobby voices have materialized in Washington, attracted by the possibility of influencing the flow of federal dollars. They can be categorized according to the general function for which they seek to channel dollars: (1) commercial; (2) professional maintenance; (3) social and educational reform; (4) general welfare; and (5) parochial schools.

(1) The commercial, private group composed of profit-making corporations is perhaps the most popular image in the genre of lobby. It does exist, but it is actually the least prominent in the political world of education. Profit-making corporations lobby in education obviously because not all aspects of public schools are nonprofit. The manufacturers and sellers of books, supplies, equipment, and other goods always seek profit, and to the extent that they can expand the amount of federal dollars available to be spent on their wares, they can expand their market and their profits. Thus they are generally supporters of federal aid to education. Their most prominent lobby, the National Audio-Visual Association (NAVA), a kind of trade association composed of corporations, acquired a sound Washington base after passage of Title III of the National Defense Education Act (1958), which made special provision for educational hardware and software. Since then NAVA has generally supported federal aid and has specifically lobbied to ensure that new laws carry provisions for federal expenditures for their goods.

To diminish any speculations that the private interests wield great influence, it is worth noting that the education market, estimated at perhaps one billion dollars, is actually rather small when it is divided among the numerous book, material, and other manufacturers. It is miniscule when compared to defense or highways and, further, the federal share of that dollar market is probably less than 10 percent. NAVA is an effective lobby, but for limited ends.

(2) By far the largest and most influential segment of the Washington education lobby is the professional maintenance groups. One distinction among them is whether they are concerned mainly with higher education or with what is more commonly known as public schooling—elementary, secondary, and vocational education. The higher education groups are sometimes referred to as "One Dupont Circle," the address of the building where many of them are located. One Dupont Circle includes such groups as the American Association of Colleges and Land Grant Universities, the American Council on Education, the American Association of Junior Colleges, and others. The public schooling category includes the National Education Association (NEA), the Council of Chief State School Officers (CCSSO), the American Association of School Administrators (AASA), the Parent Teacher Association (PTA), the National School Boards Association, and also more specialized groups like the American Library Association, the American Vocational Association, and others.

The key similarity of these groups is that they represent some aspect of the established school and university institutional structure. Their goal is to gain more resources to bolster the segment of education that composes their membership. For example, the American Association of Colleges and Land Grant Universities is made up of member institutions drawn from some of the nation's largest universities. The job of the association is to seek to channel federal dollars to relieve fiscal stress in hard times and to expand in good times. The giant NEA is composed of more than 1.1 million classroom teachers. Its impressive building houses many functions, but the political function is to raise federal dollars to increase teachers' salaries and to do it under conditions that will protect the teachers' status. Between 80 and 85 percent of all education dollars go for the support of teachers' salaries, so any increase in federal dollars ultimately benefits the NEA members. Just as the higher education lobby seeks to preserve and strengthen the current institutional structure, the public school groups seek primarily to preserve their interests, all of which rest on the preservation of well-financed locally controlled public education, mainly oriented on the basis of a student-teacher-classroom relationship.

(3) A third category of groups is the reform lobbies. Their vested

interests do not lie in maintenance of the status quo basic structure of schools. Rather, they see themselves as change agents, ranging from gadflies to revolutionaries. By advocating social, technical, and organizational changes in education they hope both to redefine the goals of the school and get the education system to do its job better. The large foundations—particularly Carnegie and Ford—have led this group. Befitting their institutional autonomy, the foundations have decided to act as gadflies to the status quo in American education. Foundation officials identify problems which they feel are significant (Ford receives proposals from the public and mounts its own efforts to grant money for both research and demonstration of alternative ideas). The foundations hope that the projects they finance will be seminal and become "seed programs" that will catch on and be adopted in public policy to receive sustaining tax-based support. By making grants for the original compensatory education projects and for public broadcasting, among others, Ford created powerful pilot demonstrations to guide and motivate the decisions of public officials.

The federal tax structure prohibits foundation personnel from lobby activity; however, by identifying a problem and granting money to nonfoundation men and women to pursue the problem, the foundation accomplishes the same end. For example, a group of higher education "progressives," led by Frank Newman, received money from Ford and with it produced *The Report on Higher Education,* which became an important document in the making of the 1972 Higher Education Amendments. Newman and others did the lobby work, which Ford officials could endorse if asked, but Ford officials were not and, by law, could not be the public front men. The true relation of foundation money to the policy process is never clear because men like Newman are independent scholars who argue their points based on their own collected wisdom. However, the foundation's selection of topics and selection of the type of people to pursue the topic is clearly an important mode of influence within the policy process.

Other reformers are found among certain college professors, intellectuals-at-large, and, to a measured extent, some of the maintenance organizations. Often they do not have a physical presence in Washington; their effect is made by their writings or disciples.

At a more radical extreme of reformers is a coalition of civil rights groups which first appeared in 1969, the Washington Research Project. They want vast reordering of educational priorities, giving first attention to the poor. They have made some impression in Washington, but remain rather small in voice compared with the professional-maintenance lobbies.

(4) The fourth category includes groups not principally concerned with education but that on occasion use their organizational resources and prestige to seek to influence education policy. The AFL-CIO, for example, is one of education's best friends and one of the most influential lobby groups. It is not predominantly concerned with education, but it has for a long time involved itself in areas that affect the well-being of its vast membership. Mass public education is seen by the AFL-CIO as a bastion of betterment for the common man. In terms of policy, the AFL-CIO is somewhere between the maintenance and reform groups. It consistently seeks to strengthen the schools as they are but has also supported virtually all legislation extending special benefits to the poor.

Other groups of this nature include the National Association of Manufacturers and the Daughters of the American Revolution, which have opposed federal aid to education.

(5) A fifth category stands by itself. This is the "Catholic Lobby," represented mainly by the United States Catholic Conference. Its primary and virtually only goal in the federal policy process for education has been to obtain federal funds for the financially ailing parochial schools in America. The Catholic Conference played a particularly crucial role in education politics before passage of the Elementary and Secondary Education Act (ESEA) in 1965. The "religious war," the stalemate between those desiring aid to parochial schools and those opposed, caused some of the most severe problems in the history of federal aid. Many of those issues were either resolved by compromise or were ended in 1973 by adverse decisions of the Supreme Court constraining expenditure of public funds for parochial schools.

Perhaps a sixth category should be listed as a lobby, or should at least be clearly recognized as effectively lobby-like. It is the executive branch, which regularly develops its legislative proposals and then actively presses them on the Congress, using many of the same tactics as a regular lobby and differing mainly because it acts within the governmental system. The Constitution provides for a separation of powers, but often it seems to be breached. Complains one "regular" lobbyist, somewhat bitterly:

I guess I take too much the point of view that congressional people do. I worked there for too long. I see a real separation of power intended by the founding fathers. When you are in the executive branch of government, you are supposed to be carrying out the law—make the law work. I do not really like all the running back and forth that exists between the executive agencies and the United States Congress. By golly, they are supposed to *administer* the laws, and they ought not be up on the Hill trying to pass bills, and that is what a lot of them do.

For good or ill, any number of administration officials, for different motives, seek to influence congressional decisions sometimes in opposition to regular lobby objectives or sometimes in an entirely different dimension.

The categories above create a broad definition of the Washington education lobby. The definition applies to those people and groups who seek some sort of advocacy position within the official decision-making process. That advocacy can be pro or con although it is most often more complex, based on conflict and compromise. All lobby advocacy is directed toward defining patterns of federal aid to education—that is, each group seeks to shape the purposes and the manner by which dollars are distributed. However, even in policy conflict, lobby advocacy almost always favors increase in aid. Thus there is a function for each lobby structured in terms of the parochial needs of its membership (teachers, parents, school board, universities, etc.) and, equally important, a function for the inchoate but demonstrative education lobby taken as a whole. As a whole, the Washington education lobby maintains constant presence and pressure for a firm and expansive federal role in education.

Anatomy of Lobby Groups

In formal settings like congressional hearings, banquets, and high level meetings, the visible tip of the major lobby group is often a front man. He may be an officer or distinguished member of the group who has limited ongoing policy responsibilities in the group. For example, the president of the NEA, a teacher who serves for a one-year term, will probably be the person who writes to or speaks with the president of the United States or a congressional committee chairman if the occasion should arise. The use of distinguished, bona fide front men on these occasions is proper form, and suffuses the event with an aura of legitimacy.

The Lobbyist

The energy force of most of a group's Washington activity is the lobbyist. He is a well-paid, full-time professional and he is the principal ongoing working link between the group (and its aspirations) and government decision makers. The lobbyist must be able to penetrate Washington institutional life. His first qualification is that he know the complexities and patterns of the federal policy process. Ordinarily he is a man or woman long familiar with the Washington scene. Virtually all education lobbyists have had experience in government, perhaps as legislative or administrative assistants to congressmen or senators, committee staff, members, or in legislative roles in the administration. Their generic understanding of government would allow them to become the lobbyist for the highway, housing, or defense industries just as well as for education. Although few of them are educators, most seem to have an abiding interest in the field.

The lobbyist's main work is to link his group's aspirations with the actions of official decision makers. The linkage involves foremost the necessity for the lobbyist to stay informed on several fronts. He must know the position of his own organization, the status of every legislative idea relevant to his organization, the positions and leanings of all relevant government officials, as well as other lobbies and interests, and the detailed facts of the pending legislation. Says one lobbyist, "One of the greatest assets a lobbyist has is information." So he talks to everyone—congressional members and staff, administration officials, his own group's membership, and fellow lobbyists from other organizations. This communications job can become extremely complicated. There are thousands of communication synapses that change as issues change, and even change dramatically as the same issue evolves in the legislative or administrative process.

"We are pros. We are professionals," says a lobbyist. By this he means to indicate more than the condition that each lobbyist is employed by his group to work for the group's ends. Most education lobbyists also identify themselves as part of a fraternity that has its own codes and values. The fraternity is an informal communications link.

If I call a guy up and say, "Where are you on this issue?" he will tell me. Or, if he calls me, I tell him—for the most part depending upon who it is.

Even if one lobbyist is working toward ends different from another, information flow is vital both to the maintenance of well-articulated conflict and to the development of compromise. In short, the policy process cannot operate even in conflict if it is disconnected.

To earn the trust of others and keep it is achieved by not lying and by adhering to all agreements. Because of the complexity of politics in Washington, many procedural agreements are made—that is, agreements about the way parties will proceed to resolve their differences or achieve their goals. It is the ability to trust the agreements about the process of work that is perhaps most vital to the lobbyist. Says a lobbyist:

The old statement that a politician's word is his bond, I think, is very true. I could not last twenty-four hours, just looking at it from a very practical standpoint, not keeping my word whether it be with a member of Congress or a fellow from another organization.

He who is not trusted gains no information, and credible information exchange is the heart of the lobbyist's job. Obedience to the basic ethical rules of the fraternity is mandatory.

Successful role play for a lobbyist requires an affable personality. They are easy to talk with and are not shy about seeking their ends. Their personality style is crucial to performance of the job and generally includes the vital attribute of providing minimum opportunity for arousing offensive feelings—anger—either in themselves or their respondents. The affability is often so ritualized that a lobbyist will speak about a respondent as his friend. Sometimes the traditional definition applies, but a Washington "friend" has a special connotation. He is a person who holds a position which the lobbyist must regularly contact and who is open and cooperative. In that sense, a friend may even be a political enemy who must be contacted. A Washington friend is not necessarily an emotionally close companion or an ally. He is someone you can call on the phone, pass a little gossip, and then get the information you need. The ritual of a growing friendship can bring this relationship into a bar where cocktails make the otherwise necessary conversation a bit more enjoyable.

Characterizing a political counterpart as a friend simply employs affability for the function of obtaining communications. To be judgmental, rigid, or formal would shut out virtually all of the lobbyist's world. The lobbyist's requirement to enter into many relationships requires an affability that does not equate the value of the person with the value of his ideological and power position. In this setting, position outweighs person. To ensure civility, the relationship is structured as more than technical and less than intimate.

Intragroup Policy Processes

The lobbyist or spokesman is the principal working contact in discussions with government decision leaders. That does not make him his group's policy-maker. Typically, he carries policy decisions from the group to the government and back to the group. Because of the expertise he gains on the realities of governmental politics, the lobbyist will probably be one of the important voices at the group's decision-making council, but his government liaison activities are circumscribed within the fundamental boundaries of the group's decided purpose. Each group has an internal formal policy development process. The technique varies. Perhaps it is best to refer to the classical model of the AFL-CIO as an example.

Unlike other education lobbies, the AFL-CIO lobbyist is engaged in many noneducation activities. He carried the union battle against confirmation of Supreme Court nominee Harold Carswell the same year he worked on additional funding for schools. One of his assignments is education, and the assignments come to him through an intraunion process to which he is only an adviser. He describes the process:

The AFL-CIO has a Department of Education. What normally happens is that in broad terms they set overall policy. They may prepare a draft about a policy question. Maybe I will work with them. When the staff people hear of a proposal [perhaps from the administration], they will start considering it. Maybe the Education Department will do a draft background paper. Somewhere down the line they will draft a policy position resolution on the matter. I will probably look at it, and it is looked at by what amounts to sort of a committee of top level staff. Then, if there is no AFL-CIO national convention, it is submitted to the Executive Council [made up of the presidents of the major national unions under the long-term presidency of George Meany]. The council will act on it, and then it becomes official policy of the AFL-CIO.

The lobbyist keeps tuned to the staff activity, advising on political realities and technical information he might have picked up, but the basic research and work is done in the Education Department. As the Education Department drafts the resolution for approval by the Executive Council, the lobbyist watches very closely. The resolution will comprise his marching orders, and he must ensure that they are viable given the political realities. "I like the resolution written broad enough so that I have a lot of flexibility in terms of what is going on on the Hill." (A lobbyist's activities thicken in political conflict when compromise is made. As the policy process unfolds, new specific choices constantly arise, and the lobbyist must then cast opinions of the group when often the group has never considered and will not consider the specific problem. If he has a general mandate, he can work toward the group's aspirations without being shackled by inflexibility.)

When the resolution is formally adopted, the lobbyist is turned loose:

Once that is done, then I am pretty free to move in terms of our general policy. Then we are in a position to start trying to have an input in terms of legislation or agency action or anything else that is going on.

The Education Department staff remains active. It will draft legislation for friendly members of Congress, provide technical information to the lobbyist, and exchange tidbits of data about problems of legislation.

At the other extreme from the somewhat bureaucratic, giant AFL-CIO is the relatively tiny Washington Research Project. It is an "advocacy group"; it claims as its constituency poor people who cannot speak for themselves. It has no individual duespayers. Its actual membership is other civil rights groups. The functioning membership is a small professional and volunteer staff that analyzes issues from the perspective of achieving more resource allocations to the poor. Within the broad goal, whatever results from the efforts of individual staff members is what the group does on a project-by-project basis. In this one organization, the staff is the policy-making council, the membership, and the lobbyists.

The large maintenance organizations also have formal internal policy processes. The general pattern follows the AFL-CIO example, where staff and national leaders mount a resolution for approval at the group's national convention or some executive body. For example, the AVA lobbyist says:

Inside the organization the most important group I work with would be the Committee on Resolutions and Program of Work. This is a committee that really fashions our legislative policy and sets our goals and directions in conjunction with the Board of Directors.

Although each organization has a way of getting its position on the record, the Washington spokesmen rely less on formal proclamations for behavioral cues than on the accrued culture of the group. For example, single-purpose groups like AVA or ALA have a relatively easy task of developing internal policy. Their objectives are clear at a general level: expand and protect the laws benefiting vocational education or libraries. Specific legislative goals then emerge easily enough, depending on the pressures in the rest of the Washington policy apparatus. It is rare for the Washington staff not to recognize when an administrative or legislative proposal is in keeping with the group's tradition and goals. For example, in 1971 AVA worked closely with Congressman Roman Pucinski (D., Ill.), chairman of the Special Subcommittee on Education, which has responsibility for vocational education, to create by law a Bureau of Vocational Education in USOE. In discussing the authority base from which the national AVA spokesmen supported the bill, the lobbyist says:

The reason we feel comfortable doing that on behalf of AVA members is because over the last ten years we have had all kinds of resolutions about the need for federal leadership at the U.S. Office of Education. Our members have told us [the Washington staff] that this needs to be done.

The other big groups—like NEA, NSBA, AASA—face a more complicated policy situation, which is resolved by what might be called "lowest common denominator politics." Their policy formulation problem is twofold. First, each group, like the NEA, is composed of diverse members who are located in all parts of the nation working under different political and professional constraints. One subgroup's favor is another's source of dismay, and the internal stability of the whole association cannot be sacrificed to anyone. Secondly, the group's members—whether they be teachers, principals, superintendents, board members, or even chief state school officers—are responsible for operating or guiding the local school, and they want to maintain that responsibility. Power is theirs. They want both to keep it and be given the resources to fulfill its expectations. Thus, to avoid alienation of the many national and regional subgroups and to remain within the requirement to preserve local control of education, the realm of major national policy objectives—one might say organizational ideology—is necessarily narrow for the maintenance groups, and they set carefully neutralized goals, mostly general goals. An NEA spokesman lays out the basic guidelines:

All the big lobbies agree on creation of a [cabinet level] Department of Education; so, we all support a Department of Education.

And, on finance, another lobbyist says:

Our position is that, in general framework, we are striving for a general aid to education where the federal government will pick up, nationwide, 50 percent of the funding. That is a long range goal. I know the NEA has theirs up to 33 percent. The difference between 33 percent and 50 percent, well, that is part of the discussion, and you do not know what the final result will be, but these are the long-range goals.

On categorical aid to education* (particularly aid to the disadvantaged), groups begin to fall out a bit, but still general goals dominate. Says the lobbyist:

We also have a position that says that there are *certain*, narrow, categorical programs which we will support because there is an overriding federal interest or nationwide interest in them. Here we speak specifically with respect to the problems of the handicapped which many times a local school district just cannot finance. (Everyone supports the handicapped.) Then we speak in terms of the disadvantaged. This is a nationwide problem. We are probably one of the few organizations that really supports ESEA, Title I [aid to the disadvantaged]. This is a strange phenomenon, but it is true. This year there are only three big groups asking for more money for Title I—no one else. But, it happens to be the three big ones—AFL-CIO, NEA, and NSBA. The three of us were the ones which withstood a terrible onslaught from the rest of the associations.

In short, we have gotten to a general position of supporting general aid and to a practical position that there are certain overriding federal interests in categorical programs which we will support. But we are not particularly interested in any new categorical programs.

The basic positions of the big groups have grown mainly since 1960, reinforced by resolutions passed by executive bodies or

---

*The distinction between categorical aid and general aid should be made clear. General aid is federal dollars granted by formula to either a state or to a local school district to be used as the state or district sees fit. That is, the money is allocated for general education purposes. Categorical aid is money allocated for specific purposes established and defined by law. Federal dollars are thus allocated for special categories, such as aid to Spanish-speaking students, aid to libraries, state departments of education, etc. There are a large number of categories. In each case of categorical aid, the federal government, not the local educational agency, determines the purpose for the money.

conventions. Periodically a major policy shift may take place (as in the 1950s and 1960s when some groups moved from opposing federal aid altogether to supporting it), but barring those infrequent occurrences custom generally tells the Washington-based staff what it is authorized to seek.

Lobby Power—Constraints

All would be well for the lobbies if they could simply pass their viewpoints on to governmental officials to be made into law. A popular myth even in Washington is that the big professional organizations "control" government education policy. That their impact is felt is beyond question; however, the impact varies in intensity, effect, and location depending on the group and the stage of the policy process.

Actually, the 1960s and the early 1970s showed the lobbies to be rather ineffectual in getting their way in authorizing legislation. The people who make laws are members of Congress, not lobbies, and, in this period congressional decision makers did not look to lobby leadership. Congressional liberals embraced a viewpoint created largely by collaboration with administration liberals and foundation-funded or university-based reformist intellectuals.

Unlike the lobbies, which basically wanted net increases in some type of general federal aid, the liberals emphasized reformist themes, particularly "equality of educational opportunity" and reform of old-fashioned pedagogy. Their dissatisfaction with the status quo, backed by the rectitude of helping the poor, put the liberals in a favorable light and on the offensive. They were able to pose the question, "Tell us why we should not install new, innovative programs?"

The lobbies, not organized for reform but wanting new federal dollars for the benefit of their memberships, were at a disadvantage. They wanted simple extensions of existing laws or simple general grants in aid to states and school districts, but being neither decision-makers nor the architects of the agendas for the decision-makers, if the big lobbies wanted the dollars to flow they had no choice but to support the liberal legislation. An AVA spokesman cites an example from his field:

I would say the AVA's impact in education has been one of supporting something that comes down the pipe that they can be for rather than going out and making educational policy. . . . In 1963 the John F. Kennedy panel recommended the Vocational Education Act of that year, and the big, tough job was to negotiate what the panel was recommending with what the vocational educators would buy. . . . So, it was a reaction sort of a thing rather than being out front with the legislative program. Same thing happened when we passed those amendments. That was not a recommendation that came from the profession; it was a presidential study group that said that certain things ought to happen. We personally had influence on the panel, but it was not the AVA legislative program. We bought the panel proposals after somebody else decided what it ought to be.

In the 1960s, particularly in the landmark Elementary and Secondary Education Act of 1965, the failure to structure the form of the legislation was a blow but not a bitter defeat for most of the big lobbies. They would have preferred to have been more influential, but since even categorical dollars end up in teacher paychecks, tax relief, school libraries, etc., they could easily support the liberal measures.

The big lobbies have sometimes fought to have their will translated into law. The AVA openly fought some important reform recommendations of the 1963 panel, and lost. The two most important pieces of legislation in this period, the Elementary and Secondary Education Act (ESEA) of 1965, and the Higher Education Amendments of 1972 engineered the bulk of dollars to be distributed on the basis of family income of students. As noted above, in 1965 the big public school lobbies chose to take dollars distributed under a reform source, considering reform dollars better than none. But in 1972, the higher education lobby united and opposed the proposal to grant higher education dollars to students—particularly economically less advantaged students—in lieu of granting the bulk of money directly to the institutions of higher learning. Their all-out lobby effort failed. (Details are described in chapter 3.)

The professional organizations do not contribute money to campaigns, and they can offer only limited benefits. One lobbyist says:

We can get congressmen speeches around, and they get honorariums for that. That is really about the only positive thing that we can do for them. Oh, I can remember a time, too, that we have used our mailing list for certain congressional districts or certain states. We wrote to all our organization's members in the congressman's district saying he has been an outstanding leader. It is kind of a nicety, but it wouldn't be enough to get them to act on a matter.

NAVA, a private organization, will contribute money to a candidate here and there, but the amounts are small and only act as a sort of symbolic show of gratitude for the member's cooperation. None of the education congressmen acknowledge either important education support or opposition at the polls. No group, including the NEA, can turn out the vote.

One lobbyist sums it up:

On the real, gut power issues I do not know of any groups in education or any one of them that has real clout in the United States Congress. Education just does not have it. You take the strictly labor issues, the real fights like minimum wage or whatever, organized labor can put some clout behind those members of Congress, and I mean line them up. Education cannot do that.

Patterns of Lobby Influence

Lobbyists are not without influence, however. Although members of Congress and staff are not controlled by the big lobbies, the lobby voice can be heard. Legitimacy of access to members of Congress is a lobby's prime asset.

A senator or congressman will seek the support of the organizations. He wants commitment beforehand. He wants to be able to go in and say that the NEA, the NSBA, AASA, AFL-CIO supports this. They will ask, "How does the educational community feel about your proposal?" They feel that is the responsibility to their constituents.

Another lobbyist says:

Our position does represent a force or a position to be reckoned with because House Education and Labor Committee Chairman Carl Perkins is very proud of his committee and the results of his committee. He would obviously be worried and upset if he found out one of the major constituencies of his committee was opposing him on something he was going to do or upset with what what he was going to do. . . . No committee chairman wants to find himself in a position that when he goes to the House floor, he is there without any grass roots support.

So, the lobby will be heard.

On the infrequent occasions when the big lobby groups try to mount full-scale opposition to a bill, their probability of winning is good. The NEA was able to kill a federal aid bill in 1963 over a clash with the U.S. Catholic Conference on aid to parochial schools. NEA remained adamant on the separation of church and state, creating an impasse that caused House members to balk and kill the bill.

Lobby Methods

Lobbies do not regularly canvass the entire Congress to achieve their goals. Contacts with selected, friendly members give each lobby an opening and a voice within Congress. The higher education lobby had Special Education Subcommittee Chairman Edith Green; the Washington Research Project had access to Senators Kennedy and Mondale; AVA had its special contacts. Says a spokesman:

AVA has a reputation as being pretty effective, and it has done that through having its members pretty close to the important folks in Congress. It was a southern oriented, rural tradition kind of thing that went along real well with the United States Congress where the positions of power were held by Southern Congressmen with long seniority. But, that is changing now as AVA and the Congress change. . . . I guess it boils down to the fact that the AVA members have had the right kind of touch or the right kind of clout with the right people. If we had to go out and massively influence 435 members of Congress, I would just have to say to you it could not be done unless they were ready to be influenced. But, if you want to pick out individuals like Carl Albert, the House Speaker, or Carl Perkins, the Chairman of the Education and Labor Committee, or others, we have got people back in their states that we can get to get them to do certain things. . . . There are six or eight members who are real crucial.

Members of Congress who take special interest in a lobby's desires will perform such services as introducing a bill desired by the lobby, arguing the cause of the lobby in hearings, inserting lines in committee reports favorable to the lobby, intervening in the administration to influence an administrative decision, and other matters.

The reasons why a member of Congress would cooperate with a lobby are various. It may be that a subcommittee chairman finds himself saddled with responsibilities and welcomes the assistance of the lobby; it may be that the member once sponsored a bill and feels obligated to protect it; or he may simply favor the issue. One means of gaining a member's cooperation is to convince him that the cause is proper. This could occur at conventional testimony at public hearings, at private meetings, or as a result of special techniques sometimes employed by the lobby to gain a member's attention. For example, all the major organizations have members who reside in every congressional district. The national organization can at times bolster its influence by relaying its desires to the congressman through one of his own constituents, particularly a prominent local citizen. For example, the NSBA has a special sort of appeal:

We have clout for a couple of reasons. One is because our members are elected public officials. Second, is when they come up and testify or talk to congressmen, the congressmen know damn well that the school board member's job, his livelihood, is not dependent upon him being a member of that school board. If that board member explains how something is not going to work and why he favors one over the other, nine times out of ten there will be no ulterior motive.

Or, again, with vocational education:

We try to get someone close to the congressman. I find out who can and keep in touch with them. For example, an important congressman is back in his state now, and I have not got the report on him which reminds me I have to call. We have a man in his state who is president of the state vocational association. He is a pretty sophisticated fellow. I was with him about three weeks ago right before the Easter recess. I told him that this bill was going to be introduced by the congressman and that we had been working with him on it. "Now," I said, "Your job is to go see him and to convince him that he should do all in his power to be getting some hearings established on this bill. You talk it through with him real good and tell him how much this means." In other words, I tried to brief our man to make him as smart as he could be and get him to ask the right questions and, you know, get him to pursue it. So, he got the appointment set up with the congressman.

Grass roots lobby pressure is actually infrequent. Members of Congress and staff know that the big groups represent real constituencies; thus, they readily supplant the requirement of grass roots pressure for face-to-face meetings with Washington-based lobbyists or group spokesmen. These information exchanges are welcomed by the members, but in varying degree. One congressman, a subcommittee chairman, says:

You just saw me complete a one and one-half hour conference here in my office on school desegregation with two gentlemen who represent two of the largest educational organizations in the country. We have gone over a great deal of detail involving this legislation. I did it personally because I am going to have to make some judgments on this bill. One man was the lobbyist for the school boards. He represents, for the most part, the school board members of the country. . . . I would not say their organization is powerful. What I would do is perhaps use the word knowledgeable. Now the lobbyist is close to the grass roots problems across the country. He is important to me as a chairman of the committee that is going to have to report this bill because he can give me kind of a conceptualization of the whole country. He has members that he is in touch with in every state. When you are dealing with a problem like desegregation, there are problems that are peculiar to southern districts but do not exist in Los Angeles but do exist in San Francisco. He has an input into his shop from school board members all over the country.

The National School Board Association is really a mosaic. While it is very true that they have their own viewpoint, that they believe in strong local control and guard it very zealously, the composite of their thinking becomes a national attitude if there is any validity in representative government. For that reason, all of these lobbies are extremely important. They are valuable tools to a member of Congress as long as they do not own you. It is one thing to call these fellows in and say, "O.K. What is your view of the problem, and what do you think your people would be willing to accept in the way of compromises." They will tell you, and you will weigh them against all the other information that you get; then you make your own judgment and decision. When they come in here and tell you this is the way it has got to be and no other way, the thing to do is just boot them out of your office.

A lobbyist says:

I have never yet run into an instance where I have not been received cordially and with interest by a member of Congress. I have never run into a confrontation with a member of Congress.

Like all legitimate lobbyists, he is welcomed by House members as well as by certain staff (particularly in the Senate) in the performance of the proper function of his job. He is a part of the process.

Another prominent House education subcommittee member says:

As far as the associations are concerned, I listen to what they have to say. I think they do have some influence on me. But I recognize, for instance, that the NEA is primarily made up of teachers; therefore, they have a selfish interest in the teaching profession. The School Board Association is acting primarily from the point of view of school board people; the AASA, the superintendents, or the chief state school officers operate from their vantage points. So, I recognize the selfishness of their positions. At the same time, I recognize the intimate knowledge they have of education, and I accept that as a valid contribution to the whole process.

The outstanding political strengths of the big lobby groups is their continual presence in Washington from which comes enduring political contacts (they know which buttons to try to push) and expertise. Whenever an issue arises that affects the group's interest, they are ready to jump into the fray and at least make their position known. Based on their grass roots constituency and the aura of legitimacy which it brings, the lobbyist or spokesman gains access and respect for his opinions. A lobby is only one voice, however, sometimes contradicted by another lobby, always supplemented by numerous spokesmen, and often not entirely in step with the biases and opinions of the men and women in government who ultimately make the decisions.

Coalition Efforts

If the major lobby groups could ally on matters of fundamental policy, their power would be, and has shown to be, geometrically magnified. One lobbyist notes:

We are not going to win or lose education legislation by ourselves. I think that when we get with other groups and form a broad base and just get a much wider constituency, you have a multiple effect—you can say power, if you like—over members of the House or Senate. By joining the coalition it makes it much harder for the elected representatives to resist a common objective. You can have the AFL-CIO, NEA, maybe the librarians, maybe some of the higher education people, the civil rights groups, the NSBA, or others all supporting a given bill. If you can all work together in an effort to have input on a given member or a given committee, you damn well do have a broad base.

This ideal is difficult to achieve. Although many of the groups share general goals, the differences are usually enough to prevent policy unification. Says one lobbyist:

A major battle to achieve a general aid bill is right now too complicated. What kind of formula can we get up? We get ourselves into that split-up battle again. We have never been able to come up with the specifics of a bill that we could get the kind of coalition support that would be necessary. That is why I made the statement that it depends on whether we are talking in terms of how much persuasion we have in Congress depends somewhat on what the other forces are doing. On a general aid bill you have the concerns of the parochial schools for one. You have concerns of the civil rights people. They do not trust anything going through the states, and they are more effective at the federal level through categorical legislation. Then you have got certain organizations that are organized basically at the federal level who are not strong at state levels. The AFL-CIO is the best example. They are not really operative in education at the local level.

In short, the self-interest of a number of organized lobby groups would not necessarily lie in unity in support of general aid to education. Many groups that have gained favor under categorical programs fear losing not only their special privileged status but also continued growth of that status. If a broad general aid bill is to come forth, government leadership, not lobby (professional) leadership, will be the principal directing force.

Between 1969 and beyond 1973, the major education maintenance lobbies plus the AFL-CIO did draw together into a strong, winning coalition to obtain additional funding for education. It is worth retelling part of the story.

From 1960 to 1969 the lobbies were occupied with obtaining new legislation authorizing new programs. During this period little attention was paid to the funding of these programs. Funding seemed to proceed normally, but the last presidential budget of the Johnson administration, which became the basic budget document for President Nixon's first year (1969), reflected administration desires to cut back. Cuts in the education portion of the budget were dramatic. Every lobby was adversely affected.

Although the lobbies do compete and disagree about many substantive issues, the lobbyists themselves are friendly. A number of them would on occasion meet and have a drink together at the old Congressional Hotel across from the House office buildings. Whatever the social benefits of these meetings, politically they served as an informal arena to breach organizational introversion. During several of these sessions lobbyists from the NSBA, NEA, ALA, NAVA, "Impact Aid," and others agreed that the budget recommendations would hurt all and help no one. Their organizational leadership agreed that it was in the interest of everyone to bring more dollars to each of the programs.

To contravene a presidential budget proposal or a decision of the House Appropriations Committee is a structurally complicated task, never accomplished without difficulty and seeming to require the absence of one element. That is, it is necessary there there be no important lobby opposition to the budget increase request. One major lobby can raise enough conflict to prevent another lobby from getting an appropriations increase—united we stand, divided we fall. Equally important, there must be great and active support from the most important as well as the lesser lobby groups.

In 1969 and in subsequent years, the giant education lobbies, joined by the AFL-CIO and many smaller groups and affiliations, set aside their differences over substantive policy and achieved a strong front by forming the Emergency Committee for Full Funding. The basis of the Emergency Committee was an agreement that for a short term (for "emergency" purposes), all participants would support one goal: to press Congress to allocate federal dollars for every education law on the books to the limit permitted in authorizing legislation, i.e., to the limits of full funding. ("Full funding" refers to the upper limits to which Congress has authorized expenditures for a certain provision. The annual appropriations process determines the actual amount of dollars to be allocated, which can be less but not more than the authorized amount.) The Emergency Committee avoided all value judgments about which authorized legislation was "best" or most worthy. Dollars were the only goal.

Groups of unequal power and diverse functions found incentives to join in mutual support. Maintenance groups like the NEA or NSBA, joined by the AFL-CIO as well as the higher education lobbies, supported the coalition because their common goal was to pump more money from all sources into the education system, on the reasoning that eventually the money reaches the causes they support, like teacher's salaries, tax relief, and expanded school and university services. As long as these groups do not oppose each other, their combined lobby power is considerable. Another vital component of the Emergency Committee coalition was the loosely organized advocates of increased support for Impacted Area School Aid. Impact Aid derives from Public Laws 815 and 874, both of which give general aid to school districts based on the number of children of federal employees attending a school district. The spokesmen for Impact Aid have considerable power—indeed, they are the foundation on which the other lobbies operate. Because Impact Aid is allocated to school districts with no strings attached, school board members and educational administrators support it. Because impact aid is a "pork barrel," that is, it is federal dollars for use in a congressman's district, and because it flows into 383 districts, it commands enormous congressional support. Like the AVA and supporters of the popular vocational education provisions, supporters of Impact Aid are needed by the other lobbies.

The weaker interests, like bilingual education, which has virtually no lobby, or loosely organized interests like aid to the disadvantaged, as well as a number of other small categories, could probably get little for themselves without support from the stronger groups. Standing alone in an appropriations struggle, they would have suffered; thus the weak needed the strong to lift their appropriations. And, because the weaker groups are backed by moral rectitude, the stronger groups embraced them to make a show of moral and professional solidarity. Public opposition by groups of poor people or handicapped children could damage the cause, so the coalition for dollars struck a commonweal.

The Emergency Committee began operations under a governing board drawn from the various education lobbies and under the management of its executive director, Charles W. Lee. The major function of the Emergency Committee was communication with the House and Senate policy makers, with member groups, and with sundry people across the country. Lee coordinated information from all sources and the resources available to gain congressional support. The committee was financed by a loan from member groups and then by a number of relatively small contributions from hundreds of sources. The total budget remained modest.

Lee was eminently and uniquely qualified for the job of executive director. As long-time aide to Senator Wayne Morse and as counsel of the Senate Education Subcommittee which Morse chaired before his reelection defeat in 1968, Lee became intimately involved with education legislation, with all of the players in federal education politics, and with the mechanics and nuances of the operation of the Senate and House. He knew education and politics and people. Most important, he was trusted by all of the lobbyists.

Lee began committee sessions with early morning breakfasts. (Early morning was not only a good hour when everyone was free, but also followed Senator Morse's folksy tactic of testing a man's dedication by seeing if he would get up early in the morning for the cause.) With policy resolved—pursuing full funding for all—the meetings dealt with tactics, including such things as getting the "right person" to act as a front for the committee (in the first year they reached into the higher education community to find Arthur Flemming, a distinguished college president and a former Republican Secretary of Health, Education and Welfare); identifying members of the House who would sponsor amendments to increase the appropriations; determining lobby methods; planning the timing of moves; solving housekeeping problems of the Emergency Committee itself, and hundreds of other details.

Emergency Committee action focused on two arenas, the Congress and "the public."

Phase 1 centered on the House of Representatives, and specifically on the Labor and Health, Education, and Welfare subcommittee of the House Appropriations Committee. This phase of the lobby effort ended quickly when a plea from the Emergency Committee to the thrift-minded Appropriations Committee resulted in an unsatisfactory compromise offer.

Phase 2. Unable to arrive at a simple solution in the Appropriations Committee, the Emergency Committee, as anticipated, had to shift the field of play to the House floor. On the floor, the agenda would be first set by the Report of the Appropriations Committee (a report that did not include satisfactory education increases). The tactic planned, a classic strategy, was for a congressman in alliance with the Emergency Committee to introduce an amendment on the House floor that, if adopted, would dramatically increase education appropriations and thus overrule the powerful Appropriations Committee.

The first move of Phase 2 brought the Emergency Committee into negotiations with a liberal Appropriations Committee member and other members who offered to sponsor the amendment. At their first meeting, Lee, speaking for the lobbies, presented an "asking list" of about a 1.3 billion dollar increase over the Nixon budget recommendations. True to Emergency Committee policy, the asking list represented full funding for education. The congressmen, who would be faced with defending the amendment on the House floor, examined the list, and after additional meetings they determined that it was feasible to offer an amendment proposing an increase of 800 million dollars. This decision was based on political calculations about what kind of package could be sold and on ideological grounds, that is, which increases made good policy.

The 500 million dollar difference between the asking list and the compromise offered by the congressmen represented cuts from full funding in all legislative areas, but some lobbies were cut proportionately more than others. The Emergency Committee itself remained aloof from the final decision to cut. Although informal negotiations between the congressmen and Lee may have occurred, at least ostensibly the congressmen took responsibility and had final power. This policy was crucial because in the final analysis it kept the Emergency Committee loyal to its pledge not to favor any of its members. Although some of the groups within the Emergency Committee lost vigor after the cuts, the coalition did not break. No lobby opposition arose. This was vital to success.

Phase 3. Although all congressmen "support education" in the abstract, most do not favor spending increases. House tradition predicts that floor action on an appropriations bill will almost always follow Appropriations Committee recommendations. Two hundred and eighteen votes are needed for passage if all members attend—a majority of the House—and many of those members had to be convinced that the priority of education finance exceeded the value of thrift. (Only a majority of those present and voting are needed to pass a floor measure, but 218, one more than half of 435, is the only safe figure from which to plan.) Convincing a majority of House members to go against the Appropriations Committee and spend almost a billion dollars extra presented an elaborate, unprecedented task that would involve intricate organization. The best strategy in this case was to mobilize a massive, grass roots movement to contact virtually every member of the House.

Mobilizing the public is the classic democratic means of influencing Congress. The fact that it occurs so infrequently perhaps testifies more to its difficulty than to its undesirability. A true grass roots movement is effective. As Lee said, "The echo creates the yell." The noises from the spaces of America can create the sound of leadership in Congress. Lee had to make certain that virtually every congressman knew that the folks back home wanted a budget increase for education.

The method of the Emergency Committee turned from closed door meetings to orchestrating liaisons among members of the House and tens of thousands of educators, school board members, administrators, businessmen, and other citizens. Each group in the Emergency Committee employed its own favored tactics to get their members to contact House members. NAVA had the salesmen from the various corporations contact their clients, AVA relied on state associations to get telegrams from localities into House offices, AASA contacted school superintendents, etc. As the floor vote neared, thousands of people were brought to Washington to make personal appearances in congressional offices. (The difficulty of this task was intensified by the unpredictable House floor agenda, where a flexible schedule often results in votes coming several days earlier or later than expected.)

The thousands of people who came to Washington were organized by congressional district into "packs," composed of representatives from as many diverse group affiliations as possible. A pack might contain a superintendent, a board member, a librarian, a teacher, an audiovisual expert, etc. At organizational meetings in the Rayburn House Office Building—with rooms arranged through the good offices of the chairman of the Education and Labor Committee—the grass roots people were instructed on how to approach their congressman. Under supervision of the lobbyist from the AFL-CIO (the Emergency Committee man with the most experience in open lobby efforts), they were told to go to the congressman, let him know that the children of America sent them (not special interests), and that they were on a selfless mission. The grass roots people were told not to be awed by the trappings of official Washington—the mahogany desk and flags in the congressman's office. They were to ask the congressman not whether he was a supporter of education but very specifically whether he intended to be on the floor to vote, and if he intended to vote in favor of the amendment. The secret of the lobbyist was revealed—be direct, be confident, and most of all know exactly what you want and ask for it exactly.

Each pack had a kit containing information about the congressman, about the benefits to be brought by the amendment to his particular congressional district, and other material to help the grass roots people. In addition, the kit included reporting sheets on which the congressman's response was recorded. This data was returned to Lee, who could then tell which congressmen stood committed, which ones were hopeless, and which ones needed more prodding. Lee then engineered special heat; home town phone calls and telegrams descended on the wavering congressmen.

Personal contact between a representative and his constituents— particularly responsible citizens, educators of his district's children— is powerful medicine. In the first Emergency Committee floor amendment effort and in subsequent attempts, the lobby succeeded in mustering a majority of House members. Despite the Nixon administration's opposition to the amendment, the winning majority included some Republicans, who on this appropriations issue were convinced to respond to the demonstrative echo in their districts.

Victory in the House set the stage for a much easier job in the Senate. The Senate is traditionally more generous than the House on education appropriations. Indeed, the Senate often votes more money than the House-passed version, anticipating a compromise cutback in the joint House-Senate Conference to a level somewhat above the original House figure. Intensive grass roots lobby work did not have to be repeated in the Senate. The liaison could be handled by Emergency Committee leaders and a few critical senators and their staffs.

The complete story of the Emergency Committee for Full Funding is much longer, extending over several years, two presidential vetoes, one veto override, and other struggles. A full history of the committee would have to include its legacy on education appropriations, which continued beyond the formal existance of the Emergency Committee. The effectiveness of the legacy is reflected in a bitter floor speech by Congressman Daniel Flood (D., Pa.), chairman of the Labor-HEW subcommittee of the House Appropriations Committee. Flood, of course, wanted the recommendations of his subcommittee upheld on the House floor. He deplored the lobby coalition effort to pass an enlarging amendment. In 1972, when the House once again was considering another large increase over Flood's subcommittee

report and over the president's budget recommendations for education (an amendment which passed, causing President Nixon to veto
the entire HEW appropriation measure), Flood remarked on the floor
of the House:

Mr. Chairman, I rise in opposition to the amendment.

Apparently, the authors of this amendment do not like the term "package."
Now [they call it] a "quality" amendment. Don't you love that . . . ? Now it is a
"quality" amendment. The name has changed, but the same people are behind
it. . . . They used to hang out in the Congressional Hotel. Now that is closed
down, of course, and they meet in some hidden, mysterious place in the dead of
night to concoct these amendments.

I am reminded of the three preparing the witch's brew in Macbeth: "When shall
we three meet again? In thunder, lightning, or in Maine?"* They call it a quality
amendment. At the shopping center we see quality beer, quality corn, or quality
bologna. No matter how thin you slice it, it is still bologna. [1]

So, in the face of powerful structural and political opposition, the
strength of coalition politics in both education authorization and
appropriations has been proven over time. Not only is a coalition
possible among elite national spokesmen, but grass roots people also
can be united. The latter requires tremendous effort and is not a
viable alternative to ongoing decision-making by representative elites.
However, the demonstrative palpability of grass root interests is more
than a ploy of power; it is proof of representative government on
these issues. Further, it is evidence that, in education, power is available if the issue is clear and shared.

Lobbies and the Administration

The relationship between the lobbies and the administration is
discussed in chapter 4. However, it should be said here that lobbies
seek to exert influence wherever possible. If a lobby can have a hand
in developing the administration legislative proposals, it will eagerly
exercise whatever influence is available. The same is true for the
administration's budgetary process although no lobby under any
administration has had a major hand in it. The differences in lobby
relations between the middle level USOE bureaucracy and the high
level policy makers is marked. This is discussed also in chapter 4, but

*"Maine" refers to the Democratic congressman from Maine who sponsored
the appropriations increase amendment, Representative (now Senator) William
Hathaway.

it is worth noting here that lobbies do better with the established middle level bureaucrats than with the more flamboyant policy makers.

Conclusion

In whatever form the lobby exists (and this chapter has used a broad definition), their political function extends to the development and representation of recommendations which they would like translated into official policy. Lobby power is thus not the ability to make authoritative decisions. It is measured as a function of getting others to grant what the lobby wants.

Lobby power is mainly "influential." Influence is the ability to generate arguments that convince an authoritative decision maker to act. There are several bases on which an authoritative decision maker might support a lobby. Some decision makers simply respect the group's prestige and respond to its pronouncements. (NEA opposition to the Kennedy bill was sufficient for many House members and, up until 1963, the position of the American Vocational Association virtually determined the federal government's vocational education policy.) Other decision makers embrace a lobby because of ideological compatability or because of ad hoc circumstances where the decision makers think the lobby is correct. Lobby power also commonly results from the lobby's ability to identify a unique issue and propose a solution (or justify reaffirmation of an established policy) that an official decision maker can support and subsequently advocate as his own position.

Most often no single voice controls. Because lobbies compete, their conflicting efforts often reveal needs and solutions that reasonably differ on the same issue (NAVA wants dollars for hardware-software and the American Library Association wants essentially the same dollars for books, etc.) The authoritative decision-maker (for example, a congressman) must weigh the influence efforts, and tends to become either an advocate for one group over another or a Solomon offering conflict-resolving compromise. Most often a final decision is the synthesis of the authoritative decision-maker's thoughts and compromises rather than of the unmodified agenda of the lobby.

In unusual circumstances, for example the Emergency Committee's efforts in the House, the lobby is not so much a direct influence as it is a vehicle for mobilizing popular opinion. Popular opinion, in American mythology and at the polls, is a higher form of authority than the congressman himself and a form of authority to which the congressman is prone to respond. In any event, even if the lobby is "powerful" and can exert firm guidance over official decision-makers, it is the latter, not the former, who make the authoritative allocation.

It is vital to note again that the big education groups do not control access to or influence with a decision-maker. A number of assorted people actively, if sometimes surreptitiously or inconspicuously, seek successfully to influence decision-makers. A powerful example, mentioned above, is the foundation-funded scholar who produces policy-oriented research (as opposed to "basic research") for the specific purpose of feeding ideas into the legislative and administrative processes. He is an expert with an agenda presenting a double-barreled thrust—information and a program. Such a person always has an advantage over those who do not know exactly what they want.

Sometimes a single expert or set of experts emerges as the principal lobby on an issue because none of the established groups possesses the expertise or wants the responsibility. This was the case with the Early Childhood Education Act, in which the big professional lobbies had minimal input partly because they had no history of concern with early childhood education and partly because the bill was developed by independent House liberals, who tend not to turn to the big groups for advice anyway.

The influential position of reform-oriented experts not associated with the big lobby groups in part reflects the inability of the giant lobbies to advocate other than a lowest common denominator program. It is also a reflection of the political realities of the 1960s and early 1970s, when ardent liberals controlled Congress and particularly the House Education and Labor Committee. The liberal winds of politics drew some advisory voices in and sent others to wander. Of course, even if the House were to become patently conservative on education (more than it has been), this does not mean that the big lobbies would then take over. A new genre of experts espousing "reform," but with a conservative twist, could gain an inside track, leaving the big lobbies in their somewhat midfield power position.

The vagaries and complexities of Congress are a story in themselves, and to that we turn in the following chapter.

Note for Chapter 2

1. U.S., Congress, House, *Congressional Record*, 92d Cong., 2d Sess., June 15, 1972, p. H5673.

3. The Congress

Representative Jamie Whitten (D., Miss.) is due in traffic court Monday following a Georgetown accident in which his car collided with another auto, jumped the curb, struck an iron fence and two trees and smashed into a wall. A third car on the other side of the wall was damaged. According to a witness the first thing Whitten did was to get out of his car and begin shaking hands.—AP News

To civics students and historians, the Congress of the United States is one of the world's most impressive, continuous democratic bodies. Its testimonial is its longevity. To daily observers of its life, Congress sometimes seems an asylum whose inmates, confined for two-year spells, struggle to make sense of the national scene by occasionally spilling out a consensual message in the form of a law. The internal life of Congress varies from the pomp of House doorkeeper Mr. Fishbait Miller announcing, as did heralds of old, that the

President of the United States has arrived, to a New York congressman, derriere protruding, sniffing exhaust from a car to dramatize
the problem of air pollution in hopes of getting a spot on the evening
television news. Congress moves from grand Senate oratory to back
room tough bargaining; from issues of war and peace to pork barrel
activities and whether or not the *Congressional Record* should be
printed on new or recycled paper; from vigorous, brilliant men in
their prime to doting codgers unable to comprehend and uninterested in the problems of their times to slick, expedient hucksters.
The Congress is a potpourri, a condensation of virtually every aspect
of American life, life-styles, character, and quality. Putting all this
under one roof and asking the participants to agree on great issues is
an awesome phenomenon.

Congress is the target of the nation's conflict and was consciously
created that way by the founding fathers. Its internal structure veri-
tably panders to conflict, preventing Congress from acting easily.
Often it is criticized because it cannot act easily for the good. The
more important quality is that Congress is easily disabled from acting
at all. It was designed to ensure compromise and to protect from
abrupt or narrow use of power. To the citizen, this is its glory; to the
political analyst, a kind of nemesis. There is little science buried in an
institution designed for irregularity. The inherent difficulty and complexity of congressional action must be kept in mind during the
discussion that follows.

The House of Representatives

The House defies any single description. At any one moment it is a
most complicated organization, and its dynamics change in myriad
ways daily, often momentarily.

Each of the 435 members is responsible first to his electorate,
which votes him up or down, as well as to his party and to the House
itself. Every member of Congress is also responsible to the "public
interest" of the whole nation. As members of committees and as
voting members of the entire House, the solons are called on to treat
issues that may have little direct relationship to their constituency or
that bear on the whole country as much as on their states or districts.
A great deal of the member's work is absorbed in intense and specific
lawmaking, involving intimate details of legislation that his constitu-

ents will never know or perhaps feel the effects of—education issues included.

No two members of Congress fulfill their responsibilities in the same way. Each congressional office is a sort of unique, private corporation, with the elected member as chairman; the work load of his employees, the political perspective, and the productivity of the office depend on the ambience he establishes. Thus a legislative aide in one congressman's office may be working on extending federal aid benefits, while in another office an aide may be working on exactly the reverse, and, in three hundred other offices, no one may be aware of or interested in what is going on in the first two.

The House is an institution that requires its variegated members to act in unison as colleagues capable of reaching consensus in a majority vote. This is a formidable goal. A majority of 435 is 218, and where each member may be at cross-purposes to some degree with every other, a majority is almost always a delicate balance.

In achieving this balance, the final floor vote is only an end point of the complex workings of the House inner space. Structured patterns and customs, imposed and self-imposed on the House, expedite its work. The most important principles of congressional order are division of labor (through the committee system) and a degree of focalization of power (through the seniority system). The committee system permits issues to find a home and possibly a specific remedy, and the seniority system, even in the modern Congress, concentrates enough power in one man or small group of men to activate procedures for processing an issue.

The Education Committees

Each bill introduced in the House that bears on education is referred by the house speaker to the full Education and Labor Committee. The committee initially does nothing with the bill; rather, the committee chairman refers it to one of the education subcommittees.

Since 1961, three education subcommittees have handled all bills designed to authorize education laws. Like the full committee, each subcommittee has its own jurisdiction, that is, areas of established legislative responsibility, and ordinarily the full committee chairman assigns bills to subcommittees according to the customary jurisdiction. For example, the Special Education Subcommittee handles higher education, the General Education Subcommittee handles elementary and secondary education, vocational education, and Impact Aid, and the Select Subcommittee has handled topical bills not in the mainstream, such as drug abuse and environmental education, as well as the larger areas of educational research and early childhood education.

Individuals on the Education and Labor Committee

All education laws that emerge from Congress have their foundations shaped by the few men and women who compose a House education subcommittee—committees are composed of individuals, and that is where the story begins.

The full Education and Labor Committee has often been the focus of America's most heated domestic strife, first in labor matters (with the most divisive moment over the Taft-Hartley Act in 1949), then in the social reform efforts of the 1960s. More than any committee in Congress, the Education and Labor Committee has attracted men and women of variegated passions, ideologies, and personal flamboyance, with pro and con slants in every direction. The following background sketches of five members hint at their varied persuasions.

Congressman James H. Scheuer (D., Bronx, N.Y.) served from 1965-72.* A committee member who was never a chairman, Scheuer represented a district of poor blacks and Puerto Ricans (most of whom do not vote) and very liberal Jews (most of whom do vote). As the multimillionaire son of a multimillionaire, Scheuer was elected to office with his own financial support and the political backing of the Reform Democratic Movement in New York City. The Reform Democrats, who were initially devoted to breaking up the New York City machine (the so-called "Organization Democrats") at the local level, advocated ultraliberal reform policies at the national level. Thus, Scheuer's active home political constituency, which in effect amounted to several hundred active members of Reform Democratic clubs in New York, expected their candidate to support militant reform of all types. Scheuer's flamboyant personal-

---

*Scheuer's defeat was a direct result of the requirement to redistrict New York State. In the 1972 race, New York City lost a congressman, and the new congressional map drawn by the state legislature pitted Scheuer against a popular incumbent. In a hard-fought contest, Scheuer lost. The winner, it should be noted, was also a Reform Democrat who held views indistinguishable from Scheuer's.

ity and publicity-seeking desires fit well into the competition among Reform Democrats to establish the most "liberal" record—the strongest opposition to the war in Vietnam, the most vigorous opposition to environmental pollution, first advocacy of abortion availability, the largest Social Security increase proposal, or advocacy of the most current and largest social welfare program. Scheuer, in both personal disposition and constituency support, freely advocated the largest increase for the broadest and perhaps most expensive education and welfare programs.

Congressman Albert Quie, the Education and Labor Committee's ranking Republican elected in 1958, is from rural Minnesota, which has Rochester as its largest city. He is elected to Congress by a virtually all-white, relatively wealthy, mostly farming or farm-related constituency. Voter turnout in southern Minnesota is very high, and the more people who turn out, the more Republicans there are to support Quie. His is a "safe" seat. His Republican constituency has no equivalent of "reform clubs," like Mr. Scheuer's. People in southern Minnesota tend to value the status quo and seek to utilize and develop it through thrift, hard work, and self-help. By his quiet and disciplined nature and based on his constituency, Quie advocates "responsible" federal programs. Although a strong advocate of federal aid to education, he favors the allocation of federal dollars to the state and then to the school districts for use as determined by local governments. He would prefer to keep federal reform programs and direct federal power, but not federal dollars, out of education.

Congressman Roman Pucinski, elected continuously from 1958 to 1972 from the northwest side of Chicago, became chairman of the Special Education Committee. His political career grew through the Chicago Democratic political organization ("the machine" under the tutelage of Mayor Richard Daley), and he worked his way up in traditional fashion to become one of the most trusted organization leaders. (Pucinski left his House seat in 1972 to run as the organization's sacrifice candidate against the very popular incumbent Senator Charles Percy, and was soundly defeated.) Like Quie, Pucinski had a safe constituency, but the characteristics differed. Pucinski's district was solidly urban, white, middle-class, and Democratic. But the congressional district from which Pucinski was elected composed only part of his real constituency. His loyalty and responsibilities extended to the entire Cook County Democratic organization, headed by Mayor Daley. A major function of his role in Congress was to bring as much money and service as possible to the city of Chicago (as well as to perform his congressional duties as creditably as possible). Beyond loyalty to the organization, his ideology, following the tradition of big city machine politics, was New Deal: modest progress toward helping people but without fundamental political reform at any stage. He favored federal aid to education in its varied forms, especially vocational education because much of his constituency was not college bound. Unlike Scheuer but like many big city Democrats, his liberalism stopped abruptly at federal efforts of any sort to bypass and dissipate local organization power. This meant discouraging or encouraging federal grants depending on how they served the organization. Most of all it meant blocking federal policies that could cost the organization votes. No issue in education, or indeed in Congress as a whole, was more perilous in that regard than the bussing of school children to obtain racial balance. Thus, one of Pucinski's most difficult trials in Congress occurred during his last year in office when his committee handled the Emergency School Assistance Act, which was designed to ease the strains of school desegregation. Pucinski was in a powerful position that could enhance his career and the interests of the Daley organization by ensuring that dollars were allocated to school districts without permitting the intensely unpopular bussing of children. The act, if passed in a "liberal" form, could have aided school bussing in the North and thus have identified Pucinski and Daley with the most unpopular issue of the day—and in an election year. Short of a public obscenity or a crime, only by supporting or even facilitating bussing could he have caused as much voter wrath against himself, and the organization. He worked hard and successfully to create a "moderate" bill without bussing.

Representative Edith Green (D., Ore.), elected continuously from 1954 as a Democrat, became chairman of the Special Education Subcommittee responsible for higher education. During the period of the 1960s and early 1970s, the florescence of education legislation, Mrs. Green perhaps more than any other member brought to the committee a viewpoint that generated conflict. Mrs. Green's philosophy developed during the 1960s from enthusiastic support of the liberal program of President Kennedy to a position perhaps best described as populist. During the Johnson years she began to develop a distrust of centralized federal power, thus she was in the position of weighing the value of federal support for education against what she perceived as the potential abuse of federal power and the ineffectiveness of centralized program planning. Her Oregon constituency, which provided her a relatively safe seat, supported her eclecticism while both her Republican and Democratic colleagues on the Education and Labor Committee struggled to fathom her exact position.

As a final example, Congressman John Brademas, a Democrat elected in 1958 from an essentially Republican Indiana district, was reelected based mainly on his highly creditable congressional record. From the outset, Brademas conscientiously billed himself as the "education Congressman." Immediately after his election he went on a lone mission to Texas to House Speaker Sam Rayburn, with a request to be assigned to the Education and Labor Committee. Brademas's motives were not like Scheuer's, to join the committee because it was the place for the greatest social reform. Brademas sought the committee for the opposite reason—because "education" is a safe issue, one on which a Democrat dependent on Republican good will and votes can survive. Liberalism in education could make the liberal Democrat Brademas a "good congressman" back home. Furthermore, by being an education congressman he could avoid becoming involved involuntarily in highly partisan issues that could ruin his necessarily neutral image. (For an in-depth profile of Brademas, see the chapter by Jack H. Schuster.)

Scheuer, Quie, Pucinski, Green, and Brademas are a sample. Each of the thirty-eight members of the Education and Labor Committee has a unique story; each has been impelled by unique motives, and seeks to affect national education policies with different needs, goals, and styles. (Committee membership changes somewhat every two years, adding to variety.) The personal and political differences represented on the committee are both widespread and conflicting, setting the stage for policy disagreements and power struggles.

The Exercise of Power in the Committee—Individual Members

Individual members of a subcommittee possess unequal power and seek unequal use of the power they have. Thus, a member who has little seniority and is not a chairman, but who works hard and takes an interest in committee affairs can affect legislation and policy. A lazy subcommittee chairman—or a ranking member who chooses to put all his time into labor issues rather than education—can have less effect than the junior man. The means for a member to affect policy are varied. Two case studies, one of an ordinary member and one of a subcommittee chairman, illustrate some of the motives and methods whereby members come to gain power and exercise influence. The two cases, drawn from the sketches above, are both majority members (Democrats): James H. Scheuer and John Brademas.

Case 1. James H. Scheuer and the Environmental Education Act. On October 30, 1970, at San Clemente, against his better judgment, President Nixon unceremoniously signed Public Law no. 91-616, known as the Environmental Education Act:

To authorize the United States Commissioner of Education to establish education programs to encourage understanding of policies, and support of activities, designed to enhance environmental quality and maintain ecological balance.[1]

The story begins thirteen months earlier under a portrait of George Washington in the members' dining room of the House of Representatives.

Fresh from a crushing and expensive defeat in the 1969 New York City mayoral election, placing fifth in a field of five candidates, Congressman James H. Scheuer returned to his congressional duties in Washington for the opening of the second session of the ninety-first Congress. Because of the mayoral campaign he had been absent from much of the second half of the first session. His record of absences, combined with the defeat, had blemished his record and caused personal discouragement, but his political problems were only beginning. New York State was to be redistricted for the 1970 congressional election, and to keep his seat in Congress Scheuer would have to seek reelection in a new district; in all probability, he would face the most difficult obstacle of a congressional election—he would have to run against another incumbent.

Like many left-liberal congressmen, during his career Scheuer had sought to be a principal sponsor of legislation. Having one's name as a sponsor of a bill is important to some congressmen because it provides them with press coverage (especially important in New York City where publicity is hard to get), material for newsletters, power in the bureaucracy where the law is administered, ego gratification, the attention of people interested in the law, organizational support during campaigns, and, perhaps, respect from colleagues. Mr. Scheuer had always been active in supporting reform legislation, and he had a few unusual successes while a new congressman as the principal sponsor of some major laws. (His most important contribution was the so-called New Careers legislation, a program for training and uplifting the poor into meaningful and promotable employment, often as "paraprofessionals." In Scheuer's case, the supporters and propagandists of New Careers publicized the program, giving him lavish credit and labeling the program money as "Scheuer dollars." Because much of his constituency was impoverished and eligible for New Careers support, it was hoped that his connection with the program—his dollars—would garner him votes. New Careers supporters even provided direct campaign support.)

Thus, at the opening of the ninety-first Congress, Congressman Scheuer, his shrewd and trusted administrative assistant Richard Brown, and his new, young legislative assistant sat down at lunch to plan a legislative strategy that would flatter the congressman's career and, it was hoped, gain him publicity and political support in the Bronx.* The congressman needed an issue—an "idea."

Scheuer had been a long-time opponent of the Vietnam War. (He was one of the first members of Congress to endorse the presidential bid of Senator Eugene McCarthy.) At the opening of the ninety-first Congress, the press and public fumed about the war, while Washington was preparing for the gigantic peace march of November 1969. But for Scheuer there remained little additional political mileage in the war. By 1969 he was one of many voices, and publicity comes to an ordinary congressman because he does something extraordinary.

At lunch, always a nervous affair with Scheuer, the administrative assistant, a witty veteran of New York politics, fingered the crystal water glass and began to talk about the crunching sound one experiences when driving through sections of the Bronx, where glass bottles

---

*Each member of Congress is provided with an office in one of three House office buildings and a staff, usually consisting of an administrative assistant (the man or woman second in command intimately involved in many aspects of the boss's life), a legislative assistant (usually a younger man who does staff work writing speeches, press releases, communication with constituents, drafting legislation, and researching problems for the congressman), perhaps another assistant or an intern, a caseworker who handles personal problems of constituents, and secretaries. In addition, money is provided by the government for an office in the member's home district. (The more of his staff budget the member spends in his district office, the less he has for Washington.) Each member also has telephones, office equipment and supply budgets, and many other amenities.

often find their end under a rolling tire. The conversation turned to pollution—bottles and cans—and one of Mr. Scheuer's major legislative thrusts was born. The legislative assistant returned to the office and in the next few weeks designed "the bottle bill," a bill that would discourage pollution by penalizing careless disposition of empty glass and aluminum containers. Now hooked on the subject, the legislative assistant noted from the *New York Times* that automobile desertions in New York City cost the city hundreds of thousands of dollars and great inconvenience, and, remembering Lady Bird Johnson's America beautification campaign, he moved from bottles and cans and conceived the abandoned automobile bill. The congressman and the administrative assistant were pleased. Although neither bill had a chance of becoming law, both were avante garde and could be introduced with the hope of some press coverage.

In early October, with antiwar pressure mounting, the congressman, who was known for conducting a great deal of his business in the House dining room, arranged to have lunch with his legislative assistant and a majority staff member of the full House Education and Labor Committee, a bright, affable fellow with no special training. A major part of his job was the special, nontechnical function of exchanging information and being an extension of the eyes and ears of the committee chairman. He characterized himself, without abnegation, as a "bullshit artist," and he lived in the center of the traffic pattern of conversations about issues affecting the committee. At lunch, the staff member was interested in the mayoral race and New York politics, and Mr. Scheuer wanted to tap into the central core of scuttlebutt about new and "politically sexy" issues.

Getting involved in an issue requires lead time. A congressman who wants to keep avante garde must be onto issues several months —sometimes a year or more—before they reach the front page. The staff member, a step ahead of the front pages, advised Mr. Scheuer to get involved broadly in the area of environmental quality. Senator Muskie had put himself in the field, but no House member had yet made a major dramatic committment; thus, the field was yet open. (With today's hindsight, the committee staff member may not seem particularly far-reaching, but it must be remembered that in fall 1969, environmental quality concerned only the hard core environmental faddists. Environment was not yet an "issue," and, to a politician looking to the future, the staff member's advice served to confirm other bits of wisdom, from the administrative assistant, that Mr. Scheuer should plunge in.)

The legislative assistant had a slightly different view than the committee staff man. The LA thought, "Bottles, cans, and abandoned autos are good issues, but what can a member of the Select Education Subcommittee of the House Education and Labor Committee do *both* to help education and to capitalize on coming political opportunities on the environmental issue?" For him, there were two masters—the profession of education and the congressman's political interests. Neither, particularly the latter, could be slighted.

At this point Mr. Scheuer's situation began to congeal. He wanted a dramatic issue for publicity purposes; he needed a reform issue because of his ideology; he was convinced that environment was a coming issue, and he was already dabbling in the area with bottles, cans, and automobiles. However, none of this had anything to do with education. Suddenly the proper synthesis emerged, and it became obvious that Mr. Scheuer should "author" legislation entitled the Environmental Education Act.

A phone call to the Select Subcommittee counsel (the direct employee of the full committee but the personal appointee of and in effect assistant to Chairman Brademas) revealed that he had already given the subject of environment some fleeting thought, but, because of work overload and lack of evidence about the priority of environment, no serious work had been done. The committee counsel was receptive and encouraging, and this was encouraging to the legislative assistant because it meant that Chairman Brademas would take an interest and perhaps hold hearings.

The legislative assistant made no further inquiries either within Congress or in the Republican administration. In dealing with flashy legislation like environmental education, covetousness and a degree of secrecy are necessary lest the idea be highjacked by a senator, a bureaucrat, or another representative before Mr. Scheuer could gain sponsorship and credit. Some members of Capitol Hill can become quite competitive.

At this point the legislative assistant drafted a policy memo to Congressman Scheuer:

Re: A Potentially High Payoff Angle to Environmental Pollution

(1) Intro.

On the question of environmental pollution and the approach you should take, several formats have been suggested during the last few weeks:

(a) Make yourself an all-around, generic "expert" on environmental contamination, including such topics as air pollution, water pollution, overpopulation, architectural squalor, and others. [The committee staff man favored this approach.]

(b) You could dabble in pollution with items like the bottle bill, junk autos, or others. This approach would utilize a dramatic stab at a number of items more for the publicity and shock benefit than to take a comprehensive approach to pollution. (This was the initial approach of our office as we began to seriously consider pollution problems.)

(c) You could sponsor a serious bill which will get hearings. Preferably, the hearings would be on one of your subcommittees where leadership on the issue would be acknowledged to be yours. This would provide you a public issue; you would build an alliance with many involved and well-intentioned environmentalists. Perhaps leadership on such a bill would draw you into a coterie of public figures in a new dimension where you have not delved. (This is the route I recommend.)

(2) The Plan

There is a need for a strong public education program on pollution and environmental abuse. The demand first comes from industry, which eschews regulation and would be eager, very eager, to support public education approaches. Secondly, there is a great deal of political mileage because no one is opposed to environmental protection particularly at the level of public education. Thirdly, from a cursory examination, public education on environmental contamination is now small scale and relegated to a few private groups and modest government activity (mostly Dept. of Interior, relating to parks and roadsides), therefore a government public education program can be easily and eagerly absorbed.

(3) The Plan for a *Public Education on Environmental Contamination Act*

The legislative format could include a range of public information programs: classroom curriculum and materials development; educational professional development along the lines of summer institutes; grants for university course development; university research grants for development of teacher education; development and disposition of materials for the media (a new Smokey the Bear program); a development of an elementary and secondary field of ecology; community action for clean cities programs; ecology in Higher Education.

(I should leave the rest of the page blank for the plethora of ideas which could come out of hearings.)

(4) Political Realities

If properly developed, it will go to your own Select Education (Brademas) Subcommittee. I understand that Brademas would be receptive to the idea, and some staff members would welcome the topic.

There is little question that this approach (a public education bill) is hanging in the air waiting to be plucked. The question is whether you want to get into the environmental field, and, if so, just how much staff time would the office be willing to spare. A major bill like this would take a lot of work and, of course, would mean sacrifice of other things. The advantage would be that the subcommittee staff would pick up much of the work load once the thing was underway.

I do not know about such problems as: Would this become a Brademas bill once it reached the committee? Is there mileage in the Bronx? How much leadership would you be permitted within the subcommittee? Will Brademas bring it to a hearing?

Mr. Scheuer read the memo and liked the ideas in it, but no commitment was immediately forthcoming. The following Saturday, a week before the huge 1969 antiwar protest, Mr. Scheuer attended a meeting in the New Senate Office Building, where leaders of several established, militant environmental groups were convened in near-total obscurity to discuss problems. Mr. Scheuer was the only elected official present, and he became a focus of the attention of a number of the environmentalists. The meeting dealt in broad, academic generalizations about the need for environmental protection, and when it ended Scheuer, the legislative assistant, and several environmentalists went for hot chocolate at a nearby hotel. The environmentalists, at that time lonely for official recognition, thoroughly reinforced Mr. Scheuer's interest and reacted positively to the proposal for an education act. To Mr. Scheuer, flattered and stimulated by his newfound company, all doubts were dispelled, and he ordered the legislative assistant to proceed in drafting the bill.

Within days a version of the drafted bill lay on Mr. Scheuer's desk. Without reading the actual content, he suggested that it be sent down to the counsel of the select subcommittee for technical brush up. Further, he wanted the title of the bill to be phrased in such a way that it would be referred to the select subcommittee, where presumably his membership would give him leadership and control. This minor decision—to send the bill to subcommittee for brush up—proved to have unhappy consequences for Mr. Scheuer.

The alternative to giving the subcommittee counsel a hand in drafting the bill would have been to send it to the nonpartisan, nonpolitical Legislative Drafting Service, where teams of experienced lawyer-technicians take a memo containing the substance of legislation and convert it into technical, precise, legal language. Using this route, Mr. Scheuer could then have had a proper bill in hand to throw into the hopper as the lone and original sponsor. However, the bill went to the counsel of the subcommittee. On November 12, 1969, the legislative assistant received a call from the select subcommittee counsel that his boss, Congressman Brademas, had introduced H.R. 14753, the Environmental Quality Education Act, with himself as principal sponsor and Mr. Scheuer and two Republicans as co-sponsors. The bill, slightly modified but clearly the work of Mr. Scheuer's office, had been highjacked, but not without good reason, and, for the sake of the bill, perhaps with desirable ends.

In 1969 Mr. Scheuer was fourteenth in seniority on the Education and Labor Committee. Although a member of Congress is entitled to introduce any bill he deems important, only a committee chairman is in the critical position of being able to call hearings on the bill and expedite its movement. It was Brademas, not Scheuer, who could launch the bill on the way to becoming law. On the Drug Abuse Education Act, Chairman Brademas encouraged and aided Congressman Lloyd Meeds's (fifteenth in seniority) effort to be the principal sponsor and legislative leader of the bill. However, on environmental education, Mr. Brademas wanted the leadership for himself. He snapped up the bill when it first surfaced, leaving Mr. Scheuer only token recognition. Mr. Scheuer was denied the opportunity to become the legislative focus of the bill, and lobbyists and other interested parties turned to Brademas.

The story of Mr. Scheuer and environmental education illustrates how the individual efforts of one nonsenior member can be mobilized to effect the policy process. In this case, the basic work done by Mr. Scheuer's office was lost to the public eye—a misfortune for Mr. Scheuer's publicity needs—but, without his spearheading, the bill may never have been launched, or if it had been the form and content might have been quite different.

Case 2. John Brademas and the Accumulation of Power. Both the general and the special education subcommittees have kept their agendas busy either renewing existing legislation or considering major, new proposals that fall within their existing realms of jurisdiction. The general and special subcommittee chairmen have not needed to create new issues because their jurisdiction gave them responsibility for the largest and most important pieces of legislation.

Created to attend to the education items of least significance, the select subcommittee could have easily and justifiably languished. When John Brademas inherited the chairmanship in 1969, the committee had responsibility for some minor laws—on vocational rehabilitation, arts and humanities, older Americans, and a few other problems. But Brademas was not the kind of legislator to let his potential power remain fallow. Even before he assumed the chair he had exhibited a propensity for creating situations that would lend him stature, recognition, and influence over legislation. (Full committee chairman Adam Clayton Powell (D., Harlem, N.Y.) in 1965 had made Brademas, then a very junior member, the chairman of an ad hoc committee on international education, from which came the International Education Act of 1966.) To make the select subcommittee important, Brademas began to search for issues. He adopted the Drug Abuse Education Act, dramatized and passed the Environmental Education Act, and held hearings on an educational technology bill, among others. Over a period of years he established a record for getting things done—even if it was passing laws no one knew they wanted until he invented them. Explaining his eventful legislative record, he says:

I'm not chairman of the general education subcommittee handling elementary and secondary. That isn't where I happen to find myself.... I'd go batty locked into solely elementary and secondary, for instance, or solely higher education. ... The nature of my job is to try to be a leader in public policy in the areas that seem to require some leadership.... If you look at our committee last year [1971], we passed about eight laws, I guess. I don't mean to put in a box score kind of play, but without any question we were one of the most productive [committees in Congress].

(Why do you pursue so much legislation?)

It is not a political motivation in the sense that I am seeking some other office beyond the one I now have. Not political in that sense. It's political in the sense that you seek to extend your impact and your influence. After all, what am I here for?

Although some of the more conservative members of the Education and Labor Committee scorned Brademas's penchant for nurturing many pieces of showy but relatively meaningless legislation, which create bureaucracies but have no real program or dollar impact, his liberal record won respect from his more liberal colleagues. He was elected as vice-chairman of the liberal Democratic Study Group in the House, and by 1970 he became one of two deputy majority House whips, putting him in a junior House leadership position.

All the while Brademas continued to collect bits and pieces of power. When offered the ostensibly meaningless post of chairman of the House Printing Subcommittee (in charge of printing House documents), he relished the opportunity because it meant he would be given more office space (a small but classic office in the Capitol building itself), more staff who might spend only a small amount of time on House printing and the rest on education matters, and an opportunity to jolt his colleagues a bit by reforming House printing policies. (For example, he wanted to print the *Congressional Record* on recycled paper as a national example of conservation. He also wanted to redesign and rewrite House "public relations" documents, involving millions of pieces of literature.) These achievements reflected the growing internal credibility and respect of Mr. Brademas by the House leadership. He was able to claim that he was one of the best-informed members of the Education and Labor Committee; he had the respect of his liberal colleagues; he could get the job done; he would not sit back and wait for affairs to come to him.

And the more you have, the more you can get. In 1970-1971 Brademas, while still select committee chairman, found a way to step up his involvement in education from the relatively small but punchy issues to the gigantic issue of early childhood education and the solid domain of educational research through the then-impending bill to create a National Institute of Education (NIE).

After President Nixon raised the issue of the NIE, Brademas read the administration bill. He says:

I immediately called HEW and said I want that bill. They saw to it that I got it, and I introduced it and had it sent to my subcommittee. I said to the HEW officials, "You had better let me have it because I will give it much more sympathetic treatment than [either of the two other subcommittee chairmen]." They understood that instantly.

One other subcommittee chairman was considered by some to be a bit lazy; a second chairman to be hypercritical of educational research. The Republican administration HEW officials saw Brademas, the outspoken liberal, as the best man—a hard worker and a supporter of research. To Brademas it meant not only that he could finally father a major piece of legislation, but also that he could count on having research as his legislative bailiwick in the future. He relished the prospect:

With jurisdiction over educational research I can go into elementary and secondary; into anything, anything.

Early childhood education was far more dramatic. Aspects of it are discussed elsewhere in this chapter, but the essence involved the Brademas concoction and House passage of a huge bill providing multibillions of dollars for a great array of preschool education. It hit the public as somewhat of a surprise. President Nixon vetoed the bill, not only because of the cost but also on ideological grounds because he and other public commentators claimed it would have virtually communized the care of every preschool child in the United States.

Debate on the merits of the bill is not appropriate here. The point that Brademas proved quintessentially was how a single member, chairman of a subcommittee designed to be insignificant, could gain considerable power to advance his own standing and raise crucial national issues in education to the extent of causing a full-scale presidential retort. He showed that with imagination and a reforming instinct a member of Congress can create issues where none had hitherto existed, and then he can largely control their fate.

The two cases above illustrate some of the variables—ideology, motivation, position, network of communication, accumulation of power—that affect the behavior of a member of the committee. Other methods of influence are available to individual members.

Hard Work—An Individual Member's Right

Even without seniority or the drive that comes from special publicity or psychological needs, a junior subcommittee member can raise issues. He can even gain notoriety in the committee by "doing his homework," that is, by attending to his committee business, following its affairs, and becoming so well-informed that no business can be transacted without his scrutiny and contribution. Pertinent questions at hearings can lead to amendments to a pending bill or changes in the bill before it is reported. A sharp congressman who attends to details can, with a few words added or deleted, benefit or hinder, expand or contract, or take from one and give to another the most desired commodity in Washington: federal dollars. Strong argumentation on an issue is listened to by colleagues and is often accepted because reason is a powerful force when men assemble to solve a problem. The reader should not be so cynical about political decisions as to discount the power of clear thought, information, and problem-solving intellect. Its exercise is an ennobling act that can give a member power even without seniority.

Only One Vote. Some members of the committee influence education policy only through their vote and contribute little to the verbal argumentation or the design of the bill. The activist members involved in education are few—perhaps a dozen, on and off—and the rest of the Education and Labor Committee members, who concentrate on labor issues or problems on other committees, are available mainly for partisan or ideological show on votes to support, kill, or alter an item during mark-up sessions. These committee members are often uninformed about the details of the issue before them. They rely on the judgment and analysis of committee opinion leaders whose general viewpoints are congruent with their own. Their presence particularly at mark-up sessions can be crucial, however, because votes usher provisions to birth.

Chairmen as Individuals

Every session a large number of education bills are introduced into the House. The subcommittees could not hear them all, and, even if it were a physical and intellectual possibility, the chairmen would not do so. To some extent, hearings are called at the discretion of the chair, and the subcommittee chairman can choose to hear a bill (thus giving it a chance at life) or kill a bill by not hearing it. Further, if the chairman wants to hear and support a particular bill or advance a particular version of pending legislation, all he need do is introduce it himself, wait for it to be referred, and then call hearings. This gives the chairman some power to set the agenda according to his tastes.

Those individual members who hold high seniority—chairmen or leaders of the minority—must, because of their central position, take an active policy stand on virtually every issue that comes before the committee. Each has his own style, and, because of seniority, each has magnified opportunity to make a personal impression on legislation.

Because the philosophies, work styles, and ambitions of each member, and particularly the chairmen (and, during the 1960s and early 1970s, specifically Mrs. Green) differ, it matters which subcommittee and which chairman gains jurisdiction of a bill. The Special Education Subcommittee chaired by Representative Green had customary jurisdiction for higher education and the 1972 Higher Education Amendments fell under her auspices. As shown later in this chapter, her power and her particular impact produced a House version of the Higher Education amendments far different from one that would have emerged had Congressman Brademas or full committee Chairman Carl Perkins handled the bill.

In the case of the NIE bill, when Congressman Brademas asked HEW to send him the bill so that he could introduce it, he in effect arranged to gain jurisdiction of the bill, thereby setting a destiny for it that could have been very different. In that case, Mr. Brademas had no customary right to jurisdiction. Indeed, over a period of years through her investigations and exposures of alleged failures of USOE research efforts, Mrs. Green had established a certain basis for jurisdiction over the area. Had Chairman Perkins referred the bill to her subcommittee, the result would probably have been a less expansive version than that produced by the more optimistic research proponent, Brademas. (Further, by capturing the bill Mr. Brademas expanded his power in the realm of education and in effect constricted hers.)

Institutional Processes

An education subcommittee is a place of little glamor; it is one of many workbenches of the House. The greater part of the agenda of subcommittee work is composed of the often technical and obscure chores of structuring issues and renewing and restructuring established legislation. The task offers little romance and no escape.

Since 1965, when the great legislative breakthrough on federal aid to education was achieved in the Elementary and Secondary Education Act, a growing number of pieces of major, complicated legislation have been added to the existing melange of laws. These laws have been designed to expire in staggering years, and some must be renewed or at least reconsidered every year. The work of the committees is thus demanding and recurrent, and is made greater by the need to develop new legislation.

The task of creating legislation—particularly education legislation, which tends to be rather unnewsworthy—is not carried equally by all members. The subcommittee, officially composed of a chairman and perhaps seven majority and six minority members, ordinarily commands the intensive efforts of only a few members. The chairman must be somewhat active and take concern because responsibility falls directly in his lap. (Some chairmen have been notably lazy; running a subcommittee is hard work, and not all congressmen relish it. But that is the exception.) Other members participate according to their interest. Chairman Brademas illustrates how it may be necessary for the subcommittee to provide a sort of song and dance to involve members in the hard work. Speaking about NIE, he says:

We are going to have a year-long graduate seminar in educational research. I have had a number of hearings so far. I have taken the subcommittee to Paris, Oslo, and Britain looking at educational research centers there. We work hard. . . . A nice place to be, in Paris for a weekend. That is part of my strategy. I have to get the attention of my colleagues. They ask, "Brademas, what are you so interested in educational research for?" I said, "It's very interesting. Come along with me to Paris, and I'll show you." You have to get the attention of the mule if you are going to teach him anything. That is the theory I use. We are going to go to the Soviet Union in August on the same subject.*

Sources of Information

The working, active House member typically informs himself about the background intricacies, and potential solutions to pending issues. He tends not to rely on staff advice about what to do. A number of information channels are open to him. The first, and most classic, is the congressional hearing.

The Hearing. During the 1960s two types of hearings—the classical and the publicity hearings—dominated the Education and Labor Committee. In the 1970s a third type—legislative oversight—appears to be emerging in importance.

Hearings are based on bills. A bill is simply a piece of proposed legislation. There are several sources for bills. The administration almost always offers its version as developed by policy officials and bureaucratic technicians. Because of manpower, expertise, and presidential prestige, the administration version is always sufficiently well-developed to become a major focus of the committee's agenda. (The

---

*Sometimes this sort of activity is pejoratively labled "a junket." That is a misnomer here. In terms of dollars, the amount of money spent for committee activity of this sort is negligible in terms of the cost of operations of Congress. Second, such hearings can not only play an important political role in gaining the involvement of congressional members, they also provide information to the public and professionals as well as to the members. In addition, as sponsor of the International Education Act, Mr. Brademas has secondary interests in maintaining international education contacts.

ranking member of the party of the president routinely introduces the administration version.) If the administration is of a different party than the majority of the House (and sometimes even if it is not), the subcommittee chairman uses his staff and whatever other aides are available—often lobby or available technical expertise—to develop and introduce another version dealing with the same subject but with different provisions.

Thus, a major piece of legislation—for example, on higher education or vocational education—comes before the subcommittee in at least two versions, Republican and Democratic. The main bills in their alternative forms are often supplemented by minor bills dealing with associated topics (like an Indian education bill associated with a larger bill dealing with postsecondary education) introduced by members at the request of interest groups or because of a concern by the member himself. (In addition, another or several different versions of the bill may be introduced in the Senate, complicating the House work.)

In the context of the classical hearing, the initial bills are only working documents. The final product—the reported bill—may well bear only partial resemblance to its progenitor because, once introduced, conflict and compromise rather than fiat determine its destiny.

With the bills in hand setting the broad agenda, hearings begin and undertake to examine the virtues, evils, benefits, and losses of the many provisions. Virtues and evils, benefits and losses, are usually relative matters that depend on whose interests are at stake. And everyone's interest is heard: at the invitation of the chairman, at their own request, and at the request of other committee members, experts and spokesmen for myriads of groups come to testify on all or parts of the bill. Each witness seeks to "build a record" of his or his group's position, endorsing or condemning provisions, adding ideas in the hope they will be incorporated into law, and providing documentation so a sympathetic committee member will have an official basis later to offer an amendment in mark-up or a line in the committee report supporting the group's interest.

There is no mystery as to how these groups and spokesmen find their way before the committee. First, the administration is always invited to offer its opinions. The secretary of the Department of Health, Education, and Welfare, the assistant secretary for education of HEW, the U.S. commissioner of education, the director of NIE, and other officials carry the official administration position.

Secondly, many subcommittee decisions determine who shall be the recipient of federal dollars. Dollars are a magnet, and all groups interested in federal resources—from the NEA seeking to raise teachers' salaries to the NAVA trying to sell movie projectors—keep tabs on subcommittee affairs. (Some groups, like the National Audio Visual Association, are so adept at ferreting out places in the law where dollars can potentially be spent on their projects, and are one hundred percent likely to lobby and testify, that the people who draft the laws seem voluntarily to include language giving NAVA a piece of the action.)

Thirdly, the committee seeks advice from experts, often university professors, practitioners in the field, or people who have established reputations in the matters before the committee. Not unlike lobbyists, experts cannot be considered neutral parties to the policy process; they are interested in seeing the law shaped according to their professional recommendations. They do not directly, ostensibly at least, pursue personal profit, but even the experts are not always pristine. They may be protecting institutional investments, or merely the prestige of their ideas. For example, in the hearings on higher education in 1970, spokesmen for large universities tried to counteract prestigious studies which urged that federal dollars be given directly to students rather than to the institutions and thus indirectly to students. The competing testimony raised a vast issue portending change in the distribution of power at institutions of higher learning. It involved a value judgment more far-reaching and controversial than a decision merely to permit the purchase of a movie projector with federal dollars.

In short, witnesses come before the committee to protect or advance their own direct interests, whether those interests are classified as mercantile, ideological, institutional, or intellectual.

The House education subcommittees tend to hold copious hearings. Many days of testimony and thick volumes of live and appended statements and data compose the typical House education hearing record. Ordinarily, no one who can show a legitimate standing is denied the right to testify. This includes the nation's great minds as well as little, selfish interests.

Although this practice sounds highly "democratic," many members think the subcommittees "overhear" bills by inviting tedious repetition and voicing of insignificant splinter opinions. In fact, congressmen cannot use a great deal of the testimony presented. Committee concerns and the feasible realm of committee action are more circumscribed than is the average witness's presentation. However, overhearing a matter may be functional, since a subcommittee member who attends hearings cannot help but become sated with the political, if not the technical issues, before him. Very attentive members like Mr. Brademas and Mrs. Green will often come to know more about an issue than the supposed expert. (Customary assignment of bills of the same category (like vocational education) to the same subcommittee also has the effect of rationalizing the legislative process. Not only do the subcommittee chairman and committee members, as well as staff, become familiar with the problems in their area, but also, all people involved—bureaucrats, lobbyists, administration leaders, and others—know over a period of time with whom they are dealing. Relationships, rapport, understanding, and a core of knowledge are built among the actors.)

Extended public hearings thus inevitably become in part a charade. Sometimes the hearing becomes more for the benefit of the witness than the member. The assumption is that if everyone is heard, regardless of how insignificant or how repetitive he is, each petitioner is thus flattered and at least somewhat gratified. He receives, in the words of Murray Edelman, "symbolic reassurance" that his needs will be considered.[2]

The real significance of the classical hearing should not be overlooked. Up to the point of redundance, they are informative, permitting choices before the committee—in terms of alternative programs available, issues of distribution of power and money, and other matters—to surface. Equally important, the hearings become a permanent legislative record. No matter how boring the process is, the record is vital to later political moves in defending amendments to the bill, writing lines in the committee report, and finally in administration of the law. Not incidentally, the written record is also a remarkable public document, baring to journalists, political scientists, and historians the logical underpinnings of American law.

The second type, the publicity hearing, is less designed to examine and resolve crucial conflicts among interested parties than it is as a forum. It serves to develop a written record, to "create a need" hitherto unrealized. Before Mr. Brademas decided to hold hearings, there existed no professional, public, or congressional interest to legislate in the areas of drug abuse or environmental education. His hearings took a general national problem, like environment, gave it an education twist, and argued that federal educational policy could play a vital role. In the process, interest groups were created, congressmen got used to the new idea, and publicity mounted. If carefully timed to current national fads, this type of nonessential hearing can be a means to a quick legislative victory.

The third type, the congressional "oversight" hearing, does not have new legislation as its first objective; rather, it is designed to examine how well the administration is enforcing the existing law and how well the law is working. From oversight hearings, attempts at passage of corrective legislation reforming old laws are a logical step. The model of this hearing has been used best by the Senate, notably in recent times by the Foreign Relations Committee under Senator William Fulbright, in his examinations of American policy in Vietnam. Oversight is follow-up. Hearings proceed officially under the guise of legislation, but are really designed to build a record on the success or failure of the administration or the previous work of Congress.

During the 1960s many pieces of education legislation were created or expanded, but great doubts were raised about their effectiveness. The compensatory education programs of ESEA and Head Start could not be shown to have had an important effect on the achievement of children, educational research seemed to be a swamp of esoteric findings neither adequately disseminated nor applied, vocational education showed little evidence of affecting the labor market —the list of vague utility goes on. In addition, the U.S. Office of Education faced chastisement from both the Congress and the Office of Management and Budget for its loose management. But Congress never stopped to look at what it had created. Says one member of the Education and Labor Committee:

I think we have moved too fast in the sixties to get tooled up to the programs. I think that we have adopted too many programs without the careful consideration of them. I thought we should have stopped, looked, and listened in about 1968 and really found out what has happened to programs we have before we go onto others.

To take a stronger hand in weeding and perfecting the existing legislation, all of the active members of the Education and Labor Committee favor additional legislative oversight—at least they favor it in principle. The constraints, however, have been very real. First, the physical and intellectual task would greatly tax the committee's resources. Representative Edith Green was the first member to try to investigate USOE policy. She did it in the area of research, but says:

Yes. We did it. That was a great sacrifice. The oversight that we had done on the research contracts was done to a large extent out of my own limited congressional office staff.

With only one or two staff people confronting the USOE or NIE bureaucracy under conditions where the bureaucracy is assumed to have a lot to hide, and with the congressional investigators also having prodigious normal responsibilities back on the committee, the paltry congressional effort does not stand much chance. Mrs. Green attempted to counter the odds by introducing and getting passed a section in the 1972 Higher Education Amendments providing money, staff, and authority to the General Accounting Office (the investigative arm of Congress) specifically for investigation of education policies of the education bureaucracy.

The second constraint lies in the conflict between a member's knowledge of what is good policy and his feelings about what would be politically good for him. Each law or each major provision has a congressional sponsor who seeks to protect and expand rather than attack it. Legislative oversight on other people's laws is one thing; criticism of one's own pet another. Thirdly, the giant educational lobbies are not inclined to pursue oversight seriously because to them the existing laws represent dollars going out to teachers and other interests. The big groups fear oversight if it means potential loss of dollars, and will support it only if assured that dollars taken from poorly-working programs would be replaced in some other way.

Oversight, while a part of the general ethic of accountability mouthed by nearly all government officials, is a multiedged sword, and often too many interests are threatened to be cut. Liberals would be inclined to perform oversight to show that the administration is underfunding and underadministering the law, and thus defeating the idealistic intent of Congress. Their motto might be "If only the bureaucracy would administer the law better, congressional goals would be achieved." This becomes an attack on the administration, on the party in power, and on fiscal constraint. On the other hand, conservatives and even some liberal critics of education would want oversight to weed out the good from the bad and to stop spending money where no results are shown. Their motto would be "If it does not work, throw it out." This becomes an attack on the committee's liberal majority and on the flow of federal dollars to education. Oversight bodes trouble, and until the promise of federal aid to education is quite secure, it is too dangerous a doctrine for the committee to embrace entl·usiastically.

Oversight functions may expand in the 1970s as some of the older members with vested interests leave the scene. Perhaps more important will be the impending change in the committee's work load. If the press for passage of new laws subsides—when there is a law covering every exigency—committees will then have more time. Further, they will have a press for action—to do something—and one area to which they can turn their energy is the refinement of what they did in the past.

Other Sources of Information for the Member. We have considered hearings, with some digressions, as a source of information for the member, but everybody who is influential does not surface at hearings, and all that is on the hearing surface is not all that is influential. Each member has private sources of information and opinion.

(1) There is first the member's staff and, in the case of the subcommittee chairman, the committee counsel. These people are employees who, as their profession, serve their boss with information and service which they judge will help.

(2) Every member, by virtue of his public position and his role, serves as an information funnel, attracting all kinds of people, including the most competent, who have valuable information and wisdom. Experts often voluntarily come forth when their field becomes a matter of public policy. (Sometimes their expertise has been created especially for the legislation. For example, the Ford Foundation funded a team of researchers for HEW headed by Frank Newman to develop the Report on Higher Education.[3] It became known as the Newman Report, and Newman surfaced on the Hill during deliberations of the 1972 higher education titles.) If the expert is sufficiently distinguished, the member or his staff will probably seek him. A typical instance would find a congressman himself or one of his staff checking out a proposal with experts or interest groups through a

telephone call, letter, or lunch talk. Often one or several experts will stay in close contact with the member throughout the duration of the bill under consideration.

Administration bureaucrats are a special type of expert who can be valuable to the member, but they are not always entirely trustworthy. The most reliable information service of the bureaucracy comes from its considerable ability to supply data necessary to the legislation. Frequently this is public information routinely gathered by USOE dealing with, for example, numbers of students enrolled in an affected program, costs of educating them, future enrollment projections and costs, and other technical matters.

A large number of USOE-NIE-HEW bureaucrats specialize in topics on the federal role in education on which Congress legislates. They often possess detailed information; however, on matters of policy (as opposed to uninterpreted facts and figures) they are under constraints set by higher level, politically motivated administration officials. The information forthcoming from them is officially transmitted only with the acquiescence of high level administration policy-makers; thus it often lacks objectivity and tends to support the administration's policy goals. For example, one well-informed HEW administration specialist served both as a coauthor of the Newman Report and as the principal HEW technician on the 1972 higher education proposals. He was a focus of information, but because the Nixon administration adopted many of the Newman precepts as its official policy, his usefulness to committee members not in agreement with Newman was limited. His job was to promote the administration's stand, and of course his opinions were not detached.

Because the public statements of bureaucrats are under policy censorship, the frank exchange of their quantity of information and often considerable wisdom can be denied to members of the committee. Some congressmen overcome this obstacle by establishing independent rapport with bureaucrats. The congressman then can obtain objective and off-the-record opinions, and the bureaucrat gains a policy role, a sense of importance, and perhaps congressional protection. There is a style to these transactions that maintains the integrity of the bureaucrat, and over the years some of them create broad congressional contacts and thereby manage to make themselves more valuable within the administration. The pattern and extent of these relationships are unrecorded—and sometimes politically illicit—but the administration's informal contributions to congressional information are almost as important as its formal input.

Another category of clearly recognized experts are the lobbyists. These people, as suggested in the previous chapter, are experts on their own problems and particularly on solutions. Virtually no education proposal comes to Congress that is not scrutinized by one or more lobbies whose basic interest lies in advancing and protecting the goals of their membership. This fact should not be viewed cynically; simply because the lobbyist speaks on behalf of his organization does not mean that his ideas are suspect and that they are not useful to the member. Lobbyists solve many problems in the legislative process; their information is usually well prepared and they are skilled at aiding the member. (They have a good bedside manner, so to speak.) The NEA deserves special citation here, not because it lobbies on policy matters with greater skill than other groups, but because its vast research department is considered by some committee members and staff to be superior to USOE, more reliable, and far more efficient. Members who want data in precise facts and figures receive quick service from the NEA.

In the less-than-expert but more-than-layman category are the media and editorial spokesmen who have "access" to the member because members read serious journalists at least when their own legislative issues are being discussed. Even lobbyists, detached from their parochial lobby responsibilities, can become unofficial consultants. Noting that he often disagrees with a certain lobbyist, one congressman asserts that he always listens when the lobbyist speaks:

He was a guy that I had respect for. When he came up before the committee, it seemed to me he had facts, and he had logic with it. So, I came to respect him as an individual. . . . I rely on him now, not because he represents [a big education lobby group], but because over a period of years I could depend on what he told me. I think that the people with whom I have worked, unless we have a strong disagreement on a particular issue, are people who did not lie to me and who represented the facts the best they could, as they knew them.

Other people who have both good information and political savvy are former administration education officials, people who have followed certain issues, or hangers-on who can gain access to a member and channel his thought. Many former administration officials who are now outside government often toil in the vineyards of Congress hoping still to affect policy. The "hangers-on"—political groupies—can have anywhere from a sexual motivation to a desire to be close to power.

(3) Each member of Congress also has trusted confidants as part of his political entourage. These people are not experts on the substance of issues; they advise on political virtues. They may be back-home politicos with their ear to the ground, long-time friends who can be trusted to enter into a helpful and confidential dialogue, paid advisers (sometimes, for example, the administrative assistant), or "contacts." Contacts, particularly on education subcommittees, include university professors, foundation officials, officials of institutions like unions or universities with whom the member has established rapport, or others. The confidants may themselves become loci for informants who want to reach the member. The size and extent of the network thus created is incalculable, but it certainly is vast, reaching deep into the educational establishment.

(4) Each member uses his colleagues in the House as sources of information. Communication takes place on the floor of the House while waiting for role call votes or during debate, in the infamous halls and cloakrooms of Congress, and on the telephone. (Unlike the administration, very little intercongressmen communication takes place through written memos.) In these contacts members of the Education and Labor Committee can have a casual exchange of ideas comparing notes on the definition of the issues and the most desirable solutions. Also, subcommittee chairmen can test ideas with colleagues whom they respect for their wisdom and good judgment. Most important, intercongressional communication gives warnings about "problems" in a bill. Because a winning coalition is needed to pass a bill, problems, as identified by regional, partisan, racial, and other elements, must be identified and taken into account well in advance of confrontation. Congressmen are not shy about letting their colleagues know their objections or desires; so the intercongressional information system can serve a vigorous and vital conflict identification as well as resolution function.

(5) Finally, the committee member is a source of information to himself. Motivated to carry on in education because that is where he finds himself in Congress, the member usually has a feeling of responsibility and sufficient pride to want to do the job well. He inexorably develops a basis to make his own judgment. As discussed above, the

intensely involved members become veritable experts. But, when all things are considered, even if he has (as he inevitably must) incorporated the judgments of others as his own, the act of voting is his, and it stems from knowledge within himself.

In this discussion of information sources, the notion that a member's subcommittee work is necessarily influenced by the people back home should be dispelled. First, members tend not to be held responsible at the polls for exercise of their legislative committee functions. One Education and Labor Committee staff man, in referring to the ranking Republican member, Albert Quie, observes:

Al Quie is not particularly vulnerable in Rochester, Minnesota, because of what the American Vocational Association or the American School Boards Association or any of those groups does. Yet he is responsive and talks to those people. They need him a hell of a lot more than he needs them, but he is responsive because they are professionally involved. His major interest in the Congress is education. It is not a political [i.e., vote getting] thing. Education really does not have political clout at the voting booth level on national offices. Some of the really best friends that education ever had in both parties in terms of really, really supporting them have been defeated without getting assistance from the education groups.

Secondly, although some people back home may be close advisers of a member, virtually all of his constituents are not. In handling technical problems with national implications, the folks back home can actually be a hindrance. One congressman says:

They are too far away. Things in Washington happen faster than they can keep track of. I would welcome advice from a consortium of people back home if they followed the issues and were knowledgeable, but they are not knowledgeable. I would just as soon have it the way it is now—leave me alone. That is because I do not like to have them contact me just on the basis of their biases. But what tends to happen is that somebody out here in Washington—for example, the National Education Association—sends a wire out to someone in my district to send a wire to me.

The result of such contact from back home is to represent a narrow view of a Washington education lobby under the guise of a grass roots movement, in order to gain consideration of a lobby position that might be rejected under objective scrutiny. Members are not fooled by this activity. The congressman says:

I have a pretty good relationship with most of the people back home, and they would give me a call and tell me the source [of such pressure activity].

Issues of the Subcommittee

Subcommittee members are not professional educators. They are politicians whose circumscribed job is to determine the proper exercise of federal power in education and, most often in this respect, who should receive federal funds for what purpose and under what conditions. This function first requires the member to acknowledge that there is a need for legislation. Then the member must answer the famous question posed by Harold Lasswell, "Who gets what, when, where, and how?"[4]

Need. Information sources, including hearings, are heavily composed of arguments that turn on need, or lack of need, for legislation. Need assessment can range from the grand issue (should we have a bill supporting general aid to education?) to the detailed (should teachers of Spanish-speaking students be provided special training opportunities?).

Ironically, need assessment, the rationale from which legislation flows, is often the least important factor in the congressional education policy process. The education subcommittees have a vantaged view of national problems. They sit near the top of a pyramid of national need-articulating agencies. By the time a House subcommittee holds hearings on a particular topic, need, at least grossly defined, is taken for granted by most people concerned. Those who are involved in the process are involved mainly in designing a way to fulfill the need. A fairly safe rule regarding education is to assume that there is not an original idea in Congress, and that virtually every education matter considered by a subcommittee is either a reconsideration of what has come before or, if the issue is "new," is a reaction to need articulation already highly developed within the nation.

This is particularly true once an initial legislative breakthrough has been made. For example, ever since vocational education entered the congressional policy agenda in 1917 it has been annually funded and periodically renewed with virtually no public question raised about its legitimacy. Likewise, in 1965, at the height of the civil rights movement, aid to the education of disadvantaged children, an issue whose time had come borne on the wisdom of the Supreme Court and the political movement represented by Dr. Martin Luther King,

Jr., was established as part of federal education policy. Like vocational education, federal commitment to disadvantaged children is likely to continue for an indefinite period. Details of the original laws will and have been changed, but change is not mainly a reassessment of need. Rather, minor changes in the form of legislative modification reconfirm the established need, and make old commitments even stronger. Once established, need dies hard. It tends to be reaffirmed and only over a period of years is it redefined through gradual modification. For example, impact aid has been redefined from aid to areas serving military installations to a sort of general aid to education with dollars carefully spread all over the country. But it has survived—indeed, flourished—still performing its old function and in addition serving as a pork barrel, making the "need" for Impact Aid even greater. Reform of Impact Aid to its original limited purpose will occur probably only when the Congress considers a general aid to education bill to supplant and greatly exceed current impact aid pork-barrel payments.

Infrequently, controversial grand issues of need arise in federal education policy that generate strong differences and cause members to stalemate over the acceptance of need. Before 1961, when the Education and Labor Committee was under the chairmanship of Representative Graham Barden (D., N.C.), the very question of legitimacy of federal aid to education was in the forefront, with Barden strongly and powerfully opposed. Indeed, the question of the validity of the need for massive federal aid had been stalemated in Congress for almost one hundred years, until the breakthrough in ESEA. In another less important example during the 1960s, Congressman Brademas, despite his prodigious legislative record, could not create a sufficient sense of need for an educational technology act. The failure was due in part to the success of the technology lobby to get a clause in each of the separate pieces of education legislation permitting money to be expended for its hardware and software. The lack of agreement on need became a major focus of the 1972 Higher Education Amendments, not because members of Congress disputed the federal role in higher education but because of a congressional debate on an antibussing provision appended to the higher education bill. If there had been agreement in favor of bussing, the controversy could have turned on the technical matters of a bussing program, and in that case, it could have been said that there was agreement on need. However, the issue was bitterly divisive with strong factions of the House committed to stopping all bussing to achieve racial balance.

Need as Determined by Members' Ideology. Just as need definition tends not to be a major function of subcommittee hearings (although it may take up a lot of time as lobbies come forth to officially endorse the bill), neither is the determination of a member's "basic perspective" toward federal educational policy created there. Through their party affiliation, constituency relationships, and general political growth, subcommittee members develop a kind of ideology to guide their involvement in policy formation. Members with different ideologies can equally support a grand need, like federal aid to higher education, but their differing ideology directs their separate inclinations when seeking answers to the question of who gets what, when, where, and how. During the 1960s and early 1970s two schools of thought have demarcated the continuum of ideology within the subcommittees.

The first school, generally embraced by liberals (mostly Democrats) conceived of the role of federal involvement in education as one of reforming or at least correcting the faults of the education system. Their central focus was to provide equality of educational opportunity to the assorted types of disadvantaged children, and to achieve this they have supported the concept of using all federal funds as "categorical" aid to education, that is, aid with a social reform policy objective. Fundamentally, they believe that the schools can play an important role in social reform, i.e., schoolmen take the initiative. Because they feel that the professional education establishment and state and local governments for education are unlikely to initiate social reform, these liberal congressmen have sought to make federal education dollars conditional on reform objectives supervised by federal administrators.

The second school, followed by less reform-minded members, was not only disenchanted with the results of federal reform efforts of the 1960s, but also holds to the view that state and local school officials know best what they need, and that the federal government should not try to impose social and educational reform from a distance. Ideally, these members would seek to determine the amount of federal education dollars needed in the nation and then develop a means of getting the dollars out to school districts without federal programmatic strings. These more conservative members are not opposed to federal aid, but they are opposed to what they see as the arrogance of the notion that local problems can be diagnosed and solved with centrally composed national policy. Says one Republican congressman:

We disagree with the Democrats most on the question of state involvement. If I had my preference, all the federal money would go through a state agency to be distributed amongst the communities. If Congressman Brademas [a liberal Democrat] had his druthers, I guess he would pass the state entirely and have it a federal-local program. . . . To me, the silliest thing imaginable is that some people want the cities to have everything.

Or summed up by a Republican staff aide:

Although education legislation tends to be bipartisan—certainly the concerns are bipartisan—the issues tend to be the extent of federal direction, strings, guidelines, controls, as opposed to state and local administration of federally financed programs with fewer guidelines. I would say a majority on the Democratic side of the committee still believe in quite tight federal reins on these programs. The majority on the Republican side tend to feel that they ought to be relaxed. Another issue that involves some of the same things is what we regard as the problem of proliferating categorical programs. When the Democrats see a problem, any problem no matter how small, they tend to immediately want to enact federal legislation to deal with it. We, on the other hand, prefer and have been seeking for a number of years to consolidate a good many of these . . . programs . . . to give a lot more discretion at the local level about how they will allocate funds. But, you cannot always draw a line and say this is a Democratic decision and that this is a Republican decision. Members tend to have a variety of feelings between the parties.

The differences between the two schools rest in fundamental judgments by members about the capability of federal power, the legitimacy of that power as an intervening force in the classroom, the desirable shape of the American education system, and the benefits received in their congressional districts. The ideological stands of members, more or less congealed a priori, form the focal points of some of the most serious deliberations within the subcommittees where one member or another seeks to establish the merits of writing a law based on his views of who *should* get what, when, where, and how. Coalitions form, often breaking down into Republicans versus Democrats, with occasional crossovers and unlikely alliances depending on a particular point.

The ideological basis of alliances is often more pragmatic than doctrinaire. The conservative members tend to represent basically rural or prosperous suburban districts which would benefit less from federal aid if dollars were distributed based on a formula designed to serve the less wealthy, educationally disadvantaged who live in big cities or impoverished rural areas. The liberals tend to represent central cities or other economically pressed areas where many poor people reside. Southern Democrats, who are not liberal on many issues, join the northern liberals because their southern districts are poor and benefit from federal aid. In effect, helping the poor helps the fiscal posture of their congressional districts. (Composition of the subcommittees reflects, if imperfectly, the variety of constituencies in the nation. Thus, when subcommittee members act in a way that would serve their district, they also act to represent the interests of districts like theirs.)

Committee Mark-up

The information-gathering period during which subcommittee hearings and other communications take place are preparatory sparring rounds for the moment of truth—the mark-up session where votes are taken, official decisions are made, and a bill is reported. "Mark-up" is a literal term designating the committee sessions where the proposed bill is rewritten to meet with the approval of a majority of the committee. An Education and Labor Committee staff member describes the activity of the mark-up session:

There is a lot of prelegislative juggling and so forth on legislation before its introduction. Then, following the hearing process, you have a mark-up in which, under the rules of the House, the bill is read section by section, and after each section is read then members can offer amendments, and they vote on those amendments. Then the bill is read through in its entirety. Mark-up can sometimes take months.

The mark-up sessions are an educational experience for those members who have not intensely involved themselves in hearings and other communications. By attending mark-up, even marginally concerned committee members have an opportunity to inform themselves about the effect of the vote they will cast. Says a staff observer:

Members certainly get pretty well educated on every aspect of a bill in a mark-up session. The bill is actually debated, and, if there are any questions, staff or other technical aides provide explanations or information. Sometimes when there is a doubtful point and there is somebody in the executive branch who can supply answers, they are called in to provide answers or data on any question. A

mark-up session is in itself an opportunity for a member to become fully acquainted with each provision, and he has adequate time to amend.

Some issues become important to a member, causing him to be
active in mark-up. Perhaps he has ongoing, intense involvement, or he
may be personally uninterested but acting on behalf of an interest
group or constituent who appeals to him. Says the staff observer:

Now, it is true that some members have keener interests in certain legislation
than they do in others. And, for this reason, you will find some members playing
a more prominent role in certain types of legislation than others.

Mark-up is the time for the member who wants to exert influence to
pursue his goals actively.

On important bills, mark-up, like a circus high wire act, with the
chairman as ringmaster, several members walking the tightrope, and
even the clown below holding some influence, is an exciting and
delicate balance. Each section of the bill, as well as the final bill as a
whole, must be approved by a majority of the committee. Although
Republicans and Democrats both support the general concept of
federal aid to education, they all have some separate interests—some
quite divergent—and to achieve their mutual goal of reporting a bill
they ordinarily must achieve compromise.

The life of a bill is fragile and is dependent on a winning coalition;
thus all proposals presented in mark-up—from Republicans, Democrats, junior and senior members—are considered, and most are considered seriously. The process of compromise can be hard work. As a
staff observer put it, "Those guys have got to take the bruises and
cuts on the votes they cast." By this he meant not only that the
process of compromise is strenuous, but also that each member
wants to win. To do so sometimes he must give up something or he
must be satisfied with a partial victory. Wins and losses are tallied.
Members become identified with positions and interest groups; constituents and fellow ideologues are watching to see who comes out
best in a power struggle. Structural pressures thus impinge on the
member's prestige and self-image, causing political battles at times to
be intense.

A member's potential power is never greater than at mark-up.
Armed with some ideas acquired before or during the hearing phase,
each subcommittee member at mark-up is able to channel a variety
of special and general interests into the bill. During this time mem-

bers become engaged in numerous, and often intense, informal meetings in their offices, at lunch or in casual places. The meetings may be with fellow members—allies plotting strategies or adversaries ironing out an agreement—or with lobbyists or experts frequently consulted when new provisions or compromises materialize. (Sometimes the lobbyist will contact the member to try to enlighten him on the lobby's view of the issue, and just as often the member will consult the lobby to find out what they see as the problems in a proposal.) Lobbyists or consultants who have the ear of a member will be in closest contact during mark-up.

To gain a literal understanding, the reader should imagine a congressman sitting behind his mahogany desk flanked by the American flag. Across the desk sits a spokesman from the National Education Association or perhaps the AFL-CIO. The men know each other and talk easily with perhaps a scattering of profanity or some frank observations about the ideas of colleagues or adversaries. The lobbyist may just offer information or perhaps try to convince the member that a certain proposal, vote, or argument in mark-up will best satisfy a particular need. The member will ask questions. If the staff aide is present, he may join in or perhaps listen silently to discuss the matter later. Perhaps the member is convinced, perhaps not. He may have a very similar discussion later at lunch with another lobbyist or a non-lobbyist expert who will give another point of view. Perhaps at the end of the day the member will review the cross-section of ideas with his staff aide or other members. By 10:30 a.m. at the next day's mark-up session, the member may be prepared to argue a case, but, if the matter is complicated, the argument may just lead to another round of consultations.

Ideological Issues. The mark-up sessions are divided, of course, on the matter of who gets how much money, but they are also places for ideological infighting. On these matters, members need no assistance (although they may need technical data supplied by staff).

Ideological divisiveness continually recurs in mark-up on such matters as whether the federal, state, local governments, or the student should control federal dollars; whether only the poor or also the lower middle class should be included in the formulae for distribution of dollars for disadvantaged; whether dollars should be used to force change, etc.

In session after session, one Republican member who strongly supports federal aid to education consistently presses to direct federal dollars through the states rather than, as the Democrats would have it, from the federal directly to the local level. On one bill he fought for his position and came up with less than the whole loaf but more than a crumb. He says:

So, this bill coming up is a compromise between our views. The state will have the main administrative responsibility outside cities of a certain size. I do not know what we will end up with; it will either be 100,000 or 250,000 [dollars]. If it is 100,000, the money will go directly from the federal government to the cities of 100,00 or above, and that amounts to 150 cities. Then the remainder of the money will go to the states making it 200 units of government the federal government will deal with instead of the thousands you would have to deal with if all transactions were directly from the federal to the local level.

The congressman reasoned that for the time being that was the best compromise he could get. The liberal Democrats gave him enough so that he could not offer a successful floor amendment, but the liberals did not have to give him too much because they controlled the committee votes. The Republican got a lot more than he would have if he had not fought the issue.

Nonideological Issues. Important nonideological issues arising at subcommittee level are often technical but crucial, and require ironing out through direct confrontation of the members, sometimes with the help of expert witnesses or heavy staff assistance. The most important in this category is solution of the question of who gets how much money. Relatively small amounts of federal education money are given out at the discretion of the federal bureaucrats. Most of it is granted by formula to states, school districts, or other recipients (e.g., directly to students in the case of some provisions of Title I Higher Education Amendments of 1972).

Beyond ideology, the question of who gets how much money is affected by the need to spread federal aid programs and federal dollars broadly enough around the country to garner support from members of Congress. For example, members may know and sympathize with the fact that the big cities are in a serious plight, but they also know that if they represent suburban or rural districts, their duty is to bring federal tax dollars back home. Says one Midwestern congressman:

I use the example of Title I of the Elementary and Secondary Education Act. I strongly oppose the formula that operates there because I see New York getting the lion's share. Secondly, I recognize that in a rural area, like I have in portions of my district, that there are so many other factors when you use the census year to determine how many children come from a poor family. Because if the rain does not happen to come one year, and that happens to be the year they take the census—like in 1960 in my district—then my constituents are considered as lower income than they normally are and benefit for ten years (until the next census) in school aid. However, if on the other hand all the weather conditions are perfect and everything grows right, and they have better crops than ever before, and they take the census that year and are considered wealthier, they will not be able to receive the money they normally should if there are droughts between the census.

Up to a "reasonable" point—always indeterminate—each member fights for equity to his district. Working toward compromise aid distribution formulae, buttering the bread evenly, can be an incredibly complex patchwork, often more like using fresh bread and cold butter, as spokesmen for each interest area seek to ensure that his area is protected.

Noncompromise. The compromise model does not always hold, however. There were two notable exceptions in 1972 were, first, the higher education provisions where, in subcommittee, Chairman Edith Green refused elaborate compromises, although accepting some, on the student aid issue (discussed below, see p. 105). She fought for a version of the bill she thought was "right," and produced a version differing in important ways from the desires of the liberal Democrats (and some Republicans). As subcommittee chairman she held certain power—particularly the power of delay—and certain prestige—because to the average House member, the opinion of the chairman or minority leader is often honored. Within the subcommittee, liberal opponents of the Green version waged a limited battle stopping short of raising a bruhaha that could have stalemated the entire proposal there. Faced with the prospect of no bill or trying to fight the Green version in different congressional domains, the subcommittee passed her version, which eventually composed the basis of the House floor-passed bill that was sent to the Senate. It is worth noting here what is described more fully below, that ability to withstand compromise at the House subcommittee stage does not ensure final victory. Indeed, lacking widely shared consensus, if refusal to compromise is sufficiently staunch at one point it almost ensures defeat at another point. Ultimately Mrs. Green lost her battle in the House-Senate conference.

John Brademas and the Early Childhood Education Act of 1972 provide another case of relatively uncompromising subcommittee action, but this time more because the affairs of his select subcommittee went unchallenged rather than because Brademas remained obstinate. The Brademas bill was designed in subcommittee with support of committee Republicans. Although broad hearings with the nation's most noted experts on children were held, the bill was virtually ignored, at least officially, by the administration as well as by the press and by most House members. It thus grew with public scrutiny and support by experts on children (each witness urging expansion of its provisions to meet with his pet ideas about children), but in relative political obscurity. Reported to the floor by the full committee, it passed the House almost routinely—with opposition only beginning to organize—as education bills not touching volatile issues like bussing are wont to do. (Brademas welcomed intrasubcommittee compromise on the issue of who gets how much money. Settling this issue tends to remove the most potent grounds for House members' opposition.) Thus, the strong liberals remained relatively uncompromised simply because of the absence of important dissent. (There was, for example, no antichild lobby, nor were there competing or established institutions in the area of early childhood education to quibble over the bill.)

But powerful dissent was real, if not previously apparent. It was not until the bill was up for the president's signature that journalists and the Republican leadership discovered that a multibillion-dollar bill designed to revolutionize childcare in America, perhaps, next to Social Security, the most important piece of social legislation ever offered in Congress, was a near-reality. President Nixon unequivocally vetoed the bill on both fiscal and ideological grounds. (The Brademas work on early childhood education, while it did not become law, established a basis for legislative battles in future years when administration support and more compromise will serve to aid passage.)

Nonissues. Some legislative matters are genuinely noncontroversial. Consensus and not discord actually characterizes discussion of most of the problems presented to the Education and Labor Committee, although the areas of consensus do not seem to be as important because they enter the legislative process smoothly. First, and overriding the House legislative process, is the general bipartisan agreement that federal aid to education is a valid goal to work for. Secondly, in every bill there is considerable "boiler plate," that is, material that turns up in one bill after another and simply attends to the many technical problems of establishing civil service or other positions, payment of funds, and other housekeeping factors. Thirdly, in many substantive areas, all members of the committee tend to agree, or fail to dissent, when points are brought forward. For example, the commissioner of education may ask for a change in the law to make it easier or less costly to administer. Most of these requests are happily received by the members. If a member has a favorite cause, like Mr. Scheuer had with New Careers, or other members have, for instance, with the handicapped or Spanish-speaking, these causes are often easily injected into deliberations. (Sometimes the only member who will remain sitting and attentive at the hearings is the member whose cause is being heard.)

Another nonissue for Education and Labor Committee deliberations is the subcommittee's power to determine how much money will actually be allocated annually to education. Education subcommittees, like all authorizing committees, are empowered merely to authorize ceilings of expenditures. In the language of the law, they "authorize to be appropriated" a certain amount of money. The actual appropriation is made annually in a separate law through a separate appropriations process under the auspices of the House Appropriations Committee. The trend of House education subcommittees is to authorize very high limits, which typically are not funded in full because of budget constraints but give leeway for growth over a period of years. These matters cause little vital controversy.

Another important nonissue: It is worthwhile to note that virtually no decisions are made requiring knowledge of professional pedagogy. Despite their broad exposure to professional data, members of the committee have politics—conflict resolution—as their function. When professional expertise enters the problem of lawmaking, members of the committee shift responsibility to the Office of Education or to schoolmen throughout the nation by writing laws in general language permitting the responsible administering agency to engage in vast arrays of educational activity within the categorical domain of the law.

The Minority. Where there is conflict, ideological or not, the careful negotiation and ironing out in subcommittee takes place for two reasons: (1) rationality, because a bill may make better sense written one way than another—the driving force here is simply the good sense of the members and their desire to make the federal dollar as efficient and effective as possible; and (2) politics, compromise to placate a minority whose support is needed.

By definition, minorities do not control a situation in which the "majority rules," but, in the House, majorities can be fragile and chimerical. Party alone does not determine how a member will vote, nor will a majority in subcommittee necessarily assure a majority in other decision-making settings—full committee, House floor, or House-Senate conference.

Education and Labor Committee members of both parties tend to be far more liberal than members of their party in the House as a whole. Thus, liberal committee Democrats tend to be more liberal than the Democratic House leadership, and committee Republicans, while probably more liberal than the Republican House leadership, tend to reflect the vital center of the House more than do the committee Democrats. This gives the Republican minority some advantages. Republican proposals tend not to be harsh alternatives to the Democratic programs—there is more fundamental agreement than disagreement—rather they shape, tint, and moderate.

In addition, the very liberal committee Democrats are constrained not only by the sobering effects (and power) of the Democratic House leadership but also by the ability of the moderate Republicans to appeal through amendments to the House floor. Since the end of the eighty-ninth Congress, whose sizeable Democratic majority was based on the extraordinary Johnson sweep of 1964, the numbers of Republicans and Democrats have become more equal.[5] When vote margins are narrow, there is a reasonable probability that moderate Republican leaders, who do not obtain adequate compromise in subcommittee, can successfully rewrite a bill through floor amendments. The greater the likelihood of such amendments, the more powerful is the influence pressing majority and minority members to accommodate one another in subcommittee. When asked if he felt at a disadvantage being a Republican on a Democratic-controlled subcommittee, a congressman responded:

Yes. I would feel better if we were in control if that is what you mean. . . . But I play a pretty dominant role on the committee. I guess it is the fact that I have worked on this legislation, and they recognize that I have got people who will vote with me not only on the full committee but on the floor and that I have developed a respect among some Democrats, too.

Says a Republican staff man:

There is no substitute for being the majority. None at all. . . . but it depends on what is being considered. If it is a matter of deep party division you cannot expect to affect it from the minority, particularly in committee. On the floor, that is another question because often enough we have the votes to do what we want to do on the House floor. Sure, we can affect legislation, even controversial legislation.

In addition, members of the minority exert influence because many of them are smart, work hard, stay informed, and bring ideas and logic to bear on the arguments.

The Full Committee and the Report

Procedurally, on a majority vote the subcommittee reports the bill to the full committee. That is, the subcommittee, having made its decisions, authorizes the full committee to evaluate and vote on the bill. The full committee can vote to kill the subcommittee proposal, modify it and report it to the floor of the House for adoption, or send it to the House floor with no change. With up to thirty-five members, all of whom have their own legislative responsibilities, the full committee is not a viable place to carry out the hard work and compromises needed to develop a bill; the subcommittee is expected to keep it until problems are ironed out. The full Education and Labor Committee can, and often does, amend the subcommittee version, but ordinarily the full committee passes the bill to the House floor mainly unchanged.

The act of reporting a bill is accompanied by a document called the Committee Report. This document is an important policy tool, because it reflects, in writing, the explicit intent of the legal language created by the committee. (One section of the report contains the exact technical version of the bill approved by the committee. Then follows anywhere from a few paragraphs to over a hundred pages prepared by the subcommittee and full committee staff containing a brief legislative history of the bill, the findings of the committee, and an explanation of the committee's intent.) In principle, the administration is supposed to enforce the law in line with the intent of Congress, so the report serves as a set of instructions—both broadening and confining—to the administration on how the law should be carried out.

Frequently the report will contain instructions not immediately evident in the law itself. If hearings have found a certain idea to be useful (like funding chemists to do educational research), then the actual law, which is necessarily written in general terms, will be supplemented with a line in the report spelling out how the funds can and should be spent. Sometimes the line is merely a condensation of more elaborate statements in the hearing record. Administrators often must go back to the hearings to fathom the exact intent of Congress. For an interest group or spokesman to get a line in the report can be as important as having the line written into law.

The report is written in terse language. Every line contains a message. Several examples from Report No. 92-554, 1971 (later to become the Education Amendments of 1972), reveal the style of the report. The sections quoted deal with the House findings and intent relating to creation of the National Institute of Education.

Educational researchers have traditionally been associated with psychology, sociology, and related disciplines, but relatively few have been drawn from a range of other disciplines now also understood to have particular relevance to education—physiology, chemistry, anthropology, computer sciences, statistics, to cite only several.[6]

This finding implicitly speaks to the intent of the committee for the NIE to broaden the scope of people considered to be educational researchers eligible for NIE dollars.

Although the National Institute of Education would conduct a small amount of in-house research, the Committee intends that most of its work would be performed by grant, contract, or other arrangement, by other agencies, institutions and individuals.[7]

This provision is designed both to authorize the employment of some full-time researchers by NIE and to ensure that NIE does not become a separate research institution supported by federal dollars. The purpose of the committee is mainly that NIE serve as an administrative unit to tap the best available resources for educational research in nongovernmental institutions.

A slightly more technical example can be drawn from the section of the report called the Occupational Education Act of 1971:

For fiscal year 1972, the Act provides for grants to the states principally for the purpose of setting up the administrative agencies and for comprehensive planning for the occupational education program. . . . It is the Committee's intention that after the establishment of the State agencies and the conclusion of the planning during the first year, almost all of each State's funds will be used for the actual operation of programs. In other words, the Act does not set a specific percentage of dollar limitation on the amount of money which can be used within a particular State during any year for State administering and planning, but the Committee expects the Office of Education in its administration of the Act to place reasonable restrictions (according to need) on each State's use of funds for these purposes in order to encourage the use of as much of these funds as possible for operation of programs.[8]

In short, the committee wants the money used for programs for pupils and not for administration, and USOE should watch closely where the money goes. Upset at the way USOE had been administering vocational education, the committee began giving detailed instructions as warnings that, unless USOE cleaned up its shop, more and more administrative functions would be removed from the discretion of the administrators and written into the law—of course, anathema to administrators. The report in this case is thus designed to carry a tough message to the administration.

Even with the report, the House is unable to detail what it expects of administrative behavior. The intent of Congress is at best sporadically spelled out in detail, and more often, congressional intent is only a sketch.

The House Floor

The House has come to expect annual as well as sporadic education bills. By the time a major bill reaches the floor, pressure for passage is high, and most issues have either been resolved or clearly defined. When the final vote comes, there is always a pass—no-pass dichotomy where if a member is simply opposed to the concept of the bill, no compromises are possible. For example, some very conservative Republicans tend routinely to oppose education bills and other social legislation on the grounds that such bills are inflationary and that they interfere with local control. These members simply vote no. Most members however, do not have so easy a task.

The average member has first the difficult chore of becoming informed about the broad outline of a bill and its "problems," that is, any elements in the bill that cause objections. A number of sources are available to help him—the *Congressional Quarterly* weekly service, lobbyists who are eager to point out the benefits or deficits of a proposal, the media, staff analysis, constituent pressure, or, most likely, party whips (members assigned to marshall floor votes and relay the position of the party leadership). Most members probably know the gist of an education bill by the time it comes to vote.

For the average member, the vote on final passage is not as difficult as a vote on floor amendments. He is frequently put in the position of being for the bill in general but not sure about his stand on a complex amendment offered by a subcommittee member who is trying to win on the House floor what was lost at the committee level. Often such amendments are technical, with the details and ramifications known only to the committee members who have previously debated them. Usually the member has guidance on two grounds in appraising the amendment. First, he asks if it helps his district. On the House floor, members tend to "vote their district," and, if they can clearly see constituent advantage, they will be heavily swayed to vote yes. More often, however, floor amendments on authorizing legislation in education can be categorized ideologically—does the amendment make the bill more "liberal" or more "conservative"? Ideology tends to be a partisan or regional matter, and members, who it must be remembered often do not understand the details of the pending amendment, look to the position of the party leadership, which usually boils down to the position of the party's ranking member on the Education and Labor Committee. (In these cases the Democrats who vote Republican on some issues, or vice versa, watch for the cues that signal their customary switch. For example, southern Democrats are likely to switch over on Republican amendments strengthening states rights but would rarely do so on an amendment to decrease aid to the poor.)

Being uninformed, or at best having only sketchy knowledge, about a bill is a common experience and can be frustrating for an ordinary House member, especially if he has a hunch that the bill on the floor has implications not immediately evident. A good example occurred at the floor debate on the final conference report of the Education Amendments of 1972, a mammoth bill with intricate and conflicting provisions. The following dialogue was provoked between a frustrated Congressman Olin Teague (D., Texas) and the chairman of the House Education and Labor Committee, Carl Perkins, who was trying to usher the bill to passage.

MR. TEAGUE OF TEXAS. Mr. Speaker, I desire to make a point of order.

THE SPEAKER. The Gentleman will state his point of order.

MR. TEAGUE. Mr. Speaker, the rules of the House limit the number of staff members who are allowed on the floor in a situation like this, and I make the point of order that [the House Education and Labor Committee] has violated that rule of the House.

Mr. Speaker, the reason I make this point of order is to point up the fact that if the debate concerning this conference report requires 10 or 15 staff members to be on the floor to tell the [Education and Labor members responsible for ushering the bill through] what to do, then for sure they must not know what is in the bill.

MR. PERKINS. . . . I regret that the gentleman from Texas who opposes the bill has made the point of order of this kind because it certainly would never have been done by the gentleman from Kentucky [that is, Mr. Perkins himself].

MR. TEAGUE. Mr. Speaker, the gentleman from Texas was merely trying to make the point that nobody on this floor knows what is in this bill.[9]

Although partisan ideology is a strong factor in considering floor amendments, the final floor vote on adoption of the whole bill is usually heavily bipartisan in the area of education. The great majority of both Republicans and Democrats endorse federal aid to education. They see it as relieving the local tax burden, as an idea whose time has come. Given this general bipartisan support, members accede to the practical pressure to approve the basic work that comes to the floor from the committee. This is particularly true because, at least since 1965, the important education bills have been extensions and modifications of old legislation. Political battles that were once fought over initial adoption of a major law are not often replayed in the House. Even though such renewals can contain significant new material, their final passage is rarely challenged because, if not approved, the old legislation that has become national policy will expire, a year or more of the education subcommittee's efforts will have been wasted, agreed-on compromises disappear, and dollars will not flow to the member's education institutions. Barring massive conflict—for example where the NEA or the AFL-CIO openly lobby against a bill—it is the battle over amendments that becomes the average member's most critical moment of choice. The final vote more often than not reflects the pressure for passage, conceals the divisions in the bill, and upholds the success of the compromise activity.

A Note on House Staff

The full committee as well as each subcommittee has a chief staff professional and other employees. The majority party members always have a larger staff than the minority. The committee staff serve all committee members of their party but take orders from the chairman or, in the case of the minority staff, from the ranking minority member.

In the House, the staff's job is many things but is mostly technical, not policy-making. Says one education committee counsel:

I make no political or policy decision with legislation. These are made by my clients—the chairman of the committee and the other Democrats on the committee. They set policy and make decisions. I think it would be a very poor method of proceeding to make policy decisions in carrying out a technical job.

When asked if he thought a staff man who tries to make policy would last very long, he answered, "Oh, certainly not!" And when asked if staff took policy initiative, one ranking congressman said:

No. As far as our own staff, some of them would like to do that. I prevent them from it. I explain to them that they should not; that they should always check with some member of Congress and go through a member of the Congress. . . . If I ever found out that a staff man was trying to make policy, I would sure get on the staff member for doing it. . . . It is the members of Congress who are elected to office and ought to be making those decisions, not the staff people creating policy in the name of their congressman.

Staff men are important to the legislative process and to the ability of the member to affect legislation. Their functions are designed to facilitate in every way the chairman and other members in their search for information, analysis, and issue identification. They provide technical assistance by developing detailed information, and the more information and staff work available to a member, the better he is equipped to raise points, advance his interests, obstruct his opponents, and develop the law. Staff can be one of the backbones of a member's influence. Further, committee staff are responsible for the myriad administrative functions involved in committee management. A partial list of staff responsibilities includes:

—Brief the committee members (particularly the chairman) on problems before the committee;

—Examine carefully all proposals to determine which matters require scrutiny of the member;

—Pass information on behalf of the member to lobbyists, Senate staff, minority staff, and the administration;

—Collect information from any sources that might be of interest to the member;

—Put together program ideas into formal, drafted legislation;

—Analyze policy proposals that come to the committee from various sources and render the analysis to the chairman or other members;

—Conceive and draft justifications and attacks for different policy positions, both to inform the chairman and for the chairman and other members to utilize in public;

—Develop hearings—arrange for witnesses, schedule them, prepare both witnesses and members;

—Prepare agenda for committee meetings;

—Housekeeping chores, such as arranging for committee travel;

—Draft proposed rules for the committee;

—Advise committee members on the judicial aspects of legislation;

—Handle legal aspects of a bill as it moves from subcommittee, to full committee, to Rules Committee, to the floor of the House, and in conference with the Senate.

—Iron out technical differences between minority and majority at staff level for the member's approval.

This last function is a most vital staff policy contribution, and it bears directly on policy-making. Some differences between members can be resolved by comparison of intricate technical data, but often they do not have the time or background to get into each data struggle. Majority and minority staffs must spend hours trying to make the alternatives clear and eliminating what is unworkable, to hone the member's decision choices to the most reasonable and possible. Members then familiarize themselves with the refined field of play. Interstaff negotiation does not settle the issue, but good staff work eliminates most ephemeral choices leaving the member with fundamental decisions.

A less technical, looser staff policy influence derives from the staff man's constant exposure to the issues, combined with his ready access to the member. The staff man is in an ideal position to structure the member's perspective by raising points he thinks will interest the member, and by discussing the alternative solutions. Undoubtedly, the staff man can influence the member's thought. The degree varies with the personalities involved. (There are instances where the administrative assistant virtually *is* the member, but this is rare.) Usually staff influence is highly circumscribed. One staff man says:

I am working full time in education ... and I am sifting information and fact daily on what is happening in education. I certainly know the legislation, and I have the advantage that I have been with the committee ten years. I know what happened seven years ago about a similar sort of thing. That is an advantage. Anyone with that kind of information is going to be sought after to provide information. But, ... I think anybody who presumes in this complicated field that he has all the answers is an idiot!—and will soon be shown an idiot. This is an area in which you try to analyze the problem, think about practical solutions and good solutions. Then you encounter political situations, practical considerations, budget problems, personality problems. There are just too many things that enter into making a member's judgment on legislative action. Staff would be very presumptious to try to suggest a course of action [transcending all the real factors pressing upon a member].

Although the staff man can influence the member, he should not be viewed as analogous to a lobbyist. Staff men hold as a strong professional attribute, and perhaps a psychological need, a sense of loyalty to their boss. Almost uniformly, they pride themselves in being able to think like the member. Thus, when the staff man influences the member, he does so with a mind geared to what the member would want to think if the member were as well informed and could see the issue clearly. (The lobbyist, on the other hand, seeks to get the member to think as the lobby wants.)

Some staff men harbor a secret arrogance (not, sometimes, very secret) that they are the true brains behind the public operation; others would be insulted at the thought that they might represent an independent force in the member's policy activities. While all staff men are independent in that they perform a function different from the member, on the House Education and Labor Committee, with its high proportion of intelligent and able members, staff performs mostly technical, advisory, and administrative chores in line with the members' policy directives.

The House in Summary

The House policy process for education does not lend itself to a neat summing up. It does have overriding unifying forces: the bipartisan agreement that federal aid to education is a proper policy goal and the reality pressures to produce bills. But the process is cumbersome and divisive, a shuffling among committee members who in early stages are more ideological than pragmatic but later, by necessity, become practical and reasonable when the clash of interests forebodes stalemate.

The divisiveness of the House education policy process is not only a product of the controversy inherent in social legislation and the committee members' diverse ideologies. It is also a product of the committee's structure. Power and organization have been fragmented. With three education subcommittees—therefore three chairmen each with his own staff, with each subcommittee allowed an almost free hand by the full committee chairman, and with a strong minority (with a staff) that acts almost like a subcommittee itself, proliferation of legislative ideas has been encouraged.

Ideological and structural fragmentation has served to dramatize the confusion of goals. Uncertainty about the purposes of the federal role in education is perhaps also a function of the relative newness of education as a bona fide legislative area. In the education subcommittees, more than anywhere else in the House, the rhetoric of social missionaries confront what are by comparison the seemingly mundane advocates of the established social order—Rousseau versus Burke. The Education and Labor Committee and its subcommittees have spawned sometimes bold social debates, pitting the reformers against the moderates, with the reformers prevailing in the 1960s and the moderates gaining more control in the 1970s. Perhaps, with time, the federal policy process for education in the House will mature and be reflected in a common understanding of the goals. Then the dynamics of the House policy process will emerge more clearly, and, although differences within the committee will inevitably continue, common understanding will ease fragmentation and smooth the committee's policy process.

The Senate

The Senate policy process for education is far simpler than that in the House due in part to necessity, because of the Senate's work overload, in part to the customs and procedures of the Senate, and in part because the issue area of education generally has not offered senators a dramatic set of policy problems.

Senate Work Load

The House with its 435 members can afford the luxury of one full committee chairman, three subcommittees each with a chairman, perhaps half a dozen activists, and up to a dozen or more fairly concerned members. Not only are numerous House members involved in education, but also the division of labor permits those members to specialize in subfields and to devote most of their legislative efforts to the fields of major interest.

In the Senate, with only 100 members, each senator sits on an average of four committees, perhaps seven subcommittees, and he may chair one of the subcommittees. There are enormous legislative demands on his time and energy. Further, the area of education claims only one subcommittee, a piece of the full Senate Labor and Public Welfare Committee (notably, the title of the full Senate committee does not even contain the word "education"). The education subcommittee is operationally composed of one active senator—the subcommittee chairman—and six other members who are at best marginally active in committee affairs and show intermittent interest on selected topics. One thin subcommittee manned by overloaded senators is responsible for considering the same legislation covered in the House.

Education has never created much competition among senators for power or headlines, let alone for the dubious opportunity of carrying out the mundane mechanics of developing legislation that commands little public attention. Education receives superficial—often only symbolic—attention from the elected member. The following remarks by Senator Harrison Williams (D., N.J.), a member of the subcommittee, relay his courtesy and his sympathy for education, but also indicate education's relative insignificance. The senator came to the hearings specifically to build a sympathetic record for the American Association of Junior Colleges. Before beginning questioning, he was impelled to make the following admission.

That is a magnificent foundation on which we can go on and build this program of necessary assistance to junior colleges. It is a great statement. I will say that my preparation and my homework [that is, the materials prepared for the Senator's examination] for your appearance here today was complete. My follow-through was not. I got in about midnight, driving down from New Jersey, and there was the information on my desk, and frankly, after a long drive, I was not up to it.[10]

Like most of his colleagues, the senator desired to be supportive of education but knew little of the particulars. This scene is unlikely to find a counterpart in the House.

Even the subcommittee chairman, who spends more time on education than any other senator, spends little of his own time on education. He can give his attention mainly to education program highlights and areas of high conflict. The most vigorous education subcommittee chairman was Senator Wayne Morse (D., Ore.), but even Morse, always a staunch supporter of federal aid to education, could serve the cause only at highlight moments. By 1965 he had become deeply involved in his role on the Senate Foreign Relations Committee; he was one of two senators who voted against the Gulf of Tonkin resolution, and one of the earliest and most persistent opponents to expansion of the Vietnam war. Without losing his affection for education, he, like many other senators concerned about education, chose to channel his energy to the subjects that seemed most crucial. In a modern Senate concerned with drama, education is lackluster. Senator Claiborne Pell (D., R.I.), successor to Morse as subcommittee chairman, sounds like a lonely legislator in the following dialogue with a witness:

WITNESS. Senator Pell, thank you very much for this opportunity to appear before this distinguished subcommittee which is dealing, I think, with a subject very, very important to the national interest.

SENATOR PELL. I would completely agree with you that what we are doing is tremendously important, and yet the public is really not greatly interested in the problem with which you and I are seized. I see one representative of the press here, and very rarely does the general public take an interest in these hearings. But, I will agree with you that they are important.[11]

Senate Hearings

The television stereotype of Senate hearings poses a vigilant senator against a recalcitrant witness (Senator Fulbright taking on Robert McNamara or Melvin Laird and the entire Defense Department or Senator Sam Ervin probing into Watergate). Often it shows cross-examination by a senator who asks piercing questions driving to the bottom of matters of dramatic national interest. The ordinary reality, particularly in education, is much different.

In education hearings often the subcommittee chairman is the only senator in attendance. Witnesses are not dramatic. Virtually all witnesses are "friendly," that is, the senator and the witness share a

goal of helping the witness make a public record of his special interests. Furthermore, Senate education hearings are short. The giant
Education Amendments of 1972, a 157-page bill reported by the
Senate in 1971, involved eleven "days" of hearings in 1971 and
fifteen "days" in 1972. (A day of hearings means convening the
subcommittee at 10:00 a.m. and adjourning at 11:30 a.m. or noon—
on occasion longer.) These twenty-six "days" represented the public
record on literally hundreds of major policy decisions affecting education.

The purpose of the Senate hearing is to build a terse record to
show: (1) the position of the witness; (2) exploration of the legislative intent of the witness, usually through a dialogue with the
Senator; (3) the position of the senator vis-à-vis the witness. Hearings
are mainly political, not intellectual, seminars on the underpinnings
of policy, records of who wants what in education and indications of
the leaning of the senator toward support of or opposition to the
request. Examples of three common types of hearings follow.

(1) The record-building hearing is the most common. It follows a
routine designed solely to build a public record of support and opposition to proposals. It is not designed to make public debate on the
substance of bills. Data is buried. To save time and reduce boredom,
the witness customarily verbally summarizes his more extensive
written testimony. The details of the testimony are inserted only
"for the record." This means that even if the senator attends the
hearings, he probably never gets to hear or be informed about many
details of the proposals he considers.

The following example, drawn from hearings on the Vocational
Education Amendments of 1972, illustrates how a witness, Dr. Edward Kabakjian, executive secretary of the American Industrial Arts
Association, sought to ensure that industrial arts received special
treatment. Senator Pell helped the witness make his point, then cast
his own policy judgment:

DR. KABAKJIAN. Good morning, Senator Pell. I am Edward Kabakjian. . . .
What I would like to do is to paint a picture of what the issues are with the hope
you will have a few questions to raise and establish a dialogue.

SENATOR PELL. The questions will depend entirely on how long a period of
time you leave me.

DR. KABAKJIAN [Dr. Kabakjian spoke for a few minutes saying in part]. Now,
there is a problem with the present 1968 vocational educational amendments, in

that there is a lack of clarity in terms of the committment by Congress for the inclusion or exclusion of industrial arts teachers, and their students and programs in that particular act. . . .

The statement in the act which seems to be raising much of the confusion is one which under the definition of vocational education states that vocational education means, and I quote: "Instruction relating to occupation or occupations for which the students are in training or instruction necessary for the students to benefit from such training."

We feel that industrial arts does contribute significantly to that intent (and should be the intent of Congress to permit funding for industrial arts programs.) . . .

And there is a serious industrial arts teacher shortage in the nation. . . . There has been a massive federal support for the improvement of industrial arts curriculum in the last ten years, and now that the curriculum has been developed, there is no vehicle for the dissemination of the findings of that research. . . .

What we need now from the Federal Government is support in our educational programs to provide facilities, equipment, and programs to train faculty necessary to prepare teachers for these new programs in the elementary and secondary school.

SENATOR PELL. In other words, you want much more—to be more specific?

DR. KABAKJIAN. We want your bill more specifically carried out.

SENATOR PELL. In other words, at this point you feel yourself in a gray area?

DR. KABAKJIAN. Very definitely.

SENATOR PELL. We will take this into account in drafting the bill and I am struck with the statistics that you mention. . . . [Am I correct in saying that] the hope is that some of these young men will find they are particularly interested in one or another aspect of the trades they are learning and will go into it following completion of high school?

DR. KABAKJIAN. Yes, very definitely. [12]

In the above dialogue Pell himself received only a vague indication of the exact desires of Dr. Kabakjian, but the intent and the result of the exchange is clear. Dr. Kabakjian, with the assistance of the senator, built a record and a rationale for including industrial arts in programs where it had formerly been excluded. Senator Pell, through his statement, "We shall take this into account . . ." indicated an interest and a modest commitment. Pell's remark will serve as a cue to his staff to examine the reasonableness of the detailed industrial arts requests.

(2) A second hearing situation closely related to the first finds the senator seeking record endorsement for his bill from a witness. This technique, a favorite of Pell, pushes the witness either to reject the

bill or to accept it in principle listing only his exceptions. The general endorsement qualified only by exceptions gives the impression of broad support for the senator's bill.

Endorsement, while not always forthcoming (some witnesses simply do not want the bill enacted into law), is usually accompanied by qualifications representing the selfish interests of the witness. The witness will say in effect, "Yes, our organization likes the bill, but we think you should add such and such or delete such and such." For example, Dr. Stanley Spector of Washington University in St. Louis testified in support of retaining Title VI, NDEA, involving area foreign language centers. Because the new higher education amendments could possibly have eliminated Title VI provisions, Dr. Spector and his associates, who had a significant professional stake in the title, remained circumspect about endorsing Pell's proposal. Dr. Spector would endorse the Pell bill but not at the expense of Title VI.

SENATOR PELL. Gentlemen, with specific regard to the legislation before us, the administration bill which extends the program for two years, and the committee bill S. 659, which extends it for a longer period consolidating it with International Education and strengthening graduate schools. . . . Do you have any preference as to which bill you prefer?

DR. SPECTOR. May I address myself to that point. . . . If the International Education Act provisions which the Senator's bill incorporates should go forward, I think this would very desirable . . . so, I think the two [NDEA VI and International Education] mesh very well, and I think the Committee should be complimented on coming forward with this idea *provided, of course, that Title VI moneys are not lost in the shuffle.* [Emphasis added.]

SENATOR PELL. Have you studied the legislation that we asked you to comment upon?

DR. SPECTOR. Yes, sir.

SENATOR PELL. Which bill do you prefer?

DR. SPECTOR. I would prefer your bill, sir, provided we could be sure that the Title VI provisions were there. . . .

SENATOR PELL. Thank you very much.[13]

In a similar example, Senator Pell found it easier to obtain an endorsement. Director of Libraries Dr. Stuart Forth, of the University of Kentucky, appeared before the subcommittee to urge retention of Title II A, B, and C—the library title—of the Higher Education Act. After a brief statement by Dr. Forth:

SENATOR PELL. As you know, we are faced with two definite choices, and we want to try to be specific about which we want to do. As opposed to the two bills, the Administration bill, S. 1123, and the committee bill, S. 659, when it comes to your area of interest do you have a choice between them?

DR. FORTH. Yes. As far as I am concerned, S. 659 is the one that we want.

SENATOR PELL. That is a nice statement which is very hard to get. Thank you. This helps us as we move ahead in the legislative process, and you will be amazed how rarely it is that witnesses will say we want this and we want that.[14]

In his last sentence, the senator meant that most witnesses want "this or that" but with complicated modifications. He must have been relieved to encounter an unequivocally supportive witness. Of course, the Pell version gave Dr. Forth what he wanted. (Many such public agreements are the result of lobby-staff prehearing work to iron out differences which can then be anointed by the senator and the witness.)

(3) The third hearing situation illustrates how hearings can allow the building of a record of difference between the witness and the senator. This type is most difficult for both senator and witness, but often it is the most important hearing held. The witnesses in the example are Nixon administration officials, HEW Secretary Elliot Richardson and USOE Commissioner Sidney Marland. The hearings were examining a proposal for the structure of the National Institute for Education, and the crucial issues revolved around: (1) whether the Congress should legislate the structure of HEW, thus forbidding reorganization at the will of the secretary, and (2) whether NIE should be a highly autonomous agency responsible only to the HEW secretary or whether the commissioner should have a strong hand in NIE policy. Briefly, the administration preferred: (1) as little congressional direction in structuring the administration as possible, and (2) to permit the commissioner to play a strong role in NIE.

SECRETARY RICHARDSON. . . . I feel it unwise policy in general to detail internal organization by legislation. Such legal specificity creates too many roadblocks to change. One of the primary needs of any organization is the need for flexibility, the ability to maintain viability by responding quickly to changing conditions. One would hardly expect the Congress to legislate the organization of an infantry division. . . . It is up to the administrator, whether a military man or educator, to organize the resources and be responsible for carrying out the mission . . . [thus] I oppose the language of Title III of S. 659 [the Pell bill which would create a Division of Education of HEW composed of the Office of Education and the NIE . . .]. [Secretary Richardson supported] the President's proposal which would permit the centralization of authority in the Secretary, to be delegated as he decided. . . .

COMMISSIONER MARLAND. . . . The National Institute of Education needs its own institutional identity distinct from the Office of Education. . . . The National Institute of Education, while requiring its own separate identity, will also need fruitful ties to other agencies supporting education or related activities. The most important of these, of course, is the Office of Education. One way to provide coordination is to make a single official responsible for both agencies . . . Secretary Richardson would delegate to the Commissioner responsibility for overseeing the Office of Education and NIE . . . and would make [the] agencies responsible to the Commissioner. . . .

SENATOR PELL. Thank you very much, Mr. Secretary and Mr. Commissioner. . . . One point . . . I would like to touch on here is that you *appear* to want the equivalent of what we are proposing in the form of an education division of HEW. However, you really want to do it administratively, and *we want to set it up by law.* [Emphasis added.] . . . I would advise you to work with staff on some modified language that would meet both the objections and the objectives.
 . . . Before getting into any specific questions, I hope you understand the reason for our proposal. I look forward to the day when we will have a separate Cabinet level Department of Education. I realize this runs completely counter to the Administration's proposals. . . .

[Later in the hearing]

SECRETARY RICHARDSON. The head of the NIE, Director of NIE, should be independent of the Office of Education in the sense that the director would not be taking orders from the Commissioner day to day but still related to him. . . . In effect, the Commissioner would be the senior. . . .

SENATOR PELL. I think I follow, but my understanding was that the Institute would be established so that in the event of a Secretary or Commissioner without great imagination or an innovative approach, the [NIE] would be able to support innovation. And while I have great respect for you and Dr. Marland, the time might come when there might be in those jobs men for whom one does not have such respect. *And I personally believe that the [NIE] would be a spot more independent than I detect* in the [table of organization suggested by the Administration]. (Emphasis added.)[15]

Plainly, the senator and the administration have come head on, albeit politely, to a major point of difference. The administration wants to design its own structure; the senator distrusts USOE bureaucracy and wants to ensure in law that the NIE gets a chance at newness and innovation by being separated from USOE. The sometimes subtle dialogue—almost always couched in friendly language—actually reflects stern differences, and the record shows it.

The above testimony bears another remark. Both the secretary and the commissioner came to the hearings with carefully prepared testimony and flanked by technical staff aides. But, as in other instances, technical data exchange is not the vital Senate hearing function.

Technical matters in the Senate quickly boil down to big policy chunks—positions into which the details fall. Senator Pell can hold his own in such hearings without his own detailed staff help because the big policy directions have been worked out over his years in public office. He tells the secretary:

I look forward to the day when we will have a separate Cabinet level Department of Education. I realize this runs completely counter to the Administration's proposals.

and again reveals his preestablished viewpoint when he notes:

I personally believe that the [NIE] should be a spot more independent than I detect in the [administration proposal].

The senator has built a record; he has laid down his biases, and, for the rest, he says:

I would advise you to work with [subcommittee] staff on some modified language that would meet both the objections and the objectives.

He has cast the policy superstructure, thus fulfilling the function of the hearings.

Power of the Chairman

The chairman of the Subcommittee on Education is the Senate's education specialist. He is expected to do his job, and, on all but volatile issues (e.g., bussing, race), no other senator is likely to take an interest, let alone interfere. The chairman's individual power is considerable and nearly exclusive. Since most issues raised in subcommittee will never have another chance to surface throughout the entire Senate policy process, the chairman's assents and dissents are vital.

Protection from abuse of the chairman's power rests in Senate custom—the so-called "club system"—and in the personal policy stands of the men who have held the job. The club system can be viewed as an institutionalized compensation for the Senate's tendency to assign ostensibly great power in a policy area to one man. Only in exceptional cases will any other senator bother to learn the details of an education issue. If he does, however, his concern will probably be honored. Assuming that all senators—particularly those with high seniority—are members of the same club, each with equal standing, then on most policy matters each senator honors the request of any other to add to or delete provisions to a bill. A senator otherwise uninvolved or only marginally involved in education may request a change to benefit a special interest in his state, to benefit a favored lobby, for idealism, to do the president or a bureaucrat a favor, or for any number of reasons. An example can be drawn from the 1972 Higher Education Amendments. Senator Edward Kennedy, as a spokesman for the dispossessed, had developed a bill to aid Indian education. As a member of the Labor and Public Welfare Committee (though not much involved in its education deliberations), he offered the bill for inclusion in the comprehensive education bill, which was gratefully received by Chairman Pell.*

Besides being an informal device to fragment Senate power, the club system expedites Senate business. Uncontentious reciprocity among members on most matters permits the Senate to reduce quibbling, thus permitting time for debate on other issues of more concern to the members.

The chairman ultimately retains the decision to be as clubby as he can without injuring the design of his bill. Senator Pell agreed with the Kennedy proposal—two liberals in the same broth. Club courtesy also works among more ideologically distant members, but only up to the point of highly partisan or fundamental matters which the chairman wants to protect and, if necessary, take to a vote. Because he is a member of the majority and therefore commands a majority on virtually every issue that would come to a committee mark-up vote, the last word is almost always the chairman's.

The club system does not touch the fundamental perspective of the chairman, so protection from abuse of his power rests in large part on his personal policy viewpoint on education. An obstructionist could retard growth of education. However, since the 1950s the men who have held the job—and the Senate as a body—have been expansive with education. Their liberal posture has caused acceptance of provisions to extend benefits in every direction, and new programs have been easily added. (Indeed, the Senate subcommittee often serves as a sort of court of appeals from the House. When ideas,

---

*If a lobbyist or interest spokesman can involve virtually any senator in an idea and can get the senator to make a proposal to the chairman, the lobby then has a powerful inroad to the final version of the Senate bill. (For example, the National Audio Visual Association has a Senate ally who is almost totally uninformed on education matters but is willing to help NAVA if needed. He can be quite effective.)

particularly liberal ideas, have failed in the House, lobbyists and spokesmen knew that they stood a good chance of getting back some of their losses in the Senate. One senator can add to the Senate version of a bill what it might take a team effort to do in the House.)

Senate Staff

If senators, even under the best leadership, treat only the highlights of policy and give little personal time to education, how does the work get done? The answer is perhaps shocking to the uninitiated, for most work and a great deal of policy is generated by senatorial staff responsible to the subcommittee chairman, who were never elected into public office by the people. In education, senators have depended upon staff, and staff exercise of policy power should not be underestimated.

One brief example shows how the staff can set the senator's decision-making agenda. Senator Gaylord Nelson introduced the Senate version of the Environmental Quality Education Act, and Senator Pell's subcommittee staff, while recognizing Senator Nelson's jurisdiction, took a hand in the bill's formation. Says a Senate staffer:

Like with Senator Nelson and the Environmental Education Bill: As far as we were concerned [on the subcommittee staff], that was the Nelson bill. He said what he wanted it to do. We suggested a change, and he said, "Fine" through his personal office staff. We did not sit down and talk to him. We sat down with Dennis [Nelson's staff man] and said, "Dennis, this is a rotten bill. Change it." He said, "Why?" and we told him. He said "All right" and went to Nelson and said, "How about it?" Nelson said, "That is a good idea. Change it." It all took thirty seconds with Nelson.

Nelson retained the final say—the senator always does—but he had nothing to do with the development of the new policy and was put in the position of reacting. Given the senator's general isolation from the details, he must react at a very general level, leaving staff sometimes considerable power to define what he will react to.

Staff is the senator's major, sometimes exclusive, source of information. The effects of his staff on what the senator hears are manifest in hearings, briefings, and policy formulation.

Staff and Hearings. Staff influence at hearings can be considerable. The committee counsel is responsible for scheduling witnesses at the hearing, thus he is able to ensure that certain voices are heard. Because the senator is unlikely to know details of matters being heard, he must rely on staff briefing. By suggesting that the senator should nurture a witness and build a record in a certain way, staff can draw out issues it sees as important. Commonly the staff prepares the senator with a list of questions he can ask each witness. Each question draws a particular response from the witness which the senator can publicly approve or reject. After the hearing, when the senator is not available for extensive consultation, the staff technician uses the hearing record as his base for including components in the Senate bill. Witnesses who have made subtle and technical points and, as a result of questioning by the senator, have won his endorsement, will likely find that the pleas of their testimony become translated into a line or section of the draft bill or a line in the all-important committee report. To the extent that staff can control hearings it controls the content of the hearing record—the officially sanctioned document of the chairman. Therefore, staff can control elements of policy.

The clearest open manifestation of Senate reliance on staff comes at joint House-Senate conference sessions. Members of the House typically know the facts and refer to staff infrequently. Senators consistently rely on staff for virtually all matters. In one conference session, Senator Morse consulted his staff aide Charles Lee to the point where House members were talking directly to Lee. This prompted one House member to remark sarcastically, "I note the addition of the one-hundred-and-first senator."

Staff, the Information Funnel. Every session the House passes a number of education bills. The Senate usually (not always) draws up one omnibus bill collecting all matters considered by the House and perhaps adding a few. This practice, necessary considering that only one man handles the work and also for the sake of conducting Senate floor business efficiently, creates a situation of great complexity. A giant bill discussing higher education, vocational education, emergency school assistance, and any number of other topics can scarcely be digested thoroughly by one senator working less than part-time on the matter. Further, except when a major issue has come to a peak and needs a formal decision to resolve differences, senators rarely see education lobbyists. Issue formulation, detailed information exchange, and negotiations between the lobby and the Senate are carried on almost entirely through the subcommittee staff.

Staff has access to the senator, which is denied most other people. Efficient use of this access requires that staff receive all relevant information, capsulize the issues, and then stay a step ahead (two steps, says one staffer) of the senator. By knowing which issues should be raised, the staff can meet the senator with prepared analyses of the problems and prepared proposals for solution. Or, if the senator raises the problem, the staff tries to be prepared with a solution. The senator routinely defers to the staff member's closeness to the data and asks for suggestions about the meaning of the data and what should be done. Since the senator is unlikely to seek alternative opinions on most points in question, the staff member's judgment often weighs heavily (indeed, it may be the only weight) in the senator's snap decision.

The Senator's Control of Staff. Lest the above description imply that the staff manipulates the senator, it should be noted that there is a correcting force: the senator himself. First, staff members are employed on the assumption that, whatever the staff member does, it must make the senator look good. Embarrassing the senator is immediate grounds for reprimand or dismissal. This syndrome has its roots not only in the hire-and-fire capability of the boss but also in the type of person attracted to the job. Even more than in the House, Senate staffers are fiercely loyal, often revering of their principal. Their sometimes pretentious claims of being the true brains behind the member's work rarely goes further than noting that the work was merely a fulfillment of the member's broad policy wishes, and never goes further than saying that the ideas generated are what the member would want if he had the time and information to think about them.

Second, although the senator may not concern himself with details, he has an overriding ideology and some pet ideas that have accumulated over the years and to which staff scrupulously attends. Aid to the disadvantaged and to low income students underlay both Senator Morse and Senator Pell's policies, and legislation reflects their beliefs. Senator Morse consistently sought to aid the handicapped, and his staff aide, Charles Lee, inserted proper language into bills at every opportunity.

Senate staff is not wildly independent, but it does have responsibility for handling details—matters that can be crucial to a lobby—

and for setting much of a senator's thought about education. Further, as the main source of access to the senator, staff has responsibility to iron out problems with lobbyists, administration officials, and others who look to the senator for broad guidance. Senate staff performs many of the functions for which elected members are responsible in the House.

The Minority

In the Senate the minority is at less of a disadvantage than in the House. Senators are less partisan, and the club system operates on a bipartisan basis. They find that by accommodating each other on as many issues as possible—fighting out only the crucial, uncompromised issues—that life in the Senate is made more pleasant for all.

Minority members also rely heavily on staff to iron out the minority position. As the education bills are assembled by the majority staff, the minority counsel carefully scrutinizes each provision. Following the pattern of the members, the staff relations between minority and majority are more that of colleagues than adversaries. The majority staff counsel describes the process.

> After the majority gets a second draft of the bill, then we sit down with the minority counsel, and we just more or less look at the bill—an explanation process. "Have you any suggestions?" I ask. He usually has suggestions. He is a great nitpicker, and he always, if there is an error, is going to find it. This is not a political discussion. This is a technical nonpartisan we-have-to-get-a-bill-through approach. At that point he knows pretty well where we are going. Then he canvasses the Republican senators and the Nixon administration and asks what they think of this and this and this. Then we go through another draft, and that is when the Republicans come in to say, "We do not like this. We do not like that. We will take this out," and tell us what is wrong with that. At this point we go back to the chairman [Pell] and say, "The Republicans find these things wrong with our draft bill. The minority counsel does not like this, and Senator so-and-so does not like that, or somebody wants to put this proposal in." And we get another policy decision from the chairman, and then we go back and hammer it out.
>
> By this time we have been through the principals and back again, and we know where the issues lie. That is where we agree to agree and agree to disagree.

Based on the member's agreements to compromise, the staff irons out differences. What remains is a decision for subcommittee mark-up vote.

> By the time senators come to oppose each other on an issue, the staff has combed the issues down to such a point that it is a yes or no. It is a very clear choice. We will have a hundred-page bill, and we'll go into a subcommittee

meeting with four issues because the staffs on the Democratic and the Republican side have agreed to virtually all of that hundred-page bill. Then we sit and debate. I'll give you an example. One of the things we always go to the committee about, of course we always win it, is this administration [Nixon] wants everything done by the secretary of HEW, and we want it done by the Office of the Commissioner. That is one we can never resolve at the staff level. So, we take it to subcommittee mark-up, and the subcommittee votes seven to five for the commissioner because we have got more votes than they do. At this point it becomes partisan.

The premark-up compromise activity among staff and senators may reduce the differences to zero or it may not, but inevitably the subcommittee mark-up session will take a vote and report the bill to the full Labor and Public Welfare Committee. Except when a volatile, truly divisive issue is present—such as school bussing—the full committee routinely refers the bill to the Senate floor.

The Senate Floor

The Senate is known for grand oratory, but education rarely evokes the best the senators have to offer. Although a dissenting senator could take his case to the floor and seek an amendment (unless the issue is a lively one, like bussing), the subcommittee chairman's will is likely to reign. The contents, particularly the details, of the bill are the responsibility of the subcommittee, and floor debate is unlikely to consider mundane, if admittedly important, matters like the organization of USOE. As long as money is equitably spread among the states, few members question the details.

That there are exceptions to easy floor acceptance has been noted above. The prime example occurred in the Omnibus Education Amendments of 1972, a 157-page bill containing proposals for over 21 billion dollars in bold, new federal aid to higher education, and numerous other provisions. The only Senate floor debate of substance occurred over appending an eight-paragraph proposal designed to control the bussing of elementary and secondary students to achieve racial balance. Virtually all public and senatorial attention, including an angry public admonition by President Nixon on the weakness of the antibussing provision, focused on these few paragraphs. The vast substance of the bill received almost no attention.

(On votes on volatile issues like bussing, each senator is his own man with his own motives. For example, bussing has given some senators a handle for back home political gain. On the 1972 antibussing proposal, however, only Senator David Grambrell (D.,

Georgia) exploited the issue in this way. Gambrell, fighting a tough up-hill battle for election after being appointed to the seat left by the death of Senator Richard Russell, faced contenders in Georgia who carried on lively public talks on the evils of bussing. Gambrell voted against the Education Amendments and proclaimed back home that he wanted a tougher antibussing proposal and would sacrifice federal dollars to education to get the tougher proposal. Senator Stennis (D., Miss.), ordinarily a tough antibusser, summed up the views of the rest of the southern senators when he said, "On balance, considering all the factors . . . I think the needs for additional federal assistance for education at all levels are so great that I should support the . . . [bill]." Seven highly pro-education northern, liberal senators voted against the bill because they thought the antibussing provision too strong! They included four members of the Labor and Public Welfare Committee. If four members of the mother committee failed to support substantive provisions of a committee bill on the floor, the probability of defeat would be high. But, on volatile issues, each senator works out his own decision.)

The Senate in Summary

This discussion has been brief, compared to that of the House. But the Senate process is fundamentally less complicated, less scrutinous, and, to the Senate, less important. No senator seeks to make his career in education. He does not have to create issues or accumulate power, nor is he checked by vigorously competing colleagues.

The Senate relies more on its technicians than does the House. Because the technicians work for one man—the chairman—the process is considerably more efficient than in the House where any number of bosses argue among themselves. When issues "bubble up," as one staffer put it, they can be assessed, and mechanisms to solve problems can be developed under one friendly tent rather than in warring camps. (This, of course, is not a paradigm for Senate policy activities in other areas like defense or foreign affairs.) The Senate is not without conflict and pressure, but because most senators hold a low salience for education and because the Senate tends to expand its policies to include the interests of all rather than stand and fight on every point, education usually remains a low conflict issue.

Even though the Senate policy process is more casual than the

House, it is not necessarily less important or less influential to the final outcome as the following discussion on the conference illustrates.

The Conference

For a bill to emerge from Congress, not only must both the House and Senate consider the same measures, but each body must pass the bill in identical form. Since 1965 the House and Senate have been accustomed to annual education legislation, but, with rare exceptions—notably the Elementary and Secondary Education Act of 1965—their versions differ.* To clear Congress, an ad hoc conference committee is required. Conference members are appointed by the leader of each body. (Conferees usually include the senators and congressmen who have worked on the bill.) Their job is to iron out differences between the bodies and report a single, agreed-on version which the floor of each body can then consider for approval. The conference report is nonamendable; its refusal by one body either kills the bill or sends it back to another conference. Approval of the same conference report by both bodies sends the bill to the president for signing or veto.

Conference is a more potent mechanism than its place in the policy timetable warrants. For a conference to occur, the full mechanisms of both House and Senate must have gone their course with each producing an output. But conference can suddenly become the most vital point in the legislative process. Conference can kill a bill. In 1960 the House simply refused to appoint conferees, ending the chance for federal aid that year. More often the conference is vital because it can undo the work of either body of Congress. Reference to the conference on the 1972 Education Amendments offers a good illustration.

The House and Senate passed substantially different versions of major sections of the 1972 Education Amendments. Both bodies had worked years on its various sections, and pressure for passage was

---

*The managers of ESEA in both bodies feared that amendments to the administration version of the bill would open a deluge of proposals and compromises endangering passage. Because the eighty-ninth Congress was overwhelmingly controlled by liberal Democrats responsive to administration wishes, the amending process was suspended. This unusual demonstration of power tagged ESEA with the title, "The Railroad Act of 1965."

strong. But over four hundred points of difference existed between House and Senate, causing an unusually protracted conference of twenty sessions, one fifteen-hour session lasting late into the night.

Many of the points to be worked out in conference involved minor considerations, such as arriving at a common name for the bill. Some decisions were crucial, however, and fall into two categories: (1) compromises crucial to success of final floor passage of the bill; (2) compromises crucial to the substance of the bill but dealing with esoteric matters or matters of indifference to the floor of the chambers.

(1) In November 1971, at the time of initial House floor action to approve what was to become the 1972 amendments, a coalition of southern Democrats, Republicans (following President Nixon's lead), and assorted other members, supported a rigorous antibussing amendment. The Senate, yielding to a similar coalition, produced antibussing language, though milder than the House. Bussing had the national eye, and it was going to be fought out in the 157-page bill that dealt primarily with higher education and assorted other benefits.

With both houses committed to antibussing although heavily loaded with probussing or neutral members, the life of the bill hung on the ability of the conferees to develop an antibussing compromise strong enough for the proponents and not too strong for the opponents. In either chamber a group of probussers angry because an amendment was too strong could easily unite with a group of antibussers upset because an amendment was too weak to form a coalition and defeat the entire bill. Scrupulous compromise, not too harsh but sufficient to cool, had to be contrived. The job fell to the liberal architects of the bill because they had been appointed as a majority of the conferees. They had the chore of saving their own work, and they succeeded by developing a provision that satisfied the symbolic needs of the antibussers without truly forbidding bussing where it was required by the court or desired by the local school board. The compromise succeeded in placating both sides.

(2) Only on the bussing issue could the bill die; therefore, only on that issue were the conferees truly responsible to their respective chambers. The independence of the conferees showed clearly in the rest of their deliberations.

If Senate and House differ markedly in their versions of the bill, one chamber or both must yield. This poses little problem when, for example, the Senate has created a proposal the House has not considered and cares little about. Often, in fact, the Senate subcommittee will make many minor "add-ons" which end up uncontested in conference.

The much tougher situation occurs when both bodies have passed radically different versions of the same issue. This occurred on the higher education titles. The bill developed by Representative Green provided that institutions—that is, colleges and universities—would essentially control the flow of federal aid to higher education. Further, she favored the notion that the great bulk of the aid be granted to students *by institutions,* based on the college loan officer's judgment of merit. Mrs. Green's version was not supported by her liberal House colleagues nor by the majority of committee Republicans, the same people who dominated the House conference delegation.* Although the House floor had passed the Green version, the House liberal conferees heartily supported Senator Pell's bill for "Basic Opportunity Grants." They voted for it, and that was the version reported from the conference. Quoting from the conference report (no. 92-789), the Pell idea is explained:

The Senate amendment established two separate programs of student assistance grants; the House amendment on its part extended and revised the existing program. *The conference substitute adopts the general pattern of the Senate amendment.* The Senate amendment established a *new* program under which students at colleges and universities were entitled to basic grants to assist them to pursue their education. The amount of the basic grant was $1,400 less the amount the student or the family of the student could reasonably be expected to contribute toward his education. (Emphasis added.)[16]

Quite simply, the Senate in its version did something the House did not—indeed, which the House Special Education Subcommittee under Mrs. Green had consciously rejected—but which the liberal House conferees accepted. The Senate version made entitlement a matter of right to each student with emphasis on financially disadvantaged students. Institutions lost control over decisions about who

*In their minority report issued in October 1971, when the Green bill was reported to the House floor, six of the eight Republicans appointed as conferees explicitly stated their endorsement of Pell. They said: "Our proposal would assure that Federal student aid . . . would be directed first at those students who can make the least contribution to their further education . . . . The amount of each [grant] would be $1,400 minus expected family contribution. . . . This formula is similar to that in the Senate-passed S. 659 [The Pell bill].[17]

would receive aid. The implications of such a national policy for mass higher education are beyond discussion here, although their importance should be obvious.

The conference report is presented to the floor of each body for a yes or no decision. In the Senate, since they won their major demands and satisfactorily solved the bussing issue, passage came easy. The problems of the conference focused on the House.

In an unprecedented action, Representative Green, who had worked three years as subcommittee chairman to produce the first House version, ironically was forced to rise and oppose the conference report. She did so under the most unpropitious circumstances. First, most members were uninformed about the substance of the bill. Secondly, they were mainly concerned about bussing and what that meant at the polls. (It was, after all, an election year for each House member.) Most debate turned on bussing even though it was essentially irrelevant to the rest of the bill and the conferees had carefully developed a bussing compromise approved by the House leadership. The matter was almost moot. Thirdly, it was now or never for the substantive content of the bill. House refusal at this point would send the entire package back to subcommittee, stalemate a new higher education bill, and possibly threaten any aid to higher education because the old law was expiring. Because a majority of members "support education," they tended to support the rest of the conference report despite its vast alterations by the conferees. Mrs. Green laid out what was at stake. Under the apportionment of time on the House floor (controlled by the bill's supporters), she was granted only four minutes to speak.

MRS. GREEN. Mr. Speaker, I regret very much that the chairman will only allow the opposition four minutes to state the reasons for opposition to many of the varied, complex, and detailed parts of this legislation; so, I hope my colleagues will forgive me if I seem to be using shorthand in my speech . . . to summarize now in the allotted four minutes . . . a $20 billion bill affecting the lives of millions of people in the next several years.

Mr. Speaker, in the eighteen years I have been in the House, I do not recall any time when I have actively participated in an effort to defeat a Conference Report. I fully realize that it is most difficult to defeat a bill in its final stages when it comes back from conference. . . .

As you know, I was the author of the higher education legislation, and I now find myself in the most regrettable position of opposing the legislation. . . . This House on November 4 [1971] voted 332 to 38 in favor of the higher education bill. In the conference drastic changes were made in several respects. The debate should not center exclusively around the bussing issue. . . . These are educational decisions of major importance. . . .

Mr. Speaker, in my judgment we are starting false courses, and we are making false promises that we will never keep. The first false promise appears in the student financial aid section . . . of the Conference Report. . . . I do not happen to believe that this Congress or succeeding Congresses in the next several years will [properly fund this legislation] . . . . The funds will not be there, and students will have a perfect right to say this is another promise that Congress never intended to keep.

Furthermore, Mr. Speaker, I do not happen to believe that every student attending an institution of higher education is "entitled" as a matter of right to $1,400 of other taxpayers' money. I think any student financial aid supplied by the Federal Government should depend on the academic achievement and the motivation of the student. . . . The existing programs—educational opportunity grants, work-study and NDEA subsidized loans and guaranteed student loans . . . were designed so that the student financial aid officer would make the decision based on the student's academic achievement and his motivation and his financial need and that of the family. Not a single one of the four programs was originally passed on the theory that any and all enrolled students are "entitled" to the money.

In the conference committee sessions a proponent of the "entitlement" theory argued that he wanted to force the college or university to pay more attention to the disadvantaged student. Does this Congress really want to pass class legislation and continue a policy which makes it more and more difficult for the middle income student and ignores their needs while we place all the emphasis on the disadvantaged and urge them to enroll at the college whether or not they do college work?

Mr. Speaker, in the original legislation, I would never have argued for Federal funds for institutional support had I not been persuaded that many of our private colleges and universities are really facing a financial crisis of major proportions. The bill which the House passed was designed to give across-the-board support to all institutions of higher education with a weighted factor for the small college. As a compromise we accepted a provision that one-third of the institutional aid would be . . . tied to the dollar amounts . . . [of federal aid to students attending the institution]. The Conference Report changed the 33 1/3 percent to 90 percent so that no undergraduate four-year institution will receive any institutional aid except that which is tied directly to the funds for needy students.

To summarize, Mr. Speaker, I cannot vote for this Conference Report because it is class legislation—with almost exclusive emphasis on the disadvantaged student—to the neglect of sons and daughters of the middle income families. . . . I cannot vote for this Conference Report because it abandons the House position of across-the-board institutional aid and the result, as I see it, will be to accelerate the pace at which private colleges will have to close their doors. . . . I cannot vote for this Conference Report because we use economic persuasion to try to force universities and colleges to change their function.[18]

Despite Mrs. Green's objections, the bill passed 218 to 180. The liberals, who had broad support outside the higher education lobbies, carried their ideas into policy. Senator Pell's unwillingness to compromise on aid to students was a risk which he won not only in the Senate where his success was never questioned, but in the House.

What the House liberals could not do in subcommittee, they could do in conference, and the rest of the House remained almost uninvolved.

The saga of the conference on the 1972 Education Amendments reveals the possibility of a subcommittee's work being destroyed (i.e., in the House in 1972) and the possibility of an alternative view, developed in the other chamber, succeeding. The once defeated House liberals ended in victory by using the structural complexity of the Congress, the art of compromise, and the opportunity for magnification of their power.

Mrs. Green would seem to have won all but the last round. She proved more indomitable, however. Defeated in her most important legislative endeavor and with her power on the Education and Labor Committee ultimately checked, she resigned her appointment to the committee. In the new Congress organized in 1973 she invoked her seniority and was appointed to the powerful House Appropriations Committee. Not yet finished, she would again confront the higher education provisions in their annual battle for funding. And so, the congressional policy process took an unforeseen and in that sense, not an unusual twist.

Conclusion

Ultimately, power is the game in Congress, and votes are the instruments. If a proposal has the votes at any particular stage, it will win at that stage. But there are many stages. Mrs. Green could muster votes at subcommittee, full committee, and initially on the House floor. What she won, others lost, and they relied on the Senate. What was lost in the House to the opponents of Mrs. Green was won by Senator Pell at subcommittee, full committee, and floor stages, and Pell and his House allies controlled the conference. With the votes at the conference and with bussing under control, final floor victory was theirs, and they ended up writing the law, not Mrs. Green.

The congressional process goes on. The same day that Senator Pell rose on the floor of the Senate to ask acceptance of the Conference Report, he made a brief but highly pregnant request, barely observable in the official notices of the *Congressional Record*. In a Senate resolution he requested new money for his education subcommittee.

Not to exceed $200,000 shall be available to examine, investigate, and make a complete study of any and all matters pertaining to the financing of elementary and secondary education.[19]

With the 1972 amendments not yet history, Senator Pell was gearing up to prepare for new legislation on a "pressing issue," as they all are, concerning the "financial crisis" of elementary and secondary education in the 1970s and the need for a greatly heightened federal commitment. Similar tooling up was beginning in the House, but that is another story, one with a different theme, a slightly different plot, and some different players.

Notes for Chapter 3

1. Public Law no. 91-616 (October 30, 1970).

2. Murray Edelman, *The Symbolic Uses of Politics* (Urbana: University of Illinois Press, 1964).

3. Frank Newman, *Report on Higher Education,* catalog no. HE 5.250:50065 (Washington, D.C.: Government Printing Office, 1971). From the inside cover: "This report was prepared by an independent Task Force funded by the Ford Foundation, and does not necessarily reflect the policies of the Department of Health, Education, and Welfare."

4. Harold D. Lasswell, "Who Gets What, When, Where and How?" in *The Political Writings of Harold D. Lasswell* (Glencoe, Ill.: The Free Press, 1951).

5. The best study of the education legislative policy process was done by Eugene Eidenberg and Roy Morey, *An Act of Congress* (New York: W. W. Norton, 1969). Unfortunately, this excellent study focused entirely on the passage of ESEA when extraordinary political conditions prevailed. The Johnson sweep had decimated Republican power in Congress. This aberration, which has not existed during passage of education since 1966, temporarily suspended the reality and, for Eidenberg and Morey, the conception of minority power.

6. U.S., Congress, House, *Higher Education Act of 1971, Report no. 92-554,* 92d Cong., 1st Sess., 1971, p. 61.

7. Ibid., p. 62.

8. Ibid., p. 75.

9. U.S., Congress, House, *Congressional Record,* 92d Cong., 2d Sess., June 8, 1972, p. H5425.

10. U.S., Congress, Senate, Committee on Labor and Public Welfare, Subcommittee on Education, hearings on the Higher Education Amendments of 1970, 91st Cong., 2d Sess., pt. 3, June 21, 1970, p. 1467.

11. U.S., Congress, Senate, Committee on Labor and Public Welfare, Subcommittee on Education, hearings on Education Amendments of 1971, 92d Cong., 2d Sess., pt. 3, April 22, 1972, p. 1222.

12. Ibid., p. 1592.

13. Ibid., p. 1238.

14. Ibid., p. 1349.

15. U.S., Congress, Senate, Committee on Labor and Public Welfare, Subcommittee on Education, hearings on Education Amendments of 1971, 92d Cong., 2d Sess., pt. 5, 1972, pp. 2180, 2182, 2187, 2188, 2242, 2243, 2251, 2252, 2255.

16. Conference Report, Education Amendments of 1972, Senate Report no. 92-798, 92d Cong., 2d Sess. (1972), p. 167.

17. U.S., Congress, House, *Higher Education Act of 1971, Report no. 92-554,* p. 243.

18. U.S., Congress, House, *Congressional Record,* 92d Cong., 2d Sess., June 8, 1972, p. H5398.

19. U.S., Congress, Senate, *Congressional Record,* 92d Cong., 2d Sess., May 24, 1972, p. S8322.

4. The Administration

Introduction

Organizationally, for purposes of education policy, "the administration" includes the president, his immediate and extended staff, the Department of Health, Education, and Welfare, the Office of Education, the National Institute of Education, and all other officials of the executive branch who affect education policy.* In common usage "the administration" refers more precisely to the government's partisan executive leadership, staffed at the top by the president

*In 1972, Congress by law altered the traditional structure of the education hierarchy. The chief education official on the organization chart became the HEW assistant secretary for education, and he stood above the coequal commissioner (in charge of USOE affairs) and a director of the National Institute of Education (in charge of research). Most of the data for this chapter was collected before the assistant secretary role became operational; thus, the term "commissioner" is generally used to denote the chief officer officially designated to lead in educational affairs. Patterns of administrative organization frequently change. Indeed, this is one major point of this chapter.

followed by his political appointees and the civil service bureaucrats who are directly responsible to the political appointees. A dynamic definition of "the administration" is the combination of policy, programs, controls, and operations that emerges under the aegis of executive branch officials whose actions define and reflect partisan leadership.

Administration officials have two functions—making and executing policy—but these functions are not distributed equally or distinctly throughout the administrative hierarchy. Generally, policy-making occurs at the highest administrative levels—the political and near-political levels—and policy execution falls to lower levels—the professional civil service—but this by no means holds up as a rigorous truth. Although the very highest officials do little execution of policy and the lowest officials do limited policy-making, the middle level bureaucrats, who are both political creatures and civil servants, do both. Indeed, their responsibility and opportunity to execute policy permits and often compels middle level bureaucrats to shape new policy or change the old.

The major policy-making functions of the administration are (1) to set presidential priorities; (2) to develop an administration legislative program in order to propose laws to Congress or react to legislative proposals originating in Congress; and (3) to develop criteria for administration of existing law in order to determine the pattern and purposes of expenditures and of executive leadership in education. In fulfilling these functions, the actual operation of the administrative policy process varies in its neatness, ranging from relatively crisp and stern high level decisions to murky middle level bureaucratic infighting, negotiations, and compromise. (Often high level policy is itself quite murky.)

This chapter outlines the administration policy process by concentrating on both the presidential high level and the middle levels. Although a great deal of time and effort is spent by middle and lower level bureaucrats on policy execution, this discussion focuses on the use of power and influence to create or to modify policy objectives, that is, policy-making. What separates policy-making from other administrative activities is not always clear; however, in this discussion a great deal of administrative work has been safely ignored, not because it is unimportant but because it is clearly devoted to the nuts and bolts of program operations.

The Power of the President

Presidential priority can be defined as the goals and values held by the president ranked in order of their importance. For example, President Nixon's first-term goal for federal educational policy was "special revenue sharing," i.e., the reduction of extant and future categorical aid programs and the development of grants of federal dollars to states for use in ways which they determine, with the single stipulation that education block grants be used for education purposes. In the ranking of Nixon administration business (a ranking that would include foreign policy, defense, inflation, housing, and so on ad infinitum), special revenue sharing for education—particularly if new federal dollars were to be added—sat very low on the list of things to be done. On the other hand, in the order of Johnson administration priorities, obtaining a major education bill and funding for it ranked high as one of the most important issues.

Presidential priority determines what will be done within the administrative branch, and, regardless of the zeal of lower level administration officials who may disagree with the president, highly effective mechanisms exist to enforce his will. His desires would be meaningless if they could not be enforced; thus, before discussing the process by which priorities are set, it is useful to discuss the mechanisms of presidential control.

Presidential Control Mechanisms

The White House is one of the smaller official buildings in Washington, but it contains an inordinate share of the master switches of power. It begins with the president. The president is a single human being. He does exist—physically and politically. Perhaps this assertion seems too evident; however, it is vital to understand that he sets the pace and direction of administration policy. Although the aides around him help shape both the character and quality of presidential policy, it is the president who determines the characteristics of the aides.

Unfolding from the presidential center is an assorted core group of immediate, "innermost," presidential aides. Since 1960 the names of Schlesinger, Sorensen, Moyer, Bundy, Rostow, Kissinger, Moynihan, Ehrlichman, Haldeman, and others have been in the news because these men have advised the president and have been responsible for handling presidential involvement in the great issues of our times. Some of them are specialists—they talk to the president only when their issue area requires his attention—and some are generalists—they offer the president "wise counsel" and clarification of thoughts—and some are both. (In the latter category are Harry Hopkins, Sherman Adams, Robert Kennedy, John Mitchell.) All are unquestionably loyal. (Loyalty does not imply that presidential aides are sycophants. *The Pentagon Papers* reveals to the public a record of conflict and difference among the aides and between the aides and the president. Loyalty implies (1) dedication to facilitating the president's work and (2) a public role that will not undermine confidence in the office of the president.)

Of all the innermost aides from the Kennedy to the Nixon years, only one man, Douglass Cater in the Johnson administration, was predominantly concerned with education. (Another aide in the Johnson White House, Joseph Califano, was also heavily involved in education.) This privileged position reflected President Johnson's vital concern with education. Both Kennedy and Nixon assigned top level White House aides to handle education if the need arose, but neither president had a man assigned exclusively to serve as an organizing and driving force for the education area. (Congressmen of both parties and high level USOE-HEW officials frequently complained about the Nixon administration that when the time came to contact the White House about education, "there was nobody down there who knew anything.") For the Nixon years particularly, White House staff involvement in education occurred in an intermittent or crisis basis, for example, bussing or the school finance scare of 1972.

The main source of authority and power for innermost aides is their access to the president. They can direct presidential attention (and often speak for the president without consulting him on the particulars), and thus can produce the scarcest power commodity in Washington: presidential prestige coming to bear on a proposal.*

The innermost White House staff man holds a crucial position in

---

*Numerous lesser White House aides—interns, junior staff men, even secretaries—call to Congress or various places within the administration, prefacing their dimly authorized activities by saying, "This is John Smith in the White House. The president wants . . ." or "the president has asked me to. . . ." This annoys congressmen and responsible bureaucrats, who will gladly respond to a genuine presidential need but would like to filter out the important from the trivial, and do not wish to be manipulated by unauthorized personnel.

the modern version of the office of the president. He can speak to and speak for the president when sometimes even cabinet officers cannot. But this considerable influence is not ordinarily exclusive. In most policy affairs, a check-and-balance system operates which permits more than one access route to the president. If an innermost aide is pressing a point with which the commissioner of education (hereafter called "the commissioner") or the HEW secretary disagrees, they, too, usually have access to the president and can, through a phone call or a memo, express their viewpoint.

Except on the most important points of policy, conflict among underlings is kept from the president. He is simply too busy to settle "minor" squabbles (which may have to do with allocations of millions of dollars!). It is the function of various top level officials to iron out their differences—to do the hard work of negotiation, leaving the president to set the large priorities and serve as the final arbiter on the key questions. However, the potential for a number of men to reach the president, even if it is not exercised, encourages resolution of differences within the administration at a level below the chief executive.

Beneath the president and his innermost policy staff is the large, but not vast, "presidential staff", composed of several thousand people and known as the Executive Office of the President (EOP), which is organized into high level policy units like the Council of Economic Advisors and the Office of Management and Budget (OMB, formerly known as the Bureau of the Budget). EOP employees, many of whom the president will never meet, provide extensive, detailed, and deep staff assistance specifically for him. They enable him (that is, the office of the president) to formulate presidential policy, control that policy within his cabinet and the giant federal bureaucracy, and advance the policy within Congress and the public. Their highly talented work efforts combined with their loyalty to his goals are his primary assets in extending presidential priorities.

Loyalty in the executive office is assured by two devices: (1) political control at the top, and (2) minimal bureaucratic entanglements. The following discussion concentrates on OMB because that is the most important EOP unit in the consideration of educational policy-making.

The director of OMB is a high level political appointee (with direct access to the president at any time), in practice outranking many of the cabinet officers. He is a man of unquestionable loyalty and sympathy to the interests of the president. Below the director lies a set of second level, politically appointed, administrative posts. The second level is responsible for specific policy areas, one of which is education, and an officeholder at this high place is a bona fide partisan servant. (Although OMB posts *are* political appointments, they are not patronage jobs. The top OMB men are politically loyal and carefully screened—they are also highly talented administrators, economists, scientists, strategists, etc.)

Immediately beneath the political top lie units of very bright, well-educated, exceptionally talented, nonpolitical, career civil servants concerned with specific issue areas including education. (They are most often attorneys by training.) The civil servants, consisting of less than a dozen technicians and policy analysts in education, come under immediate scrutiny of OMB political appointees, and it is here that OMB structure for educational policy formulation stops. There is, therefore, direct political supervision of policy-involved civil service staff ensuring that the president's interests within the EOP will not be lost in an unfathomable bureaucratic depth. In addition to the close political supervision, the task of ensuring loyalty to the president is made easier because the OMB civil servants maintain a disciplined, professional spirit which, regardless of their personal beliefs, bind them to serve the president whoever he may be and for whatever priorities finally evolve. If they cannot abide with what the incumbent president wants, they leave. (After a brief vacation between the Johnson and Nixon administrations, some of them remained, creating a core of continual knowledge on their subject.)

Although OMB is frequently described as "inscrutable" or "mysterious," its techniques are actually quite simple. (Certainly OMB is more easily comprehended than USOE.) With their loyalty and function clear—to help establish and to enforce presidential priorities—and with clarification of those priorities at hand through public presidential messages and the frequent person-to-person and memo communication among the president, his innermost aides, and top level OMB officials—OMB officials become an ideal screen through which all policy ideas and proposals generated in cabinet departments are filtered.

All proposals from the cabinet departments are submitted to OMB for clearance, where they are judged against presidential ideology, and, within that context, judged against presidential priorities as expressed in the annual presidential budget. (The budget of course reflects the ideology and favored programs of the president. Ideas and words are free and abundant, but, if the ideas become operating programs, they cost money, which is scarce. OMB's job is to ensure that those dollars that are available are used to try to fulfill the highest presidential priorities.)

Proposals received by OMB civil servants are examined, and decisions are rendered through written recommendations discussing the ideological and budgetary merits. If the issue is small, the written opinion will receive cursory appraisal from a political appointee. If the issue is important, involving, for example, fundamental proposals strongly backed by the HEW secretary or the commissioner, the OMB political men as well as White House aides may become intensely involved. Ultimately, OMB officials render decisions, which are more than mere opinions, essentially vetoing any proposal outside the priorities, approving satisfactory proposals, or entering into negotiations to iron out differences between HEW or USOE-NIE aspirations and presidential objectives. In addition to formal policy proposal reviews, OMB makes prior review of public speeches, congressional testimony, draft legislation, and virtually any potential public acts of administration officials. OMB thus strikes out clandestine or inadvertant public statements that could commit the administration to a nonpriority course.

If OMB determines that an administration employee, from the HEW secretary to a low level USOE bureaucrat, cannot publicly promote a policy proposal, then (unless the employee can somehow raise the discussion to a higher level to redefine the existing priority— perhaps appealing to the president) it is as if the president himself has issued the prohibition. Federal officers do not often act outside of OMB clearance.

OMB's small staff for education is an effective match in policy control over USOE-NIE and HEW, which employ thousands. Actually, in HEW and USOE-NIE only a few dozen people make high level policy; the rest predominantly execute it. The few HEW-USOE-NIE policy people are easily supervised, and, when necessary, directed from OMB.

In effect, OMB issues work directives to the departments based on presidential desires. This process is negative—vetoing departmental proposals—as well as aggressive. Based on high level White House policy decisions, OMB may issue policy directives ranging from a memorandum outlining the president's broad intent to a detailed, fully drafted piece of legislation which the department must defend in Congress. (OMB would prefer not to do the heavy staff work like drafting legislation, but sometimes, when White House control is crucial, it does.) From a practical viewpoint, HEW and USOE-NIE are not free to promulgate just any good-sounding ideas. Unless the highest level White House decision-makers can be convinced that priorities should be changed, USOE-NIE and HEW education policy-makers walk a taut line trying to prepare proposals that will satisfy OMB and at the same time meet their own education priorities, which may be quite different. This brings OMB and White House level people into negotiations with HEW and USOE-NIE officials (particularly on budgetary matters), with OMB usually having the upper hand. (At one time cabinet level officials performed many of the functions of OMB (some still do). However, having a loyal, highly intelligent cadre at his disposal to enforce his will—a palace guard, so to speak—has become a powerful tool of the president as the size of the bureaucracy has grown. Education is perhaps more strictly con-trolled through OMB than are other areas—for example, the Justice Department and particularly the FBI or the CIA.)

Setting Presidential Priorities

The "viewpoint" of the president arises from characteristics of the man—his philosophy, his record, his values, his aspirations, his leader-ship style and approach to handling conflict—and establishes the first basis for his priorities. For example, Presidents Kennedy and John-son, as activist, New Deal-style Democrats, envisioned a positive social welfare mission for the federal government, which included federal intervention in public school goals, curriculum, and social composition. President Nixon, on the other hand, as an activist, con-servative Republican, believed in the minimal use of federal power which might serve to interfere with functions of established state and local school districts, and he believed that as president he should not lend his prestige for such programs.

Presidential viewpoint is also influenced by an assortment of sub-stantive "needs." The needs are manifest as political pressures or petitions within the political system in various forms like constituent or lobby pressure, reports of public opinion, lawsuits, scholarly reports and analyses, etc. If the petitions are received they are reflected in such places as the party platform, campaign promises, or court decisions. For example, in the 1964 presidential campaign President Johnson, speaking in Texas, asked Mexican-Americans to support Democratic candidates. Through previous cueing based on contact with Mexican-American leaders, Johnson appealed for their vote in a context of articulating his commitment to their desires for greater federal education support. Upon his election, the campaign promise was translated into a new Mexican American Affairs Unit in USOE, created with considerable strength under presidential benevolence. In another example, when the U.S. Supreme Court, in *Swann v. Mecklenburg* (1970), permitted court-required bussing to achieve racial balance in the schools, subsequent outbreak of public pressures pro and especially con created a need for an administration policy. In this case, President Nixon responded by developing an "antibussing policy."

When, as in the Kennedy and Johnson years, "the public" remains largely indifferent to federal education policy, elite leadership, rooted in presidential viewpoints, serves to define issues and to create priorities. When, on the other hand, public interest is rife or when the courts or Congress bring issues to the fore (e.g., bussing), then presidential priorities relating to these issues tend to develop passively as a reaction to pressures, and only the content of the reaction as opposed to definition of the problem is defined by the viewpoint of the president.

Given that the president usually has an action priority on education (even if that priority is to cut back), then detailed priorities—programs, dollars, administrative techniques, specific goals—emerge based on technical data gathered by presidential appointees. As strong as President Johnson's commitment was to advancing the federal role in education, close aides report that he probably never fully digested the detailed components of ESEA. He wanted a bill—the right bill—and rightness was to be determined by educational need and political feasibility, an area of detail that ordinarily lies beyond sustained presidential attention. Details emerge through high level policy groups inside the administration or from devices like "the Conversation."

High Level Policy Group—The Reactors

If a problem is acute or is foisted upon the administration (like bussing), most likely the administration will lead by reacting. Reaction is also a favored mode for a nonactivist administration which has low priority for initiating education policy. Reaction tends to be a defense, and, as such, important policy details (in the case of the Nixon administration) are likely to emerge almost entirely from a high level administration policy group composed of White House aides (with access to the president) and others depending on the issue, like assistant secretaries from HEW, Justice, Treasury, or Agriculture, the USOE commissioner, the NIE director, a second or third level OMB official, and any others thought to have a legitimate contribution to make. This group, which may sometimes meet in one of the White House chambers, will set the parameters of policy, and one of its members will be assigned responsibility to follow through on details using his staff to develop refinements. As unforeseen problems arise, he may reconvene the group to iron out the difficulties and obtain a high level consensus.

The Task Force and the Conversation: The Initiators

The high level policy group is best used as a reactor to forces or ideas imposed on the administration. If presidential priority requires active leadership—that is, clear identification of the problems and their possible solutions—then details will probably be sought from various sources: from a presidential task force or commission, from USOE, NIE, HEW, or OMB professional staff memos, or other sources like lobbies or university or foundation research. Ideas solicited from these sources can then be brought to a high level policy group and ultimately to the president for their reactions, to secure presidential commitment or rejection of program priorities.

An active leadership role by the president is thus more complicated than simple reaction because the process must first consciously extend outside high administration levels and outside government—that is, it must go beyond the high level policy group. A favorite mechanism for doing this is the task force. Presidents-elect Kennedy, Johnson, and Nixon each appointed a task force on education. A task force operates as a board of elites, a relatively small number of men and women, some in government, most out of government, who possess acknowledged distinction and wisdom. Isolated from overt public pressure but reaching outside government to define and shape policy, their function is to make recommendations for the use of government power—that is, to direct the activities of the officials in the high level policy groups. The Kennedy Task Force on Education, chaired by former Purdue University president Frederick Hovde, produced a dramatic document urging that the fruitless federal aid to education efforts of the Eisenhower years must be vindicated by passing major legislation attacking the problems of disadvantaged children, urban education, segregation, teacher training, research, library and media development, and other points. It became the basic Democratic agenda accepted in principle by President Kennedy and Commissioner Francis Keppel. After the 1964 election President Johnson received a similar report from a task force chaired by John Gardner, who became secretary of Health, Education, and Welfare. The Gardner Report, not made public until Johnson left office, became a working document, backed by the obvious prestige of the President and Secretary Gardner, setting the administration agenda to fulfill the Hovde recommendations and particularly to advance the cause of federal aid to disadvantaged children. Backed by presidential priority for education under Kennedy-Johnson, the task force reports were important policy papers. In effect they became the content of the presidential commitment and a guideline—although not a gospel—directing the coordinated (and often necessarily conflicting) policy activities of USOE, HEW, OMB, and other affected agencies.

The Nixon administration has posed a different model. The Nixon task force, chaired by Alan Pifer, a foundation president, mainly followed through on the Democratic agenda supporting continued development of the federal role and particularly emphasizing the problems of equal educational opportunity and racial integration. Dr. James Allen, President Nixon's first appointee as commissioner, read the Pifer report and assumed that the suggestions would compose the president's education program. Not until serving some time in office did Commissioner Allen realize that in effect President Nixon had rejected the report and had no intention of utilizing its suggestions. Rather than expanding federal involvement, President Nixon vigorously supported budget cuts in existing legislation, and he imposed a freeze on New Deal-type reform legislation. Instead of assuming an active leadership style, one that would promote the recommendations of his own task force, the Nixon administration withdrew to a combination of active cutbacks and a "shoe pinch" method of politics, that is, action as a reaction to political pressures. If the president's priorities do not include active leadership, then outside policy aids such as the task force assume little power, and detailed priorities are likely to emerge almost exclusively from an in-government, high level policy group.

Underpinning and supplementing the task force has been a phenomena which a former commissioner called "the Conversation." The Conversation is both formal (as the task force) and informal among policy oriented men—government officials, congressmen, professors, leading citizens, etc.—who know each other or can come to know each other because of shared interests. It is an elitist seminar (although it may never formally convene) transcending institutional barriers. It could be considered analogous to the old, big city politics where the back-room boys make decisions later to be ratified by government officials; however, it is nothing so geographically isolated, formal, powerful, or easily identified.

Several Conversations exist. Progressive educational reformers of the Keppel and Howe years composed a Conversation whose members gave heavy concern to increasing categorical federal aid, racial integration, aid to the disadvantaged, and developing more adaptive modes of school administration. This group maintained a decade of influence over USOE and federal education policy, and remained ascendent in top policy levels until the resignation of James Allen as commissioner. Other Conversations exist although none had been so influential at the top levels. The maintenance organization leadership (from NEA, NSBA, AASA, etc.) communicates and powerfully influences Congress and middle and lower levels of USOE. (This Conversation is discussed in terms of the education lobby in chapter 2.) Another Conversation exists among conservative reformers, which in the early 1970s attached itself to the "accountability" movement.

In the period from Keppel to Allen, high level administration policy-makers, guided by the so-called Progressive Conversation, were seeking to advance educational "reform" in the face of reluctance from middle or lower level bureaucrats, some members of Congress, the lobbies, and other interests. Because the success of the leadership of the Conversation was a function of Kennedy's and Johnson's reform dispositions, the Progressive Conversation could maintain its ascendence but almost exclusively on the base of its presidential support. When that evaporated in the Nixon years, the Progressive Conversation as a real, if always somewhat ineffable, policy tool, fell into desuetude, leaving mainly high level administration policy groups to passively react rather than actively lead in federal education matters.

Pragmatic Compromise

Finally, presidential priorities and substantive proposals are inevitably modified by pragmatic compromise that emerges from the political realities of clashes among interested parties, both within the administration and between the administration and others (Congress, lobbies, and other publics). Power is fragmented and widely distributed in the education policy process, and with rare exception, no single hand, not even the President's, can exclusively dominate. It is futile to try to list all possible patterns of conflict among the interested parties that cause pragmatic reassessment of priorities. An unsubtle example from the Nixon years will suffice. Through the proposal of revenue sharing President Nixon and OMB consistently sought to block new categorical aid programs and consolidate old programs in order to achieve block grants to states. If he could have had his way, President Nixon seemed to desire block grants to states or no grants at all. However, liberal members of Congress succeeded with equal consistency to increase annual appropriations for the categorical aid programs. (See chapter 2 on the activities of the Emergency Committee for Full Funding.) President Nixon could not stop annual congressional increases for categorical aid without literally shutting down HEW; thus, ultimately, one of his highest education priorities could not be acted upon.

HEW-USOE Autonomy

Configurations of power within the administration vary over time and with conditions. The intensity as well as direction of presidential commitment to education determines the patterns of power (who shall govern) and extent of authority (what the governors can do) granted to the commissioner of education and the secretary of HEW. The contrast between the Kennedy-Johnson years and the early Nixon years is striking.

Background: The Times, and Presidents Kennedy and Johnson

After near successes in the Eisenhower years, marred by President Eisenhower's reluctance to support clearly and overtly a federal aid bill, both Presidents Kennedy and Johnson entered office without major elementary and secondary federal education legislation on the books. Obtaining a first breakthrough in federal aid was high on the national agenda and became an important issue in the Kennedy campaign and a clear-cut commitment in the 1964 Johnson campaign.

Unlike Eisenhower, Kennedy did not fear federal domination of the nation's schools; however, in the 1960 campaign, Kennedy placed a fatal constraint on his education priority. As the nation's first Catholic president, he publicly promised that he would not allow any federal aid to parochial schools. When the crunch came on his aid bill before Congress, and the national Catholic Welfare Conference ("the Catholic lobby") threatened to kill a bill that contained no allowances for parochial schools, Kennedy could not intervene to reach a compromise. The bill failed; his pledge had stopped him short.

President Johnson, a Protestant and not on record against aid to parochial schools, was not similarly confined. Like Kennedy he personally placed high priority on federal aid to education, but he could go a step further by unreluctantly using his office to solve the religious war. He did the job effectively, witness passage of ESEA.

Authority of the Commissioner and USOE. Although the Kennedy bills failed in Congress, his sincere intent became translated into permanent bureaucratic power and élan for education. To dramatize his intent, President Kennedy moved profoundly to change the U.S. Office of Education from a statistical and data gathering center into a vigorous policy tool. Searching for the kind of unorthodox leadership needed to shape a new USOE policy-making organization, he appointed the dean of the Harvard Graduate School of Education, Mr. Francis Keppel, as commissioner of education. Keppel, the youngest man ever to serve as dean of the Graduate School of Education at Harvard and the youngest to serve as commissioner, had risen to his position without the traditional doctorate and without experience in public education. Although the merits of Keppel's qualifications have been debated on many grounds, from the point of view of the policy process his unquestioned superior administrative skills and extraordinary intellect reflected and fulfilled Kennedy's expectations for vigorous departures in federal education policy.

Keppel met with Kennedy on occasions and received personal

assurance from the president that, up to the point of a holy war, the office of the president stood behind Keppel's leadership for new policy for both elementary and secondary as well as higher education. Although the two men were not close personal friends, they hit it off well with mutual trust. Kennedy on at least one occasion even called Keppel directly to discuss strategy in handling Congress, and Keppel never had problems contacting innermost White House aides like Ted Sorensen to gain presidential blessing on an activity.

Soon after Johnson's election, Keppel, a Kennedy man who stayed on, attended a White House meeting on education policy. Understanding the fate of the Kennedy bill and determined to settle the holy war, Johnson bluntly stated, "I want a law." The presidential priority now reigned unequivocally. Given his marching orders by the president, Keppel both literally and figuratively received the White House phone number, and to aid Keppel's efforts Douglass Cater, an innermost White House staff aide, was assigned by the president to facilitate in every way the passage of education laws.

The commissioner could ask for no more authority, for none remained to be given. The president gave him the equivalent of cabinet status on education issues. Although the secretary of HEW maintained interest in Keppel's work, primary responsibility rested with the commissioner.*

Background: The Times, Nixon's First Term

Contrasting the Kennedy-Johnson high priority for education with President Nixon's high intensity for his low priority, a different pattern of White House—HEW-USOE relationships appear.

With the passage of ESEA in 1965 followed by numerous other Democratic education laws, the 1968 presidential campaign did not include a significant education issue. Candidate Nixon's main public

---

*Another example, not dealing with legislation, demonstrates the requirement of presidential priority as a prerequisite of bureaucratic power. When Harold Howe II became commissioner after Keppel, the Johnson education legislative agenda had been passed; however, USOE faced the volatile responsibility of enforcing racial integration and civil rights provisions of the law. Howe, bent on enforcing the law in order to provide national leadership toward attainment of equal educational opportunity, confronted President Johnson with the problem. Johnson, himself a southerner and facing heavy congressional pressure for lax civil rights enforcement, stood behind Howe. The extent to which this injured Johnson's standing with influential congressmen is impossible to measure, but, under presidential protection, Howe proceeded, often dramatically.

pronouncements on domestic affairs dealt with "crime on the streets" and the failure of federal social welfare programs. No issue concerning public education, including bussing, then seemed vital in the public agenda.

Personally uninterested in the issue of education—presumably because he considered it a local matter—and committed to lowering the federal budget and lessening the federal actions that interfere with local matters, President Nixon showed no intention of instructing his staff to pursue innovations in federal aid.

The president's first meeting with his newly appointed commissioner, Dr. James Allen, set the tone. Around a White House fireplace, Dr. Allen, armed with an agenda for advances in federal action, itched to pluck the document from his breast pocket while he listened to the president expound on the problems of law and order. After about thirty minutes the president gave indications that the meeting was over, and Dr. Allen finally asked the president what he expected from his new commissioner. The president replied that he would desire a restoration of discipline to the American classroom. Although the president was prepared to move boldly on welfare reform as a domestic issue, he had no ideas or intentions to bolster the federal role in education.

Authority of the Commissioner and USOE. The inauspicious first meeting between President Nixon and Commissioner Allen foreshadowed impotence in USOE. Instead of giving the commissioner the White House phone number, the Nixon high command engineered an emasculation of USOE.

A flashback is helpful here: Because Keppel and Howe had built the leadership in USOE, the civil service-tenured, middle level policy managers tended to be quite liberal. Many were convinced that good will, more money, and federal guidance in the advancement and enforcement of equal educational opportunity would bring about the solution to America's educational problems. Commissioner Allen stood in this tradition. He had a long-established public record supporting advancement of equal educational opportunity through racial integration and educational reform. Indeed, before Keppel's appointment, President Kennedy in 1961 first offered the commissionership to Allen. (Allen refused the offer in 1960 because as Commissioner of Education in New York State, he possessed more power and national influence than did the U.S. commissioner at the time.)

The appointment of Allen either was designed as a sop to the liberal USOE constabulary or was a mistake on the part of the conservative Nixon policy leaders, but they did not delay in taking corrective action. By denying priority to growth of the federal role in education, President Nixon in effect issued a license for lower level administration officials not to cooperate with USOE.

The impetus for noncooperation came from two directions. First, since the Johnson years, the permanent staff of OMB had built up a distrust and dislike for USOE administrative policy. The efficiency and effectiveness oriented OMB men were chafed because federal education dollars could not be made to show a difference in the quality of the nation's education. With the Nixon license to cut back, OMB could unleash its attack on the efficiency and effectiveness of USOE programs, reflecting their doubts through proposals for vast dollar cuts in the presidential budget.

Secondly, two tendencies of USOE challenged the values and security of the Nixon administration. USOE bureaucrats naturally sought to expand federal education programs and obtain greater amounts of federal dollars. The Nixon administration opposed both. In addition, USOE and HEW, charged by law to enforce racial integration provisions of the law, glared out early in the Nixon years as a potential source of hottest domestic political strife. Racial integration, bussing, freezing of federal funds to force compliance, and powerful moral suasion all had gained degrees of credence at high levels of USOE under Keppel and particularly Howe, and the new Nixon administration was determined to defuse it.

How does the president of the United States keep a constant watch and leash on his commissioner of education when the commissioner is dedicated to values that contradict the president's? The answer is a cruel and fascinating story which helps illustrate that negative presidential priority can be as powerful as the positive in controlling bureaucratic action.

President Nixon had appointed his personal friend Robert Finch, then California lieutenant governor, as secretary of Health, Education, and Welfare. It fell to Finch to control USOE (with a boost from OMB). To supervise high level policy in the area of education, Finch appointed his close personal friend, Lewis H. Butler, to the office of assistant secretary for planning and evaluation (ASPE). ASPE nominally performed the function of planning national goals and performing special evaluations of ongoing programs on which future programs could be planned. In fact, ASPE was the political action arm of the secretary. Butler employed a staff of extremely bright, well educated, and in some cases politically talented men and women whose function became to review virtually every policy proposal generated by USOE and to generate from within ASPE the major proposals that USOE would publicly advance. Although Butler played no figurehead, public relations role to the education community—very few people, even Washington education lobbyists, knew about him or his operation—on matters of education policy, he became in effect the commissioner. His deputy busied his days considering policy proposals and developing and ironing out flaws and problems in what would become the Nixon administration education program. He and his staff drafted legislation and prepared workups for the education section of the presidential budget. The deputy had immediate access to Butler, and Butler had immediate access to Finch and the White House. For the purposes of policy, Commissioner Allen had neither.

Allen meantime attempted to take control of the USOE bureaucracy. He never got a foothold, partly because he was himself a poor administrator, but decidedly more because Butler and the White House systematically thwarted his independence. Allen's first attempts to appoint his own deputy and other members of his personal staff (men whose functions parallel those of the president's innermost staff in the sense of serving the immediate policy and organizational guidelines of the top man) were aborted when the White House refused to give political clearance for any of his nominees. The Nixon White House offered Commissioner Allen a selection of bona fide Republicans—at least one of whom was from industry with no experience in public education—but Allen rejected them, pressing for candidates known to him or suggested to him by a team of distinguished educators he had organized and consulted for this purpose. Finally, after using up considerable energy, Allen was permitted by the White House to appoint as his deputy Dr. Gregory Anrig, the former chief of Title IV, Civil Rights, a staunch integrationist, Democrat, and anathema to Republican goals! As a policy-making organization USOE became a pariah.*

---

*Allen's one policy success came as an ironic twist and as a dividend of his justifiable bureaucratic paranoia. (By then he knew Lewis Butler and others were looking over his shoulder.) Allen, determined to exert some leadership as commissioner and desirous of aiming at problems of disadvantaged students, con-

In high level educational policy affairs, the office of the secretary of HEW can play a strong or weak role depending mainly on whether the president holds a high priority for education. In general, it is probable that the higher the positive priority, the less involved is the secretary. If the president supports education, the commissioner as a distinguished member of his profession tends to be given considerable direct autonomy and has access to White House decision-makers without intervention by the secretary. Under Keppel and Howe, the secretary proved to be supportive, but not regularly involved in policy development. In short, the commissioner is easily given expansive authority, but, in constrictive periods, the secretary (e.g., through Assistant Secretary Butler) aided by a negativist OMB can take direct control over negotiations, approbation, and veto of matters affecting USOE.

To shut out the influence of the Progressive Conversation dominant during the Keppel-Howe-Allen years, the Nixon administration first permitted USOE to fall into policy shambles. Once the Progressive Conversation lost access, USOE could be rebuilt in a more Republican image. The Nixon appointment of Dr. Sidney P. Marland to succeed Allen as commissioner gave the administration a more responsive, inside control at USOE, and, with Butler's departure from government, USOE resumed at least a voice in its own affairs. In the new Republicanized USOE, the commissioner (later elevated to the level of HEW assistant secretary for education) assumed management

---

ceived a new proposal for USOE: "The Right to Read." (Briefly, the proposal would have dedicated the federal government to stamp out functional illiteracy by concentrating both available resources and moral leadership on the problem.)

Allen knew that if he sent the right-to-read proposal through channels, it would be either decimated at HEW (Lewis Butler) or at OMB: thus, in an unorthodox move, he presented the ideas without clearance at a major public appearance in Los Angeles. The press immediately picked up the pronouncement and interpreted it as a major new commitment of USOE. Allen, still in Los Angeles, was called to the telephone where the president, personally lauded the proposal, adopted "right to read" as the administration education motto, and suggested that the first lady become honorary chairman of a right to read national committee. However, although the president personally adopted the right-to-read slogan, presidential priority for education remained unchanged. No new dollars or well-designed programs came forth from the all-precious White House backing.

Allen's unorthodoxy could have resulted in court-martial, so to speak; instead it led to praise. When Allen broke with the president on Cambodia and publicly renounced the invasion, he was cashiered out of office within weeks. By then, the role assigned to Allen by the administration had become untenable anyway.

but not clear policy power, which is to say that Marland, under the circumstances, agreed not to press for new policy inconsistent with Republican priorities and values, and in exchange he could be given authority to manage his own shop.

(It is impossible to promulgate a hard rule predicting the assignment of power to any established bureaucratic unit. If a president other than Nixon has an expansive priority for USOE, maintenance management of the available resources at USOE would be considered insufficient leadership, and presumably HEW, the White House staff, or OMB could take over responsibility for creating new programs and dollars. President Kennedy avoided this situation by recreating USOE into an activist policy tool. In so doing he facilitated the relationship between the administration and the education community. The powerful policy position of HEW Assistant Secretary Butler served as a safety valve for the administration, but it should be considered an anomaly. HEW supervision of USOE is a serviceable check and balance within the administration, but HEW hegemony over USOE or NIE (or White House staff hegemony) isolates the education community from free access to the administrative policy process.)

In juxtaposing the Kennedy-Johnson and Nixon settings the important point is not the twists of bureaucratic life, rather it is the fact that presidential priority ranks foremost in achieving progress toward a policy goal. Without that priority the machinery of government can easily be set against action; with it, the power of the presidency can back the work and efforts of high and middle level bureaucrats. The president may not win all he wants when he takes his proposals to Congress or into the field, but very little can even begin to happen within the administration without his support.

Openness of the Administrative Policy Process

The pattern of administration power can vary in its degree of openness in the sense of whether the process utilizes a wide range of governmental and public contacts or whether policy develops within a narrowly circumscribed zone of official government policy-makers. Comparison of techniques used in the Johnson and Nixon years provides two models.

The Johnson Years

President Johnson made broad use of the task force. He received at least twelve formal task force reports on education and numerous others that affected education problems. The task force, combined with the informal Conversation welcomed by Keppel, Howe, Cater, and others, drew varied men with different types of institutional affiliations into the most intimate top level policy development processes. Further, because the Democratic Congress sought to cooperate with Johnson's legislative programs, administration officials in the White House, HEW, and USOE maintained easy and regular channels to key solons. Also, top level White House, HEW, and USOE officials reported intensive contacts with spokesmen for the proeducation lobbies and groups. For example, shortly after Francis Keppel's appointment, President Kennedy had innermost White House aide Ted Sorensen himself drive Keppel over to meet spokesmen for the Catholic bishops. Sorensen introduced Keppel on behalf of the President. This act opened channels which Keppel nurtured and which ultimately led to fruition in the negotiations on parochial school resource sharing under ESEA. Keppel himself maintained an open office and telephone to petitioners, and he assigned his assistant commissioner for legislation the nearly full-time job of contacting any and all interested parties to gather their desires and test the feasibility of emerging administrative proposals. Some of this activity is well documented in two studies of ESEA.[1]

Although primary responsibility for developing the administration's final draft of ESEA (and other bills) lay with Keppel and Cater, and although the draft of ESEA remained a well-kept state secret until release, the composition of the bill reflected long and careful negotiations. Keppel, Cater, and ultimately President Johnson each retained power of review—real power—but none of these men sustained inflexible idealism or ideology. They constantly sought to assess the balance of wisdom, conflict, and power as each portion of the bill reached degrees of hardness. Thus, they sought to obtain substantive gains for education within political realities. This is less than government by idealism and more than government by compromise and by lowest common denominator; less than fiat, more than abdication. It is far less than direct democracy, but it is not antidemocratic. Underlying the process is a strong assumption that elite leaders of groups representing large numbers of people and institutions affected by a decision can transmit "public" interest to a small number of elite government leaders charged with formalizing decisions.

The Nixon Administration, A Closed System

An extreme alternative model demonstrating administration closedness is taken from the development of the Nixon Higher Education bill (1971-72). Under pressure because the Higher Education Act of 1963 (amended in 1968) was due to expire, a Nixon position on higher education necessarily had to be developed. Peter Muirhead, a long-time high level USOE official, held as his duchy the USOE involvement in higher education. Anticipating the need for renewal legislation, USOE contracted with a consulting firm to develop a report on higher education that might serve as a basis for legislation. Mainly, Muirhead advised extending the Higher Education Act as it was passed by the Democrats and expanding funding for existing student aid programs (particularly the very popular National Defense Education Act provisions).

Within ASPE, a Butler senior staff member, who eventually gained principal responsibility for coordinating technical development of the Nixon bill, argued against the Muirhead and USOE position. After discussions within ASPE, Butler became convinced that President Nixon should have his own position, that is, the higher education bill should not merely extend what the Democrats had done previously. At least two reports existed (one developed in ASPE under the Johnson administration, and one developed for the HEW secretary from a grant by the Ford Foundation) which urged major shifts in the pattern of federal aid to higher education. The crux of these proposals were "student aid," reminiscent of the GI Bill, that is, most money would be granted directly to students on the basis of eligibility formulae, to be spent by them at institutions of their choice. Butler adopted the idea, convinced the HEW secretary, and got him to convene a top level policy group plugged into and meeting at the White House.

The group consisted mainly of subcabinet men who ordinarily did not see the president but were at most a step away: Lew Butler; Herbert Stein, then a member of the Council of Economic Advisers;

Richard Nathan, the OMB political appointee, second level with jurisdiction for education; Commissioner James Allen; Ed Morgan, a
White House staff member not as influential as the other group members but able to keep an eye on the procedures; Daniel Patrick
Moynihan, counselor to the president and with direct access to him;
a Department of Treasury representative because of the large amount
of money involved in student loans; and a Department of Labor
representative. Sitting in the anteroom were aides to some of the
group members.

Based on briefing papers and occasional consultations with aides,
the group members, meeting a number of times over three months,
outlined what they thought were the issues. The result of the discussions led to an agreement on a "Republican-Nixon" policy for higher
education based primarily on student aid. A set of guidelines
emerged, and Butler took responsibility for development of the technical details. As Butler's senior staff man began the actual job of
writing detailed provisions, he frequently consulted with Butler
about the decisions of the group. As the interpreter of the group's
intent, Butler held power to shape details of a Nixon bill within
limits laid out by the top levels.

Work on the bill remained almost exclusively in the office of the
secretary of HEW, particularly ASPE, with USOE barely consulted.
The Nixon administration policy process on the higher education bill
did not admit congressional interests, lobbies, or broad consultations
with people in the field. Lobbyists as well as members of Congress—
including Republicans—received the Nixon proposal without prior
consultations. Even within the HEW administration, dissent remained
severely quashed. One high-ranking HEW official in the office of
legislation who had clear and honest contacts with Congress fought
internally for prior negotiations and compromise from the Butler
position in order to appease the dissenting higher education lobby
and its congressional supporters. He subsequently faced bureaucratic
reprimand—transfer and loss of power. An internal outcast, the van-
quished HEW legislative man had, however, soundly reflected reality.

While administration work proceeded in near-total isolation, other
forces prepared their agendas. A closer examination of Muirhead's
proposals shows that he reflected the expressed concerns of the
higher education lobby for heavy federal involvement in simple,
direct aid to institutions. The beleaguered colleges and universities

around the country claimed they needed operating revenue and wanted it with minimal federal control. Their leaders reasoned that the Nixon proposals for student aid would, paradoxically, pose a burden to most institutions rather than a relief because federal aid to students would mean that more people would be able to attend university, and particularly more culturally disadvantaged people. Since virtually every public and most private universities cover only a fraction of the expenses of education from tuition, each additional student would produce increased cost to the university, and, in the case of the disadvantaged, the cost would be multiplied because of their need for special services.

Not only were the college and university lobbies unanimously opposed to the Nixon bill, but also the House subcommittee chairman in charge of higher education, Representative Edith Green, sympathized with them. Other members of Congress, while disagreeing with each other, almost unanimously rejected the Nixon proposal. Indeed, the ranking Republican on the Education and Labor Committee, Congressman Albert Quie, who traditionally introduces major legislation on behalf of the administration, introduced the bill with a statement on the House floor that he could not support some of its key provisions.

Thus, instead of having ironed out differences through the administrative policy process, the Nixon higher education proposal reached the public as a morass of conflict in the form of an administration bill, a separate Senate bill, several House versions, and vigorous dissent from the lobbies.

Under Kennedy-Johnson, the Conversation, while elite, served to form close consensus *before* the bill was submitted to Congress through negotiation with principal interest groups and power figures in and out of government. When administration officials iron out problems before sending the bill off, they, not the Congress, become the focus for conflict resolution. Administration officials are then in a stronger position to control and shape the policy agenda based on their proposals, and they enhance the opportunity to give up the least of their ideals and save the most. This procedure steals away congressional prerogative and power in policy shaping (and is often resented by congressmen) because if negotiations directed by the administration are successful, then legislation, when introduced, gains immediate support of important groups. Congressional hearings then become a parade of endorsements or minor dissents; congress-men lose the opportunity to use their ideas to determine the policy agenda around which compromise takes place; congressional action approaches being prefunctory and the power of the administration is magnified.

The closed method, as it worked in higher education under President Nixon, drew only on high level political appointees and technicians loyal to the appointees. It too was elite, but it was inaccessible to divergent opinion and subsequent negotiation and compromise. Administration officials can if they choose remain aloof, seeking to produce an "ideal" proposal suited to circumscribed standards. (As much as the Kennedy-Johnson and the Nixon processes differ, in both the underlying premises established by presidential priority remained unchallenged; even under Kennedy-Johnson, openness was a matter of degree determined in their case by boundaries of the élan of liberal, New Deal reform.)

The administration, however, does not pass laws; all proposed legislation eventually goes to Congress, which is necessarily open to public petition. If a proposal is controversial, as in the case of higher education, and if members of the executive branch are not willing to iron out conflicts as the legislative proposal is developed, then the burden will fall to Congress, and most likely the administration proposals will be vastly altered and the appearance of legislative leadership will be stolen from the president. (The 1972 Higher Education Act remained in Congress for two-and-one-half years in a convoluted and often bitter state; ESEA, on the other hand, having been negotiated by the Conversation, spent less than three months on the Hill.)

The Technician and the Policy-Maker

The scarcest commodity in Washington is power, and everyone likes to think he possesses it. It is common in Washington to find interns and low level staff aides who work closely with powerful decision-makers who claim that they in fact wrote a certain bill, did the work attributed to a public celebrity, or conceived the idea mouthed by a superior. Sometimes the claim is true. More often, particularly in complicated matters, the staff aide has worked intensively on a fragment of the entire policy problem. Many people who participate in decision-making have only a "technical" contribution as opposed to policy-making power. Their contributions are vital to good policy, but the contribution is of a specific kind.

The role of the technician is: (1) information gathering—he collects and condenses information about a problem to inform the decision-maker; (2) developing alternative proposals—viewing the problem, he presents an array of means to solve it; (3) analyzing—he determines the costs and benefits and the utility of various proposals; (4) problem solving—once the decision-maker has chosen, the staff aide works with the decision to shape a detailed proposal. In this last capacity, the technician may communicate and negotiate with other interested parties. The decision-maker may indeed devolve some preliminary negotiating authority onto the technician; however, all commitments are brought back to the decision-maker if conflict arises.

The creation of an idea by a technician is not the same as creation of a policy even when the idea finally emerges as policy. Ordinarily, many ideas fall into the policy hopper—where dollars are likely to be spent, ideas materialize. However, ideas only come to life by gaining approval of authoritative policy-makers who, at high levels, are direct political descendents of the president. Virtually any new proposal that will cost money or a decision that will allocate large amounts of existing money gains review at a political level.

The policy role, as opposed to the technical support role, can be distinguished; the two exist as a division of labor. (Power is logically distinguished from technical input even when the two are combined in the same person.) For example, a policy matter would be: should dollars be utilized for aid to higher education by giving them directly to students or directly to institutions? Further, assuming a decision is made for student aid, another policy question would be: should financially disadvantaged or middle class students receive most of the aid? Technical contributions would be, for example: determination of the cost of each program both to government and to the universities; assessment of the political impact of aid to the disadvantaged versus aid to the middle class; development of alternative policies and development of procedures to mobilize the policy (e.g., proposals about devices to distribute aid to students). The technical contribution enlightens the policy decision.

The president has very little technical input but great policy power; a lower level staff aide may have high technical input and almost no power. A man who moves between the highest policy people and the technical people may have a significant proportion of authoritative power as well as administrative and technical chores. He can be called a "middle level" bureaucrat.

Middle Level Policy Affairs

Below the top policy levels of the administration, that is, beneath the White House, OMB, HEW, and the commissioner (in his role as top level policy maker), exist a number of "middle level" USOE and NIE officials vested with considerable policy prerogative and influence capabilities. Although their titles change so that the appelations associate, deputy, assistant commissioner, or bureau chief have varying meaning depending on the current reorganization and locus of power, middle level officials can be considered to be one, two, or perhaps three steps below the commissioner or the NIE director. Their policy power can be paltry or plentiful. At least one second level official has been reduced to an office with no staff and no explicit functions, while others make direct contact with members of Congress, control information flow to the top level administration decision-makers, spend so-called "discretionary money," evaluate and monitor USOE programs, and work in various ways to assert their particular interests.

Office of Legislation

The goal of middle level bureaucrats is to obtain power. This means that they want foremost to have what they do affect policy. The opportunity to exercise power is a major reward of the job; however, the opportunity to exercise power comes and goes to the same bureaucratic unit. For example:

The top bureaucrats of the Office of Legislation maintain an important internal role in USOE by gleaning the attitudes of members of Congress and their staffs. One or two of the top bureaucrats from the Office of Legislation roam Capitol Hill picking up the ideas and leanings of members of Congress (and staff) and relaying positions of the administration. They bring back to other USOE policy-makers the political realities of Congress; thus, they are in a position to challenge the ideas of the administration in the name of political practicality vis-à-vis the Congress.

In the Keppel and Howe years, when open communication formed the basis for administration policy formulation, the information and analytic advice of top Office of Legislation bureaucrats was vital. They were among the most important people in the education policy process and they had power. The Nixon years tended to show a disregard for congressional postures. Although the Office of Legislation maintained the information conduit between Congress and USOE, it entered minimally into policy decisions leaving the bureaucrats mostly on the policy fringe and away from power.*

Middle Level Bureaucrats in Program Administration

The Office of Legislation was only one of many bureaucratic units vying for power. Over the years hundreds of men and women have occupied numerous middle level positions affecting a myriad of programs involving innumerable goals and utilizing infinite varieties of political strategies. A comprehensive catalogue of the patterns of utilization of power by middle level administrators is impossible; however, their "political space" can be broken into five areas: (1) relationship with superiors (top level policy-makers); (2) control over their own bureaucratic bailiwick; (3) relations with Congress; (4) relations with the lobbies and professional groups; (5) relations with "the public." Two examples drawn from the experiences of second level USOE officials—immediately below the commissioner—provide a taste and array of their activities.

Case 1. Dr. Grant Venn, Associate Commissioner of Vocational-Technical Education 1966-1970. Grant Venn had been appointed as associate commissioner for Vocational-Technical Education because the job opened up during the Johnson years when "reform" was a catch word in everyone's mind, and Venn stood nearly alone as an author and spokesman for freshness in the area of vocational education. Venn's ideas were known to HEW Secretary Gardner and to Commissioner Howe. He was hired to clean up the archaic federal vocational education program.

Since 1917 when the Smith-Hughes Act first established a federal

---

*On minor legislative matters, the Office of Legislation is consistently helpful. Periodically the office sends out a call to the bureaus of USOE requesting proposals for minor changes in the law. This permits bureaucrats responsible for administering the law to obtain revisions that facilitate solution to problems unforeseen when the law was initially enacted. If the proposed changes are noncontroversial, they can be passed along to Congress with relative ease.

role in vocational education, policy had been controlled mainly by the American Vocational Association (AVA) working closely with Congress. (Secretary Gardner once cited the AVA as one of the most effective lobbies in Washington, competing in effectiveness with the best defense lobbies.) AVA's organization reflected the structure of Smith-Hughes, which created categories of vocational educators— home economists, trade and industrials, distributive, etc. Rural and predominantly southern interests controlled AVA, particularly the most powerful category, the home economists.

Although no one could legitimately chastise the "vocies," as old-line AVA members are somewhat pejoratively called (for their rural membership and emphasis on building strong and clean minds and hearts in American youth), the thrust of that kind of vocational education seemed somehow irrelevant in the late 1960s when man-power training and retraining for both the disadvantaged and for increasingly sophisticated skilled technicians dominated the national agenda.

The old-line "vocies" in the AVA and their compliant counter-parts in the Bureau of Vocational Education in USOE, over which Venn took control, opposed change. Mainly, they wanted more money for the old programs, which translated into maintenance of the status quo.

Commissioner Howe gave support and approval to Venn's reform élan, but the commissioner's main concern, forcing school desegrega-tion, caused Howe to conserve his political energies. An all-out battle between USOE and the AVA would overshadow desegregation, and, to Howe, vocational education reform, while desirable, could not receive top priority. Thus, Venn worked with the blessing but not the powerful support of the commissioner. Venn entered office as an uncrowned head over a body that mostly had no intention of coop-erating.

With both the lobby and much of his own staff politically anta-gonistic, Venn's only resource was Congress, and his timing was pro-pitious. In 1968 the authorization for the 1963 Vocational Educa-tion Act expired. The opportunity for renewal and thus redesign of the 1963 act gave Congress power. A special provision of the 1963 act which required the appointment of an advisory committee to review the act and recommend changes provided Venn with an im-portant policy tool in relation to Congress. He knew that the advisory committee's recommendations could set the congressional agenda for 1968. It could be made into a powerful influence, and at any rate it remained his most potentially useful resource.

Technically, under the law, the president appointed the advisory committee based on recommendations of Commissioner Howe. Howe permitted Venn to suggest and in effect handpick the members. Availing himself of the opportunity, Venn selected prestigious and mainly reform-oriented educators, many of whom had personal access to members of Congress. (Venn had to make some concessions, like the appointment of old-line vocational spokesmen like the executive director of AVA, but the majority were progressive.)

Presumably, once the committee members submitted their report, they would stand behind it and give it active support; thus, the report's contents became the primary matter for Venn. From his previous experience, he had a good idea of which progressive provisions he wanted for vocational education reform and, to ensure their appearance in the report, he supervised every step of its development. He attended all advisory committee meetings, acting as their executive director like a school superintendent (as he once was) guiding his board to decisions he wants. Further, he supervised the staff work and ultimately the drafting of the report. Once armed with the report, ostensibly the work of a prestigious committee who would in fact defend it in public, Venn, as a public official, could present Congress with an agenda bearing far more weight than the mere opinions of himself as one government bureaucrat.

The process whereby administration officials contact Congress is a bit precarious. Technically, bureaucrats are forbidden by their superiors to talk or meet directly with members of Congress without a formal invitation and clearance. High level administration policymakers for obvious reasons do not like lower level people to make independent contacts with Congress about policy matters handled at top levels or about matters that top level people oppose or are ignoring. Further, members of Congress often resent being "lobbied" by administration officials, but there is an etiquette and technique to violation of the separation of powers. Middle level bureaucrats who want to pursue in Congress policy objectives favorable to their concerns must create channels of contact. The devices are almost unlimited and fascinating. For example, under the prestige umbrella of noted advisory committee members, Venn could justifiably present the report and its views on their behalf, and in that way could most effectively carry forth his own ideas. When Venn wanted to "lobby," he was able to get advisory committee members to arrange invitations to meet with congressmen, so he could then personally explain the proposals. Members of Congress and their staffs read the report and heard it explicated by Venn in hearings and conferences.

Because Venn stood as the single administration source of support for reform of vocational education, for a number of senators and representatives deeply involved in Great Society as well as education reform, he became the logical man to contact. Some members of Congress offered a sympathetic and powerful welcome, in particular Senator Wayne Morse and his staff aide Charles Lee. Lee, who almost single-handedly drafted the Senate version of the 1968 act, readily latched onto Venn's proposals for concentration of some resources on the disadvantaged, stronger federal and state monitoring of use of vocational education monies, and, because home economists could not be removed from the legislation, the budgetary distinction of vocational education dollars for home economics from dollars for genuine manpower training. In both Houses of Congress job training oriented members listened to Venn and supported many of his and their own related reform ideas. Although neither Venn nor the congressional reformers could eliminate the powerful influence of AVA, 1968 brought some clear distinctions between the old and a new vocational education.

While acting boldly, Venn covered himself at all times. Armed with the advisory committee's report and the approval if not the active support of Commissioner Howe, he obtained high level administration clearance for his proposals, signaling at least half-hearted, surely not negative, endorsement of the president. Without at least this much administration support, the AVA could have fought off most change.

As the legislative policy process developed in the Bureau of Vocational-Technical Education, Venn carefully fended off destructive forces which could waylay reform. One path that could have destroyed his efforts lay within his own bureau. When he took charge, the Bureau of Vocational-Technical Education staff all paid allegiance to AVA. The small size of the bureau permitted Venn personally to monitor much of the division's work, and he could personally review all grants; however, his employees, while not openly against him, tended toward skepticism. Venn knew, for example, that even a whisper of a policy change would immediately be broadcast both to AVA and the state departments of education around the nation. (The lower level bureaucrats have long-established telephone contacts with their counterparts in every state department of education and even at the county and district level.)* Too much pressure by Venn could bring an almost instantaneous grass roots protest, which, if too volatile and combined with AVA attack, could cripple the bureau and eliminate Venn as an effective policy-maker. Thus, if Venn pressed for vocational education reform, a dangerous effort at best, he had to avoid all unnecessary conflict with his staff. This required considerable tact and amiability as well as some tough decisions. One day Commissioner Howe called Venn into his office to inquire why the Bureau of Vocational-Technical Education paid so little attention to desegregation. The Commissioner urged Venn to make a dramatic effort to "desegregate" the bureau and presumably bring national influence for desegregation into the entire vocational education establishment. Venn resisted the drama. In fact, he quietly hired blacks and brought them into the organization as a matter of routine. However, if he had made a great cause out of the effort, as Howe requested, he would have provoked a forest fire of protest among the virtually all-white and dominantly southern vocational education professionals (in AVA) and their southern congressional sympathizers. He would have lost all effectiveness on vocational education reform, which included the important provision for concentrated aid to disadvantaged, and mostly black, youth. This points up a general fact that political success, particularly in the bureaucracy, is not only a matter of aggressiveness, but also it is a function of sound defense.

All defenses are not perfect, of course. For example, when Venn approved an adult education project grant to Operation Breadbasket, a black organization on Chicago's South Side led by the Reverend Jesse Jackson, who was an outspoken opponent of Mayor Richard Daley, he found that within hours he stood in the office of HEW Secretary Wilber Cohen. Cohen had just concluded a phone conversation with a boiling and furious Chicago Congressman Roman Pucinski, one of the most trusted Daley organization politicians. Pucinski

---

*By dialing eight and then zero, all federal bureaucrats may obtain free, unchecked access to the FTS (Federal Telecommunication System), an open long distance line permitting unlimited calls anywhere in the nation.)

(who in 1972 was slated for the Democratic candidacy for the U.S. Senate in Illinois) could barely contain himself at the thought of a vocational education grant to support enemies of the Daley organization. After all, Pucinski sat as the chairman of the General Subcommittee on Education, which handled all vocational education legislation! Venn, whose political savvy would never have permitted a direct confrontation with Pucinski, was aware of the Chicago political scene before approving the grant, but he had sought and received assurances from the head of the Adult Education Division that the Daley organization and Operation Breadbasket (Jackson) had agreed on the grant. However, Venn had been misinformed and fell into a hole not of his own making. In this case the policy implications of an action by a middle level official were interpreted as sabotage of a local (Chicago) politician. Such dangers occur infrequently, but they can upset the ability of a middle level official to carry on with his principal work. (Indeed, some bureaucrats become so paranoid about such occurrences that they hesitate to make any decisions unless safety is absolutely assured.)

As Venn proceeded with administration of the 1968 vocational act, he tried to operationalize his legislative victories, which had once been only policy papers and aspirations. Armed with the new law, he, as a middle level bureaucrat, could affect education policy in the states. Before 1968, vocational education dollars were allocated to states on a matching formula. Dollars arrived with no federal control over programs; thus, the bureau in USOE had a small role in the pattern of vocational education services. The Vocational Education Amendments of 1968 changed the situation somewhat. The 1968 law required each state to submit to the commissioner a state plan for the use of vocational education dollars. Although the Washington officials did not attempt to dictate the content of the plan, the plan imposed a federal impact in two ways. First, states and, thereby, local districts engaged in vocational education were forced to commit themselves in writing about the intended use of their money. The very creation of "a plan" meant that local and state officials had to review their own programs and approve or disapprove them. The new law did not prescribe a federal curriculum, but the new administrative patterns the law laid down required states to prescribe their own. Secondly, to enforce the state plan provision during the first year, Venn rejected every state plan at least once, necessitating a second state-level review and revision.

The extent to which a federal education official can push state and local officials is undetermined, but if moderate limits on federal power are maintained, some federal influence can enter the policy process, and middle level bureaucrats can affect the quality of programs funded with federal dollars.

Case 2. Leon M. Lessinger, Associate Commissioner for the Bureau of Elementary and Secondary Education (BESE). The name of the superintendent of schools in San Mateo, California, Leon Lessinger, came to the attention of then Vice-President Hubert Humphrey. In all likelihood neither Humphrey nor Commissioner Howe knew details about Lessinger's ideas, beyond the established fact that he had demonstrated an ability to effect change, and BESE badly needed change. Lessinger took control of BESE at a time of chaos in its administration. The honeymoon of ESEA had lapsed and in the wake of idealism remained a leaderless morass dedicated mostly to getting dollars to school districts with little control over their use. Federal administration of ESEA had not reached a point where leadership guided the dollar flow.

Lessinger entered the job somewhat naive about the federal policy process but eager to make an impact. He was then beginning to develop his ideas of "accountability" (he eventually became tagged as "the father of accountability"),[2] but abstract ideas do not run programs; the federal government is not as easy to influence as a school district, and good intentions are not power. He had to find a political strategy that would provide him power to influence the policy.

Within a short time after entering office Lessinger began a series of staff seminars to discuss his views of accountability. Although a sound idea in principle, it proved fatal to his power. Within BESE were numerous duchies directed by third level (two steps from the commissioner) bureaucrats. Each bureaucrat had a vested interest in maintaining control over his area. Lessinger's seminar signaled an intent to break up their hitherto unchallenged control, and many of them, who had strong political bases of their own, became especially uncooperative.

With or without the seminars, Lessinger faced a powerful inertia. He began a search for a power resource and, unlike Venn who found his power in the making of a law, Lessinger saw his opportunity for power in enforcement of existing law: in Title VII (bilingual education) and Title VIII (dropout prevention) of ESEA. These titles allowed Lessinger to allocate "discretionary" money; that is, he as associate commissioner could set the criteria and could strongly influence how the dollar grants should be made. Lessinger reasoned that by expending Titles VII and VIII monies on pilot projects demonstrating accountability techniques for federal leadership, the principles of his experiment could then be transferred to Title I, the largest federal aid program providing a billion and a half dollars in aid to the disadvantaged.

Such an undertaking is risky at best, but under any circumstances it would take at least tacit support from key members of Congress who supported and protected ESEA. (If the pilot projects were later successful, Lessinger could hope to move his inert internal bureaucracy with congressional prodding.) To make contact with key congressional protectors of ESEA, Lessinger had to arrange meetings, but because of bureaucratic prohibitions against his making direct contact he needed a helping hand. Lessinger turned to his assistant, B. Alden Lillywhite. Only in a bureaucratic sense an assistant, more like an army master sergeant to a new second lieutenant, Lillywhite was an old hand in Washington bureaucratic politics. Over many years he had established trusted relationships with congressional offices; thus, although Lessinger could not readily contact the office of Senator Wayne Morse (a key sponsor of ESEA), Lillywhite could. An appointment was arranged, and Lessinger went to meet with Charles W. Lee, Senator Morse's most trusted aide on education. Lee invited other Senate and House staff from both sides of the aisle to hear Lessinger's ideas. The meeting concluded with satisfaction to the congressional people. They encouraged Lessinger to try to go ahead, to take hold of Title I and ESEA and lead BESE. This meeting led to no law or even recorded hearing, rather it provided essential road paving, short-term assurance that Lessinger would not receive congressional harassment if he tried to shake up administration of the nation's most important federal education law.

The elimination of congressional dissent, ordinarily a reassuring sign to a bureaucrat wishing to make changes, only cleared the air for an explicit diagnosis of Lessinger's bureaucratic problems. Real power and achievement for Lessinger meant control of Title I. It had virtually all of the money, but gaining control of Title I proved impossible.

As the associate commissioner, Lessinger ostensibly had the official superior position, but Title I Director John F. Hughes, technically subordinate to Lessinger, had firm control of his own bailiwick. After years of favors given and broad contacts, Hughes ruled Title I. To bring change, Lessinger had to unseat Hughes from control. However, his attempts to do so unveiled a deeper layer of the raw issues facing Title I reform. Hughes "managed" Title I; he did not lead it. Under his administrative eye and in the tradition of the fear of federal control, money got to the states and districts with an absolute minimum of federal policy involvement. (The control was so minimal that, by 1970, serious questions of local mismanagement of Title I dollars were raised by the Washington Research Project, causing reaction by Commissioner Marland.[3]) Hughes, however, was essentially competent and in tune with both congressional and high administration sentiment to avoid federal-local control conflicts. His dismissal by Lessinger would have signaled a major policy change—direct federal involvement in accounting for the effects of Title I money spent by local districts—rather than a mere management shakeup.

A full-scale reform of the federal role in Title I, although intellectually compelling, had no priority or backing within the administration. Commissioner Howe, who was ready to leave USOE near the end of the Johnson administration, declined to initiate a major disruption and policy shift toward the end of his tenure. When Howe left, a series of acting commissioners and then James Allen, who from the start had been stripped of power, all lacked power and will to reorganize Title I. At the top President Nixon, seeking to define a "new federalism," set a policy standard discouraging new flexing of federal control muscles. Hughes, technically the subordinate, had structural support for his position that Lessinger could not alter.

Lessinger had some recourse. He could not act internally on Title I reform so he struck outside USOE. By using ESEA Titles VII and VIII as demonstration projects, Lessinger had limited but graphic material to enchant public educators around the country to embrace accountability. He took to the road, making hundreds of speeches across the nation and gradually building grass roots support for his position.* The public relations effort reached upward as well. One of

*At Lessinger's level public officials have virtually unlimited travel and expense money, permitting them to go anywhere they are invited (or to invite themselves).

his Title VIII projects gained the front page of the *Wall Street Journal,* and, alerted by that article, the White House took notice. Daniel Patrick Moynihan, the presidential counselor involved in education, called Lessinger to the White House. The 1969 presidential message on education subsequently contained much of Lessinger's thinking.

Although Lessinger's appeal at both grass roots and the top seemed to grow, the job of bureaucratic change using outside pressure is slow. Without structural modification based on strong action from the commissioner or a higher level, the bureaucracy tends to maintain itself. In the long run grass roots thinking can come to control top level policy, but the time lapse is great and evidence slow to materialize. Rather than simply try to maintain his survival and watch tiny, incremental change, Lessinger resigned his post, after leaving a mark but falling short of the goal.

A Note

The examples of Venn and Lessinger represent a special type of middle level USOE bureaucrat: the man who seeks change. Change agents stand out in the analysis of the policy process because they seek to paint a vivid red stripe on a pastel background, but it is a mistake to assume that change agents dominate middle and, particularly, lower level USOE bureaucracy. In less than the span of one presidential term, both Venn and Lessinger left public office, having used up their change oriented resources of power.

Most middle and lower level bureaucrats who seek long-term careers, men and women who watch presidents, commissioners, and change agents come and go, concentrate on bureaucratic maintenance efforts—maintenance of themselves and their programs—and they value survival above all else. Only if change facilitates their survival do they embrace it. Their course can be perilous, but the basic rules are inviolate: Do not antagonize anyone with more power, i.e., educational professionals, lobbies, Congress, superiors, well-placed bureaucratic inferiors, or public school officials. When in doubt about the repercussions of an action, do nothing. Act autonomously (and perhaps imperiously) only when your mandate is absolutely clear. When action is finally taken, be assured it occurs at the lowest common denominator of conflict leaving the bureaucrat free of criticism. (Corollary: Make a dramatic move on occasion in order to maintain status, but only when the move has been verified as safe.)*

Middle Level Bureaucrats and Their Political Space: A Compendium

Both change agents and maintenance bureaucrats constantly act within various political spaces.

Middle Level Bureaucrats and Superiors

Gaining high level priority unquestionably stands as the most direct route to policy influence for middle level bureaucrats. Taking the approval of Commissioner Howe and Secretary Gardner, Grant Venn could proceed quite autonomously pursuing vocational education reform. Had President Nixon's priority for education been higher, Lessinger, having won over Daniel Patrick Moynihan and others, could perhaps have gained a free hand to reform Title I. Lessinger did affect his superiors but not enough, and the difference between having the mandate (Venn) and not having it (Lessinger) made the crucial difference in each man's effectiveness.

The route to influencing superiors ordinarily requires that lower level people find a way to get higher level people to agree with them. Lower level bureaucrats must usually present an idea that serves an interest of the superior. Superiors give off cues about preferred policy directions, and lower level people try to expand their own operations by finding a way to satisfy their superiors.† In this process, a

---

*Some career bureaucrats at the middle level seem to survive on a base of ether. One long-term veteran, who at varying times through his career held responsible posts, sits ensconced in a large office with accouterments fitting his high official rank but without any apparent function, program responsibilities, or staff. His survival base is gossip—that is, over the years he has come to know thousands of educators and educational decision-makers. He talks to them revealing USOE gossip, and in return receives inside dope about the affairs of their school systems and educational organizations. Although commissioners have been wary of him as a type of security risk, each commissioner admits that his "inside dopester" activities have occasional value in policy formation.

†A fascinating autobiographical case study of a middle level bureaucrat who sought development of his agency *against* the cues of high level policy makers is that of Leon Panetta, who as director of the Office of Civil Rights (HEW) was the first official in the Nixon administration to resign publicly over differences with the Nixon policies on desegregation of schools. See Leon Panetta and Peter Gall, *Bring Us Together* (New York: J. B. Lippincott, 1971).

principal resource of middle level bureaucrats is their relative ease in gaining access to higher level policy-makers. Their methods of gaining access are through memo writing; frequent policy and idea meetings; casual conversations in hallways, taxis, and at lunch where ideas are "unofficially" offered, refined, and trust is built; public exposure, which feeds back to high level decision-makers; and virtually any available communication media.

Sometimes control by the middle level over superiors occurs by blatant power. A middle level bureaucrat may have acknowledged grant-making authority which the superior would like to control, or the middle level bureaucrat can in fact count on greater structural support (e.g., Jack Hughes over Leon Lessinger). These situations give the middle level bureaucrat "leverage" with his superior and allow the middle level to make a trade-off with the higher level in the form of future support for the middle level bureaucrat's program.

On occasion, a middle level bureaucrat will exercise hitherto un-challenged authority in a controversial way hoping that the idea will gain support from some source of power (Congress, his close supe-riors, the president, "the public"). Lessinger's support of accounta-bility through "performance contracting," Commissioner Allen's proclamation of the "right to read," and Leon Panetta's attempt to enforce hitherto soft-pedaled aspects of civil rights provisions all stand as examples.[4] Each man, although subordinate to another level, had authority resting in his office which could at least be tested one time before superiors cut him off.

Middle level bureaucrats always hold some power over their supe-riors because, without cooperation of the middle, superiors become exhausted and stymied trying to do their job. Thus middle level bureaucrats, who are particularly career minded by comparison with change agents, are often coy with superiors because giving coopera-tion at one moment is a valuable resource for gaining autonomy later. (A favored way for superiors to get middle or lower middle bureaucrats to offer satisfying policy is to be able to hire the right man for the middle level job. Then, when middle level bureaucrats "get their way," it is likely to be the same way as the superior wants. The problem is that middle level bureaucrats are on civil service tenure, and high level policy makers are often stuck with them, unable to hire like-minded men.)

Middle Level Bureaucrats and Their Own Bureaucratic Bailiwick

High level priority is simply a license to act. Once that license is issued, the middle level bureaucrat must mobilize his resources toward the favored goal. (Although Venn had a license to lead vocational education reform, no one was going to do the job for him.) The ability to do the job—to produce—depends in part on the middle level bureaucrat's own efforts and in part on how well he can get his staff and subordinates to work toward his ends. (Venn knew that his own staff could be his greatest obstacle, and he carefully nurtured them to ensure that he would not have to face their opposition.) Getting subordinate staff to do something, and to do it in pursuit of goals set by the superordinate, is always problematical in a large bureaucracy. The ability of subordinate staff to stalemate a project through interminable "legitimate" delays is one of the most frustrating and sometimes fatal pitfalls for the middle level bureaucrat. (One associate commissioner reports, for example, that he could not meet a deadline set by law to submit a major report to Congress because he could not control his subordinates, who kept insisting that more time—and money!—was needed to complete seemingly endless computer runs and analyses.) The middle level bureaucrat thus tends to face the same sort of bureaucratic game playing—fights over power and priority—with his subordinates that he himself plays with his superiors.

Middle Level Bureaucrats and Congress

Every bureau in USOE and NIE and their subparts are created by or for some provision of the law. Each law has its congressional sponsors and sympathizers. Most congressmen are proud of their legislative track record and are willing to protect, preserve, and expand the provisions they helped create. Because bureaucrats have a vested interest in the protection and growth of their policy areas, and because congressmen seeking to protect their laws benefit from the direct knowledge of their administration held by bureaucrats, congressmen and bureaucrats both have strong incentives to get together to aid their mutual interest. (Thus Lessinger went to see Charles Lee.) The liaison between a bureaucrat and a member of Congress seems inevitably open when the program interests of the middle level bureaucrat are in an area that the member of Congress feels is of concern. (Venn sought and found members of Congress interested in emphasizing manpower training rather than old-line vocational education.) The potential for contact applies also, although somewhat more problematically, to situations in which the congressman is critical of an administration program or the administration does not pay sufficient attention to the pet interests of the congressman. Contact is then a medium of political antagonism, but it brings the member and the bureaucrat together. (Representative Brademas notes that he phoned and contacted administrators of the Environmental Education Act because they were not vigorously carrying out the law. And, in the example in chapter 3, Representative Edith Green sought out bureaucrats and facts in the administration to mount a criticism of educational research activity.) Intrigue sometimes accompanies these communications; sometimes there is hostility, sometimes respect, but the communication between members of Congress and middle level bureaucrats goes on with many purposes: sometimes to bolster a congressional proposal, sometimes to undermine it; sometimes to aid the administration, sometimes to undermine it.

Middle Level Administrators and the Lobbies

The education lobbies as big professional associations are more concerned with the ongoing administration of federal programs at the middle level of policy formation than they are with the machinations of the top level. Since the time of Commissioner Keppel, the top administrative levels, guided by the Conversation, have been reformist, producing a relatively moderate but consistent slant toward allocating federal dollars to achieve equality of educational opportunity and to create alternatives to the programs and management of the conventional schools. The lobbies, as large maintenance organizations seeking additional dollars for teacher's salaries and ongoing programs, have been less effective at the top administration levels. To influence top level policy, the lobbies have turned to Congress.

Middle and lower level administration officials, have, however, continually embraced the lobbies. Their motivation is pragmatic. The middle and lower level people must administer the ongoing programs that ultimately become the programs of the lobby's membership. Lobbies can provide USOE people with information and facilitation, which eases administrative problems when federal programs are applied at the state and local levels. Likewise, lobbies cause conflict and, because bureaucrats dislike conflict more than anything else, lobby aid and support is welcomed.

A particularly good example of cooperation occurred between Dr. Don Davies and the NEA. Before his appointment as the first administrator of the Education Professions Development Act (EPDA, a law to enhance varied aspects of teacher training), Davies had worked for the NEA on research and reports that served as important underpinnings of the EPDA legislation. Engaged in development of the act, known by NEA officials, and trusted, from the NEA viewpoint Davies made an ideal appointment as administrator. This did not mean, however, that NEA ran EPDA. It did mean that, since Davies fashioned the expenditure of considerable discretionary dollars, he could work in close communication with NEA as well as university and foundation advisers so that decisions made in government would raise minimum conflict.

The power brokerage role played by Davies was not entirely voluntary. Rather, it was in part structurally defined, a necessity based on real NEA power within the administration and in Congress. Had NEA not been a political match for USOE, Davies could have reduced his power brokerage function in favor of autonomous power—"educational leadership" (that is, he could have spent federal money with fewer constraints from outside government). However, under the structural circumstances of shared power, Davies was caused to act consistently to minimize the potential for disruptive conflict between NEA and USOE. From this, he salvaged personal prestige and a political space of his own to direct innovation in EPDA programs.

On one hand, lacking political shrewdness or lacking the will to link NEA and USOE, Davies could not have survived in this particular job. (Lacking neither of these, he flourished.) On the other hand, his concern for providing government-based leadership in the use of EPDA dollars, while probably dispensable, enhanced Davies' career. He moved shrewdly between his personal ambition to use USOE dollars as a change agent and NEA's proclivity to view USOE activism skeptically, and thereby avoided being branded either as a mere maintenance bureaucrat or a boat-rocking trouble maker. This was a center course—the happy road to bureaucratic success and power.

Lobbies and Guidelines

One of the lobbies' most powerful methods to influence USOE policy is exercised during the drafting of a law's "regulations" and "guidelines." After the president signs a bill into law, the original wording of the law is broken down and reshaped into language that facilitates the tasks of administration. The first chore, ordinarily a nonpolicy function performed by USOE attornies, is to draw up "regulations." Regulations are a simple restatement of the law but reorganized and made more easily understandable. Drafting "guidelines," however, is a vital policy function performed under the auspices of middle and lower middle level bureaucrats. Guidelines go well beyond mere restatement of the words of Congress. They are *interpretations of the intent* of the regulations. Once published in the *Federal Register,* these interpretations carry the force of law, instruct state and local school officials and all other people and agencies affected by a law, and explain exactly what they can do with the funds. Although regulations must reflect the "intent of Congress" as laid down in hearings, committee reports and the actual law itself, middle level administrators often exercise a great deal of discretion over their content, and often the content of guidelines changes according to political pressures.

Before publication of guidelines, the big lobbies traditionally review them and exercise varying degrees of veto power over their content. Working closely with USOE middle level bureaucrats, representatives of the NEA, NSBA, AASA, AVA, etc., check the wording and intent and actually participate in drafting alternative wording of guidelines. Lobbies therefore participate heavily in determination of prescriptions that have the force of law. When unchallenged, this power is considerable; it thoroughly integrates the public which is ostensibly regulated by government with the government regulators.

USOE bureaucrats welcome this cozy cooperation because it leads to smooth relations between themselves and most of the public they serve. Instances where public issues arise over the content of regulations are surprisingly rare, but they occur, and when they do the protagonist is almost always a group that was not privy to the prepublication guideline review.

One conflictual incident arose in 1970 over the use of Title I money. Regulations did not allow the expenditure of Title I dollars for anything but school materials and manpower. Certain civil rights groups examined the guidelines and petitioned the commissioner and the secretary to change them to permit expenditures for clothing for children. The big lobbies, who originally participated in drafting the guidelines, vigorously opposed the change, mainly because they represent the maintenance of the schools and teachers salaries and did not want scarce federal education dollars siphoned off to meet individual needs not directly provided by the schools. Despite considerable public protest in Washington supported by newspaper coverage and editorials, the guideline remained unchanged.

Another conflictual instance between middle level bureaucrats and lobbies began as an issue of enforcement of existing guidelines. The Washington Research Project (see chapter 2), basing their protest on their own research drawn in part from published government reports, published the so-called "Martin-McClure Report."[5] In it they presented evidence that administration of Title I dollars failed to comply with regulations and guidelines requiring rigorous federal enforcement of targeting of dollars to the poor. The Martin McClure Report cited instances where Title I money was used for general aid to school systems benefiting all children, not just the poor. To ensure closer control of the dollars—local enforcement to supplement weak federal enforcement—the group proposed a guideline change to require creation of parent councils in every school with power to review and determine Title I expenditures.

Visions of "community control" and administrative agony in the local schoolhouse prompted the large education lobbies into aggressive opposition to the Washington Research Project move. Ostensibly a compromise was reached between the civil rights advocates and the lobbies by changing the guidelines to require parent councils on a school districtwide basis with symbolic but not real review and control authority of Title I. In this way the big lobbies could be in favor of "local control" of education while continuing to focus power on education professionals.

The two examples described above took place at the guideline level. No laws were passed, no hearings held, no votes taken. The administrator's interpretation of the law prevailed, and that interpretation had its base in the desires of the big lobbies. In these cases, the civil rights groups demonstrated less powerful impact than either the administration or the big lobbies. Although civil rights groups could raise the issue, without support from elsewhere—Congress, a split among the big lobbies, the president—the middle level administration could simply absorb the temporary public flack. (Notably, the ability of the Washington Research Project to raise an issue and in the process develop limited congressional support won their leaders an invitation to some future prepublication guideline review sessions. Their power, however, remained limited.)

If the NEA or AASA or other large group had sought a change in guidelines, their position would have been quite different from the civil rights groups, and middle level administrators would have reacted accordingly. The big lobbies are backed by the moral force of their professional constituency, the ongoing reciprocal relationships with bureaucrats (many of whom are members of the organizations or were once employed by them), and strong support from Congress. An NEA guideline proposal, for example, carries a natural credibility with the bureaucrats which civil rights groups have a difficult time creating. A USOE career bureaucrat, who probably views himself as an "educator," is more likely to conclude that, if the NEA wants it, it must be a serious, "proper" proposal in the interests of public education. Civil rights groups tend to be viewed as somewhat "radical," not in touch with the real problems of the schools, and supportive of a shift of power from educators to the open community. In short, civil rights groups (as well as the Chamber of Commerce, the National Association of Manufacturers, and many other lobbies) tend not to be considered the natural public of USOE, and these groups have not carried political "clout" with the middle level administrators of the law.

Middle Level Administrators and Discretionary Money

Federal education dollars are divided into "formula aid" and "discretionary money." Middle and lower level bureaucrats have virtually no policy function in distribution of formula aid because all money is allocated to states and school districts as a matter of entitlement and by a method written into law. For example, Title I ESEA dollars are distributed to local school districts strictly according to the number of "disadvantaged" pupils in the district; Impact Aid (Public Laws 80-874 and 80-814) allocates dollars to school districts according to the number of children of federal employees attending school in the districts, etc.

However, many acts of Congress do provide "discretionary funds" usually designated generally for use in research or for demonstration projects which are to be allocated according to decisions made by federal bureaucrats. It is their ability to determine the nature of these expenditures that is the middle level bureaucrat's most direct form of power.

"Discretionary" money is not just loose change in the pocket of the USOE commissioner, NIE director, or HEW assistant secretary for education. Although each high level administrator has wished otherwise, much of the money is attached to programs like vocational education, dropout prevention, bilingual education, environmental education, etc., and it is only within these programmatic boundaries that bureaucratic discretion is permitted. Further, although the commissioner or HEW secretary technically may have charge of discretionary money, the organizational reality of USOE has been that middle level bureaucrats responsible for the program areas to which the money is attached actually have controlled most of the expenditures. Thus, control over discretionary dollars remains scattered throughout middle levels.

Before the post of HEW assistant secretary for education was formalized in law, the USOE commissioner was the top education official, and each commissioner since Keppel reported that he had tried to gather a chunk of discretionary dollars which he could control and direct for coordinated policy purposes. The effort was uphill and mostly thwarted. As a start, ESEA Title III, which provided large sums for innovative programs in education, was originally administered entirely by the commissioner. This placed considerable dollars at his disposal; however, the "Quie Amendment" of 1968 transferred all but 15 percent of Title III money to control by state departments of education, leaving the commissioner with a pittance. Each commissioner has tried to gather other discretionary money for his own use, but finding the funds, setting them aside, and protecting them from the middle level bureaucrats, who would otherwise spend them, is difficult and low yield. Commissioner Howe reported trying for over a year to collect four million dollars out of a total USOE budget of over three billion dollars in order to underwrite one of his own priorities. In 1971 Commissioner Marland made the boldest effort to consolidate all USOE discretionary money in the office of the commissioner in order to fund "renewal centers" that could be directed through the commissioner's office instead of the middle levels of

USOE. This move met strong resistance from within USOE, where middle level authorities saw their power evaporating. Further, members of Congress sharply objected on the grounds that: (1) their pet projects written into categorical aid laws would become subsumed and lost under a commissioner's single umbrella; (2) concentration of power in the office of the commissioner forbodes increased federal control of education policy. (The "Quie Amendment" already supported this sentiment.)

The extent to which a commissioner or the HEW assistant secretary can concentrate discretionary funds under his control remains problematical. In education Congress has supported the view that fragmentation of federal power, with its attendant inefficiency, is preferred to the threat of "central control." If a commissioner or HEW assistant secretary insists on pressing for too much power, Congress can write into law that middle level bureaucrats responsible for program administration of a particular law are also responsible for expenditure of discretionary money. If Congress by law designs the organizational structure of middle level USOE, the commissioner and assistant secretary will lose even more of their already tenuous control over the middle level, and, in addition, will lose the chance for flexible bureaucratic infighting which now allows them to periodically gain control over pieces of discretionary funds.

As the federal role in financing education increases, Congress will probably provide the commissioner and/or assistant secretary with a token amount of discretionary money—only enough for him to demonstrate and disseminate a few carefully chosen ideas and educational designs consistent with his leadership function. Most dollars will continue to flow by formula. And in between, the middle level bureaucrats will probably continue to control the fragments of discretionary funds attached to categorical programs. Of course, constant intrabureaucratic battles will continue to be fought between contenders for the funds.

Discretion and Power

Although relatively small amounts of money are available for discretionary uses, they can translate into considerable power, particularly if concentrated. So, for example, when in 1971 USOE officials decided to fund a national program of research and information dissemination on career-vocational education, the result was a nation-

wide deluge of propaganda to enhance that particular area. By directing all discretionary vocational education dollars into "career education" and by elevating the program with the commissioner's vigorous
public support, many people and institutions which had previously
avoided the area of vocational education were drawn toward the
dollars, and they created projects at state, local school district, and
university levels.

What is a small amount of money when measured against the
entire USOE budget may be a very great amount to one researcher or
institution. If a USOE commissioner or the director of NIE "lets it
be known" that USOE or NIE is interested in researching a certain
idea, many individuals or institutions will offer a proposal to do the
work. Thus, an idea favored within USOE or NIE will receive research and public dissemination. The power to decide what the
money will be spent for is the power to encourage particular ideas.

Sometimes USOE project money is made available with the intent
of encouraging contributions of ideas from "the public" outside
USOE-NIE. For example, in 1972 NIE made money available for
field-initiated research. NIE invited scholars from diverse fields to
design their own research problems and compete for NIE funds. In
another instance, using Title VIII dropout prevention money, Associate Commissioner Lessinger let it be known through a request for
proposals that, within certain standards of "accountability," innovative ideas were welcome and would be considered for funding.
Through this broad request, a man named Charles Blaschke walked
into Lessinger's office and offered a new idea of performance contracting whereby contractors would bid to provide educational services to a school district; if the levels of service bid were not delivered
within a specified time, the company would lose its payment. Lessinger had never met Blaschke before, but this idea fit into the
broader theory of accountability. Lessinger funded the experiment,
creating the first of a number of widely publicized performance-
based educational experiments.

Sometimes in making grants the "buddy system" operates. Certain
trusted researchers have personal, friendly, or old school ties with
government officials who allocate money. USOE or NIE officials
often personnally know researchers, professors, universities, corporations, or school districts that can be relied on to "do a good job,"
which can mean anything from not causing any problems to holding

the proper ideology, to possessing the determination and resources to attempt solid research or program innovation. The crucial political variable here is access: the ability of a researcher to contact a USOE-NIE official who will fund a pet idea, or, the other way around, the knowledge by a USOE or NIE official that a certain man or woman will find it in his interest to advance a USOE or NIE idea.

One technique, a maximization of the buddy system, allows allocation of federal dollars without having to act through official channels. On occasion, large grants have been made to organizations or researchers for broad and vague purposes under an implicit agreement that the researcher or organization can use a piece of the money for his own research or project purposes, but the bulk of the money will be preserved for subcontracted projects designated by the government official who made the grant. In this way intrabureaucratic squabbles as well as the bidding system, delays, and compromises are skirted. Further, this permits officials to act imperiously, supporting friends and favored ideas, and opposing enemies and avoiding the checks and balances of government.

However, discretionary power, even at the level of program particulars, remains limited. First, middle level bureaucratic authorities necessarily act within gross priority perimeters set by law and at high political levels. Secondly, at the elemental level of dollars and cents, members of Congress who may be unconcerned with the particulars of a program still want their districts to benefit financially. Discretionary grants tend to be spread around the nation conscientiously, so that at the minimum key members of Congress have their districts benefit; USOE officials are usually scrupulous about spreading grant money geographically to avoid any congressional clamor on this ground. Because the criterion of dollars is so easy to measure and because congressmen quickly hear from home if their district is slighted, USOE officials routinely prepare geographic breakdowns of dollar distribution.

Another source of interference with middle level bureaucratic grant-making authority comes from the office of the secretary in the Department of Health, Education, and Welfare (and perhaps through the office of the secretary of the White House). Interferences of this sort are usually purely political. That is, the high level administration wants to grant a favor or ease a burden for a political ally in some part of the country. Perhaps the president can win votes in Congress by suggesting that a USOE grant will be made in a certain congress-man's district, or a local political supporter has asked the White House for help (as when President Johnson acted to create a Mexi-can-American affairs unit in USOE). Documentation of such in-stances is extremely difficult, but middle level administrators do re-port receiving "suggestions" from the office of the secretary of HEW to make a grant to a certain school district or institution disregarding established criteria for the grant. These matters are handled quietly and politely. The secretary may not be personally involved in trying to persuade the middle level authority; rather, an emissary who clear-ly represents him may do the leg work. Sometimes similar requests come directly from senators or congressmen, but infrequently.

The most active manifestations of this kind of power politics have occurred in the area of funds cut off (rather than grants made) to school districts not in compliance with provisions of the Civil Rights Act. There are several instances, some well documented. The most dramatic case, that of Commissioner Francis Keppel, brought sharp and instant reversal from the White House when he cut off funds to the City of Chicago School District for noncompliance with civil rights.

Middle level authorities who are trying to control and manage their program responsibilities ordinarily resent such power politics interference. Being technically subordinate to the secretary, even the most recalcitrant official will reverse himself and comply with a di-rect written order, but, except in the area of civil rights, high level authorities are reluctant to act so blatantly. Public knowledge of favoritism reflects badly on the administration in power (columnists like Jack Anderson as well as reform-oriented Congressmen and oth-ers thrive on these incidents), so high level officials can best get their way if they can gain voluntary compliance from middle bureaucrats. Of course, some middle level bureaucrats find value in the subse-quent trade-off; they find that cooperation in the instances of exer-cise of power politics is worth the sell-out because it leaves them freer to exercise the legitimate activities of their office at other times.

Clearly, it would be too cynical to think that discretionary grants are made only because of power politics, because of privitized views of federal bureaucrats or the buddy system. Without being naive about the constraints of making grants, it is safe to say that merit—

that is, conscientious effort to comply with the law and to advance education—dominates the decision-making process. Even within the bounds of merit, however, honest men differ about the preferred course of action. Choice implies possible conflict and subsequent efforts at influence and negotiation; therefore, where discretion over the expenditure of money exists, politics abounds.

Middle Level Bureaucrats and Monitoring and Evaluation

Recent education legislation has contained requirements that responsible administering officials "monitor" federal projects to assure that money is spent in accordance with the law, and "evaluate" the projects to determine if the "goals" of the program were achieved. Monitoring and evaluation seem to be straightforward functions, but beyond the many technical, methodological, and philosophical problems, politics dominates monitoring and evaluation policy. It is a most politically tender area.

The principal political issues stem from: (1) fear of federal control; (2) threat to survival of authorization and appropriation legislation; and (3) maintenance of the prestige of middle level bureaucrats.

Strongly applied, the power to monitor and evaluate state and local educational programs financed with federal funds is the power to pass judgment on the suitability of state and local educational expenses, and to assess programs and use the assessment as the basis for federal policy decisions. Through monitoring, federal authorities could in principle provide detailed guidelines outlining prerequisites for "proper" use of the money and then follow up the guidelines with on-site inspection of program operations. Through evaluation—either generated at the federal level or carried out locally under federal constraining guidelines—federal officials could measure program outcomes and use the measurements to advise themselves on program standards that are monitored. In short, if monitoring and evaluation functions were carried to an extreme, federal officials would determine what it is they are going to monitor and then set standards and enforce them.

Although it is doubtful that even the loosest interpretation of any education law by the most aggressive federal bureaucrat would permit this degree of federal control, the description is not even useful as an archetype of what happens. Vigorously manifest use of federal power to control local educational programs is in any case politically abhorrent. "Local control" has been a most cherished educational myth, both locally and at the federal level. Coercive attempts by USOE officials to prescribe detailed educational programs or to pass judgment on the "success" of those programs at the local level would face recalcitrant opposition from local school boards and administrators, opposition in Congress, and, in the Johnson through Nixon years, intervention from top level administration officials. USOE bureaucrats know this and are aware that the minimal influence they have over the categorical aid programs continues because they do not transgress on the local control myth. (Racial integration of the schools alone has brought intense direct "federal control" in local school districts. Actually, federal administrators acted only in the wake of federal court action and notwithstanding this power base, the issue of racial integration—bussing and the neighborhood school— has become one of the nation's most important national issues, even invading the heart of presidential politics.)

Finally, bureaucrats in charge of programs have vested interests of personal prestige and professional career patterns determined by the "success" of their work. Outright "failure" of their program does not advance their image; neither does political conflict due to overly ambitious attempts by the federal bureaucrat to oversee a particular project. Therefore, to the bureaucrat, monitoring and evaluation are potentially more sources of distress than resources for personal career development.

Since monitoring and evaluation have been seen as more opprobrious than useful as political resources, neither monitoring nor evaluation seems to be carried out with rigor. Monitoring functions are understaffed at USOE. With the exception of occasional spot audits, federal officials rely on statements originated by the states and school districts informing USOE that the money is being used as intended by law.[6] Evaluation is either performed by the local educational agency delivering the services (this is the pattern in Title I projects), or, if performed at a federal level, the bulk of evaluation on contracts seems to be given with the tacit understanding that the final report be either favorable or so obfuscating that it will have little use as a basis for policy analysis. Evaluation contracts are made with universities and, most often, private consulting firms. A number of corporations and consultants who have proven their ability to walk the evaluation tightrope seem to be awarded numerous contracts over the years.

Although monitoring has not given much power to bureaucrats and evaluation has not had much impact on policy decisions, there are notable exceptions. In the case of monitoring, the Washington Research Project through its private efforts brought to light in the Martin-McClure Report a number of obvious violations of the law in local district use of Title I funds. This caused Commissioner Marland to tighten USOE monitoring efforts and even to attempt to recall some token federal funds improperly spent.

The two most extraordinary exceptions to the unconvincing pattern of USOE evaluations are not really attributable to USOE at all. *Equality of Educational Opportunity,* the so-called "Coleman Report" (1966), shook the education world by finding among other points that the amount of money spent on a student does not seem to make any difference in his level of achievement. Policy implications from this have been enormous. It is notable that *Equality of Educational Opportunity* was not an evaluation at all, but rather a study mandated to USOE by the 1964 Civil Rights Act, and its publication was not entirely welcome at USOE. (The other major document was an evaluation of Project Headstart by the Westinghouse Corporation, which showed that the small gains made by Headstart children were not retained in later years.)

USOE Failure and Congress as a Corrective

The weakness of USOE monitoring and evaluation has prompted some critics, notably Representative Edith Green, to publicly raise the issue that it makes little sense for the same agency (USOE) to be responsible for the administrative success of a program and for its evaluation. Speaking on the floor of the House, she said:

At the present time the Office of Education has 50,000 live contracts and grants that require some degree of monitoring. The General Accounting Office has said the Research Department is absolute chaos and confusion. . . . There is no attempt to evaluate the results of the 50,000 contracts and grants now in effect.[7]

Some members of Congress and USOE officials would disagree; however, the sentiment she expressed became translated into law. Section 417 of the 1972 Education Amendments establishes authority and funding for the comptroller general of the United States, an agency of the Congress, not of the administration, to examine and evaluate administration practices in enforcement of education laws. What the bureaucrats refused to do internally, the Congress has chosen to do externally. This crimp in administration autonomy can make bureaucratic life quite unpleasant. (A strong evaluation arm of Congress can provide badly needed information about federal program operations; however, it also raises the spectre of federal control of education.)

Research

Perhaps the most profound failure of USOE leadership has been in the area of research, USOE's oldest and clearest policy mandate. From Keppel to the first Nixon administration, research functions remained low priority, taking a back seat while top level policy men concentrated on passing legislation and fighting civil rights battles. Lacking internal bureaucratic support as well as research expertise to link government research policy to the real world of education, little came from federally financed efforts to make substantial changes in American pedagogy, learning theory, or in the organization and control of American schools.

Recognizing this, in 1972 Congress created, with Nixon administration support, a National Institute for Education (NIE). NIE is designed to consolidate and coordinate at new, higher funding levels virtually all USOE efforts. The way in which the NIE was created showed Congress's deep skepticism of USOE ability to handle the responsibility. Indeed, NIE was created because USOE failed to fulfill its research function.

At hearings before the Select Subcommittee on Education, after making a deliberate and articulate statement that NIE's relationship to the Office of Education "must be a particularly close one," U.S. Commissioner Sidney Marland heard the sentiment of congressional skeptics as expressed by Subcommittee Chairman John Brademas:

Let me start by asking a question about a matter to which both you [and the HEW Secretary] made reference, that is, the relationship between the Office of Education and the NIE. I had a letter this morning from a very distinguished leader of American education commenting on precisely that issue. . . . My correspondent remarked that, on the contrary, NIE must be able to spit in the eye of the Office of Education. I must say that my instinct is to think that he is quite right. . . . I am rather apprehensive that anybody who is serious about American education is going to take seriously the NIE if it is thought to be a captive of the Office of Education.[8]

The law establishing the NIE, as explained in the conference report, subsequently required that

The Director [of NIE] shall perform such duties as are prescribed by the Secretary of Health, Education, and Welfare and shall be responsible to the Secretary and *not to or through any other officer of Health, Education, and Welfare.* The Director . . . is further prohibited . . . from delegating any of his functions to any other officer who is not directly responsible to him. (Emphasis added.)[9]

New and innovating research functions have clearly been taken away from USOE, and the commissioner of the USOE bureaucracy shall have no hand in NIE if the intent of Congress is followed.

If the NIE director and his middle level bureaucrats can protect their organization from becoming a political football and pork barrel —akin to the protection J. Edgar Hoover was able to provide for the early and beneficent years of the FBI—NIE can assume a position of power which, although circumscribed, will be legitimate and workable. Should it fail in its mission to contribute knowledge about an essential theory of pedagogy or fail to realize and protect the legitimate boundaries of its own power (and this probably will mean confining its activities to developing facts, theories, and ideas rather than seeking to control public policy formulation), NIE will melt into the obscure history of ineffectual middle level USOE bureaucratic energy dissipation. The latter is not inevitable.

Conclusion

Since Keppel, top level USOE administration decision-makers have been of a different ilk than middle level bureaucrats. Unlike the bureaucrats, top level administration education policy-makers have hardly even masqueraded as education professionals. They act as highly politicized officials specializing in the politics of education.

In the isolated excitement of Washington, the machinations of middle level bureaucrats intensify, exhaust, and restore their lives, but in moments of frankness many acknowledge that, from their view down as well as from the schoolhouse up, their activities make precious little impact on American public education. The policy machinations within middle level USOE remain dabblings with educational ideas, projects, and modestly concentrated foci of special program interests. While not inconsequential, these dabblings render only a small portion of the character of American public education. Now and then they develop into a striking idea.

Although some of these officials have sought to engineer both educational and social reform through the design of their policies, in the main decisions have boiled down to not much more than the amount of fiscal relief local school districts can obtain from the federal government. Under whatever legislative title or pretense— ESEA, Impact Aid, Emergency School Assistance, etc.—the bulk of federal dollars translates into fiscal relief. In the past couching this relief in terms of "aid to the disadvantaged," especially in the case of ESEA, has facilitated passage of bills, but at least some of the intent and most of the effect of the decisions have been less programmatic, leading most palpably to a steady enlargement of the federal share of school finance.

If the American local tax system for financing public education falters in its ability to support the cost of education, the locus of political action in education will shift significantly to the federal level, where relief dollars can be found. If then the amount of federal money available to local school districts increases dramatically, paranoia of "federal bureaucratic control of the schools" will swell, and, at the outset of expansion at least, top level decisions will probably move toward flat grant provision of dollars to states or school districts, untainted by program policies generated in a federal bureaucracy. It is unlikely, although structurally it is neither inconceivable nor impossible, that middle level bureaucrats will gain controlling power over local school policy. The long-run possibility cannot be dismissed, however.

This description has not been intended to present a static image of the "way the administration works." On the contrary, the point is that issues change, priorities appear and disappear, some people are at one time in and at another time out, and structures change. Politics is made in process, not fixed, and the purpose of this discussion has been to reveal some of the fundamental patterns by which administration politics are created and how they, sometimes quickly, sometimes very gradually, change.

Notes for Chapter 4

1. Two independent studies cover this matter: Eugene Eidenberg and Roy Morey, *An Act of Congress* (New York: W. W. Norton, 1969), and Stephen K. Bailey and Edith K. Mosher, *ESEA: The Office of Education Administers a Law* (Syracuse, N.Y.: Syracuse University Press, 1968).

2. Leon M. Lessinger, *Every Kid a Winner: Accountability in Education* (New York: Simon & Schuster, 1970.).

3. *Title I of ESEA. Is It Helping Poor Children?* (Washington, D.C.: Washington Research Project of the Southern Center for Studies in Public Policy and the NAACP Legal Defense and Education Fund, 1969).

4. Leon Panetta and Peter Gall, *Bring Us Together* (New York: J.B. Lippincott, 1971).

5. *Title I of ESEA. Is It Helping Poor Children?*

6. See the study by Jerome Murphy, "The Education Bureaucracies Implement Novel Policy: The Politics of Title I of ESEA, 1965," in *Policy and Politics in America,* ed. Allan P. Sindler (Boston: Little, Brown and Co., 1973).

7. U.S., Congress, House, *Congressional Record,* 92d Cong., 2d Sess., June 8, 1972, p. H5401.

8. U.S., Congress, House, Education and Labor Committee, Select Subcommittee on Education, *To Establish a National Institute of Education: Hearing on H.R. 33,* 92d Cong., 1st Sess., 1971, p. 113.

9. Conference Report, Education Amendments of 1972, Senate Report no. 92-798, 92d Cong., 2d Sess. (1972), p. 204.

5. The Recreative Policy Process

The federal policy process for educational decision-making seems to elude regularities and general principles, yet it can be organized into a conceptual scheme that not only provides a framework through which the reader can think about both the particulars of federal policy-making—as well as his own participation in it—but the framework also provides a theoretical base from which some policy predictions can be made. This chapter builds the conceptual scheme and then discusses one of its implications for the prospect of growth of federal aid to American education.

Structure

In a search to identify some regularities of the policy process, the focus turns to structure. In structure is found what can be called "picture-frame regularities," in the sense that a picture frame sets distinct boundaries for the creative forms contained within the framed painting. The frame does not control the picture's forms; it does, however, constrain the field within which the forms work.

The Senate, the House of Representatives, and the president as well as the courts are permanent structural fixtures—the picture-frame regularities—as long as the United States Constitution of 1789 prevails. At a very general level this structure determines the pattern of interactions within the policy process by requiring one set of political actors to be observed and evaluated by, and partly dependent upon, another set of actors. The founding fathers called this "checks and balances." The function of checks and balances was to ensure that a proposed policy is examined from several angles, and also that virtually any group or interest seeking to influence an education proposal will be heard and have some opportunity for access to the policy process. The federal policy process for educational decision-making would be very different if the picture-frame regularities of the American government as we know it were not kept stable. (The picture-frame regularities of the American government are not immutable, of course. All political systems are fragile and can deteriorate from neglect and abuse, or can be restructured by intentional action.)

Picture-frame regularities explain structure at a general level but do not account for the detailed structure or dynamics of daily political machinations. On any particular issue the structure of the policy process can be represented more specifically only by identifying the network of specific roles that develop within each of the constitutionally designed, picture-frame units. For the purpose of this political analysis the concept of roles can best be substituted by the notion of "nodules of power." A nodule is a point at which surrounding vibrations or activities converge, like a senator in an environment of information and implorations all meant to be digested in his mind. In the network, some nodes may be imagined as larger, that is, more powerful, than others; however, each is a point of convergence and to and from each flows information. A House education subcommittee chairman, an OMB specialist, a lobbyist, a staff aide to the president, and hundreds of others are all nodal points absorbing information and either exercising power directly or facilitating the exercise of power.

Qualities of Nodules

The qualities of the nodules give the policy process color, form, and meaning. The determinants of the qualities of the nodules can be identified generally in structural and ideological terms.

There are two important structural criteria of policy nodules: (1) the mere existence of a node, and (2) the probability of its interaction with other nodes within the picture frame.

On any particular policy matter, the existence of a particular node can be problematical. For example, the Johnson White House staff included a ranking specialist for education, Douglass Cater, whose responsibility was to facilitate passage of new education laws. The Nixon White House had no such specialist. Rather, the counselor to the president, John Ehrlichman, and other staff men had general responsibility for domestic legislation with no special interest in advancing education. Or, in another example, a lobbyist representing higher education will appear throughout the picture frame on all higher education matters but probably will not come forward on early childhood issues, while the National Education Association spokesman will probably appear on both. A more subtle example—an example of diminished existence of a nodal role rather than of its nonappearance or disappearance—ties the official nodal role of House subcommittee chairman, which exists durably over time, with the power of the person who holds the position. Thus, in consideration of the 1973 Higher Education Amendments, Mrs. Green exerted considerable power as subcommittee chairman. When she left the Education and Labor Committee in 1973, the subcommittee chairmanship she had held receded as a formidable element in the education policy process. The chairmanship continued, but the characteristics of its importance temporarily disappeared.

The second characteristic of structure is the variable paths of communication permitted between and among the nodules. For example, although a congressman can have considerable contact with the HEW assistant secretary for education, he is unlikely to have contact with high level officials of the Office of Management and Budget. House members do not often consult or conspire with senators before a conference committee comes into being. However, the AFL-CIO seeks to maintain vigorous contact with members of both houses of Congress, trying to get from one what they cannot get from the other, or trying to protect in one what they did get in the other. (Determination of nodule interactions is heavily dependent on patterns of power, a subject discussed below.)

Ideology

To further understand the interactions among the nodule actors, the effect of the distribution of ideology among them must be considered. As used here, ideology is broadly conceived to be the accumulation of favored choices embraced by a particular nodule actor. The choices may be long- or short-range interests, but at the time of action they are the set of ideas that guide decisions.

The American federal system, being structurally fragmented, is designed to permit exposition of diverse and divergent ideologies at many counterbalancing places. Previous chapters have shown how structure of the administration permits and often encourages officials to disagree among themselves and to compete to obtain their goals; how nodules in Congress are separated among educational liberals, moderate conservatives, and eclectics; how Congress and the administration spawn advocates of special interests who do not enter into the liberal-conservative debate but do seek to accumulate and exercise power to define policy more in accordance with their own views; and how each lobby argues that education will be improved if its own special interests are met. The fragmented structure of decision-making provides shelter for fragmented viewpoints and policy objectives.

Conflict

The result of the structural and ideological fragmentation in the federal policy process is diversity of interest representation. Structured diversity nurtures conflict, because the greater the ability of more than one ideological viewpoint to be raised and sustained at one or more nodules, the more separate interests and disagreements can potentially occur among the nodules. Conflict is best conceived as a relationship of distance consciously structured that way because of disagreement.

The effect of conflict can be to retard or to expand federal educational resources. The most potent condition under which conflict serves to retard growth of education as a federal policy area finds the major nodules aligned in some sort of polar antithesis. Such an antithesis existed until the early 1960s when the split took the form of support for and opposition to the concept of federal aid itself. The opponents, who had prevailed for almost one hundred years, were successful in preventing almost all federal aid to education. Structurally, a rather simple educational policy process existed in the federal government during this period because there was little policy to consider except the policy of having no policy.

Conflict was also polar and paralyzing in the period immediately preceding the birth of the 1965 Elementary and Secondary Education Act. Most members of Congress and administration officials as well as the lobbies were by that time in favor of federal aid. However, polarization continued. Critical nodule actors polarized for and against federal aid depending on whether the proposal made provision for the ancillary matters of racial integration or aid to parochial schools.

Conflict is most often nonpolar where the question is not answered yes or no. Rather, the question is How much? and the answer can span an infinite number of points none of which will be yes or no. Many decisions on federal aid to education do not threaten anyone's interest. The decisions tend to be over annual battles on dollar appropriations to determine which group gets how much, and, more important, how much education gets relative to other federal program areas like highways, defense, or simple budgetary cutbacks. Decisions also center on whether or not a special interest like American Indians, the Spanish-speaking, audiovisual manufacturers, etc., will be given a provision in new laws.

In both appropriations and expansion of coverage of federal aid programs, the victory of one interest tends not to detract from the potential for victory of another interest. Indeed, expansion of structural and ideological fragmentation serves generally to strengthen education as an issue. Up to some point, thus far indeterminate, expansion of the number of nodules, expansion of the range and numbers of ideological advocates concerned with education, and the consequent increase in conflict within the process result in a more substantial political presence of education matters in the federal government.

The politics of education at the federal level is not necessarily a zero sum game with a limited amount of policy and a limited amount of resources that must be split up by an ever-expanding number of beneficiaries. In a sense, the aphorism "the more the merrier" represents the case of expanded fragmentation, and can be rephrased "the more conflict or petition in the system, the bigger the policies the system develops and the more resources that can be expected to be delivered."

Where and in what pattern such a spiral stops is uncertain. One can expect that at some stage of growth, perhaps when the federal government provides one-third or one-half of the total cost of elementary and secondary education in the nation—up to twenty billion dollars—the issues of expansion of federal aid will lose their legitimacy. When education's share of federal resources stabilizes and federal education politics is a zero sum game, all interested parties who can still compete in the policy process will compete against each other to ensure that their needs are met. If the stakes of federal education politics should grow to massive size, it is not clear what patterns of conflict would survive. However, to get to the stabilization point, conflict must remain in the system causing nodule actors to enlarge the resource pool incrementally and reconfirm the commitment to growth of federal aid.

Conflict Reduction

If conflict is distance in a relationship consciously structured by disagreement, then the reverse of conflict—coalescence—is agreement, a coming together based on at least temporary mutuality. To form a policy, critical conflict must dissolve; that is, a sufficiently critical set of nodules must reach ideological convergence and establish authoritative approval of a policy. (The formation of a policy will rarely signal the absence of all conflict, but the criterion is one of "critical conflict" and this is measured in terms of power.)

The conflict arising from structural fragmentation is rarely (but, when it occurs, dramatically) overcome by "natural" ideological homogeneity resulting from a broad sweep of like-minded people into the most important nodes of the structure. The very unusual historical moment of the eighty-ninth Congress in 1965, when the Johnson administration carried a huge congressional majority, displaced outright opponents of federal aid. Great Society liberals, actively pursuing passage of a major education law, controlled crucial nodes in Congress, the administration, and the lobbies. Sharing the same basic ideology, they all submitted to strong executive leadership to produce the ESEA and other laws. The shared ideological viewpoints greatly reduced the effect of structural fragmentation, and thus reduced conflict and permitted ready negotiation of the relatively minor remaining differences.

Because structural fragmentation is rarely overcome by natural ideological homogeneity, when two or more decision-makers who hold different ideologies seek to coalesce to develop a policy, they must enter into negotiation. Negotiation can result in stalemate (and no policy, in itself a decision) or in negotiated convergence of ideology (that is, compromise). Compromise is the art and occupation of the political trade. Those role players who hold structural positions at policy levels can both assert their ideology *and* change their minds. Without the latter, there would be little policy coming from government.

Successful compromise does occur, and when it does it represents a convergence of ideology sufficient to coalesce enough nodule actors to, for example, support provisions of a bill or administrative guidelines, or obtain votes and passage of a bill, or establish circumstances for effective administration.

The process of compromise is negotiation, an activity that takes up the bulk of policy-makers' time and energy. Negotiation often involves, at the surface, formal meetings. Whether they be public House subcommittee meetings (hearing or mark-up), or Emergency Committee for Full Funding meetings in a hotel room, or administration meetings in the executive offices, often these meetings are the place where policy compromises are ironed out. They are often preceded (sometimes supplanted) by telephone calls, memos, or smaller meetings. Each set of communications among nodule actors, or among the coterie of staff and subservients to the nodule actors, results in an information transmission affecting a decision (or nondecision) that makes possible (or impossible) agreement with other nodule actors. Incalculable numbers and networks of communication occur on minor as well as major issues. There is no way to predict who will say what to whom; as in other fast games, the moves of the actors depend on the evolving structure and on each other's reactions.

The pattern of the communications described above should be demystified, particularly for a reader who intends to participate directly in the system. The fundamentals are simple. People who have interests—and they may be within or without government—prepare ideas and communicate them to people who are in a position to advance the idea and/or render an authoritative decision. If conflicts are apparent, one communicator tries to convince the other that he should go ahead. If this cannot be done, each side tries to understand what is constraining the other side and then tries to alter the proposal so that each is able to consent to a decision that meets enough of the interest of the other to bring about at least partial gratification. Sometimes an actor wins, sometimes he loses, or he wins some and loses some.

Conceptually, the work of negotiation is simple and should not be veiled by an aura that the workings of high government affairs are a dark mystery. The difficulties of comprehending high government affairs arise not because they are conceptually abstruse but because the interactions within the policy process can become complex because of complex structure; because the data from which policy is formed are often technical and complicated; and because the actors often engage in stylized behaviors causing noninitiates to the process to appear awkward. Often the work of policy-making becomes the chore of well-paid professionals who master the technical details and history of an issue, are intimate with government structure, and know the rules of behavior for negotiation within the system.

Power and Process

Compromise achieved through negotiation within the fragmented structure and ideology of the policy process is successfully reached because one or a set of nodule actors is able to cause others to accept some version of his ideology. That is, nodule actors exercise power. Power is the indispensable concept in any political analysis to account for the ability of one set of nodule actors to achieve dominance or satisfactory compromise of its ideology within the structure. The policy process is in fact the way in which power is either utilized or not utilized; magnified or minimized.

Power is a quality of a relationship. It affects a relationship in that one or more nodule actors are able to grant or to deny resources needed for development of a policy proposal. In educational decision-making in the federal government, two of the most common factors of power are:

(1) The ability to grant or to deny a proposal through holding a nodule position whose approval is needed (e.g., the president and his veto power, a majority of a subcommittee required to report a bill, an OMB official responsible for approving the HEW budget, a lobbyist reflecting denial of approval by his group, etc.);

(2) The ability to grant or deny information without which other nodule actors cannot operate (well-informed people of all kinds within and outside of government shape policy by virtue of their knowledge).

For an authority who holds official position, a major resource needed to enable him to exercise power is information about which policy should be pursued. One power resource, thus, is being in a position to be able to make a decision. A resource deficiency of this position is lack of information about what constitutes the best decision. For the nodule actor who holds no official authoritative position, a major resource is having a set of ideas, and the deficiency is the lack of authority to enact them. Thus, a major determinant of power is the ability of a nodule actor with ideas to form a link with an actor who occupies an authority nodule within the process. Power is dependent on the ability to cause an idea to be embraced by an authoritative decision-maker at the point in time in the policy process when his action will shape a decision.

When an idea is merged with an authority willing to sponsor it, both the purveyor of the idea and the actor holding the authority position exercise power. As the process becomes more complex, authorities who hold partial power (not enough to control a policy decision) become bearers of ideas that must be linked through the policy process to other authorities with different ideas who also hold partial, but vital, components of power. Thus, power is a relationship, and in a complex system, power becomes an increasing aggregation of relationships. The formation of power is the policy process.

Complicated relationships are almost inevitable in the federal policy process because of the fragmented federal structure, which inevitably requires consent of more than one nodule actor. Power is rarely sufficiently concentrated at a single nodule to permit that actor to obtain a decision unilaterally. In lieu of concentration of power at one *nodule,* policy development, based on compromise, requires accumulation of sufficient power of various nodule actors on one policy *proposal.* Thus, an essential minimum of nodule actors must accept a single policy before it can be enacted, and, to a lesser extent, before it can be effectively administered.

The measure of an "essential minimum," and thereby prediction of patterns of power and compromise, is variable depending on the place within the policy process at which a compromise is needed. At one point it may mean a majority of the members of the policy board of the AFL-CIO or NEA or other group; at another point it may mean the consent only of a House subcommittee chairman; at another point a majority of the House of Representatives, or, in the case of a veto override, two-thirds of the House and the Senate, etc.

Complexity is increased because compromises at later phases can alter previous agreements at a time when the earlier critical nodule actors are unable any longer to exercise power. The essential minimum of one point does not necessarily survive a different point, where nodule actors and the grounds for compromise have changed. For example, after Chairman Green permitted a version of the 1972 Higher Education Amendments to leave her subcommittee and thus her auspices, her work, which was developed in cooperation with the higher education lobby, became the "property" of the House-Senate Conference Committee, a liberal coalition of Senate (under Senator Pell) and House liberals (led by John Brademas), which undid her work and negated the power she had earlier exercised.

Thus policy formulation is not necessarily a linear function. Events occur simultaneously that later affect each other, and later events are not necessarily bound by previous events. The degree to which simultaneous events or earlier and later events affect each other is problematical, depending on the pattern of power that emerges on an issue.

As noted before in the discussion of polar conflict, compromise is not always possible. When that point is reached, decisions are made on the basis of showdown manifestations of power rather than further compromise. If a nodule actor holding authority has come to embrace one set of ideas and has compromised those ideas as far as he finds warranted, the relationship he has established between himself and the ideas will preclude negotiation with a different set of incompatible nodules. For example, the administration's legislative proposal for a design of the National Institute of Education was finally approved by HEW Secretary Richardson. But, when Secretary Richardson came to the Senate hearings and faced Senator Pell, Pell disagreed with Richardson, no relationship was formed, and Pell proceeded to enact an NIE design based on ideas he had come to embrace from sources other than Richardson. Because of the place in the policy process of conflict—Senate hearings—Richardson needed Pell, but failed to link his ideas with Pell's authority, and Richardson thereby did not exercise power.

The Process Shapes the Policy

A stable, predictable structure of a policy process would assume stable, predictable patterns of exercise of power; however, within the picture-frame regularities, the structure of the policy process is not permanent. The potential permutations of nodules are vast, and power relations vary significantly.

The structure's design depends a great deal on the alternative patterns through which power is exercised. That is, power recreates the process. The structure and the content of the process are not highly predictable because they adapt to patterns of power. Because of its adaptability, the process itself should be considered as a vital determinant of educational policy, not only because the process itself is capable of being shaped by power, but also because, through reshaping, the new structure of the process affects future policy.

For example, one policy outcome of the process is to permit authoritative nodule actors to build a structure that can control the rate of growth of the federal role in education. The Nixon administration provides an example of the exercise of executive power to design a structure within which power is exercised to fulfill an ideology intended to slow the rate of growth of the federal role in education.

President Nixon's ideology was to shut off as best he could increments in both federal funding and federal authority over the local control of educational policy. By exercising presidential power, he used the adaptability of the process to minimize nodules that carried expansive ideologies and to maximize nodules and their relations that slowed the growth of federal educational policy. This was accomplished first by stripping power from the liberal commissioner of education, James Allen (and other liberal U.S. Office of Education hierarchy) and by granting an assistant secretary of HEW, Lewis Butler, authority both to supercede Allen and to create policy independently. In addition, Nixon-appointed officials in charge of education at the Office of Management and Budget rejected new education proposals and refused to endorse any education spending increases. Further, the president did not use nodule actors, like the powerful White House staff, to nurture and develop policy. No staff member had specific assignments to advance educational policy proposals; consequently, lobbyists and members of Congress as well as administration officials could not build new policy in cooperation with the administration. And the president used the formal authority of his own powerful nodule to veto both substantive legislation and education appropriations.

President Nixon used these nodules, including himself, in the reverse manner of Presidents Kennedy and Johnson. The Nixon administration developed a structure of authority relationships and ideology to retard those nodule actors who sought to link power with expansive policies, while Presidents Kennedy and Johnson sought to build a structure to develop and expand educational policy. Kennedy began by assigning power to the U.S. commissioner and then by elevating nodule actors who were ideologically dedicated to reform and to the expansion of education, first appointing Francis Keppel as U.S. commissioner, and then permeating the policy levels of the U.S. Office of Education with like-minded people. Kennedy and Johnson both exercised the option to utilize nodules at the Office of Management and Budget and the White House staff to encourage development of new policy. (Douglass Cater and Joseph Califano in the Johnson White House had major responsibilities for developing policy.) Through the policy of open support, Johnson and Kennedy invited and facilitated communication among lobbies, Congress, and the White House to gain compromise when conflict threatened to block legislation. Both men also used the powerful nodule of the presidency to build public and congressional support and dramatize the high priority of federal involvement in education. In short, Kennedy and Johnson added educational nodules and invited interaction among nodules from all sources, whereas Nixon reduced the ability of supportive nodules to function and discouraged interaction among those nodules who sought to expand federal educational policy.

It is noteworthy that the structure, though flexible, is not necessarily easily manipulated. By the time of the Nixon administration,
the legitimacy of the federal role in education was firmly established
through the major legislation passed under Kennedy and Johnson.
Although Nixon did not seek to expand federal involvement, he
could neither obliterate the existing laws nor reduce the vibrancy of
nonadministration nodules like John Brademas, the AFL-CIO, etc.,
who sought to protect and expand the laws. By the decade of the
1970s nodules in the education lobbies and Congress had gained
some structural durability, and, even during the Nixon administration, they could continue their efforts, although with reduced success.

The structure and interactions thus are somewhat malleable. Both
can be shaped by those who hold power to encourage some policy
outcomes while making others difficult or impossible. Therefore, the
policy process itself is a factor in the shaping of educational policy.
To repeat: within limits, power shapes the process, but the process in
turn shapes the exercise of power. The federal policy process for
educational decision making is young, really only a product of the
1960s. As the process matures and the goals of the federal government take clearer and more durable form, the unpredictability of the
process will decrease, and then malleability of the process will be less
important than tradition in federal educational policy formulation.

Conclusion

The structure, content, and dynamics of the federal policy process
for educational decision-making has more meaning than the fact that
it exists and that it is complicated and interesting. The process ultimately produces policies that affect the well-being of the American
educational system at local and state levels. Categorical aid to special
interests—disadvantaged children, vocational education, audiovisual
firms, contractors, ad infinitum—as well as general aid to support the
operation of the public schools are issues that make a difference in
schoolhouse operations. Chapter 6 considers the limits of federal
educational policy.

6. The Limits of Federal Educational Policy

Our system is not such a delicate Swiss watch as all that.
—Paul Goodman

It is now well established that within the federal policy process there is a viable structure for educational decision-making vested in lobbies, Congress, and the administration.[1] Where power and the machinery for power exist, power can be used. Indeed, the very existence of machinery of federal power in education policy formulation is a result of its growing and continued use. But where power can exist there is no inevitability that it be exercised. It does not have to be used and perhaps should not be used. This bias is a cardinal principle of republican democracy. Before the existing power potential of the federal policy process is exercised in a new and greater spurt for expansion of the federal role in American education, it is the scholarly and political task to evaluate what the prospects are of such aggregation of power for the welfare of American public education. Such an evaluation need be neither idealistic nor strident; rather, it should set federal education power humanely and responsibly within the aspirations of the American society.

Policy and Program

To the mid-1970s the federal role in education has been what Daniel Moynihan calls "programmatic."[2] In the context of established, ongoing, locally controlled, vastly decentralized public education systems, the federal government, in the general spirit of "tireless tinkering," has allocated limited sums of federal dollars to be used to bolster school operations where they have appeared to be failing. The major program has been aid to the disadvantaged through Title I of the 1965 Elementary and Secondary Education Act, but numerous other programs such as bilingual education and educational research also aid the existing systems. Federal programs have also sought to encourage skills and values deemed especially important to national well-being, for example, vocational education or the broad National Defense Education Act, which fostered science, math, and foreign languages. These federal programs leave the established structure of schooling intact.

There has not been yet what Moynihan would call "social policy" in education. He best distinguishes social policy from programmatic change in his book recording the history of the Family Assistance Plan.[3] As a proclaimed liberal, but also as the most important adviser on domestic affairs in the Nixon administration, Moynihan proposed a sweeping, new, comprehensive, family income policy—a "quantum leap" of policy—to replace the worn and failing county-based system of public welfare in America. Moynihan argues that the widely acknowledged failure and personal degradation of the extant system of public welfare made the early 1970s a propitious time to reject both the old policy *and* a strategy that would create proposals to fix up and repair the old policy with piecemeal new programs. The time was right, he thought for a new, comprehensive, nationwide, federally planned and administered policy that would enhance individual dignity and preserve the cherished values of family unity and the values of work.

In another context, Moynihan is more explicit.[4] He argues generally that piecemeal programs do not solve problems in a society that has become a "system"—that is, where everything is related to everything else. Although idealists or old-fashioned thinkers may not like it, Moynihan and many others argue that recognition that the United States is a system is now necessary, and this means that for a given problem, a policy, not programs, is required. Moynihan does not specify that the federal government need promulgate all policies, but, because a social or economic problem necessarily ramifies throughout the system among social institutions unbounded by geography, his viewpoint obviously requires policy planning to take place at the suitable central, and therefore mostly federal, level.

As long as the federal role in educational finance remains at the mid-1970 level of 7-9 percent of the total cost of education in America, a broad federal educational policy is impossible. The smallness of the federal involvement requires that it be stated in limited programs punctuating the sustaining structure of education in the nation's sixteen thousand school districts. But, to systemic thinkers sharing Moynihan's general view, the decentralized and seemingly inchoate pattern for delivery of education may be a basic problem awaiting a propitious time for a "quantum leap" in policy. If for any set of reasons, such as real strains on local tax ability to support schooling, pressure materializes to increase dramatically the federal role to perhaps one-third or one-half the total cost of education throughout the country, then the possibility for a federal education policy in Moynihan's sense will become quite real. (By the early 1970s major national education lobbies like the National Education Association and the National School Boards Association had already put themselves on record favoring such a policy.) Considering the pressures for local tax reform and the presence of powerful educational structures in Washington, the contingency of an expanded federal role should be taken seriously.

Liberalism

Since the New Deal, discussion of governmental intervention to promote the well-being of the lives of citizens has been tantamount to analysis of the concept of liberalism. Moynihan and other men of affairs who identify themselves as liberals have embraced Nathan Glazer's formulation: "The liberal stance is [that] for every problem there is a policy."[5] In a humane and compassionate spirit, American liberals identify social failures—often problems faced by the poor, aged, powerless, or others who are discriminated against. In Glazer's words, "In the liberal view . . . we have a sea of misery, scarcely diminished at all by voluntary charitable efforts."[6] Government *should* and *can* correct the faults:

Government then starts moving in, setting up dikes pushing back the sea and reclaiming the land, so to speak. . . . The typical stance of the liberal in dealing with issues of social policy is blame—not of the unfortunates, those suffering from the ills that the social policy is meant to remove, but of society, of the political system and its leaders.[7]

Liberalism so conceived is a style of governance that became institutionalized at the federal level during the New Deal. Based on the analysis that social problems are tied to economic structures—to the distribution of wealth and the relationship of citizens to the means of production—only the federal level was thought to be a viable point to solve social problems because there labor, business, and advocates for national interests intersected with government in the context of Keynsian economics. Thus, because of the structure of the system, liberals could not be localists. Ultimately liberals became identified with both the use *and* the protection of centralized, federal power.

Liberalism, however, has had a much broader definition historically. Instead of viewing liberalism as an action—that is, first as an indictment of government and then as governmental program and policy—or as as a style of government located at the federal level, liberalism is best conceived as a goal. Liberalism has always been a philosophy of individualism, and the role of the state, while shifting in liberal thought, has always had the function to maintain the qualities of individualism. John Dewey traces the roots of liberal thought to 1688, the "glorious revolution," and John Locke.

The outstanding points of Locke's version of liberalism are that governments are instituted to protect the rights that belong to individuals prior to political organization and social relations. These rights are those summed up a century later in the American Declaration of Independence: the rights of life, liberty, and the pursuit of happiness.[8]

He adds:

The whole temper of this philosophy is individualistic in the sense in which individualism is opposed to organized social action. It held to the primacy of the individual over the state not only in time but in moral authority. It defined the individual in terms of liberties of thought and action already possessed by him in some mysterious readymade fashion, and which it was the sole business of the state to safeguard.[9]

The goal of liberalism is a humane and dignified social existence which permits personal development. In an entirely different context, and writing for a different epoch, Nevitt Sanford characterizes one aspect of what Locke and Jefferson may have meant by personal development:

Development in the ego is intimately bound up with the freeing of impulse and with the enlightenment of conscience. . . . It follows that ego growth (development of the individual) is hampered by authoritarian or overprotective regimes and by permissive-chaotic ones. The former do not give the functions of the ego a chance for exercise; the latter, through too much stimulation of impulse with consequent anxiety, may put too heavy a strain upon the developing ego.[10]

With the happiness of the individual and not the needs of organizations and institutions as the primary goal, in liberal thought the state is bound to be neither overly strong nor overly weak; it must act when and where necessary, but not ideologically. It is not an ideology of the state to which liberalism addresses itself; it is a view of the individual.

(For the sake of a logical alternative, liberalism can be posed as different from conservatism on the basis of goal. Whereas liberalism focuses on the individual, conservatism, as used here, focuses on the sanctity of organizations and institutions. Thus, to a conservative, government is more important than individuals under the assumption that the individual's destiny is the effect of the destiny of government. The extreme example is organic theory—Hegel in philosophy and fascism in politics. Glazer notes that most Americans who call themselves conservatives are actually, in the main, "slow liberals." That is, American conservatives in the vein of eighteenth-century liberals, like Jefferson and Locke, generally value stability in social order and minimal government involvement in the name of individual welfare. American conservatives most fit the definition used here when they value corporate capitalism—economic institutions—rather than individuals as the basis of society.)

The role of government in liberal thought has shifted over the years. In the context of eighteenth-century agrarian society, the pursuit of individual welfare seemed incompatible with interference by government.

Liberalism inherited this conception of a natural antagonism between ruler and ruled, interpreted as natural opposition between the individual and organized society.[11]

Minimal state involvement continued as a hallmark of liberalism into the period of industrialization, and appeared at first well suited to laissez faire capitalism. The "invisible hand" described by Adam Smith, not palpable action of the state, seemed suited to economic progress, and economic progress seemed in the interest of all. By the nineteenth century, however, the obvious practical defects of laissez faire capitalism became evident. Urbanization changed the cultural context of the lives of individuals and the toll of industrialization and urbanization made liberalism incompatible with the philosophy of laissez faire. The British Utilitarians, not losing sight of the individual, sought a calculus whereby collective political and economic policy would be designed to bring the greatest happiness to the greatest number of individuals. From Jeremy Bentham to Franklin Roosevelt, liberalism gradually became a collective policy using government power, but not for the organic purposes of the state, rather for relief of strains on the individual caused by industrial life.* Dewey writes that even by the nineteenth century, liberalism

came surely, if gradually, to be disassociated from the laissez faire creed and to be associated with the use of governmental action for aid to those at economic disadvantage and for alleviation of their conditions.[12]

Dewey himself represents a dual tradition of modern liberalism. In his pedagogic writings at the turn of the century (e.g., *Democracy and Education*) he, and clearly his disciples, advocated an individualism which stated that, through schooling, individuals could learn to adapt to and participate in the industrial economy. The state had the minimal function, he felt, not of controlling the social and economic order but of aiding people to adapt. By the mid-1930s he advocated a liberal interpretation which said that the state should transform the economy for individuals rather than the other way around. He wrote:

Regimentation of material and mechanical forces is the only way by which the mass of individuals can be released from regimentation and consequent suppression of their cultural possibilities. . . . The notion that organized social control of economic forces lies outside the historic path of liberalism shows that liberalism is still impeded by remnants of its earlier laissez faire phase with its opposition of society and the individual. . . . We must reverse the perspective and see that socialized economy is the means of free individual development as the end.[13]

---

*The collectivist view carried so far that it became an academic discipline of sociology. In his classic work *Suicide*, Emile Durkheim, through his concept of anomie, argued that for an individual, life itself had no meaning outside meaningful role relationships. Marx, in his radical economic analysis, envisioned individual man existing as part of a social class, and, as a member of a class, exploited or favored. Individual interest was in fact class interest.

Although liberals like Moynihan and politicans like Lyndon Johnson were not willing to go as far as Dewey recommended, the differences between them and Dewey is only one of degree and strategy, not of fundamental philosophy. All liberals in the mid-twentieth century believed that economic growth was progress and that when economic growth impeded social and individual welfare, corrective political action both to change individuals and to change the effects of the economy on individuals should be taken. Liberal government relied on two factors: (1) informed intelligence created by social and economic technicians about problems and proper remedial policy; and (2) the use of government power to change the relation of individuals to the means of production as well as their very life-styles. In housing, highways, employment, aged or indigent persons, and a myriad of other categories, the federal government acquired a primary interest in seeking to maintain economic growth and ensure that human beings benefited in the process. (The failures of liberalism, where they occurred, should not detract from understanding the philosophy which motivated it.)

Liberalism and Education

Having identified liberalism with systemic federal action, at this juncture in history, when the federal government is able and likely to expand its role in educational finance, is it illiberal to doubt the virtue of such a policy? The answer, of course, depends on whether one considers liberalism to be an ideological political style or to be a philosophical goal. If it is a style, there is no doubt: federal action is liberal. If it is a goal, Dewey, the quintessential American pragmatist, would probably be more circumspect. Might he turn to the Utilitarians and ask, Is it not necessary to make decisions based on what brings the most benefit to the most people as individuals? In a society collectivized by urbanism, what policy would benefit the largest number of people? The pragmatic question is worth exploring although it is always more difficult to answer than the ideological question.

In a liberal calculus, the proper relationship of education, the individual, and the state is based on the relationship of the individual to his culture at a point in time. It is not said to be "proper" for moral reasons, but because of structural realities. Education and the individual develop within a cultural context. It has been amply demonstrated that schools are structured by the culture. From the start of the twentieth century public education never became a part of a federal social policy; yet, remarkably, without a central government policy, for the most part every child was able to attend school and did so for a similar purpose: because the social and economic opportunities—that is, the social structure of American life in the context of corporate capitalism—made school attendance necessary to individual and social welfare. Joel Spring writes:

After all, the original purpose of social education at the turn of the century was to fit man into the industrial world. Education did turn men into things that had to be trained and molded for the requirements of society. . . . As long as the public schools take responsibility for the socialization of the child, social adaptation to the institution becomes inevitable.[14]

Just as culturally defined social roles and economic opportunity were filtered through schooling during the period of American industrialization, individual development in an emerging postindustrial period will require an adaptation of education—adapted to the cultural context of different, postindustrial times. Some indicators of those times are now apparent.

America today is evolving toward a culture based on increasing leisure, a work force increasingly engaged in nonproduction occupations, and an end to unlimited material growth. This last implies an end to the illusion of improving one's personal status through increased material consumption. The American in the last part of this century is less and less tied to rote industrial and work structures—as well as less tied to family structure—and more dependent on individual personality development as a source of growth.* Automation, cybernetics, and system planning in industry ironically undermine the basis for systems planning in educational policy because job roles, as well as private recreation and fulfillment, come increasingly to depend on decisions by individuals about their proper relationship to materiel, to others, and to themselves.

If the trends in the economic and social structure toward individ-

---

*The concept of personality development cannot be explored here, but the interested reader is referred to work done in the 1950s and 1960s by Eric Erickson, Abraham Maslow, Nevitt Sanford, and others. Increase in the individual's capacity to mature—to differentiate his view of the world and integrate his own personality—is the goal of personality development. This goal is distinguished from, although not necessarily antithetical to, development of the economy or one's status within it.

ual personality development are real, and if they continue to be valued, then what will be needed in the future, as in the past, is education for individuals tailored to their emergent needs within *their* viable cultural context. If the goal of individualism is cherished, the institutional delivery system for education will be less like that of the past, when it was designed to adapt individuals to industrial roles, and should become increasingly flexible and adaptive to personal development. This would seem to require myriad education policies depending on local and small group circumstances (pluralism) and individual need, and seems directly opposite to what can be expected from a large-scale federal involvement in educational policy.

Two Reasons for a Federal Education Policy

Two major arguments for creation of federal policy are currently offered: (1) the need to aid the disadvantaged, and (2) the need to reform the system of educational finance.

Federal policy in elementary and secondary education has been geared primarily to remediation of the disadvantaged (poor, handicapped, discriminated against) or remediation of skills (math, science, foreign languages, vocational training.) For the most part federal policy has attempted to help the individual adapt to the local school program, and thus was mainly in line with the goals of locally controlled schooling. (The major point of divergence came with the federal commitment to equal educational opportunity through racial desegregation; however, this was a decision of the courts based on constitutional, not education, principles, and could not be said to constitute a federal education policy.) Federal policy was not reformist in the sense that it attempted to alter the structure or values of American public education.

On its face, federal support to help bring underachieving children (mainly black and other minority) up to the norms of the American white middle class seems to be a classically liberal goal. It would seek to increase individual welfare by increasing individual ability to compete in the economic structure, on the assumption that school achievement is related to economic well-being. Such a goal is a limited federal education commitment to aid the dispossessed. Pursuit of the goal is not ostensibly deleterious to the overriding dominance of decentralized education outlets, and thus has negligible effects on the redistribution of power to control education.*

Although the effects of compensatory education seem negligible and the social effects of emphasizing achievement in schools seem only slightly discriminatory, the policy of compensatory education is relatively harmless—at least in comparison with the problem raised by attempts to equalize teachers' salaries throughout the nation.

Correction of the relationship of workers to the means of production is a classic liberal goal best illustrated in the 1935 Wagner Act. Because American schools are organized into districts of unequal wealth, the amount of dollars spent on children, that is, dollars for teachers' salaries, varies widely among and within states. (In practice, dollars are not spent on children. Approximately 80-85 percent of education dollars go for teachers' salaries and benefits.) A system of federal finance of schools under an equity dollar distribution formula could correct the disparities among school district salaries, and, within tolerable differences, provide teachers throughout the nation with essentially similiar salaries for performing essentially similiar work regardless of whether they reside in a poor or a rich school district.

Although the goal of equity to teachers meets liberal criteria for goal setting, the antiliberal (patently conservative) potential of such a

---

*Pursuit of compensatory education has other problems, however. According to the research reported in *Equality of Educational Opportunity*, [15] the so-called Coleman Report and reanalyzed by Christopher Jencks et al., in the book *Inequality*, [16] compensatory education does not in fact serve to increase achievement. The academic achievement of children seems crucially dependent on their cultural background and relationship to their families, and is only marginally dependent on their public institutional relations. Also, failure of the pedagogic aspects of compensatory education is perhaps not as important as the social implications which a federal commitment to equal educational achievement encourages. Jencks infers in *Inequality* that the credentialing system—the granting of status through diplomas and certification through schooling—is a discriminatory criterion for economic achievement if credentials are based on school achievement measures. The number of years spent in school is a better indicator of where an individual will fit in the stratified economic system than is school achievement. If Jencks is correct, then it follows that disadvantaged children should be supported by governmental action in a way that will keep them in school for more years or by an action that intervenes in the custom of credentialing rather than a policy designed to raise their test scores (and presumably drive them from school if they "fail"). Another way of saying the same thing is that by encouraging improvement of test scores *and* permitting social selection to be based on test scores, children of the poor—particularly blacks—are somewhat discriminated against. This is a social goal away from liberalism.

policy for the nation's sixty million school children is enormous. If the federal government becomes the source of new dollars in education and if most education dollars are currently spent on teachers' salaries, logic would lead to the conclusion that teachers would organize power into large national unions capable of negotiating with Congress and the administration over teacher salary increases. Predictably, the source of dollars draws political petitioners, and teachers would not be alone. Virtually any set of interests—school districts, principals, superintendents, building contractors, reformers, reactionaries, etc.—would look to the federal level as its most effective political unit.

In the least complicated model of massive federal involvement, dollars would be allocated to state legislatures (or school districts) to be spent as state and local officals deem. Even in this model with no programmatic federal policy attached, the net result is a profound institutional shift of educational politics to a nationwide, centralized focus from where the dollars emanate. In more complicated models, massive federal involvement with powerful organized interests could seek federally promulgated education programs, or, in Moynihan's term, education policy. This can even occur tacitly as established interests seek to maintain their institutional roles, thus denying the validity of options. Teachers in particular have a short-run vested interest in maintaining the classroom-based schoolhouse with fixed student-teacher ratios. A yet more complicated model would find specific education policies promulgated in the "national interest" with the effect of homogenizing curriculum and student experiences across the nation. Given the proclivities of the federal policy process for educational decision-making to compromise in the face of conflict, a vast amount of general aid dollars for education could easily be eroded to meet the demands of organized interests. Social policy in education within this context would require "expert" planning—technocratic diagnosis of problems and technical prescription of solutions—and this would create a new cadre of vested interests.

An adequate theory of education must be more than pedagogy—the art of instruction. It must, in the postindustrial era, include a theory of institutions, a theory of personal individual development, and, ultimately, a view of the relationship of individuals to institutions. In considering these factors, the result of massive federal involvement in education would predictably be conservative—as defined above—with focus on organizations and institutions and *their* vested interests making not only the members of the organization, but also its clients (children), the servants of the organization. The classic reason for centralizing social policy is to gain increased power leverage for classes of interest, but children, from a practical view-point, do not, and in an individualistic theory, should not, compose a viable class in the context of power and dollars within the federal policy process. Centralization of power in education in the interests of individual development of children seems a poor risk.

Critics and decision-makers must look beyond short-range problems of finance or momentary national need to the longer-range issue of the permanent institutional shifts that accompany short-range decisions. In education, a short-term policy of increasing the federal role in educational finance to relieve tax burdens and obtain teacher salary equity or *for whatever reasons* carries with it the long-term installation of nationally vested teacher interests which will bring similiar power aggregations for other groups and interests. Creation of heavily vested long-term power blocks makes increase in federal educational finance profoundly illiberal, and therefore, in the con-text of American culture, unwise.

Conclusion

If individualism in the sense of personal development is to flourish as a fundamental goal of American education, then federal education policy must be limited to at most a piecemeal programmatic effort to support selected special interests like research or aid to the disadvan-taged. A liberal relationship of individual to education institution means preservation of vastly decentralized educational outlets with the potential for the relationship of individuals and the educational outlets to adapt to changing social and economic conditions.

New social and economic conditions evolve slowly, and schools even more slowly, but the matching of education to the evolving culture, which is the same as saying that human values change as conditions of life change, does take place. Before people give up their old securities, they need to test new adaptations; thus slowness has the virtue of helping people maintain continuity with their environ-ment and themselves. The direction and rate of change in education should be free to respond to social and economic change and should not be restrained by limited vested interests of well-established power blocks. The words of Federalist No. 10 still seem sound:

> It is in vain to say that enlightened statesmen will be able to adjust these clashing interests and render them all subservient to the public good. Enlightened statesmen will not always be at the helm. Nor, in many cases, can such an adjustment be made at all without taking into view indirect and remote considerations which will rarely prevail over the immediate interest which one party may find in disregarding the rights of another or the good of the whole.

Notes for Chapter 6

1. See the substantive chapters in this book, as well as Eugene Eidenberg and Roy Morey, *An Act of Congress* (New York: W. W. Norton, 1969), and Stephen K. Bailey and Edith Mosher, *ESEA: The Office of Education Administers a Law* (Syracuse, N.Y.: Syracuse University Press, 1968).

2. Daniel P. Moynihan, *The Politics of a Guaranteed Income: The Nixon Administration and the Family Assistance Plan* (New York: Vintage Books, 1973), chap. 8.

3. Ibid.

4. Daniel P. Moynihan, "Politics versus Program in the 1970s," *The Public Interest* (summer 1970).

5. Nathan Glazer, "The Limits of Social Policy," *Commentary* 52, no. 3 (September 1971).

6. Ibid., p. 51.

7. Ibid.

8. John Dewey, *Liberalism and Social Action* (New York: Capricorn Books, 1935), p. 4.

9. Ibid., p. 5.

10. Nevitt Sanford, *The American College* (New York: John Wiley & Sons, 1965), p. 279.

11. Dewey, *Liberalism and Social Action*, p. 5.

12. Ibid., p. 21.

13. Ibid., p. 90.

14. Joel Spring, *Education and the Rise of the Corporate State* (Boston: Beacon Press, 1972), p. 171.

15. James Coleman et al., *Equality of Educational Opportunity* (Washington, D.C.: Government Printing Office, 1966).

16. Christopher Jencks, Marshall Smith, Henry Ackland, Mary Jo Bane, David Cohen, Herbert Gintis, Barbara Heyns, and Stephan Michelson, *Inequality* (New York: Basic Books, 1972).

PART II

SUPPLEMENTARY ESSAYS

Federal Courts and
Federal Educational Policy

JOHN E. McDERMOTT

The paramount theme in education for the last quarter-century has been egalitarian: the search for equality of educational opportunity. Closely related, perhaps inseparable, is the concern with improving the quality of education for all children, now more urgent as discouragement and pessimism deepen over whether the nation's schools can achieve their historic objective of being the gateway to social equality. No one seems to know precisely the formula for achieving equality of educational opportunity, nor what quality education is, let alone how to improve it. Whatever the definition, the power to pursue these aims derives from control over the financing and the administration of educational programs. Control over the method of raising and spending revenues—the power of the purse, as it were—is often congruent with control over program, and is frequently utilized to promote educational policy objectives. Federal categorical aid programs to local school districts are a conspicuous example. Control over how an educational program is administered determines how well that program achieves its objectives within the limits of its financial resources, and includes decision-making authority over a variety of nonfinancial matters that constitute the bulk of educational policy-making—content of curriculum; classification and assignment of students, teachers, and administrative personnel; hiring and firing of teachers; methods of teaching; rules, regulations and discipline of students; etc. This rough model of power relies on a distinction between finance and program that is often blurred, though the paradigmatic contours of each can fairly be described.

The scope and significance of the federal government's participation in the policy-making framework—that is, its power in the process—is the subject of this book. No discussion of federal educational policy would be complete without examining the role of the federal judiciary in shaping and defining the nature and limits of that policy. This chapter will first examine the nature of federal judicial power in resolving educational disputes and then will describe the scope of judicial review of conflicts relating to the financing and administration of school programs.

I. Education and the Nature of Federal Judicial Power

Ours is a national government in which powers, limited to those delegated to it, are separated, a doctrine to which the federal judiciary owes its origin and character. Adjudication of disputes, which is the business of courts, is an essential part of the federal policy process. The scope of federal judicial power is described in Article III of the U.S. Constitution and, in terms relevant to education, extends to "all Cases, in Law and Equity, arising under this Constitution, [and] the Laws of the United States."[1] Judicial authority over matters relating to education thus derives from two not always divisible sources: the Constitution and statutes enacted pursuant to authority delegated thereunder.

The doctrine of judicial supremacy, established early in our history in the seminal case of *Marbury v. Madison*,[2] vests the federal judicial power with the ultimate authority to decide the meaning and effect of the rights, powers and duties declared by the Constitution. Were it otherwise, the Constitution might have three independent and coequal meanings, and the "checks and balances" system of government implied by the principle of separation of powers would be defeated. Federal courts therefore review the constitutional validity of federal legislation and federal administrative action. In litigation of disputes that relate to education, the primary constitutional imperatives enforced by federal courts on the legislative and executive branches of the United States government are the protections of freedom of speech and religion, and the prohibition against governmental establishment of religion (each contained in the First Amendment), the guarantee of due process of law (Fifth Amendment), and the separation of powers restraint on congressional and administrative action beyond those powers delegated by the Constitution. Apposite instances include the challenge, now being considered by the U.S. Supreme Court, to provisions of the Elementary and Secondary Education Act of 1965 (ESEA) extending Title I compensatory education benefits to parochial schools, allegedly in violation of the establishment of religion clause of the First Amendment[3]; the nullification of congressionally imposed racial segregation in the District of Columbia public schools by the decision in *Bolling v. Sharpe*[4]; and recent attacks on the Nixon administration's impoundment of federal funds earmarked by Congress for educational purposes, allegedly in excess of executive power and in denigration of congressional power.[5]

Article III also vests the judiciary with authority to interpret and apply congressional enactments and to secure federal administrative compliance therewith, as witness *Adams v. Richardson*,[6] in which the Department of Health, Education, and Welfare was ordered to begin compliance proceedings under the Civil Rights Act of 1964 against segregated state universities and school districts receiving federal financial assistance. Judicial review of the constitutionality of congressional and administrative action, and of the conformity of administrative action with federal legislation, is essential to the separation of powers principle of government, serving to safeguard the balance of power among the three branches of the federal government.

Federal courts are also empowered to review (1) the constitutionality of state and local policy-making and administrative action, and (2) the conformity of state activity with the requirements of federal legislation. Where state legislative or administrative action contravenes the U.S. Constitution or acts of Congress, the federal supremacy clause contained in Article VI of the Constitution invalidates the former:

This Constitution, and the Laws of the United States which shall be made in Pursuance thereof . . . shall be the supreme Law of the Land; and the Judges in every State shall be bound thereby, any thing in the Constitution or Laws of any State to the Contrary notwithstanding.

The specific constitutional guarantees relevant to education that are preserved against state infringement all derive from the Fourteenth Amendment: the equal protection clause, the due process clause and the First Amendment protections held to be incorporated in the latter. The equal protection clause is the basis for litigation asserting the right to equality of educational opportunity and the right to racial equality in public education. Of the latter, the penultimate case is *Brown v. Board of Education of Topeka*,[7] which declared racial segregation in public schools unconstitutional. Fourteenth Amendment claims are those most frequently in dispute in federal courts, and occasion the broadest exercise of judicial power in the educational policymaking process. Federal courts also assure proper implementation of federal legislation by state and local educational agencies, as in the enforcement of ESEA requirements that local and state expenditures in Title I schools be "comparable" to expenditures in non-Title I schools before application of Title I funds, so that federal funds supplement, not supplant, local efforts.[8]

The scope of federal judicial power over educational disputes is markedly confined. Aside from the obvious restraints imposed by case-by-case adjudication, the separation of powers doctrine limits the activity of the federal judiciary to powers delegated to it by the Constitution, that is, to "Cases" and "Controversies". The Constitution makes no explicit delegation of educational decision-making power to the federal government; nor has congressional legislation supplanted state control of education. Consequently, because the federal policy role in education is itself small, so also limited is the role of federal courts. The doctrine of federalism, forbidding unnecessary intrusions by the federal government into state and local decision-making prerogatives, also limits the power of the federal judiciary in education. As an implementation of that doctrine, federal courts are courts of limited jurisdiction, that is, federal courts may exercise power over a dispute only where the Constitution or federal legislation expressly confers the power to do so. Educational policymaking, in short, is ultimately a state and local power reserved under the Tenth Amendment.

The twin restraints of separation of powers and federalism are traditional doctrines, part of a pattern of principled adjudication in which a judge "is buttressed against the world, but what is perhaps more significant and certain, against himself, against his own natural tendency to give way before waves of feeling and opinion that may be as momentary as they are momentarily overwhelming."[9] Yet judicial restraint conflicts with the sense of urgency and necessity that has marked the egalitarian quest in America. The federal judiciary, the only branch of the federal government whose members are not elected, is a forum where right prevails, not majoritarianism, where the potentiality exists—was even realized during the Warren Court era—for the law to become an instrument of social reform. To some this notion is but "statesmanship superimposed on the democratic political process, . . . its final test . . . the future."[10] Nowhere has the tension between these competing philosophies of the judicial process been more evident than in litigation of educational disputes.

II. Federal Judicial Review of School Financing

Interdistrict Expenditure Inequalities

Recent years have witnessed growing concern with the fairness of state educational financing systems for public elementary and secondary schools.[11] Because of heavy reliance on local district taxation of real property, in every state except Hawaii there are substantial disparities in interdistrict expenditures per pupil.[12] It has been alleged that the quality of education is a function of local district wealth, because wealth-produced spending variations result in inequalities in the educational opportunities afforded children.[13] Although the effect of such gross systemic spending irregularities on student outcomes has been vigorously disputed,[14] school districts are demonstrably unequal in (1) financial capacity to raise revenue for education, (2) the amount of money spent on each child, and (3) the educational resources and inputs made available to children—unequal, in other words, in the opportunity to pursue academic excellence. Money can be misspent and is by no means synonymous with quality, but money can be said to be a necessary and precipitating, if not sufficient, factor in creating and maintaining a sound educational program. Certainly a presumption in its favor should be indulged where the reason for inequitable apportionment is the fortuity of the amount of local taxable wealth within a school district's boundaries. Taxable wealth is haphazardly distributed and bears no relationship to the educational needs or costs of a school district. The only justification advanced for permitting educational revenues to depend on local wealth is that local fiscal control enhances responsiveness to local educational needs and to community spending priorities, an authentic claim were the spending inequalities not so outrageous, the benefits of local control equally available to all school districts, and feasible alternatives for financing public schools unavailable that would preserve the prerogatives of local decision-making. However "equality of educational opportunity" is defined, state systems of financing public education fail to satisfy even minimal or threshold standards.

The U.S. Supreme Court was presented with the opportunity to invalidate one of the worst of these school financing systems in *San Antonio Independent School District v. Rodriguez,*[15] decided on March 21, 1973. A group of Texas school children, primarily poor and Mexican-American, challenged the constitutionality of the Texas school finance system, alleging that the wealth-produced expenditure disparities, created by the finance system and not adequately offset by the state's equalization efforts, denied them equality of educational opportunity in violation of the equal protection clause of the Fourteenth Amendment. Had the Court held for the plaintiffs, the school finance systems in nearly every state would soon have succumbed to similar constitutional attack, opening the door to a potentially unlimited prospective involvement by federal courts in educational decision-making. That the Court felt restrained from doing so portends serious long-range implications for federal judicial power within the educational policy process, at least as far as equal protection theory is the basis of any claim for relief.

Careful consideration is due the legal claim in *Rodriguez* that denial of equality of educational opportunity violates the equal protection clause of the Fourteenth Amendment. The relevant language of the amendment provides, "No State shall make or enforce any law which shall abridge the privileges or immunities of citizens of the United States; nor shall any State deprive any person of life, liberty, or property, without due process of law; *nor deny to any person within its jurisdiction the equal protection of the laws.*" (Emphasis added.) Equal treatment of persons by state governments is thus a guarantee of United States citizenship. The language indicates that the deprivation or infringement must be the result of *state* action. Yet nearly all legislation draws distinctions between people or treats them differently. The Supreme Court, however, has traditionally disfavored certain types of "invidious distinctions," such as racial classifications and infringements on the right to vote, and in recent years has adopted a dual test for measuring the validity of legislative distinctions against the equal protection clause.[16] Ordinarily, a challenged statute is vested with a presumption of constitutionality, the validity of a legislative classification depending on whether the statute bears some rational relationship to a conceivably legitimate state purpose. This is the so-called "rational basis" test and is typically applied in cases where the legislation involves some economic regulation. On the other hand, where the classifications drawn by a challenged legislative scheme are "suspect" (or "invidious") or touch on "fundamental interests," the Court has subjected such classifications to "strict scrutiny," requiring the state to establish that the distinctions drawn are *necessary* to the attainment of a *compelling* state interest. In *Rodriguez,* the plaintiffs alleged that both a suspect classification, i.e., wealth (district and/or family wealth), and a fundamental interest, i.e., education, were present, thereby triggering "strict scrutiny" judicial review of the Texas statutory scheme of school financing. In practice, whether the rational basis or the strict scrutiny test is selected as the standard to apply in measuring legislative classifications against the equal protection clause very often determines the outcome, a rigidity that has generated criticism from commentators and from which the Court has itself departed on occasion.[17] The Court nonetheless employed the two-level test in *Rodriguez,* holding that the particular wealth discrimination alleged—district wealth—was not a suspect classification, nor was education a fundamental interest for purposes of the federal equal protection clause. Strict scrutiny review was thus rejected; the Court, per Mr. Justice Powell, held further that the reliance of the Texas school finance system on local wealth was rationally related to a legitimate state objective, that is, the enhancement of local control and decision-making over both finance and program. The *Rodriguez* decision will have a major impact on educational litigation in both federal and state courts.

The wealth classification urged by the plaintiffs as suspect was that of district wealth, a classification which defines every child in property-poor districts as disadvantaged by the school finance system. The classification was designed in response to a 1968 federal district court decision, *McInnis v. Shapiro*,[18] in which plaintiff school children, attacking the Illinois school financing system, alleged that the equal protection clause of the Fourteenth Amendment required that school expenditures be made only on the basis of pupils' educational needs. Equality of educational opportunity was thus constitutionally compelled. The court ruled that a lack of judicially manageable standards rendered the case "nonjusticiable." The court regarded "educational need" as a "nebulous concept" incapable of providing the judiciary with a yardstick for determining "when the Constitution is satisfied and when it is violated," and ruled that plaintiffs' claims were more appropriately pursued in the legislature than in the courts. To avoid this separation of powers objection, school finance reform lawyers erected a negative standard that would enable courts to adjudicate the issue of interdistrict expenditure inequities: the quality of education must not be a function of wealth other than the wealth of the state as a whole.[19] This standard did not require a state to distribute expenditures to respond to need, nor did it require equal expenditures per pupil; only expenditure differences that were the result of disparities in local wealth were alleged to be unconstitutional. Several state courts and lower federal courts adopted this approach in invalidating state school finance systems, the most notable case being *Serrano v. Priest*.[20] But in *Rodriguez* Justice Powell reasoned that district wealth was unlike wealth classifications previously invalidated by the Court. Present in previous cases were both a class fairly definable as indigent, and an absolute, rather than a relative, deprivation of some desired benefit. Poor people do not necessarily live in property-poor school districts, resulting in a disadvantaged class that Powell described in *Rodriguez* as "large, diverse, and amorphous . . . unified only by the common factor of residence"[21] in low wealth districts. Neither was the benefit of an adequate education totally denied plaintiffs, for the Texas' Minimum Foundation Program financing plan guaranteed a minimum level of expenditures for every child. The Court thus held that the district wealth discrimination in the Texas school financing scheme was not a suspect classification because the discrimination did not operate to the "peculiar disadvantage" of any suspect class, nor did it have any of the "traditional indicia of suspectness: the class is not saddled with such disabilities, or subjected to such a history of purposeful unequal treatment, or relegated to such a position of political power-lessness as to command extraordinary protection from the majoritarian political process"[22]

The distinction between absolute and relative deprivation of benefit carries important implications for future education litigation involving indigent plaintiffs. Presumably, intradistrict expenditure disparities challenged in federal courts would suffer the same fate as interdistrict expenditure disparities, at least where the disadvantaged class is defined as poor persons in the affected schools, or all children in lower expenditure schools, regardless of personal wealth (unless, of course, the inequities were shown to be arbitrary or irrational). The requirement of an absolute deprivation also would seem to foreclose litigation in federal courts by impoverished children asserting the right to compensatory education designed to meet their specialized needs, at least where such programs would require additional expenditures beyond the level provided ordinary children.[23] Even where the claim is not for a program requiring more dollars but simply for a different kind of program—that is, a program designed to fit the deprived child's educational need—plaintiffs must overcome the objection voiced in *McInnis* that "need" is a judicially indefinable standard and thus an inappropriate basis for judicial intervention in educational policymaking. *McInnis* perhaps can be distinguished in that the relief called for would have required identification of *all* educational needs, whereas in a compensatory suit the needs of only one particular, clearly definable class of poor persons would be in issue—but such a result is doubtful. Any showing less than that the education afforded generally by a school district is wholly inadequate in either expenditures or program would contravene *McInnis*. Even were race the standard, no relief would be likely unless it could be shown that the disability alleged was the result of state action, which is the only activity proscribed by the Fourteenth Amendment. The only apparent forum for relief is that of state judiciaries, as most states have constitutional provisions giving the right to education preferred status among the liberties protected. (The prospects for such state judicial relief are discussed below.) After *Rodriguez,* wealth classifications are thus of only limited constitutional significance, a fact which, when coupled with the view expressed in *McInnis* that any reordering of educational programs to more nearly approximate pupil need is beyond the scope of judicial power, can only mean that, constitutionally, the federal courts have little or no power over state and local methods of school financing.

Powell's analysis of the constitutional significance of education gives added force to this observation. Justice Powell recognized the vital role of education in American society, but reasoned that "the importance of a service performed by the State does not determine whether it must be regarded as fundamental for purposes of examination under the Equal Protection Clause."[24] Absent specific constitutional declaration, judicial self-restraint compels against any such policy judgment:

It is not the province of this Court to create substantive constitutional rights in the name of guaranteeing equal protection of the laws. Thus the key to discovering whether education is "fundamental" is not to be found in comparisons of the relative societal significance of education as opposed to subsistence or housing. Nor is it to be found by weighing whether education is as important as the right to travel. Rather, the answer lies in assessing whether there is a right to education explicitly or implicitly guaranteed by the Constitution.[25]

Mr. Powell held that education was not a fundamental interest, because it was not among the rights afforded explicit protection by the United States Constitution, nor did it appear to be implicitly protected. Strict scrutiny judicial review was thus rejected.

The majority holding in *Rodriguez* that education was not a fundamental interest was seen by Justice Marshall, dissenting, as "a retreat from our historic commitment to equality of educational opportunity."[26] This alleged commitment originates from the Court's famous decision in *Brown v. Board of Education,* in which state-imposed racial segregation in public schools was held to violate the equal protection clause of the Fourteenth Amendment. The decision was not based solely on the invidiousness of the racial classification, but also appeared to rest on the paramount importance of education:

Today education is perhaps the most important function of state and local governments. Compulsory school attendance laws and the great expenditures for education both demonstrate our recognition of the importance of education to our democratic society. It is required in the performance of our most basic responsibilities, even service in the armed forces. It is the foundation of good citizenship. Today it is a principal instrument in awakening the child to cultural values, and preparing him for later professional training, and in helping him to adjust normally to his environment. In these days, it is doubtful that any child may reasonably be expected to succeed in life if he is denied the opportunity of an education. *Such an opportunity where the state has undertaken to provide it, is a right which must be made available to all on equal terms.*[27] (Emphasis added.)

Although *Brown* was decided before the development of the two-level test for measuring legislative classifications against the equal protection clause, the language above suggests a special and independent judicial concern with equality of educational opportunity. Not one word in the quoted passage refers to or is limited in its application to racial discrimination, suggesting several questions: Was *Brown* a race case? an education case? or both? If *Brown* attaches special meaning to education for purposes of federal equal protection theory, what is the scope of that protection? How far does it extend? Does the protection exist independent of race? Do inequalities in educational opportunities demand strict judicial analysis? These questions have intrigued commentators since 1954, and *Brown* can fairly be said to have been responsible for spawning extensive litigation asserting the right to equality of educational opportunity. *Rodriguez* in large measure resolves the speculation about the constitutional importance of education that *Brown* generated and clearly defines the limits of federal educational policy originating under the equal protection clause of the Fourteenth Amendment. *Rodriguez,* which cannot be squared satisfactorily with *Brown,* dealt a crushing defeat to those who regarded the federal equal protection clause as an instrument of educational reform.

Powell's disposition of the constitutional character of education was heavily influenced by considerations of federalism. *Rodriguez* confined the scope of federal judicial review of state legislation under the Fourteenth Amendment to constitutionally guaranteed rights and interests, thereby avoiding undue interference by federal courts with state legislative freedom:

[E]very claim arising under the Equal Protection Clause has implications for the relationship between national and state power under our federal system. Questions of federalism are always inherent in the process of determining whether a State's laws are to be accorded the traditional presumption of constitutionality, or are to be subjected instead to rigorous judicial scrutiny . . . it would be difficult to imagine a case having a greater potential impact on our federal system than the one now before us, in which we are urged to abrogate systems of financing public education presently in existence in virtually every State.[28]

Education is not explicitly protected by the Constitution, nor is there any role delegated to the federal government in educational decision-making at the state and local level. Education is essentially a state function, the power over which, not having been delegated to the federal government, is reserved to the states under the Tenth Amendment.

Education litigation in federal courts under the equal protection clause of the Fourteenth Amendment is not entirely ended. In *Rodriguez,* the Court, after rejecting the strict scrutiny standard of review, applied the "rational basis" test and held that the Texas school financing system was rationally related to the legitimate state objective of promoting local district control over both school finance and program. Thus, although education is not a fundamental interest commanding special judicial attention, inequalities in educational opportunities can and will no doubt continue to be tested, but against the less rigorous "rational basis" standard. Otherwise the Court would be abdicating its responsibility to enforce the Fourteenth Amendment guarantee against irrational or arbitrary treatment by state governments. The survival of a limited doctrine of equality of educational opportunity under the equal protection clause is supported by several pre-*Brown* "separate but equal" cases. In *Sweatt v. Painter,*[29] the plaintiff was denied admission to the University of Texas Law School on the basis of race. Although he was offered a place in a separate law school for black students, Sweatt chose to challenge his denial of admission to the University of Texas because the legal education offered at the black law school was not substantially equal to that offered at the University of Texas and was therefore not in compliance with the separate but equal rationale of *Plessy v. Ferguson.*[30] The Court ruled in *Sweatt:*

[W]e cannot find substantial equality in the educational opportunities offered white and negro law students by the state. In terms of number of the faculty, variety of courses and opportunity for specialization, size of the student body, scope of the library, availability of law review and similar activities, the quality of the Texas Law School is superior. What is more important the University of Texas Law School possesses to a far greater degree those qualities which are incapable of objective measurement but which make for greatness in a law school. Such qualities to name but a few include reputation of faculty, experience of the administration, position and influence of the alumni, standing in the community, traditions and prestige. It is difficult to believe that one that had a free choice between these law schools would consider the question close.[31]

A similar decision was reached in *McLaurin v. Oklahoma State Regents for Higher Education,*[32] in which a black student, admitted to the graduate school of education because Oklahoma had no separate graduate school of education for black students, was assigned segregated seating in classrooms, in the library, and in the cafeteria. The Court struck down these restrictions, stating that such restrictions "impair and inhibit his ability to study, to engage in discussions and exchange views with other students, and, in general, to learn his profession."[33]

In each of these cases, the issue was whether the educational opportunities offered to the plaintiff were quantitatively and qualitatively equal; the decision did not turn on racial discrimination since that issue was not before the Court. Doctrinally, these cases are education cases, not race cases, and can be distinguished from *Brown,* in which white and black schools were assumed to be equal. *Sweatt* and *McLaurin* stand for the proposition that a state may not arbitrarily discriminate among its students in terms of the educational opportunities provided. Presumably, equality of educational opportunity survives as a doctrine at least where the state draws legislative distinctions arbitrarily and irrationally. Indeed, one lower federal court recently decided that Pennsylvania's exclusion of handicapped children from the educational system was irrational and arbitrary on the basis of evidence that such students are educable.[34] The court ruled that every child has a right to an education, at least where the state is providing it for other children. However, the instances in which legislative classifications do not survive the rational basis test are few, and unless some intermediate level test is devised the prospect for extensive relief from federal courts under the equal protection clause of the Fourteenth Amendment is limited at best. Perhaps continued litigation will result in abandonment of the present two-level equal protection analysis, although in view of *Rodriguez* that seems unlikely.

An unexpected result of *Rodriguez,* and one consistent with the value of federalism, is the challenge in state courts under state constitutions to interdistrict expenditure inequalities created by state school financing systems. In fact, school finance lawsuits pending at the time *Rodriguez* was decided asserted claims under both federal and state constitutional provisions, although the latter were not being vigorously pressed.[35] State constitutional claims are commonly based upon provisions that mandate the legislature of a state to establish "uniform and general"[36] or "general uniform, thorough"[37] systems of public education. Many state constitutions also contain some version of an equal protection guarantee similar to that in the Fourteenth Amendment, and many pending school finance suits allege a denial of such guarantee.[38] What, then, is the effect of *Rodriguez* on the outcome of state court challenges against school financing inequalities? For challenges of the former type, *Rodriguez* can have no binding effect, as state supreme courts are the ultimate authority in interpreting state constitutions. Thus, one month after *Rodriguez* was decided, the New Jersey Supreme Court declared that state's financing system to be in violation of a state constitutional provision guaranteeing a "thorough and efficient" school system.[39] As for the latter challenges, Justice Powell has perhaps provided a surprising answer to the question posed. In *Rodriguez,* strict scrutiny review was rejected because education was not a fundamental interest afforded explicit protection by the Constitution. Yet the constitutions of forty-eight of the fifty states do offer explicit protection of education,[40] often mandating the legislature to establish a system of public education. In California, article 9, § 1, of the constitution provides, "A general diffusion of knowledge and intelligence being essential to the preservation of the rights and liberties of the people, the legislature shall encourage by all suitable means the promotion of intellectual, scientific, moral and agricultural improvement." If state courts, in interpreting the equal protection provisions of state constitutions, employ the same two-level test used in *Rodriguez,* then, according to Powell's own standard, education may properly be regarded as a fundamental *state* interest triggering strict judicial review. Had such language appeared in the U.S. Constitution, Justice Powell would have been compelled by his own logic to find education a fundamental federal interest and would have thus struck down the Texas school financing system. In other words, education, while not a fundamental *federal* interest, *is* a fundamental *state* interest, a claim consonant with the control over education reserved to the states under the Tenth Amendment.

Therefore *Rodriguez* may presage more extensive state litigation regarding inequalities of educational opportunities and greater development of an independent body of state constitutional law. The shift in judicial power from federal courts to state courts in educational litigation asserting a denial of equal educational opportunity is perhaps historic, as federal courts have been the traditional forum for litigation involving personal rights and liberties, the forum where law might be used offensively as an instrument to effect change and to provide relief when none could be achieved through the majoritarian process. *Rodriguez* foreclosed that potentiality, remitting litigants to state courts in which, even if they are not traditionally favorable or sympathetic forums, the legal claims are far stronger and certainly deserving of exploration before abandonment of such claims altogether. This prospect for future educational reform litigation exemplifies the most pervasive feature of federal educational policy: the primary responsibility for educational decision-making is a state, not federal, function.

Rodriguez by no means implied that state legislatures were thus freed of the obligation to seek greater equity in financing public education, the ultimate objective sought through litigation. While regarding the method of finance as a legislative matter, the majority opinion recognized that "the need is apparent for reform in tax systems which may well have relied too long and too heavily upon the local property tax"[41] thus directing public notice to where the ultimate responsibility for reform rests. One of the purposes of activist reform litigation is, if not to prevail, at least to inform the public of injustice and the need for reform, a role that may itself produce the desired result. School finance reform has occurred in Florida, California, Utah, Michigan, Kansas, Oregon, Maine, and Washington, and is under serious reconsideration in many other state legislatures.[42] In response to *Rodriguez*, Senators Mondale, Stevenson, and Javits have submitted a "quality education bill" that would provide four billion dollars, double present federal spending on public elementary and secondary education, in financial assistance to states to relieve spending inequities caused by overdependence on the local property tax.[43] Win or lose, the point has been made.

Federal Courts and Federal Financial Assistance

Although the constitutional scope of federal judicial power over disputes involving state and local financing of schools is severely restricted following *Rodriguez*, the federal government nonetheless exerts considerable influence over how schools spend money for education. Congress has appropriated over $3 billion[44] in support of (1) elementary and secondary education, (2) higher education, in the form of aid both to institutions and to students, and (3) noninstructional activities such as public libraries and the National Institute of Education. Federal aid programs are nearly all "categorical," that is, to secure the benefits of federal categorical assistance, state and local educational agencies must agree to use the funds provided for only the purposes specified in the legislation and in accordance with regulations promulgated by the Office of Education. A table of such programs appears on pp. 215-217.

Program specifications and conditions, often extensive, must be satisfied. For example, the Smith-Hughes Vocational Education Act of 1917 appropriates money to the states for the purpose of paying the salaries of teachers of agricultural subjects, the salaries of teachers of trade, home economics, and industrial subjects, and the preparation of teachers in both categories. To receive assistance in the payment of salaries for teachers of trade, home economics, and industrial subjects, state and local agencies must agree to no fewer than fourteen conditions:[45]

(1) Education in such subjects shall be given in schools under public supervision and control;

(2) The controlling purpose of such education shall be to fit for useful employment;

(3) Such education shall be designed to meet the needs of persons less than college grade but over fourteen years of age;

(4) The state or local community shall provide the necessary plant and equipment determined by the state, with HEW approval, as the minimum requirement for education in a given trade;

(5) The amount spent for maintenance of education shall not be less annually than the amount fixed by the state, with HEW approval, as the minimum for such schools or classes;

(6) Schools or classes for persons not entered upon employment shall require that at least half of instruction be given to practical work on a useful or productive basis, extending over not less than nine months per year and not less than thirty hours per week;

(7) One-third of appropriation for salaries shall be applied to part-time classes for workers over fourteen years of age;

(8) Part-time classes shall include not less than 144 hours of classroom instruction per year;

(9) Evening industrial schools are limited to persons over sixteen and confined to instruction which is supplemental to daily employment;

(10) Teachers of any trade or industrial subject shall have the

Table of Federal Programs

1. Aid to Elementary and Secondary Education

Category	Act	Statutory reference	Purpose
1. Vocational	Smith-Hughes Vocational Education Act (also known as Vocational Education Act of 1917)	20 U.S.C. §§ 11-15, 16-28 (1969)	Teaching of agricultural, trade, home economics and industrial subjects
	Vocational Education Act of 1963; Vocational Education Amendments of 1968	20 U.S.C. §§ 1241 et seq. (1969)	Improvement of existing programs, development of innovative occupational education programs and work-study programs for vocational education students
2. Impact	Act Sept. 30, 1950	20 U.S.C. §§ 236 et seq. (1969)	Assistance for local educational agencies in areas affected by federal activity
	School Facilities Construction Act	20 U.S.C. §§ 631 et seq. (1969)	School construction in areas affected by federal activity
3. Compensatory	Elementary and Secondary Act of 1965, Amendments of 1966, Amendments of 1967, Amendments of 1970	20 U.S.C. §§ 241a-244, 331-332b, 821 et seq. (1969)	Assistance to local educational agencies for the education of children of low-income families; educational research and research training; grants for educational materials, facilities and services, and strengthening of educational agencies
	Bilingual Education Act (1968)	20 U.S.C. §§ 880b to 880b-6 (1969)	Bilingual education programs

1. Aid to Elementary and Secondary Education (*continued*)

Category	Act	Statutory reference	Purpose
	Indian Education Act, Indian Elementary and Secondary School Assistance Act (1972)	20 U.S.C. §§ 241aa *et seq.*, 887c, 1119a, 1211a and 1221f-1221h (1969)	Financial assistance to local educational agencies for education of Indian children
	Johnson-O'Malley Act (1931, 1934)	25 U.S.C. §§ 451 *et seq.*	Education of Indian children
	National School Lunch Act (1946)	42 U.S.C. §§ 1751 *et seq.* (1970)	Free and reduced price school lunches
4. Special Education	Education of the Handicapped Act (1968)	20 U.S.C. §§ 871-880a (1969)	Education of handicapped children
	Handicapped Children's Early Education Assistance Act (1968)	20 U.S.C. §§ 621-624 (1969)	Early education programs for handicapped children
	Education of the Handicapped (1970)	20 U.S.C. §§ 1401 *et seq.* (1969)	Improvement of existing programs; training personnel for education of handicapped; research; instructional media; special programs
5. School Desegregation	Emergency School Aid Act (1972)	20 U.S.C. 1601 *et seq.* (1969)	Assistance to local educational agencies to eliminate minority group isolation

2. Aid to Higher Education

Category	Act	Statutory reference	Purpose
1. Land Grant Colleges	Morill Act of 1862 (also known as Act of July 2, 1862); Agricultural College Act of 1890 (also known as the Second Morill Act); Bankhead-Jones Act	7 U.S.C. §§ 301-08 (1970); 7 U.S.C. §§ 321-28 (1970); 7 U.S.C. §§ 329 (1970)	Establishment of agricultural colleges

2. Veterans' Benefits	Veterans, Widows and Orphans Act	38 U.S.C. §§ 1650 *et seq.* (1959)	Veterans' education
3. Academic Institutions	National Defense Education Act of 1958; Amendments, 1964	20 U.S.C. §§ 401 *et seq.* (1969)	Student loans; financial assistance for strengthening instruction in science, math, and foreign languages
	Higher Education Facilities Act of 1963	20 U.S.C. §§ 701 *et seq.* (1969)	Construction of academic facilities
	Higher Education Act of 1965; Amendments of 1965; Amendments of 1968; Education Amendments of 1972	20 U.S.C. §§ 711 *et seq.*, 1001 *et seq.* (1969)	Improvement of existing programs; student financial assistance; library assistance; community service programs
	Education Professions Development Act (1965)	20 U.S.C. §§ 1091 *et seq.* (1969)	Teacher training and improvement

3. Other Aid

1. Research	Cooperative Research Act (1965)	20 U.S.C. §§ 331-332b	Educational research and research training
	General Education Provisions Act (1972), creating National Institute of Education	20 U.S.C. §§ 1221 *et seq.* 1969)	Educational research
2. Educational Services and Facilities for General Public	Library Services Act (1956); Library Services and Construction Act (1964), Amendments of 1966; Library Services and Construction Amendments of 1970	20 U.S.C. 351 *et seq.* (1969)	Public library services and construction

minimum qualifications determined for such subjects by the state, with HEW approval;

(11) Not more than 20 percent of money appropriated for salaries of such teachers shall be expended for the salaries of teachers of home economics subjects;

(12) No state shall receive any appropriation for salaries of teachers of trade, home economics and industrial subjects until it shall have taken advantage of at least the minimum amount appropriated for the training of such teachers;

(13) Appropriations for such salaries are to be devoted exclusively to the payment of such salaries, the cost of any supplementary instruction to be borne entirely by the state and local communities;

(14) The money for such salaries shall be conditioned that for each dollar of federal money so expended the state or local community shall expend an equal amount for such salaries.

Congress uses the power of the purse to achieve national educational program objectives. The matching funds condition, also present in the National School Lunch Act of 1946, even affects how state and local school bodies deploy their own financial resources. As a result of the "strings" attached to federal assistance, such programs have "exerted important programmatic or financial leverage in certain areas of national policy . . . [providing] a small but strategic proportion of total revenues for American public education."[46]

Federal courts are empowered to give meaning and effect to congressional intent and to assure that federal moneys are properly spent and the conditions upon its acceptance fully satisfied. Administration of federal programs is vested with state and local school authorities and, because the review of compliance with federal guidelines by the U.S. Office of Education has in practice been only perfunctory, litigation to enforce federal law has been meager, and often generated, where it has occurred, not by governmental parties but by individuals intended as the recipients of federal largesse. An example of the latter is litigation to secure the rights of impoverished children to free and reduced price lunches under the National School Lunch Act of 1946. That legislation, requiring participating states to provide three dollars for every federal dollar, was enacted both to encourage domestic consumption of agricultural commodities and to safeguard the health of school children. In *Shaw v. Governing Board of the Modesto School District,*[47] a federal district court in 1970 invalidated the practice of a financially pressed California school district of restricting the number of needy children served free or reduced price lunches by raising eligibility standards from 100 percent of poverty level to 80 percent of poverty level. The court ruled that 42 U.S.C. § 1758 requires that schools participating in the federal lunch program, must, as a condition upon receiving federal funds, provide every needy child with a free or reduced price lunch. Federal courts also ruled, however, that, in the selection of recipient schools, participating states and school districts are not required to give priority to those schools whose children are in greatest need.[48] Although a provision of the Act provides that "need and attendance" shall be taken into account in school selection, the legislative history and declared purpose of Congress was to encourage lunch programs for all children in order to benefit farmers and the economy. One court, rejecting the priority claim, still found a Colorado school district in violation of the act on a showing that it had entirely ignored considerations of need.[49] In *Briggs v. Kerrigan,*[50] however, a practice of excluding schools that lack kitchen facilities for preparing meals was held permissible in light of the substantial additional local expenditures required. Unsuccessful litigation of the need priority claim dramatized the need for remedial legislation, and in 1970 the act was amended to require that state school authorities must establish lunch programs in neediest schools first and provide free or reduced price lunches to the neediest children first, in effect overruling *Briggs.*[51]

The use of federal money to achieve national policy objectives occurs not only as a result of "strings," but also from the power to entirely withhold or terminate federal assistance. The most illustrative example, and certainly the most controversial one, is Title VI of the Civil Rights Act of 1964, which prohibits racial discrimination in any program or activity receiving federal financial assistance.[52] The federal courts, in enforcing the act, have required school districts to desegregate or have financial assistance withdrawn.[53] Recently, in *Adams v. Richardson,* the District of Columbia Court of Appeals declared that HEW had been derelict in securing compliance with Title VI by schools and universities receiving federal money, and ordered the agency to institute compliance proceedings against ten state-operated systems of higher education, and to commence enforcement proceedings against secondary and primary school districts found to be in noncompliance with Title VI.[54]

Administrative power to withhold federal funds is not done without judicial scrutiny. The Nixon administration's impoundment policy, designed to reduce inflation by reducing federal spending, has been challenged in over fifty cases in the federal courts.[55] Several of these cases involve impoundment of federal educational funds. Despite separation of powers arguments raised by government lawyers that the courts lack jurisdiction over the president, in each case thus far decided the impoundments were invalidated. An Oklahoma district court ruled that allotments to states under the Library Services and Construction Act were mandatory; the impoundment was thus in violation of the clear mandate of the act, as no discretion existed to support an impoundment.[56] The impoundment also violated Articles I and II of the Constitution, the Administrative Procedure Act, and the administration's own regulations. In another case, release of Indian education money was blocked by nonimplementation. The president was required to appoint the National Advisory Council on Indian Education prior to the appropriation of money under the act. A federal district court ordered the president to make the appointments so that the money could be released.[57]

Despite the range of federal programs, the role of the federal government in the educational policy process is lilliputian. Federal educational expenditures are but 7 percent of total expenditures on public education in the United States from all sources, federal, state, and local.[58] The General Education Provisions Act,[59] part of the Education Amendments of 1972, does not leave this perception of limited federal involvement unexpressed. The Office of Education is stated to have no authority other than that expressly provided for by statute, and federal control over local educational programs is expressly prohibited.[60] Even more important, perhaps, is the explicit requirement in nearly every federal assistance program, that federal funds shall be used only to supplement local programs, not to supplant them, a policy that promises both a limited federal involvement in educational finance and a program impact of maximum significance.[61]

Two aid programs in which the courts have been called on to enforce this policy are those of impact aid and compensatory education. Impact aid legislation was first passed in 1950 to relieve financial burdens on local educational agencies that occurred as a result of federal activities. Operating funds were provided to ease financial burdens where federal ownership of real property reduced local taxable wealth, where local agencies were providing education for children who were residing on or whose parents were employed on federal property, or where there was a sudden and substantial increase in school attendance as a result of federal activities. The School Facilities Construction Act of 1958 provided financial assistance for construction of minimum school facilities in school districts that had substantial increases in school attendance as a result of new or increased federal activities.

Several states, approximately fifteen, developed state aid apportionment formulas for state assistance to local school districts in which the amount of federal impact aid received by a district was reduced from the share otherwise allocable to the district by the state. Virginia, for example, deducted from its Minimum Education Program expenditure per child, guaranteed to all students from a combination of state and local money, an amount equal to 50 percent of all federal impact aid received by a district. The amount of state support was thereby reduced by 10 million dollars. The Virginia legislature also provided that if federal funds were conditioned upon exclusion from the state financing scheme, then the state was to exclude not only the impact funds but the "federal" children as well, thus achieving the same result. Virginia's financing plan was invalidated in *Shepheard v. Godwin*[62] because its effect was to defeat the congressional intent to supplement the state and local income of particular school districts and to substitute federal aid for state revenues. The court held that the purpose of the federal legislation was to compensate local school districts for losses in *local,* not *state,* revenues. The legislation, in other words, was not intended to lessen state efforts. As a result, the practice of deducting impact aid from otherwise allocable state apportionments was declared unconstitutional under the supremacy clause of Article VI. The alternative statute, excluding federal children from the state distribution formula, was declared a violation of the equal protection clause as a discrimination without justification. Similar state financing arrangements were soon voided in South Dakota, Kansas, Nebraska and California.[63] Congress also responded by amending the impact aid statutes to provide the U.S. Commissioner of Education with an administrative remedy to reduce where appropriate federal aid to local school districts in an amount equivalent to any reduction in state educational expenditures.[64]

A similar program, but one considerably more difficult for courts to enforce, beleaguers proper implementation of compensatory education funds under Title I (ESEA). Title I is by far the most ambitious federal aid program in our history, providing over $1.5 billion each year (roughly half of all federal expenditures for education) for the education of more than 9 million children from low income families in 16,000 schools across the country.[65] State departments of education are charged with the responsibility of administering the program, which, like all federal programs, is designed to be supplementary only. However, financially pressed school districts utilized the funds for basic support programs, defeating the congressional purpose,[66] and in 1970 Congress amended the law to require that expenditures by school districts in Title I schools, before application of Title I funds, be "comparable" to expenditures provided in non-Title I schools.[67] Congress specifically empowered the Office of Education to terminate assistance to noncomparable districts after July 1, 1972. The Office of Education, although it issued regulations prohibiting a state from approving grant applications from noncomparable districts for the 1972-73 fiscal year,[68] has not vigorously enforced the comparability requirements. State educational agencies have been relied on for enforcement. Proposals to achieve comparability, required of districts not comparable, have been approved regardless of adequacy, and in some instances funds have been allocated to districts that submitted no plan at all.[69]

Litigation was thus inevitable. On February 8, 1973, Navajo Indian students won a judgment against the Gallup County School Board and the New Mexico State Department of Education for diversion of Title I funds intended for impoverished Indian children to pay for basic program costs and for using instructional equipment purchased with Title I funds in noneligible schools.[70] In a similar suit, *Nicholson v. Pennsylvania Department of Education*,[71] parents of Title I children in Philadelphia filed an action to prohibit the Pennsylvania Department of Education from approving Philadelphia's $20 million funding application for 1972-73 because 138, or nearly 80 percent, of Philadelphia's Title I schools were noncomparable in 1971-72. The Department of Education withheld funds pending the outcome of the suit and Philadelphia utilized local funds to pay for Title I programs until the expected eventual approval of their application. On July 2, 1973, HEW denied a request from the Pennsylvania Department of Education to disburse the approved funds to Philadelphia, and the appropriation was lost.[72] On August 9, a federal district court in *Nicholson* enjoined the Pennsylvania Department of Education from approving any Title I applications from Philadelphia for the 1973-74 fiscal year, unless (1) the applications show compliance with HEW's comparability requirements or contain adequate assurance that comparability will be achieved and maintained during the funding period, (2) an affirmative showing is made that no supplanting violations exist, and (3) the applications demonstrate that Title I funds will be spent in schools with the greatest concentration of children from low-income families. On June 28, 1973, moreover, the Office of Education issued revised comparability regulations[73] providing that districts not comparable on October 1, 1973, are ineligible to receive Title I funds for 1973-74 unless a revised report showing reassignment of resources to achieve comparability is submitted by December 1, 1973. If a district is noncomparable after that date, the state education agency is required to disapprove the application and is further required to submit information to USOE demonstrating that recipient districts are comparable or that funds have been denied. Noncompliance by the state could mean the loss of the entire state allotment.

Congressional control over financing of educational programs may be ebbing, however, as there is growing dissatisfaction with federal categorical aid programs and with the postulation of program objectives in Washington that may bear little relevance to local need. In 1972 Congress enacted a general revenue sharing bill, making $6 billion available to state and local agencies to meet local fiscal needs.[74] Two-thirds of this money was "passed through" to county and city governments subject only to the requirement that revenue-sharing funds be spent for five areas of general priorities. Education is not one of the priorities included, nor are school districts recipient agencies. State governments, however, received one-third of state revenue-sharing allotments—money without restriction that can be spent for education if desired. In 1972 the California Assembly apportioned its entire revenue-sharing allotment, $215 million, to support a school expenditure equalization plan and categorical aid programs for early childhood education and compensatory education.[75]

In addition to the enacted general revenue-sharing bill, President Nixon's original revenue-sharing proposal contained a special revenue-sharing program for education in the amount of $3 billion,[76] but that proposal was not enacted by Congress, which instead cautiously chose to adopt a five-year general revenue-sharing plan to see whether revenue-sharing is a feasible concept. Obviously, if federal aid to education moves in the direction of general aid, the role of the federal government in educational policy-making will diminish, and with it the scope of federal judicial power over school financing, for few federal educational objectives would be left to enforce. The federal role would be limited to determining the amount of assistance; federal educational policy would be a nonpolicy, although the appropriation of general funds in support of education is itself policy. A possible exception is suggested by a controversial case[77] in Georgia, where a city chose to substitute federal general revenue-sharing money to pay for its current fire department programs, one of the priority areas. The displaced local revenues were then utilized to finance nonpriority programs. A federal judge ruled that the city's use of federal funds violated the intent of Congress, which was that local revenue-sharing money be spent for specified priorities. The federal desire for accountability may imply the perpetuation of categorical programs, even in a revenue-sharing plan. The role of the federal government and of federal courts in educational financing is very narrow, perhaps even contracting, but is not likely to cease as long as Congress continues to appropriate money for education.

Federal Courts and Aid to Parochial Schools

Federal judicial involvement in educational financing is narrowly constrained, but every proposition has its exception. The First Amendment prohibits Congress from enacting any law "respecting an establishment of religion, or prohibiting the free exercise thereof." The wall between church and state thus erected to avoid their excessive entanglement is made applicable to the states by the due process clause of the Fourteenth Amendment, which protects the fundamental personal rights inherent in United States citizenship against state infringement. In recent years, the increasing financial distress of non-

public schools has spurred numerous challenges to these constitutional principles as state legislatures have enacted a variety of
measures designed to aid the secular educational purposes of parochial schools.

While some limited assistance that is distinctly secular and neutral
has been upheld by the U.S. Supreme Court (e.g., bus transportation,
school lunches, public health services and secular textbooks), in a
series of recent decisions the Court has severely limited the permissible scope of state financial assistance to private religious schools.
Invalidating state assistance laws in Rhode Island and Pennsylvania,
the Court in *Lemon v. Kurtzman*,[78] decided in 1971, established a
three-level test for determining conformity of state parochial school
assistance legislation with the First Amendment: "First, the statute
must have a secular legislative purpose; second, its principal or primary effect must be one that neither advances nor inhibits religion . . . ; finally, the statute must not foster 'an excessive governmental entanglement with religion.' "[79] Both statutes were found to
foster excessive entanglements between government and religion. The
Rhode Island case involved a statute that provided a 15 percent
salary supplement to teachers in nonpublic schools which are below
the average for secular schools in the state; the Court distinguished
teachers from textbooks: "We cannot, however, refuse here to recognize that teachers have a substantially different ideological character
than books. In terms of potential for involving some aspect of faith
or morals in secular subjects, a textbook's content is ascertainable,
but a teacher's handling of a subject is not. We cannot ignore the
dangers that a teacher under religious control and discipline poses to
the separation of the religious from the purely secular aspects of
pre-college education. The conflict of functions inheres in the situation."[80] The statute was further defective in that its benefits were
extended only to teachers of courses taught in public schools, who
used only materials appropriate for public schools, and who agreed
not to teach courses in religion. These restrictions would necessitate
ongoing government surveillance of religious schools. Governmental
involvement would also be necessary to determine which expenditures were secular and which religious for eligibility purposes. The
Pennsylvania statute offended the religion clauses on similar grounds,
containing the additional flaw that the funds for teachers' salaries
were administered through the religious schools rather than paid di-

rectly to the teachers. Both statutes, said the Court, had the potential for engendering divisive political activity.

Applying the standards set forth in *Lemon,* the Court recently struck down three New York programs providing direct money grants to nonpublic schools for (1) maintenance and repair of school facilities and equipment, (2) tuition reimbursements to parents, and (3) state income tax deductions to parents for each parochial school child.[81] The facilities grant was struck down because aid was not limited to facilities used only for secular purposes; the statute's primary effect therefore was to advance religion. The Court felt that the latter two features of New York's financing plan were direct subsidies to religious schools and thus an advancement of religion. Another New York law providing state reimbursement to private schools for the cost of tests and records required by the state was soon invalidated on the same grounds,[82] as was a Pennsylvania statute reimbursing parents for parochial school tuition expense.[83]

Paradoxically, the Supreme Court has been more lenient with federal programs providing assistance to parochial schools. In *Tilton v. Richardson,*[84] decided in 1971, the Court upheld the constitutionality of federal construction grants to sectarian institutions of higher learning under the Higher Education Facilities Act of 1963. The grants were limited to construction of facilities to be used only for secular instruction. Arguing that less potential for entanglement was present, the Court distinguished college education from elementary and secondary education, in that (1) college students were not so impressionable, (2) religious indoctrination was not a substantial purpose of religion-affiliated colleges, (3) facilities, unlike teachers, are religiously neutral, (4) the aid provided is a one-time grant requiring no continuing involvement, and (5) little potential was present for political aggravation and dissension. The Court did, however, invalidate a provision of the act limiting federal interest in the facilities to twenty years, because the use of valuable property after that period amounted to a government contribution to a religious body.

Now pending before the Supreme Court is an important challenge to federal financial assistance to private, parochial schools under Title I. Title I provides that compensatory education funds should be made available to educationally deprived children attending private schools in meaningful programs comparable in size, scope, and opportunity to those provided eligible public school children, and that such programs may require that public teacher services be provided in private schools. Parents of private school children in *Barrera v. Wheeler*[85] have challenged the refusal by the state of Missouri to provide the allotted funds to nonpublic schools. Missouri claims that the law violates the religion clauses of the First Amendment. The distinction in *Tilton* between college and precollege education is not applicable here. Providing public school teachers to parochial schools is a direct subsidy which advances religious schools. Entanglement abounds. *Lemon* declared teachers to be inherently nonneutral and, although in *Barrera* the teachers are from public schools, the Court found the Rhode Island statute in *Lemon* invalid despite the fact that many of the recipient teachers were lay teachers who were forbidden to teach religious courses; the teachers are also paid directly by the state in *Barrera*, as they were in *Lemon*. Not only is the aid in *Barrera* continuing, but state educational agencies must assure that services provided by Title I meet comparability and concentration requirements, are not used to supplant other funds, and are regularly evaluated. As in *Lemon*, to make such determinations would necessitate governmental scrutiny of the financial affairs of religious schools in order to separate secular and sectarian expenditures. If federal assistance to private schools is found unconstitutional in *Barrera*, the validity of similar federal assistance programs, such as the National School Lunch Act, will be drawn seriously into question.

III. Federal Review of Program Administration

Federal Courts and School Segregation

In 1954, the Supreme Court in *Brown v. Board of Education*[86] declared that state-imposed racial segregation in public education violated the equal protection clause of the Fourteenth Amendment. *Brown* and its progeny have occasioned the most extensive exercise of federal judicial power in adjudicating educational disputes. Because it is the ultimate authority in interpreting the meaning of the Constitution, the Court has been the primary source of federal educational policy on racial equality in public schools.

Yet *Brown* is as ambiguous as it is famous. Earlier alluded to was language in the opinion that suggested that inequality of educational opportunity was a cognizable and independent constitutional claim, a premise now partially disregarded by *Rodriguez*. A further uncertainty is the precise nature of the racial harm, and thus—and of greater moment—the extent to which school districts must achieve racial equality and by what methods. The Court held in *Brown:*

> We come then to the question presented: Does segregation of children in public schools solely on the basis of race even though the physical facilities and other tangible factors may be equal, deprive the children of the minority group of equal educational opportunities? . . .
>
> To separate them from others of similar age and qualifications solely because of their race generates a feeling of inferiority as to their status in the community that may affect their hearts and minds in a way unlikely ever to be undone. . . .
>
> We conclude that in the field of public education a doctrine of separate but equal has no place. Separate educational facilities are inherently unequal.[87]

Is the psychological harm the Court postulates as the result of school segregation the premise of the decision? If so, then *all* segregation, whether state-imposed or not, is unlawful and school districts must be constitutionally compelled to integrate in order to eradicate that harm. Or was state-imposed discriminatory treatment the cause of the harm? Or, put still differently, is only the harm that results from state-imposed racial separation judicially actionable and remediable? In any event, the minimum *Brown* demands is that state-enforced exclusion of black children from white schools be eliminated. Yet merely invalidating state segregation statutes did not desegregate school systems. When a school board changed from a racially segregated system to one based on neighborhood schools ("free choice" plans), the schools were still segregated, primarily because of racially restricted residential housing patterns, and even a unitary system could become segregated through residential migration. Several issues emerged that demanded resolution. Did *Brown* mean only that states must be neutral, allowing freedom of choice as to the schools to be attended, as long as the choice was genuinely free of official restraint? Or did *Brown* require affirmative state action to integrate school systems where de jure segregation previously was present, in order to suspend the psychological harm caused by state-imposed segregation? If the Court intervened to require affirmative school integration to relieve that harm, would not de facto school segregation also be unlawful?

Fourteen years were to pass before the first two of these questions were to be answered; the third remains unanswered. In resolving the former, lower federal courts were understandably divided. One controversial decision declared that the Constitution "does not require integration. It merely forbids discrimination."[88] Only governmentally imposed segregation was thus thought to be infirm, not segregation which was the result of free choice or "voluntary action," because the Fourteenth Amendment is not a limitation upon individual action, only state action. In *Green v. County School Board*,[89] the Supreme Court boldly resolved the issue by holding that school boards in the South where there had been a history of prior de jure segregation were "clearly charged with the affirmative duty to take whatever steps mights be necessary to convert to a unitary system in which racial discrimination would be eliminated root and branch."[90] The test, said the Court, was whether a desegregation plan "promises realistically to work, and promises realistically to work *now.*"[91] The Court's concern with results, with the disestablishment of dual systems, caused by whatever reason, was so consuming that the doctrinal basis of the decision was left unclear, although the Court was obviously attempting to eliminate de jure segregation as well as to accelerate that process.

The decision in *Green* has been criticized because the segregation was regarded not as the result of de jure discrimination, which had ended fourteen years earlier, but of residential housing segregation and racial migration over which school officials had no control.[92] *Green* thus was thought to treat southern school districts unequally by comparison with similarly de facto segregated school districts in the North and West. Although such an argument can scarcely be justified on the facts in *Green,* where various state efforts stalled any desegregation until 1965,[93] the argument's validity gains credence as years pass and segregation can no longer be easily assumed to be the result of de jure segregation in force in 1954. De facto segregation has thus emerged as a central issue of constitutional policy. Some courts have held that segregated schools are unconstitutional because racial separation, by whatever reason produced, denies equality of educational opportunity,[94] a position now clearly repudiated by *Rodriguez.* Others have regarded segregated housing patterns, caused by restrictive covenants enforced by local zoning commissions, as governmental action requiring desegregation, regardless of the good faith of school boards.[95] Still others did not view the equal protection clause as extending that far.[96] The issue was finally presented to the Supreme Court (albeit, unfortunately, in fractured form) in

Keyes v. School District No. 1,[97] the Denver school desegregation suit. The district court had found a deliberate segregative intent by the school board that was responsible for the racially segregated schools in the district's Park Hill area and ordered desegregation. The district had refused to order desegregation of the city's core area schools because no de jure intent was established. The stage was set for resolution of the de facto issue. However, Justice Brennan, writing for the majority, ruled that the school board's de jure acts in a substantial portion of the district created a prima facie case of unlawful segregated design and shifted to the school board the burden of proving that other segregated schools in the district were not also the result of de jure acts of segregation. The Court thus retained the distinction between de jure and de facto discrimination, ruling that *"purpose* or *intent* to segregate" is the test of the former.[98] Justice Powell roundly criticized Brennan's "intent" test for not being the same as the "effect" test used for southern school districts. Justices Powell and Douglas, concurring in the result, would have abolished the distinction, agreeing that purely adventitious de facto school segregation was the product of segregated housing patterns which governmental action had a role in fostering. The policy expressed by Justice Powell may eventually become declared majority doctrine when a pure de facto case is presented, as his concurrence appears more soundly reasoned than is the Brennan majority opinion.

Brown's ambiguity over whether racial segregation is a constitutionally cognizable harm only when state imposed has also surfaced in suits seeking interdistrict metropolitan school desegregation. In *Bradley v. School Board of City of Richmond, Virginia*,[99] a district court order requiring consolidation of the Richmond district, 64 percent black, with two adjoining nearly all-white county school districts, was reversed by the Fourth Circuit. All three districts were formerly segregated but had achieved unitary systems. While the court recognized the desirability of better racial balance, it found no evidence of "joint interaction between any two of the units involved (or by higher state officers) for the purpose of keeping one unit relatively white by confining blacks to another."[100] In other words, there must be interdistrict discrimination in establishing and maintaining district boundary lines, either long ago or recently for the purpose of perpetuating racial segregation. Neither could the court find any evidence of white outflow from Richmond to the two adjoining county districts. Since all three districts are unitary, and the boundary lines have not been discriminatorily drawn, there exists no invidious state action and no constitutional violation, so ruled the Court. Considerations of federalism, expressed in the Tenth Amendment, deny authority to a federal district court to order consolidation absent such a violation. On appeal, the Supreme Court split 4-4 (Justice Powell abstaining because of his prior Richmond school board membership), leaving the Fourth Circuit's reversal unaffected, but the metropolitan consolidation issue unresolved.

The problem of interdistrict racial segregation was handled quite differently in *Bradley v. Milliken*.[101] There, the Detroit school system, 64 percent black in a metropolitan area 81 percent white, was found to be de jure segregated. De jure acts of segregation by the state board of education were also found to exist. The court noted that metropolitan interdistrict segregation could be no less harmful to minority students than if accomplished within a single district and ruled that no plan involving only the Detroit system could achieve desegregation. Refraining from the consolidation approach, the court then ordered a study of the feasibility of pupil reassignment among Detroit and fifty-three other school systems in the metropolitan area. The decision was upheld by the Sixth Circuit and has been appealed to the Supreme Court.[102]

The questions explicitly and implicitly presented are weighty and difficult. What is the causal connection between de jure acts of state officials and interdistrict racial segregation? Must there be one? What is the responsibility of the state for education? Can cross-district busing be ordered in the absence of a finding that the fifty-three outlying districts are not unitary? Was there joint interaction among school districts (and the state) to establish and maintain boundary lines for the purpose of creating or perpetuating racial segregation? Must there be? Whatever the answer, de facto segregation and metropolitan desegregation suits are probing the outer parameters of *Brown* and the Fourteenth Amendment. The failure to define the harm sought to be eliminated, the concentration on effect and on the result to ameliorate that effect, have enmeshed federal courts in hopeless ambiguity and confusion and demonstrated the inefficacy of judicial solution to a problem not primarily or even significantly educational.

No other aspect of school desegregation litigation has stirred more public reaction than the judicial remedy of forced bussing, upheld by the Supreme Court in *Swann v. Charlotte-Mecklenburg Board of Education.*[103] Court-ordered busing to achieve racial desegregation has generated angry congressional and administrative response, and led to enactment and threatened enactment of legislation to limit the remedial options of federal courts. Congress, as part of the Education Amendments of 1972, prohibited the use of federal funds to transport students if designed to overcome racial imbalance or to carry out a plan of racial desegregation.[104] Congress further provided that the effectiveness of any district court order would be postponed pending appeal, where the order requires a transfer or transportation of students for the purposes of achieving racial balance. The statute applied only to lower federal courts and only until all appeals were exhausted. (Article III of the Constitution empowers Congress to establish and provide for the jurisdiction of all federal courts save the Supreme Court; Congress may not limit the jurisdiction of the Supreme Court, which was constitutionally defined.) The Supreme Court upheld the right of Congress to postpone the effectiveness of district court bussing orders, but interpreted the statute to apply only to bus transportation designed to achieve racial imbalance. The statute, said the Court, did not apply to bus transportation designed to achieve desegregation.[105] The bussing controversy has resulted in congressional and administrative attempts to place ceilings on the amount of transportation that can be ordered by a federal court and even constitutional amendments to outlaw bussing.[106] The dispute is far from resolved, although it is clear that some limited form of bussing is acceptable to a majority of the Court and is believed necessary to achieve racial equality in public education.

Constitutional policy regarding racial segregation in public schools[107] can be summarized as follows:

(1) The equal protection clause of the Fourteenth Amendment requires not only an end to state-imposed segregation of black and white students in the nation's public school systems, but has been interpreted by the Court as imposing an affirmative duty on de jure segregated school systems to produce an integrated school system.

(2) The Court is as yet unwilling to abandon the de jure–de facto distinction and find segregation, resulting from whatever cause, unlawful, although two justices as ideologically divergent as Justice Powell and Justice Douglas both believe the distinction should be

abandoned and that de facto segregation should be abolished because it is caused by racially restricted segregated housing patterns enforced by state action.

(3) With the presence of Justice Powell on the Court, and with the sentiment already rooted in Congress and the administration, federal policy on school desegregation can be expected to evolve toward a more national policy, rather than a sectional policy in which southern school districts are treated differently than their counterparts in other sections of the country.

(4) Desegregation suits are beginning to spread across school district boundary lines to the entire metropolitan area in which racial segregation in public schools exists, a development that presages more of judicial limitation than of constructive constitutional policy.

(5) It is permissible to employ bussing as a technique to achieve racial desegregation, but, because of the tension that exists among the federal judiciary, Congress and the administration over the extent to which bussing should be used, its use will continue but in perhaps a more limited fashion.

Federal Courts and the Right to Bilingual-Bicultural Educational Programs

The Supreme Court was called on this term—October 1973— to decide whether minority students are denied equality of educational opportunity when a school district or the state fails to provide bilingual-bicultural programs for minority students who speak a language other than English. In *Lau v. Nichols,*[108] the Ninth Circuit ruled that a state was not required to provide bilingual education for Chinese students in the San Francisco Unified School District because there was no showing that the language deficiencies of Chinese children were related to any past discrimination by the state or the school district. Because neither the state nor the school district created the language deficiency, no affirmative obligation existed to relieve the deficiency, so held that court. The *Lau* case was then appealed to the Supreme Court.

In a case contrary to *Lau, Serna v. Portalef Municipal Schools,*[109] a New Mexico district court held that Spanish-surname students were denied equality of educational opportunity in that the educational program was designed for middle-class Anglo students without regard to the educational needs of Spanish-speaking children. That court relied on a showing that Spanish-surname students had lower IQ and achievement scores than did Anglo students, and rejected arguments that the special needs of Spanish-surname students are not the result of state action or that financial incapacity made expenditures for bilingual, bicultural programs impossible. The school district was ordered to employ enough Spanish-speaking teachers to meet the needs of that community.

The *Lau* and *Serna* cases can be distinguished from a case in Texas, *U.S. v. Texas*,[110] in which the court ordered compensatory education programs for Mexican-American children, including bilingual-bicultural programs, after a showing that the school system in Texas had discriminated against Mexican-American children. In *Lau* the Ninth Circuit distinguished the Texas case, because there the deficiencies of Mexican-American children could be said to have been created by the school district's racially discriminatory actions; in *Lau*, no such showing was made concerning Chinese children. Put another way, *U.S. v. Texas* is a race case, where federal courts will exercise jurisdiction, while *Lau* is an education case, in which, according to *Rodriguez*, the federal courts will not intrude unless a school district acts arbitrarily or irrationally. The relevant issue is not whether education is a fundamental interest, but whether financial inability represents an irrational or arbitrary basis for failing to provide compensatory education programs or bilingual-bicultural programs. Given the holding in *Rodriguez*, plaintiffs in *Lau* seemed destined to fail.

The Court, however, entirely avoided the constitutional issue presented, ruling that the failure of the San Francisco school system to provide English language instruction to Chinese children violated Title VI of the Civil Rights Act of 1964 forbidding discrimination in any program receiving federal financial assistance.[111] Although a narrow holding on an issue not seriously considered below, *Lau* does provide a glimmer of hope for future educational reform litigation.

The Federal Courts and School Classifications

An emerging area of federal constitutional policy in the area of program administration is the validity and fairness of school classifications and labels in sorting children.[112] Classification problems typically arise in two ways: (1) the exclusion of handicapped or retarded children from the educational system of the state for allegedly being "uneducable," and (2) misclassification of children for purposes of placement in ability tracks or special education classes. Two recent cases nullified state laws excluding handicapped children from public schools in Pennsylvania and the District of Columbia, as a violation of the equal protection clause of the Fourteenth Amendment. The plaintiffs in *Pennsylvania Association for Retarded Children v. Pennsylvania* [113] offered proof that the legislative declaration that handicapped students were uneducable and untrainable lacked a rational basis in fact and therefore denied to such children the right to an education provided other children in the state. The case does not declare that the state must provide an education for all children; only that, if the state undertakes to provide education, it must do so for all children, including handicapped children, unless it can be demonstrably proven that the children sought to be excluded are entirely uneducable and untrainable. The District of Columbia case, *Mills v. Board of Education,* [114] also held that the exclusion of handicapped children cannot be excused by the claim that there are insufficient funds, for financial consideration may not bear more heavily on handicapped children than on any other type of child. The equal protection analysis in these cases is not fully articulated, although it seems that the rational basis test was being applied rather than the strict scrutiny standard. The exclusions are not being invalidated because of any finding or belief or holding that education is a fundamental interest. The rule is simply that government cannot act arbitrarily in providing benefits to the public, a finding or ruling that would be as applicable with respect to any other benefit as it would be to education.

The Pennsylvania and District of Columbia cases are also important, perhaps chiefly so, for making applicable to school classification procedures the safeguards of due process of law assured to children under the Fourteenth Amendment. The procedural due process mandated by these cases would make available to the child and his parents the right to notice and to a hearing where the appropriateness of the classification label being imposed on the child can be challenged. [115] Due process would permit a child to transfer among ability tracks, if his performance improves substantially to justify this. These due process safeguards will enable federal courts to ensure that children will not arbitrarily be denied the level of education most appropriate to their needs, if such education is being offered to other children.

The classifications themselves are far more difficult to attack. Commentators have suggested that placing children in ability tracks on the basis of cognitive skills is irrational, for schools have other educational priorities, such as in the affective and psychomotor domains.[116] But these substantive challenges to tracking or to any classification label go to the heart of educational policy and are not likely to be viewed as a subject for federal adjudication (though they may be so under state constitutions), but left to the legislative and executive arms of state and local governments. One exception to this rule is where the classification is arbitrary and irrational, as in the Pennsylvania and District of Columbia cases. Another is where race is involved. Judge J. Skelly Wright in *Hobson v. Hansen*[117] "abolished" the Washington, D.C., track system because racially biased ability tests consigned disproportionate numbers of black children to lower ability tracks. Similarly, in *Larry P. v. Riles,*[118] Judge Peckham found that the tests used to place children into mentally retarded programs were culturally biased, resulting in a disproportionate number of black students being placed in such classes. In an attempt to avoid the rigidity of the two-level equal protection test commonly employed, Judge Peckham found a prima facie violation of constitutional rights because of the de facto racial discrimination, and shifted the burden of proof as to the rationality of the classification procedures—ordinarily carried by the plaintiffs—to the school district. Under the test used by Judge Peckham, plaintiffs need only show a de facto discriminatory effect, whereupon it becomes the burden of the school district or the state to show that the procedures used have a rational basis. Judge Peckham borrowed his test from the employment discrimination provisions of Title VII of the Civil Rights Act of 1964. Again, however, the basis for such a departure was the racial imbalance in the special education programs, not the fundamentality of education which guarantees equality of educational opportunities or a quality education appropriate to the needs of every child. The classification itself was not challenged, nor would such a challenge be likely to encounter much success. Once a child is justifiably placed in a special education class or in a lower ability track, neither does it appear that any obligation exists on the part of the school district to affirmatively provide that child with compensatory or specialized education appropriate to the child's needs. Federal constitutional policy does not extend to matters of legislative or administrative policy.

The Federal Courts and Protection of First Amendment Rights

Freedom of Expression. An emerging theme of federal constitutional policy in the administration of the nation's public junior and senior high schools is protection of First Amendment freedoms, chief among them freedom of expression. In *Tinker v. Des Moines Independent Community School District*,[119] the U.S. Supreme Court declared that the free speech clause of the First Amendment limits the power of local school districts to prohibit student political protest in secondary schools. There, students wore black armbands during school hours to protest the Vietnam war, which prompted school officials to pass a regulation forbidding such activity. When the students failed to comply, they were suspended. The Court ruled that the wearing of black armbands to protest the war was a symbolic act closely akin to pure speech and protected by the free speech clause. The Court conceded that schools have authority to control the administration of local educational programs, but reasoned that school officials must tolerate nondistracting expression in class and nondisruptive conduct outside of class. Schools may control student political expression on campus and in the classroom only where such expression and activity "materially and substantially interferes with the requirements of appropriate discipline in the operation of the school."[120] As a result of *Tinker*, federal courts have demonstrated greater willingness to apply constitutional prohibitions to the actions of school officials, invalidating prior restraints on printed matter and bans on distribution on school premises of political handbills and leaflets protesting school policies and practices of school administrators.[121] Even more extensive is judicial insistence that the safeguards of due process be extended to students in disciplinary proceedings, requiring notice and a hearing prior to expulsion or suspension for any substantial period of time.[122]

The application of constitutional requirements to public institutions at the college and university level is even more extensive. In addition to the rights of due process in disciplinary hearings, federal courts have upheld the right to demonstrate, the right to pass out handbills on public campuses, the right to have controversial speakers.[123] These constitutional safeguards have not, however, been extended to private universities, which are held not to be agencies of the state for constitutional purposes.[124]

Judicial protection of First Amendment activities of students also extends to congressional enactments designed to control student conduct. Because of the campus unrest during the 1960s, Congress placed a condition on student financial assistance under NDEA that any student found guilty of a crime involving a serious disruption of a university campus shall have his benefits under those acts immediately terminated.[125] In *Rasche v. Board of Trustees of the University of Illinois,*[126] a state university's termination of assistance to a student who engaged in a peaceful demonstration was overturned, the federal district court holding that a trespassing violation was not a serious crime nor a substantial disruption of university activity. The court also struck down the entire statute as unconstitutionally vague in its restriction on the freedom of expression. Another case, *Green v. Dumke,*[127] overruled a university's termination of student financial assistance under the Higher Education Amendments Act of 1968 because of a lack of proof that the particular crime was committed in order to disrupt the institution.

These First Amendment protections also extend to teachers, who may not be dismissed or penalized for protected activity. Given special protection is a teacher's right to run for political election, to hold political views and join political associations, to participate in the determination of school policy, to participate in activities outside the classroom and to criticize publicly school board policy.[128] Freedom of expression and of association are rights protected by federal courts against state loyalty oath requirements, where refusal on First Amendment grounds to answer questions regarding loyalty results in termination of employment. Many of these statutes have been overturned for overbreadth and vagueness, and therefore for infringing upon an individual's right of belief, expression and association.[129] Federal courts vigorously protect individual rights guaranteed under the First Amendment against federal and state administrative infringement.

Freedom of Religion. Another constitutional policy deriving from the First Amendment that affects school administration and of which federal courts are the ultimate guarantors is the right to freedom of religion. The First Amendment contains two protections: (1) the prohibition against legislation "respecting an establishment of religion," designed to prevent an excessive entanglement between politics and religion; and (2) the free exercise clause, which guarantees to every individual the right to hold whatever religious beliefs and opinions he chooses, without infringement by the state on those beliefs. With respect to the establishment clause, the U.S. Supreme Court in *Epperson v. Arkansas*[130] invalidated an Arkansas statute forbidding the teaching of evolution in state-supported schools or universities because the statute was not religiously neutral but was designed to advance the Christian faith. The First Amendment, ruled the Court, "mandates governmental neutrality between religion and religion, and between religion and nonreligion."[131] The Court has also invalidated school policies of released-time religious instruction, where religious teachers are permitted to come into schools during hours set aside for secular teaching and substitute religious teaching for secular teaching[132]; although such released-time sectarian instruction was done at no expense to the schools and was not compulsory, nonparticipating students were still compelled to attend school, tax supported property was being used for religious instruction, and, together with the state's compulsory education system, the Court felt that the practice violated the establishment clause (although a similar practice was upheld in *Zorach v. Clauson*[133] because attendance was at religious centers outside of school).

The Court has also acted to nullify school board requirements demanding that a specific prayer be recited aloud before school each morning or that Bible verses be read.[134] The Court felt that such practices violate both the establishment clause and the free exercise clause, and are politically divisive. These school prayer decisions created considerable public furor, even resulting in proposals to amend the Constitution to specifically permit prayer reading in schools. The Supreme Court has also protected to some extent the practices of particular religious faiths under the free exercise clause, where those practices conflicted with state law or school regulations. In a historic decision in *Pierce v. Society of Sisters,*[135] the Court struck down an Oregon statute that prohibited attendance at nonpublic schools, upholding the right of parents to send their children to sectarian schools. The Court has also invalidated school board policies requiring all children to salute the flag and recite the pledge of allegiance, where to do so would offend a child's religious beliefs, thereby preventing state infringement of the free exercise of religion of certain faiths.[136]

Judicial enforcement of First Amendment protections of religion and expression exemplifies a federal judicial role most nearly consistent with that historically perceived. The constitutional policy is plainly declared: Federal courts engage in no policy-making, no departure from established doctrine to achieve desirable social ends, invade no province reserved to the states. The federal courts merely enforce the law. This is not to say, however, that the tensions between individual freedoms and state regulation are resolved; only that the role, authority, and responsibility of the federal courts in the process of resolution is clear and unambiguous.

IV. Federal Litigation and the Lobbies

The principal role of lobby organizations is legislative, to effect enactment of legislation that furthers the objectives of the organization or the defeat of antithetical legislation. The motives of lobbies are not limited to achieving legislative objectives, but lobby activity can fairly be said to be directed primarily at legislation. Federal court decisions often precipitate lobby activity in support of legislation which would overrule a court decision, as, for example, congressional attempts to end forced bussing as an available judicial remedy. Court decisions often dramatize the limitations of existing federal legislation or of the Constitution, generating lobby activity for remedial or supplemental legislation, as in the case of the National School Lunch Act or efforts subsequent to *Rodriguez* to provide federal funds to equalize interdistrict school expenditures. Again, these are legislative activities of lobbies and are described in more detail elsewhere in this book.

Lobbies also affect litigation directly. Lobby organizations often participate in litigation by filing amicus curiae, or "friend of the court," briefs, presenting to federal courts the special perspective or interest which the organization seeks to protect—a petitioning process not unlike the legislative role, though far less influential. In *Rodriguez,* for example, lobby organizations supporting plaintiffs as amici included the National Education Association, American Association of School Administrators, National Congress of Parents and Teachers, and the AFL-CIO; against plaintiffs were, among others, the Securities Industry Association, Inc., which regarded *Rodriguez* as a potential impairment of school district bond obligations. Lobbies and quasi lobbies also participate in litigation by providing financial assistance to legal organizations engaged in litigation of educational disputes. Private foundations, for example, extensively support public interest law firms engaged in educational litigation.

V. Conclusion

Federal judicial power in resolving educational disputes loomed large in the aftermath of *Brown*. Indeed, the last two decades have witnessed a considerable expansion and development of that power, as the body of case law has now grown to proportions that permit characterization and definition of the role of federal courts in education. Federal courts have been decisive in resolving educational disputes arising under the equal protection and due process clauses of the Fourteenth Amendment, the First Amendment protections of religion and expression, and congressional enactments providing financial assistance to state and local educational agencies. For the most part, the federal judiciary has acted in a prohibitory fashion, i.e., to prevent infringement on constitutionally and statutorily created rights and interests. Only in the area of desegregation, where the Supreme Court has enunciated an affirmative duty to integrate school systems, has there been judicial foray into constructive policy-making, a venture not so successful as gallant. Such restraint is consistent with the limited role of federal courts, conceived not as a policy body but as a dispute-settler.

The outer contours of the judicial power latent in *Brown*, a power with the potential for policy-making, have also been realized, although the tension between the desire for reform and the inherent limitations of the judiciary leave the exact boundary lines indistinct. Educational policy-making is ultimately a state and local function, a power reserved under the Tenth Amendment. The federal government exercises only a limited control over either the financing or the administration of educational programs; federal dollars are but a small percentage of total expenditures on education from all sources. *Rodriguez* held that education is not a fundamental federal right for purposes of the equal protection clause of the Fourteenth Amendment because it is not explicitly or implicitly guaranteed by the Constitution. Federal judicial power in litigating educational disputes, moverover, is not concerned with truly educational matters but with broader social and libertarian interests, such as racial equality, free speech, and religious neutrality. An exception, albeit not extensive, is judicial enforcement of congressional educational policy. Federal courts and the federal government, granted but a small role in the framework of educational decision-making, generally have little power in the policy process.

Perhaps the most significant aspect of the scope and nature of the federal judicial role in education is the tension between the necessity for educational reform and the restraints of federalism and separation of powers. The Warren Court set aside restraint to champion reform, and "only history will know whether the Warren Court has struck the balance right."[137] Others question the choice to "bet on the future," and challenge "the intuitive judicial capacity to identify the course of progress."[138] Courts, it is argued, are not designed to be policy-makers:

The judicial process is too principle-prone and principle-bound—it has to be, there is no other justification or explanation for the role it plays. It is also too remote from conditions, and deals, case by case, with too narrow a slice of reality. It is not accessible to all the varied interests that are in play, in any decision of great consequence. It is, very properly, independent. It is passive. It has difficulty controlling the stages by which it approaches a problem. It rushes forward too fast, or it lags; its pace hardly ever seems just right. For all these reasons, it is, in a vast, complex, changeable society, a most unsuitable instrument for the formation of policy.[139]

Such a perception of the federal judicial process, however valid, gives little comfort to those members of our society who suffer most from the pervasive inadequacies of a creaking, archaic educational system sadly in need of repair. However, the tension between egalitarian urgency and judicial self-restraint is a propelling, organic, and essential characteristic of constitutional policy regarding education, a perpetual process of definition and limitation. That the tension exists at all is a testament to the capacity of each branch of government to create, generate, and contribute to a dialectical process that is even more primary than the policy resolutions it demands, a testament to the living, life-giving fabric of justice.

Notes

1. U.S. Const., art. III, 2. The full scope of federal jurisdiction as defined by § 2 of Article III is as follows:

"The judicial Power shall extend to all Cases, in Law and Equity, arising under this Constitution, the Laws of the United States, and Treaties made, or which shall be made, under their Authority; to all Cases affecting Ambassadors, other public Ministers and Consuls; to all Cases of admiralty and maritime Jurisdiction; to Controversies to which the United States shall be a Party; to Controversies between two or more States; between a State and Citizens of another

State; between Citizens of different States, between Citizens of the same State claiming Lands under Grants of different States, and between a State, or the Citizens thereof, and foreign States, Citizens or Subjects.

"In all Cases affecting Ambassadors, other public Ministers and Consuls, and those in which a State shall be Party, the supreme Court shall have original Jurisdiction. In all the other Cases before mentioned, the supreme Court shall have appellate Jurisdiction, both as to Law and Fact, with such Exceptions, and under such Regulations as the Congress shall make."

2. 5 U.S. (1 Cranch) 137 (1803).

3. *Barrera v. Wheeler,* 475 F.2d 1338 (8th Cir. 1973), *rev. granted,* No. 73-62, 42 U.S.L.W. 3213 (1973).

4. 347 U.S. 497 (1954).

5. See page 220.

6. 42 U.S.L.W. 2021 (D.C. Cir. June 12, 1973).

7. 347 U.S. 483 (1954).

8. See page 222.

9. A. Bickel, *The Supreme Court and the Idea of Progress* (1970), p. 82.

10. Ibid., p. 38.

11. J. Coons, W. Clune, and S. Sugarman, *Private Wealth and Public Education* (1970); A. Wise, *Rich Schools, Poor Schools: The Promise of Equal Educational Opportunity* (1968); Horowitz and Neitring, "Equal Protection Aspects of Inequalities in Public Education and Public Assistance Programs from Place to Place Within a State," 15 *U.C.L.A. L. Rev.* 787 (1968).

12. Berke and Kelly, "The Financial Aspects of Equality of Educational Opportunity," in *Senate Select Committee on Equal Educational Opportunity, Issues in School Finance,* 92d Cong., 2d Sess. 96-97 (1972) (hereinafter cited as *Issues in School Finance*).

13. J. Coons et al., *Private Wealth and Public Education.*

14. J. Guthrie, G. Kleindorfer, H. Levin, and R. Stout, *Schools and Inequality* (1969); C. Jencks, *Inequality* (1973); U.S. Office of Education, *Equality of Educational Opportunity* (1966) (Coleman Report); D. Moynihan and F. Mosteller, eds., *On Equality of Educational Opportunity* (1972).

15. 411 U.S. 1 (1973).

16. *Police Dept. of the City of Chicago v. Mosley,* 408 U.S. 92 (1972); *Dunn v. Blumstein,* 405 U.S. 330 (1972); *Graham v. Richardson,* 403 U.S. 365 (1971); *Shapiro v. Thompson,* 394 U.S. 618 (1969); *Loving v. Virginia,* 388 U.S. 1 (1967); *McLaughlin v. Florida,* 379 U.S. 184 (1964); see also Comment, "Developments in the Law—Equal Protection," 82 *Harv. L. Rev.* 1065 (1969); Tussman and ten Broek, "The Equal Protection of the Laws," 37 *Calif. L. Rev.* 341 (1949).

17. Gunther, "Foreword: In Search of Evolving Doctrine on a Changing Court: A Model for a Newer Equal Protection," 86 *Harv L. Rev.* 1 (1972); see Justice Marshall's dissent in *Rodriguez,* 411 U.S. at 98-110, for identification and analysis of cases departing from the two-level test and for a proposed alternative standard for measuring the validity of legislative classifications.

18. 293 F. Supp. 327 (N.D. Ill. 1968), *affg. mem. sub nom., McInnis v. Ogilvie,* 394 U.S. 322 (1969).

19. J. Coons et al., *Private Wealth and Public Education.*

20. 5 Cal.3d 584 (1971).

21. 411 U.S. at 28.

22. Ibid.

23. See, e.g., Horowitz, "Unseparate for Unequal—The Emerging Fourteenth Amendment Issue in Public School Education," 13 *U.C.L.A. L. Rev.* 787 (1968).

24. 411 U.S. at 30.

25. Ibid. at 33-34.

26. Ibid. at 71.

27. 347 U.S. at 493.

28. 411 U.S. at 44.

29. 339 U.S. 629 (1950).

30. 163 U.S. 537 (1896).

31. 339 U.S. at 633-634.

32. 339 U.S. 637 (1950).

33. Ibid. at 641.

34. *Pennsylvania Assn. for Retarded Children v. Pennsylvania,* 343 F. Supp. 279 (E.D. Pa. 1972).

35. *Issues in School Finance,* pp. 166-190.

36. Oregon Const., art. VIII, §3.

37. Idaho Const., art. IX, §1.

38. *Issues in School Finance,* pp. 166-190.

39. *Robinson v. Cahill,* 62 N.J. 473, 303 A.2d 373 (1973).

40. 411 U.S. at 111-112.

41. Ibid. at 58.

42. State legislative reform in the absence of a court order may not be complete or permanent, and of those states recently enacting legislation only Kansas, Maine, and Florida give lasting relief. Justice Marshall, dissenting in *Rodriguez,* expressed similar doubts about the probability of legislative relief, a belief instrumental to his willingness to have the judiciary intervene. 411 U.S. at 71-72.

43. S. 2414, 93d Cong., 1st Sess. (1973).

44. Berke and Kirst, "The Federal Role in American School Finance: A Fiscal and Administrative Analysis," 61 *Geo. L.J.* 927, 933 (1973).

45. 20 U.S.C. §§13, 16, 19, 21.

46. Berke and Kirst, "The Federal Role in American School Finance," p. 933.

47. 310 F. Supp. 1282 (E.D. Calif. 1970).

48. *Briggs v. Kerrigan,* 307 F. Supp. 295 (D. Mass. 1969), *aff'd* 431 F.2d 967 (1970); *Ayala v. District 60 School Bd. of Pueblo, Colo.,* 327 F. Supp. 980 (D. Colo. 1971).

49. *Ayala,* supra note 48.

50. *Briggs,* supra note 48.

51. See 42 U.S.C. §1758 as amended. see also Note, "The National School Lunch Program, 1970: Mandate to Feed the Children," 60 *Geo. L.J.* 711 (1972).

52. 42 U.S.C. §2000d (1969).

53. See discussion at note 107 infra.

54. 42 U.S.L.W. 2021 (D.C. Cir. June 12, 1973).

55. Committee of the Office of Attorney General, National Association of Attorneys General, *Memorandum: Impoundment of Federal Funds* (September 20, 1973); Note, "Impoundment of Funds," 86 *Harv L. Rev.* 1505 (1973); Note, "Protecting the Fisc: Executive Impoundment and Congressional Power," 82 *Yale L.J.* 1636 (1973).

56. *State of Oklahoma v. Weinberger*, 360 F. Supp. 724 (W.D. Okla. 1973). A similar result was reached in *Commonwealth of Massachusetts v. Weinberger*, Civil No. 1308-73 (D.D.C. July 29, 1973), holding that no discretion existed over the allotment of NDEA funds.

57. *Minnesota Chippewa Tribe v. Carlucci*, Civil No. 175-73 (D.D.C. May 8, 1973).

58. Comm'n on Educ. Finance, National Education Association, *1972 Financial Status of the Public Schools* (1972), p. 40.

59. 20 U.S.C. § 1221 et seq. (1969).

60. Ibid. § 1232a.

61. See, e.g., 20 U.S.C. § 1263(a)(11) (Vocational Education Act of 1963), § 241 (Impact aid), § 832(a)(5), § 845(e) (Title I), § 880(b)(c) (Bilingual Education Act), § 1413(a)(4) (Education of the Handicapped Act), and § 1005(a)(4) (Higher Education Act community service programs).

62. 280 F. Supp. 869 (E.D. Va. 1968).

63. *Douglas Independent Sch. Dist. No. 3 v. Jorgensen*, 293 F. Supp. 849 (D.S.D. 1968); *Hergenreiter v. Hayden*, 295 F. Supp. 251 (D. Kan. 1968); *Triplett v. Tieman*, 302 F. Supp. 1244 (D. Neb. 1969); *Carlsbad Union Sch. Dist. of San Diego County v. Rafferty*, 300 F. Supp. 434 (S.D. Cal. 1969), 429 F.2d 337 (9th Cir. 1970).

64. 20 U.S.C. § 240(d) (1969).

65. Berke and Kirst, "The Federal Role in American School Finance," p. 951.

66. Martin and McClure, *Title I of ESEA. Is It Helping Poor Children?* (1969).

67. 20 U.S.C. § 241e(a)(3)(C) (1969): "State and local funds will be used in the district of such agency to provide services in project areas which, taken as a whole, are at least comparable to services being provided in areas in such district which are not receiving funds under this subchapter: *Provided,* That any finding of noncompliance with this clause shall not affect the payment of funds to any local educational agency until the fiscal year beginning July 1, 1972, and *Provided further,* That each local educational agency receiving funds under this subchapter shall report on or before July 1, 1971, and on or before July 1 of each year thereafter with respect to its compliance with this clause."

68. 36 Fed. Reg. 199, pp. 20016-17 (October 14, 1971), 45 C.F.R. 116.26 (1971).

69. Lawyers Committee for Civil Rights under Law, *Title I Comparability: A Preliminary Evaluation* (September 1972).

70. *Natonahah v. Board of Educ. of Gallup–McKinley High School District*, 355 F. Supp. 716 (D.N. Mex. 1973).

71. No. 72-1596 (E.D. Pa. 1973).

72. See Badger and Browning, "Title I and Comparability: Recent Developments," 7 *Clearinghouse Rev.* 263 (1973).

73. 38 Fed. Reg. 124, pp. 17126-28 (June 28, 1973), 45 C.F.R. 116.26 (1973).

74. 31 U.S.C. § 1221 et seq. (1969).

75. S.B. 90, Ch. 1475 (1972); see also S.B. 90 Conference Report (November 22, 1972).

76. S. 1669, 92d Cong., 1st Sess. (1971); H.R. 7796, 92d Cong., 1st Sess. (1971); see also President's Message to Congress Proposing Educational Revenue-Sharing, 117 *Congressional Record* H2469-71 (daily ed., April 6, 1971).

77. *Mathews v. Massell,* 41 U.S.L.W. 2525 (1973).

78. 403 U.S. 602 (1971).

79. Ibid. at 612-613.

80. Ibid. at 617.

81. *Committee for Public Education and Religious Liberty v. Nyquist,* 413 U.S. 756 (1973).

82. *Levitt v. Committee for Public Education and Religious Liberty,* 413 U.S. 472 (1973).

83. *Sloan v. Lemon,* 413 U.S. 825 (1973).

84. 403 U.S. 672 (1971).

85. Supra, note 3.

86. 347 U.S. 497 (1954).

87. Ibid. at 493-495.

88. *Briggs v. Elliott,* 132 F. Supp. 776 (E.D. S.C. 1955).

89. 391 U.S. 430 (1968).

90. Ibid. at 437-438.

91. Ibid. at 439.

92. See the concurring opinion of Justice Powell in *Keyes v. School District No. 1,* 413 U.S. 189, 217 (1973).

93. 391 U.S. at 432-433 (1968).

94. *Barksdale v. Springfield School Committee,* 237 F. Supp. 543 (D. Mass. 1965), *rev'd on other grounds,* 348 F.2d 261 (1st Cir. 1965); *Jackson v. Pasadena City School District,* 59 Cal.2d 876, 382 P.2d 878 (1963); see also Wright, "Public School Desegregation: Legal Remedies for De Facto Segregation," 40 *N.Y.U. L. Rev.* 283, 298-301 (1965) ("The touchstone in determining equality of the law in public education is equality of educational opportunity, not race." Ibid. at 301).

95. *Blocker v. Board of Education,* 226 F. Supp. 208 (E.D. N.Y. 1964); *Branche v. Board of Education,* 204 F. Supp. 150 (E.D. N.Y. 1962); *Jackson v. Pasadena City School District,* 59 Cal.2d 876 (1963).

96. *Bell v. School City of Gary, Ind.,* 324 F. 2d 209 (7th Cir. 1963); *Downs v. Bd. of Educ. of Kansas City,* 336 F.2d 988 (10th Cir. 1964); *Deal v. Cincinnati Bd. of Educ.,* 369 F.2d 55 (6th Cir. 1966), *cert. den.* 389 U.S. 847 (1967).

97. 413 U.S. 189 (1973).

98. Ibid. at 208.

99. 462 F.2d 1058 (4th Cir. 1972), *aff'd per curiam,* 412 U.S. 92 (1973).

100. 462 F.2d at 1065.

101. Nos. 72-1809, 1814, 41 U.S.L.W. 2192, 2841 (1972).

102. Ibid. at 42 U.S.L.W. 2022 (6th Cir. 1973), *app.* 42 U.S.L.W. 3169 (1973).

103. 402 U.S. § 1 (1971).

104. 20 U.S.C. § 1651 et seq. (1969).

105. *Drummond v. Acree,* 409 U.S. 1228 (1972).

106. See Bell, "Congressional Response to Busing," 61 *Geo. L.J.* 963 (1973).

107. The interplay in attempting to end racial discrimination in the nation's schools among the courts, the Congress, the Office of Education, and the Justice Department deserves special mention. As noted, Title VI of the Civil Rights Act of 1964 requires the termination of federal financial assistance to any school district engaged in racially discriminatory practices. The Office of Education was to assist the federal courts in bringing about the end of dual educational

systems; the Justice Department was authorized to bring suit to compel desegregation. For several years, the Supreme Court deferred to the Office of Education on matters of desegregation policy. The USOE issued guidelines for determining whether dual school systems could qualify for federal financial assistance, and even withdrew federal funds from some school districts. Yet HEW guidelines, which were limited by the Civil Rights Act to desegregation only and were not to correct all racial imbalance, did not go far enough for the courts, which had begun extending the *Brown* decision to a policy requiring an affirmative duty to achieve a unitary school system. (See the discussion of *Green* at p. 229.)

The break finally came in 1969 in *Alexander v. Holmes County Board of Education*, 396 U.S. 19 (1969), in which the Supreme Court reversed a lower court decision permitting additional time to desegregate thirty-three Mississippi school districts—a delay agreed to by the Justice Department—and ordered an immediate termination of the dual systems. See Note, "The Supreme Court, 1969 Term," 84 *Harv. L. Rev.* 1, 32-46 (1970); Note, "The Courts, HEW and Southern School Desegregation," 77 *Yale L. Rev.* 321 (1967). HEW's statutory restriction, together with the Nixon administration policy against forced bussing to achieve racial balance, resulted in a failure by the USOE and the Justice Department to aggressively enforce desegregation. The federal courts alone were left to enforce the equal protection guarantees of the Constitution. Recently, however, in *Adams v. Richardson* (supra, note 6), HEW was specifically ordered to enforce both the Civil Rights Act and its own guidelines for desegregation. HEW had found ten states operating segregated systems of higher education in violation of Title VI of the Civil Rights Act, 42 U.S.C. §2000d (1969). HEW had also found several school districts in violation of Title VI. HEW had ordered the ten states to file proposed compliance reports, but five had not done so at all and the plans submitted by the others were totally inadequate. HEW was ordered to begin compliance proceedings if satisfactory plans were not submitted within 120 days. The rule of law requires uniform treatment, regardless of the political ideology of the administration in power, and the federal courts act to demand evenhanded administration.

108. 472 F.2d 909 (9th Cir. 1973), *cert. granted*, No. 72-6520, 41 U.S.L.W. 3644 (June 11, 1973).

109. 351 F. Supp. 1279 (D.N.M. 1972).

110. 321 F. Supp. 1043 (E.D. Tex. 1970), *aff'd* 447 F.2d 441 (5th Cir. 1971), *stay den.* 404 U.S. 1206 (Black, 1971).

111. _____ U.S. _____ (1974).

112. See the exhaustive discussion in Kirp, "Schools as Sorters: The Constitutional Policy Implications of Student Classification," 121 *U. Pa. L. Rev.* 705 (1973); see also McClung, "School Classification: Some Legal Approaches to Labels," *Inequality in Education* (July 1973), p. 17.

113. 343 F. Supp. 279 (E.D. Pa. 1972).

114. 348 F. Supp. 866 (D.D.C. 1972).

115. See the extensive procedural guidelines set forth in *Mills*, ibid. at 878-883.

116. McClung, "School Classification: Some Legal Approaches to Labels," 24.

117. 269 F. Supp. 401 (D.D.C. 1967), *aff'd sub som. Smuck v. Hobson*, 408 F.2d 175 (D.C. Cir. 1969).

118. 343 F. Supp. 1306 (N.D. Cal. 1972).

119. 393 U.S. 503 (1969).

120. Ibid. at 509, citing *Burnside v. Byars*, 363 F.2d 744, 749 (5th Cir. 1966).

121. *Shanley v. Northeast Ind. Sch. Dist.*, 462 F.2d 960 (5th Cir. 1972); *Eisner v. Stamford Bd. of Educ.*, Civil No. 13220 (D. Conn. 1970) (prior censorship); *Scoville v. Bd. of Educ. of Joliet Township High School District*, 425 F.2d 10 (7th Cir. 1970) (ban on handbill distribution). But cf. the relatively unsuccessful litigation regarding hair length. See, e.g., *Ferrell v. Dallas Independent Sch. Dist.*, 392 F.2d 697 (5th Cir. 1968), *cert. den.* 393 U.S. 856 (1968).

122. *Sullivan v. Houston Independent Sch. Dist.*, 475 F.2d 1071 (5th Cir. 1973); *Pervis v. LaMarque Independent Sch. Dist.*, 466 F.2d 1054 (5th Cir. 1972); *Vail v. Bd. of Educ.*, 354 F. Supp. 592 (D.N.H. 1973).

123. *Dixon v. Alabama State Bd. of Educ.*, 294 F.2d 150 (5th Cir. 1961) (due process in disciplinary proceedings); *Hammond v. South Carolina State College*, 272 F. Supp. 947 (D.S.C. 1967) (right to demonstrate); *Jones v. Board of Regents of the Univ. of Ariz.*, 436 F.2d 618 (9th Cir. 1970) (general right to pass out handbills on public campus); *Brooks v. Auburn University*, 412 F.2d 1171 (5th Cir. 1969) (right to have controversial speakers).

124. *Powe v. Miles*, 407 F.2d 73 (2d Cir. 1968); *Browns v. Mitchell*, 409 F.2d 593 (10th Cir. 1969).

125. 20 U.S.C. §1060(a) (1969).

126. 353 F. Supp. 973 (N.D. Ill. 1972).

127. 42 U.S.L.W. 2048 (9th Cir. 1973).

128. See discussion in Emerson, Haber, and Dorsen, *Political and Civil Rights in the United States*, vol. 1 (1967), p. 902 et seq.

129. *Keyishian v. Board of Regents*, 385 U.S. 589 (1967); *Whitehill v. Elkins*, 389 U.S. 54 (1967); *Elfbrandt v. Russell*, 384 U.S. 11 (1966).

130. 393 U.S. 97 (1968).

131. Ibid. at 104.

132. *Illinois ex rel. McCollum v. Bd. of Educ.*, 333 U.S. 203 (1948).

133. 343 U.S. 306 (1952).

134. *Engel v. Vitale*, 370 U.S. 421 (1962) (prayer); *School Dist. of Abington Township v. Schempp*, 374 U.S. 203 (1963) (Bible verses).

135. 268 U.S. 510 (1925).

136. *West Virginia State Bd. of Educ. v. Barnette*, 319 U.S. 624 (1943); *Goetz v. Ansell*, _____ F.2d _____ (2d Cir. 1973).

137. Cox, *The Warren Court* (1968), p. 133.

138. Bickel, *The Supreme Court and the Idea of Progress*, pp. 99, 173.

139. Ibid., p. 175.

The Flow of Federal Funds for Education

JAMES W. GUTHRIE

> *No money shall be drawn from the Treasury, but in conse-*
> *quence of appropriations made by law . . . .*—U.S. Consti-
> tution, Art. I., § 9, ¶ 7

As surprising as it may seem, the fact that John Brademas and
James Scheuer succeeded in gaining enactment of "their" bills in no
way guarantees that the federal treasury will ever issue a check to
fund programs authorized by those bills. For the money to flow it is
necessary that separate, though related, sets of executive and legislative branch machinery be set in motion. Our purpose here is to
describe that machinery.

Background

In order for there to be a federally funded program it is necessary
that there be both "authorization" and "appropriations" legislation.

The first is a product of the politics and procedures described earlier in this book. "Authorizations" provide shape and substantive legality for federal government action. They establish and describe the purposes for which federal funds can be spent. Frequently they also specify a dollar ceiling for the amount of money that annually can be spent on the endeavor at hand. However, with very few exceptions which will be described later, the federal government does not issue a "check" unless there is also an appropriations bill specifying the amount to be spent in a given year for the purposes authorized in substantive legislation.

Authorization procedures occupy the time of most congressional committees. However, each house of Congress also has an appropriations committee. These committees do not deal directly with substantive legislation, with "authorizations." Rather, they concentrate their efforts exclusively on determining dollar amounts to be allocated to already authorized federal programs. The beginning point for actions of the appropriations committees is the president's proposed budget for the forthcoming fiscal year (FY). Following appropriations committee actions, a money bill ultimately comes for approval before the full House and Senate. It is then returned to the president for his signature, and proceeds to executive branch agencies for implementation. The process is best described by beginning with the formation of the president's annual budget.

Preparing the President's Budget

A budget is a document that states the purposes for which future expenditures are intended. It can be viewed as a spending plan; it guides the purchase of materials and services. This is true whether it is a budget for a single family, for a business, or for the entire federal government. Like almost any plan, it can be altered should expected levels of income change or if added expenditures are thought necessary. Indeed, once published by the Government Printing Office, the president's budget has little prospect but to be changed. Almost immediately after it is submitted to Congress, the budget is divided into several pieces to be dissected and acted on by appropriations subcommittees, and it is never completely reassembled. Nevertheless, even if it is compiled only to be divided, the president's budget is important. It is a succinct summary of proposed national priorities.

Subsequent congressional debate, political trades, and compromises will alter the arrangement of some of these priorities. However, the outer boundaries for the debate are generally established by the president's proposed budget.

The president's budget is like any other fiscal plan in that it represents a set of proposed spending priorities. However, it differs from most other budgets in two ways. First, the U.S. government's budget is larger by many magnitudes than almost any other budget one can conceive. For example, for fiscal year 1974 (which began July 1, 1973), the Nixon administration's federal budget proposed expenditures totaling almost $269 billion; of this, the president proposed to spend in excess of $10 billion for education and manpower.[1]

The dollar magnitude involved brings us to the second feature that distinguishes the federal government budget from its private sector counterparts. In addition to establishing proposed program priorities, the federal budget is a primary instrument for planning and exercising control over the nation's entire economy. Federal fiscal policy (taxation and spending) has been a principal tool since FDR's administration for attempting to alleviate periods of inflation and depression. Here we come upon one of the major distinctions between the politics involved in authorization and those associated with appropriations. Federal education expenditures are not only subject to the political conditions that surround aid to education as a substantive issue, but also school dollars must survive the political conflicts around national economic and fiscal policy. Thus, the politics of the appropriations process are doubly complicated.

The president's budget functions to frame and initiate the debate over national priorities and doubles as a prime tool for tuning the nation's overall economy. Given these complicated functions and the remarkable dollar amounts involved, how is such a crucial document pieced together?

The Office of Management and Budget

The Office of Management and Budget (OMB) is responsible for compiling the president's budget, which contains the expenditure plans for all units of the federal government. However, the U.S. government has not always had a unified budget. Before 1921 each department was free to determine its own expenditure priorities and amounts and submit its individual budget before congressional appropriations committees. The Agriculture Department, Army and Navy, Department of Interior (of which the Office of Education was then a part), and the other departments, were all generally free agents when it came to requesting and lobbying for their respective financial resources. The president had little ability to control their expenditure patterns or their relations with Congress. As federal government complexity and expenses increased, the lack of a consolidated budget began to have grievous results. Such an uncontrolled system operated principally to the disadvantage of the president. To be sure, he appointed department executives and they also served as members of his cabinet. However, he had no direct authority over their budgets. Moreover, his lack of control over their relations with Congress meant that it was almost impossible for him to initiate and sustain a coherent legislative program. By using or threatening to use his veto power, the president could exercise negative influence. He could prevent major governmental actions that were antithetical to his position. However, the veto is a weak weapon for launching a positive program.

Woodrow Wilson well understood the degree to which budgetary fragmentation eroded the president's power. In the later years of his administration he authorized a presidential commission, chaired by Charles Dawes, to study government budgeting procedures and to recommend reforms. Its recommendations were embodied in the Budgeting and Accounting Act, signed into law by President Warren G. Harding on June 10, 1921. The act provided for a budget director, who was housed with the Treasury Department. Mr. Dawes was appointed the first director and he became responsible for consolidating executive branch budget requests so that they could be submitted to Congress in one comprehensive piece.[2]

In 1939 the Bureau of the Budget was removed from Treasury and installed as one of the critical units within what is known as the Executive Office of the President.[3] As of 1972 its name was changed to the Office of Management and Budget (OMB), a label that better connotes its expanded role. From its simple beginnings as an agency designed to coordinate federal government budget policy, OMB has grown to be the clearinghouse for almost all executive branch activity. "Central clearance," the coordination and monitoring of communication, is necessary on all major interactions of an executive branch agency with Congress and it is OMB officials who perform the clearance function.

These management and budgeting activities have become so crucial for presidents that the OMB has gradually evolved into one of the most important units within the executive branch. Its staff has increased substantially over the few dozen who were initially employed by Dawes. Nevertheless, OMB is not the huge bureaucracy one might envision necessary to perform such important tasks. In 1973 OMB contained only 660 permanent positions (as specified in the federal government budget for fiscal year 1973). The office makes its presence felt by the extraordinary competence of most of its staff members, and it multiplies their capabilities by utilizing the services of officials throughout the executive branch bureaucracy. It is these OMB professionals who have primary responsibility for assembling the president's budget. We will turn shortly to a description of the stages in that process. First, however, we wish to explain elementary relationships between the budget and national fiscal and economic planning.

Federal Spending and the Nation's Economy

In building the president's budget, great consideration must be given to the general state of the nation's economy. This is so not only because federal expenditures are partly determined by anticipated federal revenues, but also because federal expenditures, or the absence of them, have their own economic impact. When the economy is not operating at full capacity, when unemployment is high and there is unused productive capability, then federal expenditures can be increased to pick up the slack and create added job opportunities. Lower taxes can work in the same direction by supplying consumers with added purchasing power. Conversely, when the economy appears overheated, when demand exceeds productive capacity and prices are in an inflationary spiral, a reduction in federal spending and an increase in taxes can act to reduce purchasing and to slow inflation.

The idea of using federal expenditure and taxing patterns to balance the economy has been current since the 1930s when the concept was employed to soften the impact of the Great Depression. However, in 1969 the Nixon administration inserted a refinement in the fiscal tuning process labeled the "full employment budget."[4] This concept provides a baseline against which to judge the desirability and degree of federal over or under spending. Using the full employment principle, calculations can be made as to what federal revenues would be if the economy were balanced and unemployment at an acceptably low level (approximately 4 percent). The amount of federal deficit spending or federal savings (an excess of revenues over expenditures) can then be determined to bring predicted economic conditions into line with what is desired.

Figure 1 demonstrates the relationship between federal government deficits and surpluses for the period 1964-1975 based on the full employment budget principle. The plus and minus conditions represent federal spending (and saving) patterns calculated to bring the economy into a balanced position. Notice, for example, that

Figure 1. Full Employment Budget—Surplus or Deficit

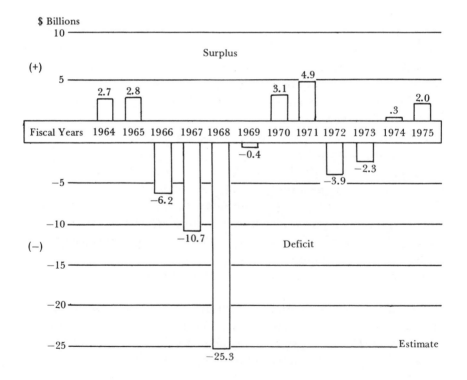

fiscal years 1971 and 1972 were projected to be recessionary. The nation's productive machinery was operating below capacity and unemployment was high. Therefore a full employment budget policy dictated federal deficit spending, almost $4 billion in 1971 and $2.3 billion in 1972. However, by fiscal year 1973 federal "pump priming" efforts were successful and the economy was predicted to be inflated. Reverse action is called for and the Treasury should take in more revenue than it disburses. Thus, by a series of successive approximations the intent is to balance the economy, with no extremes of either inflation or recession.

When the state of the economy dictates that federal expenditures should be speeded up, slowed down, delayed, or drawn out, education expenditures tend to be among the first affected. This is so because dollars for school-related programs represent one of the few places in the budget where the president has a degree of discretion. Many of the other federal government programs have mandatory expenditures built into the statutes authorizing them. For example, Medicare payments to the aged and medical payments to the poor, Social Security payments, and veterans' pensions are substantially beyond the president's ability to control. The government must disburse whatever is owed under such programs. When, for example, predictions of the economy dictate a reduction in federal expenditures, the president cannot gain much leverage on the situation by manipulating built-in expenditures of the kind listed. Rather, attention must be given to the relatively few discretionary areas in the budget, for example, school aid funds.

This is not to say that the president can recommend reductions in federal aid to education without running the risk of political reprisals. Every government expenditure has an attached clientele or constituency, and school funds are no exception. Education lobbies resist tenaciously when cuts in appropriations to education are proposed. Whether or not the president's proposals can withstand the onslaught of such political actions is a complicated question that requires description of the entire funding cycle. The point here is that, political consequences aside, aid to education is one of the points at which federal budget reduction and expansion decisions can be exercised, and what the president proposes by way of education expenditures is a function not only of where education stands in his list of national priorities, but is also related to the state of the economy and whatever overall federal fiscal policy the president believes is necessary.

In the final analysis, the president's budget is but a set of *proposed* priorities. Congress can, and usually does, alter the president's plan. Does this mean that the somewhat delicate fiscal tuning procedures contained in the president's proposals are thereafter emasculated? If Congress decides that more or less should be spent or taxes should be lower or higher than the president proposes, is all hope of manipulating the economy lost? The answer is no. [There do exist a number of "automatic" economic stabilizers which can go into effect relatively free of presidential or congressional action. Transfer payments (e.g., unemployment and welfare payments) and taxes are the two best examples. In a recession or depression, unemployment payments increase and personal income tax payments decrease; both place more disposable income in the hands of the public. In a period of inflation, the converse is the case. In addition to such automatic fiscal stabilizers, there exist possible alterations to monetary policy, e.g., federal reserve interest rates, which are outside the boundaries of immediate control by either the president or Congress.]

Congressional action contrary to the budget undoubtedly makes economic planning more difficult for the president, but it does not eliminate his planning capability. He has several cards remaining at his disposal after Congress plays out its hand. First, if the president deems congressional action to be "irresponsible" in one direction or another, he can veto the particular appropriations bill or bills involved. It is true that Congress can attempt to override such a veto, but because it takes a two-thirds majority of both houses to do so, it is infrequently the case that such happens.

Secondly, should the president feel that a veto is unwise, he may resort to various means for delaying or stretching out the spending of the money. For example, if an appropriations act allocates $1 billion for student loans, the president may order the OMB to withhold a substantial portion of the amount until the third or fourth quarter of the fiscal year. This would slow down the effect of the money entering and fueling the economy.

Indeed, if the president so chooses, he may not spend appropriated funds at all, a procedure known as "impounding." This is an extraordinarily controversial action, the constitutionality of which has yet to be determined. Because it has been employed with increasing frequency during the 1970s, it is a topic to which we will return in greater detail later.

Vetoes, delays, and impoundments are all procedures that return the reins of fiscal control to the president. However, he pays a political price for wielding them. When he does so he counters the expressed will of Congress and invites the antagonism of a variety of constituencies. Consequently, it is substantially to the president's advantage to have Congress cooperate with him in establishing and implementing fiscal policy. Presidents have attempted to do so overtly by explaining in detail why they have adopted particular overall expenditure and tax plans. In addition, they have requested of Congress that it reform its procedures for handling the budget so that there might be the same degree of coordination and centralization in congressional responses to the president's proposals as there is in compiling those proposals. Presidents hope that Congress can see its way to adopt a spending ceiling for each fiscal year and then adhere to it. If done in agreement with the president's calculations about the amount of the fiscal target, it would be a giant stride toward cooperative economic planning between the executive and legislative branches, and the president would be relieved of his relatively lonely role as guardian of the nation's economic stability. (Of course, he is by no means totally alone, even if Congress "abandons" him. The Federal Reserve System can exercise a range of monetary policies to exact control over the economy.)

The "Unified Federal Budget"

Before turning to a detailed description of how the federal budget is assembled, it is important to clarify one additional concept. There are a number of ways in which federal fiscal policy could be reported. Until the middle of the 1960s different administrations used different budget formats to report their fiscal plans. These variations, whatever their benefits, served only to confuse congressmen, the press, and the public. Consequently, while in office Lyndon B. Johnson appointed the President's Commission on Budget Concepts in March 1967. The commission recommended that the federal government move to a "unified budget," and, with a few exceptions, this was adopted for the fiscal 1969 budget and has been employed since that time.[5]

Several features distinguish a unified budget from other types. Foremost is its comprehensive nature. It includes: (1) budget authority being requested by the president as well as existing authority which will become available even in the absence of presidential action; (2) all receipts, intended expenditures, and loans; (3) the budget surplus or deficit; (4) the means by which the deficit or surplus is to be financed; and (5) the impact of the proposed federal budget on federal debt outstanding and federal debt held by the public. In the unified budget, receipts from special trust funds such as health, Social Security, old-age, survivors, and disability trust funds, are included under expenditures and receipts. The unified budget also carefully distinguishes between loans and other kinds of expenditures. It even takes federally guaranteed or insured loans into account.

The unified budget can be contrasted with other budget formats that have either been used previously or proposed. For example, the previously used administrative budget excluded mention of funds that were federally controlled but which, technically speaking, were not federally owned. And, in another administrative budget, the expenditures and receipts that take place under federal trust accounts were not mentioned. Similarly, from time to time it is proposed that the federal government move to a "capital budgeting" system wherein the budget is separated into (1) current and operating expenditures and (2) capital accounts.[6] The latter, as in businesses, would be expenditures for nonrecurring purchases of durable goods. Federal loans used to obtain capital assets would not be listed as deficits because the government had acquired a balancing asset. The federal government's ownership of capital assets would be more completely acknowledged and such assets could be depreciated in a systematic fashion.

Opponents of capital budgeting argue that thus arranging receipts and expenditure items would grant unfair political advantage to proponents of capital outlays. Expenditures would not have to be noted as deficits and thus would be politically more acceptable than deficits incurred for services. Whatever the relative merits of various budget formats, the unified budget now draws our attention. By compiling such a document, the president, the Congress, and the public have the basic information necessary to determine both national economic policy and priorities for programs such as financial aid to education.

The Budget Cycle

Surprisingly, it takes longer to prepare and to reach agreement on the federal government's budget than it does to spend the funds the budget specifies. The fiscal year for which budgets are geared lasts for twelve months, but the budget planning and approval cycle lasts for eighteen months. Following transmission to Congress, usually in January prior to the July 1 beginning of the fiscal year for which the budget is intended, it takes at least six months for all appropriation processes to run their course. Indeed, frequently Congress has not completed work on all appropriations bills before the beginning of the fiscal year. Then a set of special arrangements must be followed for federal programs and agencies to continue operating; these will be discussed later in this chapter.

We turn our immediate attention to the first two-thirds of the budget cycle, the executive branch assembly efforts.

January to June. The budget cycle begins almost immediately after the just-completed budget is sent to Congress. Thus, after the president delivered the fiscal year 1974 budget to Congress in January 1973, work began on the fiscal year 1975 budget. The early weeks of the budget cycle are characterized by a number of broadscale planning activities. OMB officials confer among themselves and with their counterparts in executive branch agencies on the information and budget studies that will be useful in assembling and justifying a particular agency's budget for the fiscal year under consideration. For example, OMB may want to assess the necessity for continuing to distribute federal funds under Public Laws 815 and 874. These two authorities grant funds to local school districts in accordance with the number of pupils whose parents either work for the federal government or who live on federally owned land. These funds are, in effect, an in-lieu-of-tax payment made by the federal government to local school districts. The degree to which federal projects and installations exert an economic hardship on a school district is debatable, and the suspicion frequently arises that PL 815 and 874 funds are an unnecessary federal expenditure. Consequently, OMB examiners have periodically requested "objective" studies of the need for such monies. Studies of this nature are the kind about which discussions would be held early in the budget cycle.[7]

A second kind of activity that begins in the initial part of the planning cycle is compilation of information about the predicted state of the economy in the fiscal year being planned. Several groups take part in these discussions. Economists from the Council of Economic Advisors (CEA), OMB, the Department of Commerce, and the Treasury Department pool their understandings of present and predicted economic conditions in an effort to arrive at an agreed-on forecast. This forecast serves as a beginning base for budget planning. It will indicate the degree to which a surplus should be created or deficit spending engaged in. By any criterion, this is a difficult task. It is substantially more tricky than shooting at a moving target, because the federal government's fiscal actions will themselves affect the speed at which the target moves. Nevertheless, by early to mid-March a general economic picture has been painted covering the next six- to eighteen-month period.

April to September. Armed with economic forecasts, the president and OMB officials compose a "budget assumption statement," which describes the general economic framework of the federal government budget. The degree to which the budget is to be balanced, a surplus accumulated or a deficit incurred, is specified, and guidelines for new obligational authority (NOA) are spelled out. ("New obligational authority" refers to the ability of an agency to encumber additional expenses, expenditures beyond those permitted by existing appropriations or automatic spending statutes.) The budget statement is discussed with cabinet officers and eventually transmitted through them and their budget officers (each department has its own budget official, generally in the capacity of an assistant secretary) to the various agencies, bureaus, and branches which comprise the executive arm of our government.

Office of Management and Budget staff have available to them from previous years the five-year expenditure projections of department agencies and bureaus. Nevertheless, all units are requested to reexamine their needs and estimates for the forthcoming fiscal year and tailor them to the president's economic guidelines. Agencies are also asked to revise and resubmit their five-year expenditure estimates. Thus, in July and August, from the smallest units embedded deep within the federal bureaucracy, budget estimates begin to percolate upward.

There are nodules along the way at which requests are aggregated, negotiated, and again passed upward to the next level. Finally, all budget requests for a particular department are aggregated. Within the Department of Health, Education, and Welfare this task is conducted by the assistant secretary-comptroller. Then, in conjunction with the secretary and other high-ranking HEW officials, the entire budget is again reviewed agency by agency. At this point, touching on education specifically, if the assistant secretary for education, the U.S. Commissioner of Education, or the director of the National Institute of Education has complaints about the manner in which his agency is being treated financially, he may appeal to this group or to the secretary himself. Speaking in terms of the formal budget process, this is their last court of appeals. (Strictly speaking, as we will see in the discussion on the congressional appropriations process, agency officials sometimes disregard executive discipline and appeal to Congress for more money than the president's budget requests for them.) However, once the decision is cast at the department level, subordinates are supposed to fall into line and thereafter be supportive.

Having negotiated a level of budgetary agreement among themselves, department officials then begin a series of discussion with OMB staff and, perhaps, with presidential advisers. The point of these conferences is to tailor department requests to the president's overall budget guidelines. OMB examiners will have combed through each agency's budget until they have a fine understanding of the expenditure items and plans. Department officials will be called on to defend their plans. Subsequently, some departments may be requested to reduce their budgets or to provide added justification for several intended programs.

By September or October, negotiations between department officials and OMB staff are usually complete. At this point, if a cabinet officer is displeased with what OMB has finally decided is appropriate for his department, he may appeal. His initial step is likely to be a further discussion with the OMB director. If he is still not satisfied, he may request a meeting with the president over the matter. However, a department executive cannot reopen his entire budget in the appeal process. He must take to the president only those few matters about which he feels most strongly and on which he believes he can make a strong case for overturning OMB decisions. In conducting such an appeal, a department head must also calculate the number of political "chits" a victory will cost him. Is the budget matter sufficiently important to warrant cashing hard-to-get political certificates of trade; what appeals, favors, or presidential decisions will he subsequently have to forfeit in order to gain his way on the budget matter at hand? (Such calculations and bargaining are most dramatic when couched in the setting of the White House or the Executive Office Building. However, the same procedures, absent the splendid surroundings, take place throughout the entire budget development process, wherever subordinates feel their "fair share" has been eroded.)

October to December. Once hearings involving OMB staff and agency and department officials are complete, and after the majority of appeals have been heard, OMB prepares a budget summary memo for the president. This provides the chief executive with a last opportunity to fine-tune the budget in keeping with whatever changes have taken place in the economy or economic forecasts since the budget process began six to nine months previously. Following that, a letter is issued from the president to each department head informing him and his subordinates of the level of their requests that will be embodied in the president's budget for the forthcoming fiscal year. At this point, a few last-minute appeals may yet be heard. However, the time schedule is beginning to act as a damper on further adjudication of differences. Also, another subtle shift, at least a temperamental shift, is occurring: the complexion of budget building now begins to change. The president, his staff, and OMB officials are beginning to loom as advocates of department and agency requests. Instead of viewing such officials as opponents on the other side of a bargaining table, for department and agency level personnel, OMB staff now increasingly assume the role of advocate as the executive branch reassembles itself and prepares for "battle" with Congress over the president's budget.

Beginning approximately in November, OMB staff busy themselves preparing the final version of the budget. This necessitates a substantial amount of detail work and last-minute checking on figures and economic conditions. Somehow, the awesome task draws to a close near the middle or end of December and the budget is conveyed to the Government Printing Office for final publication. Simultaneously, work is initiated on the president's budget message to Congress. This message, which may be accompanied by a presidential economic message, is submitted to Congress along with the budget in January, usually shortly after the president delivers his State of the Union address.*

At this point, the initiative shifts to the legislative branch.

Congress and the Appropriations Process

As we commented earlier, budgets and appropriation bills are the embodiment of spending priorities. In them is determined to a substantial degree what services the federal government will offer, what goods and services it will purchase, who and how many it will employ, and so on. Just as important, the outcome of the budget and appropriations process determines the expenditure items for which federal funds are not likely to be spent. These dollar directions have a substantial influence upon the future direction of the nation. At a somewhat lesser level, the outcome of the appropriations process shapes constituent views of the president and congressmen and influences who is returned to office. In short, how the federal government's dollars are spent is a matter of vast political importance, and that fact is not lost on Congress.

Moreover, appropriations may become an issue over which the legislative and executive branches strongly disagree. The president's budget may not represent congressional priorities. This is especially likely to be the case when Congress is controlled by the opposing political party. However, differences in perspective from the White House and from Capitol Hill can make for differences in points of view about the budget even among a president, senators, and representatives of the same party.

During the Federalist period (1789-1801), the congressional appropriations process was exceedingly simple.[8] The mode of operation was for Congress to approve but two lump sum amounts, one for support of civil endeavors, another for support of the military. The two political parties, the Federalists and the Republicans, held opposing points of view regarding appropriations. The Federalists

---

*The submission of the budget and budget message is usually followed by a battery of additional presidential messages on other topics, education among them. However, the president's new plans for education are already partially unveiled in the budget, at least insofar as any new education plans necessitate new expenditures.

believed in a strong executive and desired that money bills be loosely worded and permissive of broad executive decision-making power. Republicans, on the other hand, were anxious that the executive's authority be curtailed and endeavored to structure spending bills so as to tie the president's hands.

Since that time, political party labels have changed, but the basic issue remains. Will the Congress or the president control the details of federal spending? It is as much a question today in the last half of the twentieth century as it was in the time of Alexander Hamilton and Thomas Jefferson. Periodically, Congress enacts legislation to restrict presidential spending discretion, but subsequently fails to enforce its will and, under one justification or another—usually the exigency of war or in an economic emergency, a strong president regains substantial authority over expenditures and the conflict cycle begins again.

Whether or not accompanied by executive-legislative conflict in any particular fiscal year, appropriations deliberations are always a serious matter for congressmen. It is invariably a complicated process and increasingly a lengthy one. Our purpose in this section is to explain House and Senate appropriations committee functions, floor action, and conference committee deliberations. We will also comment on the role of lobbyists and interest group spokesmen in the appropriations process.

The Constitution specifies in Article I, § 7, that revenue bills must arise in the House of Representatives. However, it is not precise as to whether or not an appropriations measure falls under the category of revenues. Despite this ambiguity, appropriations bills traditionally received their initial hearings in the House and were then passed on to the Senate. In recent times this sequence of events has increasingly been altered. Today, it is not uncommon for a Senate appropriations subcommittee to begin consideration of a bill simultaneously with, or very shortly after, its counterpart in the House of Representatives. Despite this contemporary development, we will initiate our description with the House.

The House of Representatives and the Appropriations Process

Until 1865, the Committee on Ways and Means in the House of Representatives had jurisdiction over both revenue and supply bills. However, after seventy-five years of executive-legislative conflict over which would control federal spending, the congressional process by which funds were approved had become overly complex and burdensome and in 1865 a specific House Appropriations Committee was created.

This committee was dominated for almost forty years by a succession of powerful chairmen. During the early years of their rule, the House had a relatively centralized set of appropriations procedures. However, during the latter stages of their reign and thereafter, something of a backlash occurred, and appropriations authority was dispersed among some half-dozen committees who became antagonistic as they attempted to promote the case for their own spheres of governmental interests. In 1920 all House spending functions were again consolidated under the jurisdiction of a single appropriations committee. Since that time, additional changes have reformed the executive branch budgeting process and have added the General Accounting Office (GAO) to assist Congress in overseeing spending. However, the basic House Appropriations Committee procedures have not been altered significantly in the intervening years.

House Appropriations Committee

An assignment to the Appropriations Committee is one of the most prestigious in all the House. Both parties carefully scrutinize their members before appointing them to this committee.[9] Typically, it takes substantial seniority even to become eligible. In addition, one must possess the correct demeanor and point of view before being likely to gain membership.

Recruitment of acceptable members is only a part of the process for assuring that those deciding about dollars are of an acceptable persuasion. Once selected, Appropriations Committee members are subjected to a strong socialization effort. Through subtle manipulation of social sanctions and political rewards new committee members are made acutely aware of the expectations held for them and learn to tailor their behavior to fit the "mold" established by long years of committee tradition.[10] By the time a House member has achieved sufficient seniority and the respect of his peers to be considered suitable for Appropriations Committee service, and after he has learned how to behave as a committee member, he may rightly feel that he has entered one of Congress's most exclusive clubs. It is a club that guards its activities closely, is protective of its prerogatives, and perceives itself as having a pivotal role in the operation of American government.

The House Appropriations Committee is composed of fifty-five members, with thirty-three members from the majority party and twenty-two from the minority. The chairman is always a member of the majority party and is by far the most powerful member. In recent times his authority has been eroded, but it is still within his capacity to shape the composition of subcommittees by appointing chairmen and by controlling assignment of majority party members. In addition, the chairman of the overall committee derives power from his role as a coordinator of subcommittee activities. By controlling communication among subcommittees and between subcommittees and the full committee, the chairman retains a substantial degree of control over all the various committee components and their activities. Should he desire, he can also sit as a member of each of the subcommittees. This is rarely done, but it remains part of the chairman's arsenal of personal prerogatives.

An Appropriations Committee chairman is a force to be reckoned with. Congressmen are reluctant to oppose a chairman, and sometimes even a subcommittee chairman, for fear of retaliation when some proposed expenditure would affect constituents in their home districts. This fear even extends across the Capitol to the Senate. Former Oregon Senator Wayne Morse was once brought to his knees by opposing a subcommittee chairman's pet project; Public Works Subcommittee Chairman Kirwan (D., Ohio) badly desired an aquarium in the Capital, and Kirwan delayed all public works appropriations for Oregon until Morse capitulated.

Even presidents are not immune to the appropriations chairman's powers. During President John F. Kennedy's term of office, the Appropriations Committee chairman was Clarence Cannon (D., Mo.). Cannon badly wanted then Vice-President Lyndon B. Johnson to give an address to a Missouri college audience. Johnson politely refused, having already scheduled an activity the same day in his home state of Texas. Cannon was not reluctant to voice his disappointment to Kennedy. Sensing Cannon's vindictive capacity, the president advised Johnson to make the Missouri speech and put a special Air Force jet at the latter's disposal to make sure that he arrived there on time.[11]

By virtue of congressional tradition, the substantial seniority necessary to gain the seat, and the subculture of the Appropriations Committee itself, the committee chairman has typically been politically conservative. Most have been personally convinced that almost every interest group, and many of their own congressional peers on other committees, have as their single mission in life conducting raids on the federal treasury. Whereas the other branches of government and the other components of Congress continually try to appease constituents and powerful lobbies by "giving away the store," the Appropriations Committee, and particularly its chairman and his selected subcommittee chairmen, take seriously their role of guarding the nation's coffers and ensuring fiscal survival.

Committee chairmen have exercised their will by carefully selecting subcommittee chairmen and by punishing members who violated committee norms. For example, Clarence Cannon, who served as Appropriations Committee chairman from 1941 to 1964 (except for a four-year period when the Republicans organized Congress), offers a good example of the power of the chairman. During the latter stages of his tenure as chairman, the House leadership—and Speaker Sam Rayburn particularly—attempted to liberalize the Appropriations Committee by assigning several new members of a spending persuasion. Cannon thwarted these efforts by assigning the new men to the committee's "Siberia," the subcommittee on Washington, D.C., appropriations. He was known to permit members who agreed with him to chair two or more subcommittees. However, a particular member aligned with Rayburn, who opposed Cannon's stringent views on foreign aid, was forced to resign his foreign aid subcommittee post by Cannon's uneven enforcement of an archaic rule preventing dual subcommittee chairmanships. He rearranged the jurisdictions of subcommittees to place the budgets of important agencies in the hands of subcommittee chairmen loyal to him. On balance, he was a force unto himself within the House, and efforts to dilute his power proved relatively ineffective.[12]

The heavy burden of Appropriations Committee work falls to the subcommittees. Typically, subcommittees are established along agency lines reflecting the structure of the executive branch. (In 1973, there were thirteen subcommittees. The large portion of the education budget is contained within the jurisdiction of the subcommittee on the Departments of Labor and Health, Education, and Welfare. This subcommittee is chaired by Congressman Daniel Flood (D., Pa.).

Appropriations subcommittees are renowned in the House for their dedication to purpose.[13] This undoubtedly is a consequence of both the recruitment and socialization processes. Cooperation between subcommittee chairmen and their minority party counterparts is very high. The committee's norms and procedures, the commonly held perceptions of the committee's role as a fiscal guardian, and the high seniority and shared congressional experience of members combine to reduce partisan concerns to a minimum. Committee work is time consuming and detailed. Vast amounts of information must be sifted and digested. Members are helped in this task by a highly competent staff which itself displays remarkable nonpartisanship; the staff is characterized by less turnover than that of most any other House committee. (The same can be said of committee members themselves.)

House appropriations subcommittees are intensely proud of their roles as budget experts. The long hours spent in committee hearings and in studying budget requests make them remarkably sophisticated observers and critics of department and agency programs they oversee. Moreover, since they almost never serve on other House committees, their attention is not diluted. They believe their Senate counterparts to be unmindful of the fiscal consequences of federal spending, and see themselves as having to compensate for the Senate's tendency to appropriate larger amounts than the House. The fact that they work so hard and become so knowledgeable about programs (compared to senators, who must because of their substantially smaller numbers serve on several committees simultaneously) imbues them with the outlook that they are staunch but unsung heroes unselfishly guarding the taxpayers' interests. The self-assumed task of members is captured in the following statement taken by Fenno from the committee's official history:

... constantly and courageously to protect the Federal Treasury against thousands of appeals and imperative demands for unnecessary, unwise and excessive expenditures.[14]

Subcommittees hold hearings on the agency portions of the president's budget that fall within their purview. Executive branch officials appear before subcommittee members to justify their requests, almost always in sessions closed to the public and to the press. (The closed sessions are justified on various grounds, e.g., committee members could not play an effective budget-cutting role if subjected to the glare of public scrutiny, administration witnesses speak with more candor in private, and there are not enough large rooms in the Capitol complex to accommodate public hearings.) Subcommittee members usually begin with the assumption that the agency in question has requested more than it actually needs to conduct the programs entrusted to it.[15] They try to identify the excess and reduce the president's request to the level that is absolutely needed. This view of their role is best illustrated by the vocabulary employed by committee members as they engage in their tasks:

> The workaday lingo of the Committee member is replete with negative verbs, undesirable objects of attention, and effective instruments of action. Agency budgets are said to be filled with "fat," "padding," "grease," "pork," "oleaginous substance," "water," "oil," "cushions," "avoirdupois," "waste tissue," and "soft spots." The action verbs most commonly used are "cut," "carve," "slice," "prune," "whittle," "squeeze," "wring," "trim," "lop off," "chop," "slash," "pare," "shave," "fry," and "whack." The tools of the trade are appropriately referred to as "knife," "blade," "meat axe," "scalpel," "meat cleaver," "hatchet," "shears," "wringer," and "fine-tooth comb." Members are hailed by their fellows as being "pretty sharp with the knife." Agencies may "have the meat axe thrown at them." Executives are urged to put their agencies "on a fat boy's diet." Budgets are praised when they are "cut to the bone." And members agree that "You can always get a little more fat out of a piece of pork if you fry it a little longer and a little harder."[16]

Occasionally there is an exception to the budget reduction frame of mind. One or more Appropriations Committee members may oversee an executive branch agency or program that is dear to them. In such an instance an administration official may be encouraged to violate so-called "executive discipline" and describe the "real needs" of his program. Under subtle questioning, a department or agency official can be enticed to "admit" that his own budget requests were reduced by OMB or the White House, and, for him to serve the public as was intended by Congress, his agency will need more money than the president's budget requests. Aaron Wildavsky's insightful research on the appropriations process illustrates this point:

> OFFICIAL. If I go into those questions my personal opinions might conflict with the Budget Report. . . . But I want to make it clear to the committee that I have acquiesced in the limiting figure of the Budget.

CONGRESSMAN. You want this committee not to increase the amount of this Budget?

OFFICIAL. Oh, no; I recognize in Congress the power to do what it wants with this Budget.

CONGRESSMAN. Do you feel that it [library service] is adequate?

OFFICIAL. It is all I am permitted to come here and ask for.

CONGRESSMAN. How much would you like to ask for?

OFFICIAL. Oh, 50 percent more.

CONGRESSMAN. What did you ask the Department for?

OFFICIAL. $885,314,000.

CONGRESSMAN. What did you get from the Bureau of the Budget?

OFFICIAL. $780,000,000.

CONGRESSMAN. Between the two, they only cut you $100 million. Did you ask for too much?

OFFICIAL. No, sir.

CONGRESSMAN. Do you think you could use that $100 million if Congress voted it?

OFFICIAL. I think we could use the bulk of it, yes, sir.[17]

Much more often, however, committee members attempt to expose administration witnesses as protecting budget requests that could be reduced. The following quote makes this point to something of an extreme degree, but the underlying message is accurate.

REPRESENTATIVE ROONEY. I find a gentleman here, an FSO-6. He got an A in Chinese and you assigned him to London.

MR. X (STATE DEPARTMENT OFFICIAL). Yes, sir. That officer will have opportunities in London—not as many as he would have in Hong Kong, for example—

ROONEY. What will he do? Spend his time in Chinatown?

MR. X. No, sir. There will be opportunities in dealing with officers in the British Foreign Office who are concerned with Far Eastern Affairs. The British have foreign language specialists as well as we do.

ROONEY. So instead of speaking English to one another, they will sit in the London office and talk Chinese?

MR. X. Yes, sir.

ROONEY. Is that not fantastic?

MR. X. No, sir. They are anxious to keep up their practice.

ROONEY. Are they playing games or is this serious business?

MR. X. This is serious business.

ROONEY. Can you describe how this would happen? This officer, who is an FSO-6, probably would not be on too important a mission to the British Foreign Office, would he?

MR. X. That is correct.

ROONEY. But he has a counterpart in the British Foreign Office who also is studying Chinese and they sit down and they talk Chinese together, is that right?

MR. X. Yes.

ROONEY. They go out to Chinese restaurants and have chop suey together?

MR. X. Yes, sir.

ROONEY. And that is all at the expense of the American taxpayer?[18]

More dramatic yet:

CONGRESSMAN. I note you have 60 people handling 268 loans; that represents about 4-1/2 loans per person. Are they not a little overworked?

HOUSING AND HOME FINANCE OFFICIAL. This . . . is . . . the most difficult program . . . with which I ever had any experience.[19]

After hearings are completed, subcommittee members meet in a mark-up session to give the final shape to the bill they wish to report to the full Appropriations Committee. With the possible exception of a visit from the full committee chairman, only subcommittee members and staff are present at these meetings. Not even members of other appropriations subcommittees attend.

The overwhelming preponderance of the provisions contained in a bill reported out by a subcommittee deals with matters immediately germane to expenditures. The committee is not permitted to vote funds unless there is an existing statutory "authorization." (However, just because a substantive piece of legislation—an authorization —is on the books does not mean that the Appropriations Committee will vote for it. For example, the International Education Act passed by substantive committees in 1966 has never been appropriated a single dollar.) However, from time to time nondollar matters are concealed in the folds of an appropriations bill. For example, in 1966 James F. Kelly, a highly respected budget officer and comptroller in the Department of Health, Education, and Welfare, was promoted to assistant secretary-conptroller by a Labor-HEW appropriations subcommittee that was particularly appreciative of his competence. His promotion was imbedded in a bill that otherwise dealt strictly with spending matters. (Subcommittee reports do frequently contain comments on a particular agency's effectiveness or efficiency.)

Once completed in subcommittee, a marked-up bill is submitted for approval to the full committee. Until this unveiling, it is highly unlikely that any other committee members have seen the bill, except the full committee chairman. Transcripts of subcommittee hearings, except for matters touching on national security, are available to the full committee. However, they are only infrequently referred to. As a rule, the full committee approves the subcommittee-proposed bill intact. Amendments are technically permissible but in practice seldom occur. This is so in part because of the reciprocal respect for the expertise of other subcommittees, and also because to interfere in the work of another subcommittee is to risk reprisal. Hence, the rule is almost unquestioned support for the work of another subcommittee.

With full committee approval, the bill is ready for action on the House floor. The full committee chairman arranges scheduling with the speaker and majority leader. (Appropriations bills are "privileged" and do not need Rules Committee approval before being taken up by the entire House.) Historically, floor debate has not been extensive, and amendments offered at this point have been minimal. Outright rejection of an appropriations bill on the floor almost never happens. This is still the mode for floor action. However, one of the noteworthy features of contemporary appropriations politics is the degree to which the full House has rejected Appropriations Committee recommendations on HEW spending. Education spending in particular has been the focus for disputes between the Appropriations Committee and the full House. We will return to this point shortly.

The Senate Appropriations Process

Many of the Senate procedures are similar to those in the House, but the Senate typically spends less time deliberating about a particular set of appropriations than does the House.

The full Senate Appropriations Committee is composed of twenty-six members, fifteen majority and eleven minority. This is less than half the membership of the House Committee. For this and other reasons, Senate Appropriations Committee hearings are substantially shorter than those in the House. In part this is true because they would otherwise simply be a replay of the earlier House hearings. Hearings are also shorter because senators, who have multiple committee assignments, have less time to devote to such activities. The Senate committee perceives its appropriation function much less intensely than does its House counterpart. For the Senate Appropriations Committee members, expenditures are a natural concomitant of the programs they already authorized in their capacities on substantive committees. Thus, the Senate tends to act as an appellate body on appropriations to which agencies can come and request reprieve from whatever "harsh" treatment they feel they received at the hands of the House.

The Senate tends to be more liberal on appropriations than the House.[20] House members claim that this is because of the Senate's lack of expertise as well as a by-product of the fact that senators run for their offices only every six years. House members who must face their constituents at the polls every two years are much more reluctant, they allege, to appear to be careless with public funds. Whatever the reasons, Senate Appropriations Committee action is likely to increase House dollar levels. Former Illinois senator and financial expert Paul Douglas expressed the situation thus:

One of the common jokes around Washington is that an agency will request more than it actually needs, depending on the House to cut its request by 50 percent, the Senate to restore the amount to 100 percent, and the conference committee to compromise at 75 percent, which is the figure actually wanted by the agency in the first place.

As with the House, from appropriations subcommittee to full committee, and from there to the floor is the Senate route. Floor action is no more likely to revise a Senate bill than is the case in the House. Even if not taken to be the budget experts of their House counterparts, Senate Appropriations Committee members are recognized by other senators as being more knowledgeable and their recommendations are usually followed by the full body.

Conference Committee Action

The likelihood of the Senate and House concurring precisely on a complicated appropriations bill is extremely slim. Consequently, a Conference Committee meeting between spokesmen for the two houses is almost invariably needed. Because such conferences deal with dollar amounts, the necessary compromises are usually easy to strike. House conferences are likely to bridle at having to agree to a higher amount than their subcommittee and full committee originally approved. Nevertheless, the outcome of a conference is usually an appropriations amount somewhere between what the Senate and House first approved separately.

Following Conference Committee deliberations, the compromise appropriations bill is returned to each house for approval of the full body. Approval can be withheld, necessitating further conference committee action, but this is unusual. Typically, both houses agree to the Conference Report and the bill is prepared for presidential action. If the president signs the bill, then our discussion of legislative appropriations activity is complete. However, should the president exercise his right of veto, the bill flows back to both houses for another vote. If subsequently approved by a two-thirds majority, the bill becomes law regardless of the president's desires. If the veto is not overridden, the appropriations process is recycled almost back to the legislative starting point. A new bill must come out of subcommittee and follow the same tortuous path through both houses, a conference, and then to the president.

With increasing frequency, congressional appropriations action and presidential approval are not complete until after the beginning of the fiscal year on July 1. Under these circumstances, a so-called "continuing resolution" is passed wherein agencies and programs affected are permitted to spend at some specified dollar level, usually less than the president's requested level. For example, it is typical for a continuing resolution to specify a spending level of 90 percent of the preceding year's appropriation. If the appropriations process drags on into late fall, as it did with education funds for both fiscal years 1973 and 1974, this can work a substantial hardship on the programs involved. Decisions down the line in USOE, the states, and local school districts, are delayed because of inprecise knowledge and unsure financial conditions. Employee layoffs may occur, hiring is delayed, services are deferred, etc. Indeed, it is possible to curtail severely a program's potential effectiveness by delaying complete funding well past the beginning of the school year.

The fiscal year 1973 budget provides an extreme example of the degree to which continuing resolutions may be employed. Because of legislative-executive conflict over the causes of an inflated economy and the right of the president to spend, President Nixon twice vetoed Labor-HEW appropriations bills in 1972. When July 1, 1972, arrived and the fiscal 1973 Labor-HEW appropriations bill had not yet cleared both Houses of Congress, a continuing resolution was enacted to prevent the affected programs from being terminated. An appropriations bill was passed in August but the amount was in excess of the president's request and he vetoed it. Meanwhile, an extended continuing resolution was necessary to keep the programs intact. A new bill was presented to the president in October, but again he was dissatisfied and refused to sign it into law, so that a continuing resolution was still necessary. This time, no new spending bill was generated; the continuing resolution was relied on for the remainder of the fiscal year.

Once presidential approval is obtained for an appropriations measure, expenditure control passes from the legislative branch to the executive branch, where it remains until the subsequent fiscal year's budget is taken up.* The primary exception to this is the possibility of an audit by Congress's own accounting arm, the General Accounting Office.

---

*An exception is the sometime necessity of supplemental or special appropriations. These typically are requested by the president near the end of the fiscal year when they may be needed because of unanticipated needs that emerged as the year developed. For example, the Department of Defense almost always needs a supplemental appropriation each year. Also, supplemental appropriations may be part of a president's political strategy. He may submit a balanced or only slightly unbalanced budget capturing the public's rewards for being so frugal. Later, when there is no public attention, he may request additional funds that he knew were necessary all the while. There is a separate appropriations subcommittee to deal with supplemental bills.

Lobbying

To say that appropriations committees in both the House and the Senate are immune to the persuasive entreaties of interest group spokesmen is too strong. Nevertheless, the closed nature of committee deliberations, the businesslike manner and air of dedication that pervades committee deliberations, and the rigorous screening and socialization procedures surrounding committee membership deter the opportunities for, and effectiveness of, lobbying. On balance, committee activity can be said to be relatively free from the influence of specialized external interest groups.

This is not to claim that lobbyists do not try to ply their trade with Appropriations Committee members. They do. The education lobbies—the NEA, AFT, AASA, and other special interest groups—all maintain a staff of individuals for legislative liaison. Until relatively recently it was difficult to argue that these organizational spokesmen had any success when they went to Capitol Hill for dollars. However, this may no longer be as true as was once the case. In 1969, a large number of special interest groups representing both higher and lower education banded together in a confederation called the Committee for the Full Funding of Education Programs.[21]

The Committee for Full Funding maintains a Washington office near Capitol Hill and employs one of the most knowledgeable and artful congressional liaison agents in Washington, Charles Lee. Lee was a congressional aide to the former Oregon senator and Senate Education Committee chairman, Wayne Morse. When Morse retired, Lee began to contribute his twenty-five years of Capitol Hill experience to the cause of the Full Funding Committee. Here he has perhaps become the doyen of Washington lobbists.

The committee is composed of approximately seventy-five educational organizations which make contributions according to the size of their membership. These donations are used to pay Lee and a secretary and to maintain an office. The "decision rule" that binds these educational organizations is the agreement to focus on appropriations; the goal is to have Congress and the president close the gap between the expenditure levels contained in authorizing legislation and actual appropriations. If the authorizing statute is on the books, then the effort is to raise the appropriations for it. If the substantive program is in existence, member groups agree not to argue over its desirability or utility. This agreement has signaled a new day. Previously, educational interest groups could be "played off" against one another to a much greater extent than is possible today. Higher education interests were seldom found supporting lower education bills, and vice versa. Similarly, school administrator groups were at odds with teachers and school board organizations frequently opposed both. Such fragmentation is today substantially reduced, and for this the Full Funding Committee is in large measure responsible.

Since the Full Funding Committee's inception, congressional appropriations actions have consistently provided education with more money than the president has requested. With a modesty motivated largely by his political sophistication, Charles Lee is quick to credit Congress's new enlightenment for the increased appropriations. However, there are those quick to give the Full Funding Committee the major credit. In fact, it is difficult precisely to explain the causes of recent congressional appropriations actions. President Nixon's effort to dampen an inflationary spiral by reducing federal expenditures is not necessarily opposed by Congress. However, Nixon's choices of social action program areas such as those administered by the Office of Education and the Office of Economic Opportunity have not been agreeable to Congress. This difference of opinion undoubtedly has been aggravated by the fact that Congress is controlled by the opposition party. Thus, as we describe below, several forces have joined to alter traditional congressional appropriations action.

In the past, the president asked Congress for a particular dollar amount and expected to settle for less. For President Nixon, to his dissatisfaction, the process has been reversed: his congressional requests for education have typically been raised. For example, the fiscal 1973 dollar picture for education was put together in the following fashion. The president's original Labor-HEW budget request was for slightly less than $29 billion. On August 16, 1973, Congress cleared an appropriations bill for slightly more than $30.5 billion. The president vetoed this amount on grounds that it was inflationary. In October, the House and Senate passed a second appropriations bill for the same amount. However, this time around they inserted a provision that the president could exercise his discretion to impound approximately $1.2 billion of the total. The president again vetoed the bill because, even with the impounding provision, it was some $500 million more than he was willing to spend. It was as a consequence of this impasse that the continuing resolution referred to earlier was invoked for the fiscal year 1973 Labor-HEW spending levels. Again, in terms of causation, it is difficult to separate partisan politics, congressional feelings of independence and pique, and the efforts of the Committee for Full Funding. Nevertheless, the difference is that the Congress—both House and Senate—did not follow their traditional pattern of cutting the president's budget. If Charlie Lee and his cohorts did not single-handedly effect this change, at least they contributed to it.

Budget Administration

Up to this point we have been concerned with describing the budget development process and congressional action on the president's budget proposals. However, from the time that both the House and Senate consent to a conference committee compromise, much of the initiative on the nation's spending returns to the executive branch. The next section explains briefly the administrative steps that follow presidential approval of an appropriations bill. A subsequent section describes the controversies surrounding a modified form of presidential action, so-called "impounding," an issue that rose to special prominence during the middle years of the Nixon administration.

Simple Presidential Approval

After both houses of Congress agree to a bill, it is printed on parchment and signed by the speaker of the house and the vice president in his capacity as president of the Senate. A clerk in the house in which the bill was initially approved delivers the signed bill to the White House for presidential action. In fact, the president, or at least his staff, already has a copy of the bill; as soon as Congress has approved a bill, but probably before it has been officially printed for the speaker's and vice president's signatures, the Government Printing Office has forwarded facsimile copies to the Office of the President for the necessary study prior to presidential action.

A facsimile copy is also forwarded to the Office of Management and Budget, which has the responsibility for advising the president about an appropriations bill. The OMB in turn sends the bill to the administrative agencies involved and requests of them a reply within forty-eight hours as to what action the president should take. In part based on the replies from agencies, but more importantly based on OMB knowledge of the degree to which this bill is consistent with the president's fiscal policy, OMB prepares a statement of advice for the president. If the bill is relatively devoid of controversy, the president probably will sign it.

Once an appropriations bill is signed, a warrant in the amount approved by Congress and the president is drawn up by the Treasury Department and is countersigned by the General Accounting Office. This warrant flows to the agency involved, which must construct an apportionment plan, which specifies the amounts of money to be obligated according to quarters in the fiscal year. The apportionment plan must be approved by the OMB. Approval hinges on the state of the nation's economy, the nature of the agency's spending plans, and the agency's prior administrative record. For example, if there is a desire to "cool down" a brief inflationary spiral, OMB might hold back or slow down an agency's planned obligation of new funds until the third or fourth quarter of the fiscal year. Similarly, if an agency has complicated contractual agreements to develop with a private sector manufacturer, OMB might decree that the funds are not to be released until the plans are in their final stages.

The procedures by which the Office of Education or the National Institute of Education decides what other agencies—state, local, or private—and people will receive the appropriated federal funds is extraordinarily complex. Some statutory authorities provide federal funds directly to local school districts. Other statutes—the majority, in fact—provide funds to states either for their own use or for subsequent distribution to local education agencies. Still other statutes provide federal dollars to universities for research and to private firms and organizations for a variety of tasks as well as research. In some instances, the dollar amount to be disbursed is determined by complicated formulae embedded in the authorizing legislation; ESEA Title I is an example.[22] In other instances, review panels weigh the merits of research proposals to determine which will receive funding and which will not.

On balance, the many ways in which federal education funds are distributed are too complicated to explain here. Suffice it to say that the political processes that have shaped the flow of these funds to this point do not now stop. Many of the same actors and interest groups, in government and outside, continue to try to exert their influence over the actual distribution of federal dollars.

When the time comes for actually spending the money approved by Congress and the president, checks are usually issued by the Treasury Department drawn on one of the twelve Federal Reserve Banks located throughout the United States. (A few federal agencies have the authority to issue their own checks drawn on federal reserve accounts. The Office of Education and NIE are not among them.) When the checks are cashed, the commercial bank involved is credited on its federal reserve accounts. The check itself is returned to the Treasury to be balanced against the spending agency's appropriations level and apportionment schedule. Revenues for the regional Federal Reserve Banks are a result of direct Internal Revenue Service deposits and receipts from Treasury Department loan actions.

Reluctant Presidential Approval: Impounding

Unlike the constitutions of a number of states, the federal Constitution does not provide the president with an item veto. He has little choice but to approve or veto an appropriations bill in its entirety.* From time to time presidents have desired to withhold funds from one or a number of spending purposes intended by Congress. However, they were not willing to accomplish their end by vetoing an entire appropriations bill, with its funds for many agencies and programs. Consequently, the practice of "impounding" selected portions of appropriations bills has evolved.

In a few instances presidents have held back funds because they disagreed with the particular purposes for which Congress had intended them, e.g., additional air force squadrons, dams, and poverty subsidies. For the most part, however, the announced justification for impounding funds has been that to spend them would in some way jeopardize the nation's economy. President Franklin D. Roosevelt brought impounding to the public's attention dramatically at the

---

*If a president feels he cannot veto a bill yet does not wish to sign it, he has two options. First, he can wait ten days and permit it to become law without his signature. On occasion this is done for political reasons important to the president. When such action—or inaction—is taken, the president usually issues a statement explaining his reasons. A second mode of inaction is to pocket veto a bill. This occurs when the ten-day period of grace expires and Congress is no longer in session. Under such conditions, a president need do nothing and the bill will be vetoed automatically.

beginning of World War II, when he believed it necessary to withhold congressionally appropriated funds for a variety of public works projects.[23] FDR's position was that construction materials and labor would subsequently be needed for defense-related purposes. He argued, moreover, that a backlog of public works construction should be accumulated to provide postwar employment. Despite Roosevelt's arguments, a number of congressmen resented any delay on their state's pet projects and a substantial presidential-legislative conflict grew over the matter.

In the late 1960s the nation's economy was caught in a period of especially rapid inflation. The situation was compounded by the expense of supporting U.S. involvement in the war in Vietnam. President Nixon desired to curtail government outlays to relieve spending pressures within the general economy, but he felt the need for continued defense spending. Many members of Congress, the latter generally controlled by the Democrats, argued that if government spending was to be reduced, it should come from the Pentagon's budget, not from social services. The tool Nixon used to obtain his way in this matter was impounding.

Records are difficult to reconstruct, but between 1969 and 1973, it is likely that the Nixon administration forestalled or forbade the spending of approximately $1 billion in education funds. Spending delays continued to be imposed even after United States involvement in Vietnam was ostensibly over, because inflation persisted. This impounding was particularly disturbing to public educational interests throughout the nation. In addition to attempts at exerting political pressure through Congress (i.e., the Committee for Full Funding discussed above), a variety of court cases were brought questioning the president's constitutional right to impound.[24]

Nowhere does the U.S. Constitution explicitly provide the chief executive with power to withhold funds from congressionally approved appropriations. Plaintiffs in the impounding cases, generally states and school districts filing class action suits, asserted that the president has the right to veto any bill with which he is in disagreement. However, if he does sign it, then he is obligated to spend the money involved. At this writing the issue has not been resolved. Most lower court decisions have favored the plaintiffs, holding that the president does not have the legal authority to withhold. On appeal, the Nixon administration has not mounted a vigorous defense. Instead, the strategy appears to be to give ground slowly, yielding contested funds at each step of the way, so as to avoid a Supreme Court ruling that might declare impounding unconstitutional altogether, a decision that would close the door permanently and leave the president no discretion. By losing "gracefully" at the lower court level, the president preserves a degree of impounding discretion, either for another point in time or on dimensions other than education.

Table 1 displays the pattern of educational appropriations for the period from 1969 to 1974 (fiscal years). The actual dollar amounts for the president, the House, and the Senate are shown.

Auditing

A full explanation of federal auditing procedures would occupy at least as much space as is given here to the appropriations process. Thus, our treatment will be superficial.

Auditing is done by several agencies and with varying objectives in mind. Whatever the source, the purpose of auditing is generally two-fold: (1) to provide assurances to both Congress and the president that federal funds are being spent legally in the manner and for the purposes for which they were intended; and (2) to provide feedback as to how well particular programs are working and to assist in designing legislative and administrative improvements.

The major auditing responsibility falls to the administering agency most directly involved. Thus, the Office of Education is charged with conducting audits of the programs under its auspices. The Department of Health, Education, and Welfare also has a separate audit agency under the direction of the assistant secretary-comptroller. Audits of HEW programs conducted by this group are more random and are intended to buttress OE's efforts and to provide the HEW secretary with periodic spot-checks on the efficiency of programs under his direction. As with GAO audits, these HEW efforts are likely to extend beyond the boundaries of a simple financial accounting of expenditure objects.

Congress has its own auditing arm, the General Accounting Office (GAO). Created by the 1921 Budget and Accounting Act, this unit provides Congress with an independent view of the effectiveness of congressionally authorized programs and appropriations. The GAO does not conduct systematic audits of agency-administered programs.

Table 1. Education Appropriations and Expenditures—1969-74 (in Thousands)

	President's budget	House allowance	Senate allowance	Conference agreement	Expenditures
FY 1969	$3,753,044	$2,669,611	$3,758,691	$3,630,758	$3,630,758
FY 1970	3,228,986	4,246,241	4,572,076	4,301,469	3,839,507
FY 1971	4,002,318	4,157,608	4,794,365	4,431,639	4,431,639
FY 1972	6,145,968	4,696,271	5,505,084	5,103,414	5,103,414
FY 1973	4,923,074*	4,001,273	4,294,431	4,137,450	Veto
Resubmission		3,647,540	4,137,450	4,137,450	Veto
Supplemental	1,109,527	Not considered	1,109,527	969,037	969,037
Other supplemental appropriations					957,752
					354,146
FY 1974	5,276,651	6,175,821	6,520,516	6,262,396	6,075,076

*$1,412,237 not considered by House or Senate. Dependent on proposed legislation.

Rather, it focuses its attention here and there at the direction of congressional committees, particularly appropriations committees. GAO auditors are increasingly interested in more than whether or not appropriated funds are spent consistent with law. Also, they are now engaged in performance auditing, an effort to assess whether or not the agency involved is spending the funds effectively, whether the most efficient means are being employed to achieve whatever legislated end is involved. In the field of education, this has meant that auditors in the HEW secretary's office and from GAO have become increasingly sophisticated about matters such as testing of pupils and educational research design. It remains to be seen whether or not such auditing techniques seriously contribute to more effective educational practices. However, the likelihood is good that they will encourage educators to be more wary of spending federal funds in overtly wasteful ways.

The Distributional Consequences of Federal Funds

We have only piecemeal evidence as to the characteristics of the populations that benefit from the flow of federal school aid funds. Scholars and analysts have given little attention to the consequences of how school aid is distributed. A significant portion of the information that does exist was gathered in a series of GAO reports, like those described in the preceding section. The evidence, gathered in the late 1960s, suggests strongly that school aid dollars do not regularly arrive at the targets for which Congress intended them. This conclusion appears accurate, regardless of the level of analysis, within a school district, within a state, or for the nation generally.

Intradistrict Distribution

At the time of enactment, Congress was imprecise regarding the intent of ESEA Title I. Much congressional testimony documented the linkage between economic deprivation and low levels of achievement in school. Indeed, the Title I allocation formula was ultimately based on the number of children within a district coming from low income households. However, it was not initially clear how school districts were to spend the newly acquired federal funds. Many districts took compensatory education dollars to be a supplement for the added costs of operating schools in large cities. This did not necessarily mean that the money was spent for the specific benefit of low income children. Some districts used the funds as though they were general aid; the dollars flowed to whatever the districts decreed to be their highest priorities: administrative costs, teacher salaries, supplies, and so on.

In 1969, a civil rights research organization in Washington, D.C., documented the degree to which Title I funds were being spent to benefit the general school population rather than students from poverty-impacted households. To a significant degree the report, *ESEA Title I. Is It Helping Poor Children?* was based on the results of GAO findings. The following paragraphs capture the report's major conclusions:

> We found that although Title I is not general aid to education but categorical aid to children from poor families who have educational handicaps, funds appropriated under the Act are being used for general school purposes; to initiate system-wide programs; to buy books and supplies for all school children in the system; to pay general overhead and operating expenses; to meet new teacher contracts which call for higher salaries; to purchase all-purpose school facilities; and to equip superintendents' offices with paneling, wall-to-wall carpeting and color television.
>
> Though Title I funds are supplemental to regular money, there are numerous cases where regular classroom teachers, teachers aides, librarians, and janitors are paid solely from Title I funds. . . .
>
> Title I funds are not to supplant other Federal program funds. But the extent to which Title I funds have been used to feed educationally deprived children, to purchase library facilities and books, to provide vocational education for disadvantaged students, raises serious questions as to whether Title I funds are being used to supplant National School Lunch, Child Nutrition Act, Title II ESEA and Vocational Education Act funds.
>
> Title I funds are not for the benefit of non-poverty children, yet teaching personnel, equipment, supplies, and materials purchased with this money are found in some of the most affluent schools where not a single educationally disadvantaged child is enrolled.
>
> And Title I funds are not to equalize racially segregated schools. Yet many Southern school systems which have steadfastly refused to comply with the Constitutional mandate to desegregate use Title I funds to make black schools equal to their white counterparts. These funds are sometimes used to actually frustrate desegregation by providing black children benefits such as free food, medical care, shoes and clothes that are available to them only so long as they remain in an all-black school.[25]

This kind of information prompted then Commissioner of Education James E. Allen to form a federal intra-agency task force to recommend ways in which such problems could be eliminated. The task force, chaired by Deputy Assistant Secretary for Education Timothy

Wirth, suggested the rudiments of what subsequently became the "comparability guidelines." These guidelines, now incorporated in federal regulations for the administration of Title I, require local school districts to document that they spend equal amounts of state and local money on poor and all other children in the district. Federal funds are then supposed to be spent in addition to such general funds. Research by organizations such as the Lawyers Committee for Civil Rights under Law suggests that, at least until 1974, the comparability guidelines were only weakly enforced by the Office of Education.[26] School districts generally were striving to reduce inequities, but not with the speed the law required.

Intrastate Distribution

Another premise at the time Title I was passed was that the newly authorized federal funds would help to equalize financial disparities existing between central cities and wealthier school districts on their perimeters. Evidence on the matter suggests that Title I *does* exert an equalizing influence, but it is too small to offset the inequities provoked by state and local funds and other federal statutes. The most complete evidence on this was compiled in a 1972 study directed by Joel S. Berke of Syracuse University and Michael W. Kirst of Stanford University. Relying on survey research information and case studies from six states, Berke and Kirst offer the following general conclusions regarding the intrastate distribution of federal aid funds:

1. Non-metropolitan areas, largely rural and small town in character, tend to receive more federal aid per pupil than do metropolitan areas.

2. While central cities get more total federal aid than their suburbs, the amount of federal aid is too small to offset the suburban advantage in local and state revenues. Suburbs averaged $100 more per pupil in total revenues than their core cities in four of the five states in the study.

3. With the exception of ESEA Title I, federal programs frequently provide more funds to suburban districts than to central city districts. Large cities appear to receive less money from programs such as ESEA II, ESEA III, NDEA III, and Vocational Education than their proportion of statewide enrollment would suggest.

4. Districts with lower income tend as a general rule to get somewhat more federal aid than districts with higher income, but there are numerous glaring exceptions. With regard to property valuation, federal aid shows no overall equalizing effect.

5. Somewhat more federal aid goes to districts with higher proportions of non-white students. However, the amounts are not in proportion to the magnitude of the added costs in educating the educationally disadvantaged.

6. During the four-year time period under study, the amounts of aid received by local districts varied erratically. Almost half the metropolitan areas in the sample reported an actual decrease in revenues during the last year of the study.

7. ESEA I has focussed needed funds in districts with the greatest educational and fiscal problems. However, its use is frequently in afterhours or summer programs rather than the core curriculum presented to the educationally disadvantaged. The failure to concentrate it on pupils most in need of compensatory education and its improper use as general aid for system-wide purposes have diluted its educational impact.

8. The amounts of federal aid are simply too small to be of anything but marginal help to financially imperiled educational systems. In comparison with total revenues from all sources which ran from $475 to $1,000 per pupil in the five states, we found total federal revenues averaging only $22 to $50 per pupil, or from 3.3 percent to 10 percent of statewide average district revenues. These amounts are inadequate in face of the massive financial problems facing education.[27]

Interstate Distribution

One of the political conflicts that prevented wide-scale federal aid to education for a number of years was over the degree to which federal funds should equalize dollar differences among states.[28] Some states, notably in the South, are less wealthy and in greater need of financial assistance if one uses wealth per capita or total taxes as a percent of personal income (an indicator of effort) as measures of need. However, congressmen from wealthy states traditionally have been reluctant to vote for federal aid funds if the bill at hand contained no benefits to their own constituents. One of the ingredients of the ESEA's political genius was the Title I poverty formula which provided aid to poor states but still directed sufficient funds to wealthy states to attract their support. The Title I formula, at least in intent, went further and focused the funds flowing to wealthy states where they were most needed, on students from low income families. Since the enactment of ESEA, there has been even more congressional discussion of the need to employ federal funds for interstate equalization.[29]

At present, however, we have little knowledge regarding the extent to which federal funds equalize across state boundaries. In a 1966 study, a comparison was made of the proportion of all federal aid funds received by a state compared to the proportion of all federal personal income tax revenues contributed by that state. This computation provided a measure of the degree to which a state received more or less in school aid funds compared to the revenues its residents contributed to the federal treasury. Using this procedure, the interstate transfer of federal funds was found to be as follows: On balance, dollars flow from northeastern, midwestern, and west coast states to states located in the Rocky Mountains, along the Mason-Dixon Line separating North and South, and the deep southern states. In particular the last benefited. However, not unlike the findings of Berke and Kirst, ESEA Title I was found at both points in time to have the greatest equalization effect. Most other federal education statutes were either neutral or anti-equalizing. These calculations were repeated for 1971 data, and the findings were substantially similar.[30] Table 2 summarizes the flow of federal dollars per pupil from region to region.

Table 2. Regional Flow of Funds per Enrolled Student

Region	"Equalization" in dollars per pupil	
	1966	1971
Northeast	−22.92	−27.93
Midwest	−19.71	−27.53
Far West	−5.44	−14.20
Plains	+4.61	−9.63
Rocky Mountain	+20.02	+26.44
Border	+20.75	+31.85
South	+36.40	+47.42

Regardless of the unit of analysis, federal school aid funds cannot be rated highly in terms of the degree to which they equalize opportunity, at least as far as equal opportunity is reflected in dollar expenditures.

Conclusion

Our analysis and descriptions of the federal appropriations process have thus far assumed a "politics of school aid dollars." In our conclusions, we would like to be more explicit about this phenomenon. There are four points at which the political processes concerned with education funding differ sufficiently from the process connected with authorizing legislation to be worthy of emphasis. We explore each of these separately to simplify our explanation, but the reader should understand from the outset that there is substantial interplay among the four.

Education Politics and National Fiscal Policy

Our detailed description of the federal budget development process was designed to emphasize the extent to which overall federal spending is an instrument for tuning the nation's economy. As an integral part of that tuning process, education expenditures are subject to the political calculations compromising the president's budget building process. As one might imagine, these calculations embrace a substantially wider sphere of political concerns, touching almost every interest group, both pro and anti expanded federal spending, in the nation. By contrast, the subgovernment dealing with education legislation in the authorizing process, though by no means narrow, is smaller and the stakes are relatively minor. When it comes to the consideration of a substantive piece of legislation, the president, congressmen, lobbyists, etc., have only to consider—no matter how complicated the discussion may be—whether they are for or against the issue. In the case of an appropriations bill connected with that authorization, all the actors must also consider the impact such expenditures will have on the nation's economy.

Authorizations and Appropriations: Quadruple Jeopardy

In his book *Obstacle Course on Capitol Hill*,[31] Robert Bendiner stresses that, in the absence of substantial reform, Congress is a thoroughly conservative institution. From its roots, it reflects the constitutional framers' intent to bridle any willful chief executive. Congress has procedures, both formal and informal, capable of impeding legislation. If a bill is to traverse successfully the congressional maze, a confluence of fortuitous events is called for. For this reason many bills are submitted, but as is widely known only a select few become law.

Whatever the quantum of political energy needed to overcome congressional resistance to authorizations, power accelerated to another order of magnitude is necessary to overcome the inertia of the appropriations process. As we have described, Appropriations Committee members are among the most conservative and careful in Congress. For them to vote new money, they must be convinced of the program's utility, the administering agency's capability, and the proposed program's political acceptability. Perhaps the difference between authorization and appropriations politics can be reduced to the following: Sponsorship and subsequent enactment of an education statute is quite possibly a platform plank from which a House or Senate Education Committee member might run for future office. Holding the line on public expenditures frequently is the equivalent plank for an Appropriations Committee member.

The Political Prospect of Centripetal Forces

The 1969 emergence of the Committee for Full Funding of Educational Programs may mark a "new day" for the politics of federal school aid. Passage of the 1965 ESEA was a brilliant exception, but educational interest groups are ordinarily fragmented and difficult to enlist in a sustained joint effort. However, perhaps due to the stringency of the Nixon administration's budget policies, perhaps to the political acumen of Charles Lee, perhaps to organizational exhaustion, educational organizations have subordinated many old feuds in order for the Full Funding Committee to present a united front on appropriations. It is difficult at this time to assess the degree to which this venture has been effective; there are too many confounding conditions. Proof of success must await several more years of concerted effort—if the group stays together that long.

Should the "glue" hold for the Full Funding Committee, the potential for political success beyond the boundaries of the appropriations process is remarkable. Although it has slipped from the pinnacle it occupied in the mid-1960s, education is still something of a national religion. One out of every four Americans is estimated to be enrolled in some kind of formal educational institution. Few if any other social services reach so large a constituency. Annual expenditure estimates for this endeavor range from $60 to $90 billion. The estimated number of employees ranges from 2.5 to 3.5 million, a number that equates with the population of the farm bloc. If united, educators have the potential for exercising political power equal to almost any interest group of which one can conceive. However, the question persists: "Can all the king's men ever put it together again?"

The Political Prospect of Centrifugal Forces

The Committee for Full Funding represents a hope of future unity, but the picture below the federal level is much less optimistic.

Even if the merger discussions in the early 1970s between the powerful NEA and AFT eventuate in a unified organization, this will do little to heal the many other breaches in the educational interest group body politic. In fact, such a merger may serve only to drive administrators and school board associations even further from the ranks of teachers. Regardless of the degree to which educators may begin to take joint action at the federal level, the likelihood is great that existing and future federal programs will continue to stop short of their potential utility. This will be so because of the inability among "professional" educators to agree, beyond the level of superficial rhetoric, that the needs and desires of clients, the lay public, come first. Our hope is that, once the costs of fragmentation are fully realized, educators will redouble their efforts to resolve differences. Then there would be substantial benefits, both for educators' political power and in terms of the practical outcomes for their students.

Notes

1. The awesome growth of our federal government is illustrated by the fact that total federal expenditures for the first sixty years of our republic barely exceeded $1 billion.

2. An excellent historical description of the Bureau of the Budget and the evolution of its functions up to the Eisenhower administration is provided by Richard E. Neustadt in "Presidency and Legislation: The Growth of Central Clearance," *American Political Science Review* 48 (September 1954): 641-671.

3. Other important units within the Executive Office of the President include the Council of Economic Advisors, the National Security Council, and the Domestic Council.

4. The "full employment budget" principle is explained more completely in the *Budget of the United States: Fiscal Year 1974*, pp. 1-7. Also, the so-called "counter budget" described by Charles Schultz et al. in *Setting National Priorities: The 1973 Budget* (Washington, D.C.: The Brookings Institution, 1972), chapter 1, provides further explanation and added perspective on the incumbent administration's budget assumptions and economic forecast.

5. An excellent description of the "unified budget" and the features that distinguish it from other possible federal budget formats is provided by David J. Ott and Attiat F. Ott in *Federal Budget Policy* (Washington, D.C.: The Brookings Institution, 1969).

6. The concept of a "capital budget" for the federal government is explained by Maynard S. Cumiez in *A Capital Budget Statement for the U.S. Government* (Washington, D.C.: The Brookings Institution, 1966).

7. See for example the study conducted by the Stanford Research Institute, *Effects of Federal Installation Phaseouts upon School Districts*, OE contract 5-99-225 (Menlo Park, Calif.: Stanford Research Institute, 1966).

8. *Financial Management in the Federal Government,* prepared by the Senate Committee on Government Operations (Washington, D.C.: Government Printing Office, 1966), provides a comprehensive history of congressional appropriations procedures.

9. House committee assignment processes are explained in Nicholas A. Masters, "Committee Assignments in the House of Representatives," *American Political Science Review* 55 (June 1961): 348.

10. For added explanation of the socialization process, see Richard F. Fenno, Jr., "The House Appropriations Committee as a Political System: The Problem of Integration," *American Political Science Review* 56 (June 1962): 310.

11. Described by Daniel Berman in *In Congress Assembled* (New York: Macmillan, 1964), p. 332.

12. Nelson W. Polsby, *Congress and the Presidency* (Englewood Cliffs, N.J.: Prentice-Hall, 1971), pp. 121-122.

13. Daniel Berman provides this anecdote to illustrate committee members' dedication: "So dedicated an economizer is Congressman Passman that in 1962 he would not permit a painful physical injury to prevent him from leading the floor fight to cut the foreign aid appropriation. Although he had fractured a humerus in four places on the previous day, Passman made a dramatic entrance on the House floor seated in a wheelchair and wearing a plastic cast on his arm and shoulder." He told awed colleagues that he questioned whether he was "in as much pain as about 187 million Americans who are going to have to foot the bill [for the foreign aid appropriation]." (From *In Congress Assembled,* p. 353.)

14. Fenno, "The House Appropriations Committee as a Political System: The Problem of Integration": 311.

15. Typically, only administration officials are called to testify at appropriations subcommittee hearings. However, there is nothing legally preventing subcommittees from calling others.

16. Fenno, "The House Appropriations Committee as a Political System: The Problem of Integration": 312.

17. From Nelson W. Polsby, *Congress and the Presidency,* p. 120.

18. Aaron Wildavsky, *The Politics of the Budgetary Process* (New York: Little, Brown & Co., 1964), pp. 96-97.

19. Ibid., p. 117.

20. Indeed, there are those who assert that the Senate generally is more liberal than the House. See Lewis A. Froman, Jr., *Congressmen and Their Constituencies* (Chicago: Rand McNally, 1963), pp. 69-97.

21. Initially it was known as the "Emergency Committee for Full Funding" to connote the crisis in funding levels as perceived by the education groups. For added details see William McNamara, "Charles Lee and the Full Funding Effort," *Change* 5, no. 7 (September 1973): 49.

22. For an explanation of the complex calculations necessary to determine ESEA Title I allocations to state and local education agencies, see the forthcoming article by James W. Guthrie and Anne S. Frentz, "Distribution and Redistribution: An Analysis of the Effects of Substituting Student Test Scores for Family Income Measures as an ESEA Title I Allocation Criterion," *Social Science Quarterly.*

23. For added information on impounding, see J. D. Williams, "The Impounding of Funds by the Bureau of the Budget," Inter-University Case Progress

Series no. 28 (University, Ala.: University of Alabama Press, November 1955), and Robert E. Goostree, "The Power of the President to Impound Appropriated Funds: With Special Reference to Grants-in-Aid to Segregated Activities," *American University Law Review* 40 (January 1962).

24. Additional information on the legal implications of impounding and related court cases is contained in James R. Adams, Deputy Attorney General of the Commonwealth of Pennsylvania, "The Authority of the President to Impound Funds Appropriated by Congress," a paper presented at the annual convention of the National Organization on Legal Problems of Education, San Francisco, November 9, 1973.

25. *Title I of ESEA. Is It Helping Poor Children?* (Washington, D.C.: Washington Research Project of the Southern Center for Studies in Public Policy and the NAACP Legal Defense and Education Fund, 1969), p. 67.

26. For added evidence on interdistrict inequities, see Charles B. Hansen, "City and Suburb: An Analysis of Educational Opportunity in a Metropolitan Setting," unpublished doctoral dissertation, University of California at Berkeley, 1969.

27. Joel S. Berke and Michael W. Kirst, *Federal Aid to Education: Who Benefits? Who Governs?* (Lexington, Mass.: D. C. Heath & Co., 1972), pp. 22-23. Conclusions from their studies are reinforced by findings presented in James W. Guthrie et al., *Schools and Inequality* (Cambridge, Mass.: MIT Press, 1971).

28. This point is explained nicely by a combination of sources: C. S. Benson, *The Economics of Public Education*, 2d ed. (Boston: Houghton Mifflin, 1968), chap. 7, and Frank J. Munger and Richard F. Fenno, Jr., *National Politics and Federal Aid to Education* (Syracuse, N.Y.: Syracuse University Press, 1961).

29. James W. Guthrie and Stephen B. Lawton, "The Distribution of Federal School Aid Funds: Who Wins? Who Loses?" *Educational Administration Quarterly* 6, no. 1 (winter 1969): 47-61.

For added evidence on this point see Joel W. Berke and Michael W. Kirst, "How the Federal Government Can Encourage State School Finance Reform," *Phi Delta Kappan* (December 1973): 241-244.

30. The author is indebted to Mr. Clive Booth for computing the 1971 figures.

31. Robert Bendiner, *Obstacle Course on Capitol Hill* (New York: McGraw-Hill, 1964).

An "Education Congressman" Seeks Reelection

JACK H. SCHUSTER

Article I, Section 1, of the United States Constitution [decrees] that once every twenty-four months Congressmen sweat blood on Election Day. To be sure, Congressmen ought to be free, and are free, to do their work, without excessive public interference, but when they have done their work, they go back to the people and stand trial for their political lives.

This observation of a noted political scientist, the late E. E. Schattschneider, was amply confirmed in 1968 in Indiana's Third Congressional District election. Commenting on John Brademas' quest for a sixth consecutive term, the *South Bend Tribune* reported: "U.S. Rep. John Brademas, trying to cope with a Nixon tide, a Wallace splinter, a GOP-flavored redistricting and an industrious [opponent] Will Erwin, will be struggling for his political life Tuesday." For Brademas and many of his colleagues in the House, the 1968 campaign had begun very soon after the previous election in Novem-

From "An 'Education Congressman' Fights for Survival" by Jack H. Schuster, in *Policy and Politics in America: Six Case Studies*, edited by Allan P. Sindler, pp. 201-241. Revised and reprinted by permission.

ber 1966. To be sure, many of the nation's 435 congressmen—well over half and probably closer to three-quarters, depending on the criteria employed—occupied safe seats; for them, general elections were little more than legitimating rituals. But for marginal congressmen everywhere, the House of Representatives was a jealous mistress; the condition for continued House membership was incessant political campaigning.

Deeply concerned about his prospects for reelection, but no less concerned to maintain his reputation for integrity, Brademas attempted to make full and legitimate use of whatever political opportunities he had and whatever special resources he might be able to tap. As a congressman, he had made his mark primarily in shaping education policy. Could he, then, he speculated, find some way to capitalize on his special relationships with educators? Could an education-oriented constituency—at national, state, and local levels—be mobilized to support him? And if so, was this potential support, in terms of volunteer help and financial contributions, significant enough to justify a sizable commitment of his own time and that of his staff? Or was the "education community" too amorphous to be reached, too impotent politically to recognize and act on its stake in the election, in all, merely an illusory asset?

In concentrating generally on Brademas's reelection efforts and particularly on his relationships with varied education groups, this study raises a more general question: how a congressman seeks to collect political debts, in the form of campaign support, from his special interest constituencies. Further, a review of the response of the education community to Brademas's appeals for assistance tells us something about how educators seek to fashion national education policy and, more generally, about the dynamics of federal education politics.

Brademas: The Man, the Politician

Addicted to "combat politics" (to borrow the term of his political hero, Adlai E. Stevenson), John Brademas is perhaps as much at ease among scholars, artists, and theologians as among tough-thinking politicians and sophisticated diplomats. As much as anyone in Congress, Brademas could be regarded as "an intellectual"; indeed, the juxtaposition of the worlds of politics and scholarship is a topic on which Brademas has reflected at length.

Intense and exacting, John Brademas nonetheless possesses a warm and engaging personality. He tackles his work with inexhaustible energy, operating from behind an unbelievably cluttered desk. ("Order," he explains with a smile, quoting Spinoza, "is in the mind.") Perennially identified by Washington social columnists as one of the town's most eligible bachelors, he is a frequent escort of chic women at embassy parties and smart Washington soirées. Always the teacher, he is ever ready to discuss, especially with students, the realities of political life.

He was born in 1927 in Mishawaka, Indiana, the eldest of Stephen and Beatrice Goble Brademas's four children. His father emigrated to this country from Kalamata, Greece, as a young man, and, before his retirement, managed a restaurant in South Bend. His mother taught in the public elementary schools and kindergartens of Indiana and Michigan for over forty years. His father is Greek Orthodox; his mother, Disciples of Christ Church, but son John was raised a Methodist. (Brademas maintained sufficient involvement in the affairs of the United Methodist Church to be designated in 1968 a delegate to the Fourth Assembly of the World Council of Churches and to be elected to its 120-member Central Committee.) He has always spoken proudly of his Greek heritage—"it was the Greeks, after all," he points out, "who were the first genuine educators of the Western world"—and until 1967 enjoyed the distinction of being the sole American of Greek ancestry then serving in Congress.

Brademas graduated from Central High School in South Bend in 1945, an outstanding student and less spectacular quarterback on the football team. Then it was on to Harvard College on a scholarship. Earning a Phi Beta Kappa key and graduating *magna cum laude* in 1949, Brademas remained at Harvard for a year of graduate study in political science. During that year, he was designated a Rhodes scholar. He enrolled in Brasenose College, Oxford University, and chose to stay beyond the customary two-year stint for Rhodes scholars to complete a doctorate in social studies. His dissertation treated the anarchist movement in Spain in the 1930's, a topic that enabled him to make use of his fluency in Spanish.

After his sojourn at Oxford, John Brademas, A.B., D.Phil. (Oxon.), returned to South Bend. In college he had developed a keen interest in politics, and in 1954, at age twenty-seven, he boldly sought the Democratic nomination for Indiana's Third Congressional District. Brademas won the nomination in a sharply contested seven-way primary, but was narrowly defeated in the general election by the two-term Republican incumbent. (His 49.4 percent of the vote left him short of an upset victory by just over 2,000 votes.)

Moving to acquire more practical experience, he served in 1955 as an aide to U.S. Senator Pat McNamara (D., Mich.) and then as administrative assistant to U.S. Congressman Thomas "Lud" Ashley (D., Ohio). In 1956 he was an aide to Adlai E. Stevenson during the first months of the Governor's second bid for the presidency; his major responsibility was preparing material on campaign issues. Later that year he again received the Third District congressional nomination, this time, on the strength of his near-victory two years earlier, without serious primary opposition. But his second bid for Congress failed; Brademas's share of the vote slipped to 46.9 percent, some 12,000 votes short. Deciding to remain close to home, Brademas became Assistant Professor of Political Science at Saint Mary's College, Notre Dame, Indiana, teaching courses in American government.

For Democrats across the nation, 1958 proved to be a bonanza year. (Though a very popular president, Dwight D. Eisenhower had limited "coattail" power in his own reelection in 1956 and markedly less influence in the 1958 off-year election.) With a net gain of thirteen Senate and forty-seven House seats, Democrats won greater margins in both houses of Congress than they had enjoyed for many years. Indiana Democrats fared especially well, defeating six incumbent Republican congressmen, picking up one Senate seat, and retaining two other House seats. (Having held just two of Indiana's eleven House seats in the previous Congress, the Democrats' new total of eight House seats represented their best postwar margin.) Brademas was one of the victors. Taking advantage of the Democratic tide, the 31-year-old bachelor handily unseated the Republican who had beaten him in 1956. Capturing 57 percent of the vote, Brademas won by almost 24,000 votes.

The South Bend Democrat won reelection the next four times. But aside from 1964, the year of a national Democratic landslide (when he garnered 60.8 percent of the vote), he never achieved a comfortable margin: 52.5 percent in 1960; 52.2 percent in 1962; 55.8 percent in 1966.

1968: John Brademas Fights for Survival

The Third District of Indiana, like the Hoosier State itself, was politically volatile. Neither Democrats nor Republicans were dominant; the party outcomes shifted uncertainly from one election to the next. Prior to Brademas's first win in 1958, the Third District had been represented in Congress by Republicans for eighteen of the previous twenty years. In all, five of Indiana's eleven congressional seats were occupied by Democrats. Of the five, only one was considered completely safe in 1968, another was regarded as relatively safe, but three of the five, including Brademas's, were thought to be very vulnerable.

Given the advantages of incumbency, five-term incumbents do not ordinarily have to "sweat blood" in their campaigns for reelection. But late in the campaign, the banner headline of an article in *Look* aptly described Brademas's situation: "Congressman John Brademas —A Liberal Fights for Survival."

As the campaign unfolded, Brademas discovered that his political life was challenged by multiple threats. In February 1968, a three-judge federal court handed down a decision which redrew Indiana's congressional district boundaries to bring about compliance with the "one man, one vote" standard for the House of Representatives. Brademas was badly hurt by the redistricting decree. The court had performed major surgery on the Third District, severing two of the counties Brademas had always represented and adding two counties that historically were quite conservative.

There were other problems. Dissension within the Democratic party in Indiana was acute. A bruising three-way presidential primary in May featured dissident Senators Robert F. Kennedy and Eugene McCarthy in their first direct confrontation at the ballot box, as well as the incumbent Democratic governor whose appeal was primarily to the party's "old guard." The deep intraparty wounds were not to heal by election time in November. Moreover, the candidacy of Richard M. Nixon constituted yet another ominous sign for Indiana Democrats. Indiana had voted heavily Republican both times Nixon had run for vice-president with Eisenhower in 1952 and 1956, and in 1960, Nixon, then at the head of the ticket, ran strongly in the Third District, and, statewide, led John F. Kennedy by 223,000 votes. Undoubtedly, Nixon's candidacy could pose a formidable threat.

Not the least of Brademas's problems was his opponent, William W. Erwin, a 42-year-old farm manager and state senator from the hamlet of Etna Green in Kosciusko County. Described by the *New York Times* as an "old-line" conservative, the Republican nominee formerly served as the state chairman of the Indiana Young Republicans and as chairman of the Indiana Advisory Commission to the U.S. Civil Rights Commission. He was an experienced and industrious campaigner, a calm, steady man. Regarded as heir apparent to the Second District seat which Charlie Halleck had occupied since 1935 and was now vacating, Erwin had unexpectedly become a casualty of the judicial redistricting decree. Erwin's home county, Kosciusko, was annexed to the Third District. In the Republican primary in May, by readily outdistancing a 31-year-old South Bend attorney, Erwin had earned his chance to unseat Brademas.

Campaign Strategies: Images and Resources

No two elections are alike and neither are any two campaign strategies. All campaign strategies, though, are shaped by certain salient factors: the particular characteristics of the constituency, the personality, style, and issue orientation of the candidate and his opponent, the availability of funds, the role that party plays, and so forth. Given those determinants, some candidates approach campaigns without highly developed strategies. In practicing their political art, they avoid tightly structured campaign formats and tend to rely on their time-tested general sense of the electorate's mood.

Increasingly, though, the age of science is penetrating electoral politics: sophisticated polling (in-depth probes on candidates and issues, "quickie" telephone and shopping center surveys to detect shifts in voter attitudes and intentions); the wonders of electronic data processing (computer-generated "walking lists" for canvassing, computer-printed "personalized" letters, computer-assisted election return analyses); thoroughly professional media campaigns—especially centered on television—utilizing every selling technique known to Madison Avenue to project a buyable image. Some observers refer to these sophisticated techniques as "the new politics"; others fail to discern in them anything fundamentally "new."

Whether novel methods or not, these technologies are invariably expensive. Hence, their principal users to date have been candidates in statewide and, of course, national campaigns—would-be governors, senators, and presidents who have multimillion dollar campaign budgets. But the resources available to most candidates for the House, unless they have access to unusual wealth, are usually insufficient to underwrite a generous use of campaign technology.

John Brademas's 1968 campaign occupied something of a middle ground between the new and the not-so-new. His campaign budget imposed very real constraints on what political goods and services he could buy. He did employ more polling than he had in the past, but it was a modest effort. He did attempt to identify key "swing" precincts through a statistical analysis of voting data and demographic characteristics, but that, too, was a relatively primitive effort. His greatest indulgence was hiring one of the nation's most renowned political filmmakers, Charles Guggenheim, to prepare most of his TV spots—and they were highly artistic creations. But on the whole the Brademas campaign featured familiar techniques.

Serious planning for Brademas's sixth-term quest began in December of 1967. Over the next several months, dozens of campaign topics were discussed at a series of meetings with staff and advisers. Detailed planning began on such matters as fund-raising, organizing notebooks on issues, monitoring the speeches of the Republican nominee, organizing "Citizens for Brademas" committees in each of the counties, locating a suitable campaign headquarters, formulating a detailed budget for the campaign, projecting the use of media, newsletters and other mailings to constituents, coordinating plans with other Democratic candidates (including access to polling information that might be available from Democratic candidates running statewide), and planning the frequency of Brademas's visits to the district.

In 1968 there were considerable risks for Brademas in being identified too closely with the Democratic party. Compare 1964, when all signs pointed to a lopsided Democratic presidential victory. Then the prospects for Democratic candidates, *qua* Democrats, were good at all levels; it was one of those infrequent years in which it was politically advantageous to be perceived by voters as an Indiana Democrat. But in 1968 a comparable emphasis on partisan Democratic identification was a high-risk strategy. Brademas needed to broaden his appeal to the political middle, to the swing voters, to the thousands of politically "unstable" voters who cast ballots in presidential contests but often not in off-year elections.

Brademas's efforts to moderate his image as a liberal Democrat was no easy task. After all, he had campaigned vigorously as a Democrat for fourteen years, unequivocally and almost invariably on the side of "liberal" domestic and foreign aid programs and civil rights. Moreover, his roll-call voting record was indisputably very liberal. Throughout his time in Congress, Brademas had consistently received high ratings from liberal groups and low ratings from conservative organizations, and 1968 provided no exception. (For example, the liberal *New Republic* rated Brademas as having voted "correctly" on eleven of twelve key votes in 1967-68; only nine congressmen received perfect *New Republic* ratings, and Brademas was one of the next tier of thirty (twenty-nine of them Democrats) with eleven "correct" votes. By contrast, the conservative Americans for Constitutional Action rated Brademas's performance at only 4 percent "correct" key votes for the same 90th Congress.)

With strong anti-liberal sentiments in the winds, Brademas's voting record, if attacked by his opponent, could prove to be a serious political handicap. The political complexion of the Third District was not by any criterion as liberal as his voting record. Indeed, Erwin, his opponent, repeatedly attacked Brademas's record, attempting to portray him as a member of the "liberal establishment," and to maneuver him into a defensive posture. "John Brademas," the Etna Green Republican charged, "would probably be a fine representative of the Eastern Establishment and New York City, but . . . there is more than ample evidence that the present congressman has lost touch with the people of the Third District."

Mobilizing the Education Community

A congressman facing a political life-or-death struggle attempts to activate all the allies he can find. Gaining and maintaining group support is an invariable campaign strategy. In Brademas's case, there were many organizations and less formal groups whose favor he sought during the course of the campaign: church groups, veterans organizations, ethnic groups, chambers of commerce, farmer organizations, rural electrification associations, and many others.

For ten years John Brademas had been a strong congressional ally of education. In 1968, because of the uncertainty of success in his reelection bid, he was determined to marshall every possible political resource. Toward that end, much of his campaign effort was directed at mobilizing an "education constituency" at national, state, and local levels. But the "education community," theoretically Brademas's natural ally, traditionally had been apprehensive about engaging overtly in partisan politics and had never been easily activated. The following section focuses on the interaction between John Brademas—an "education congressman"—and the "education community."

The Washington "Education Lobby"

The relationships between lobbyists and their allies in Congress acquire a unique focus when viewed in the context of electoral politics. To what degree will an interest group commit itself in trying to assist a friend in Congress whose career may be in jeopardy? And, conversely, to what extent will a politician, locked in a tough fight for reelection, attempt to mobilize his "special interest constituency"? Such questions relate to important but little examined aspects of the national policy-making process.

At one end of this lobbyist-politician relationship is the diverse sprawl of education interest groups in Washington. Dozens of education associations—some powerful, others barely visible—constitute a very loose-knit education lobby. Reflecting American education's rich pluralism, the interests of these education groups differ markedly. Some, like the American Library Association, have relatively narrow policy objectives; others, like the National Education Association, concern themselves with a wide range of education issues. Some represent the interests of a single institution (the University of California maintains a Washington office); others are large "umbrella" organizations (the American Council on Education purports to speak for over 1,300 member colleges and universities). Some, like the United States Catholic Conference, represent religious interests; others, such as Protestants and Other Americans United, seek to preserve secularism in public education. Some, like the AFL-CIO or the NAACP, are not primarily education oriented, though they engage in education lobbying. Almost all represent nonprofit institutions, but a few, such as the National Audio-Visual Association, speak for the interests of a group of profit-making businesses. Some represent the interests of states (the Education Commission of the States or the Council of Chief State School Officers) and the cities (the Research Council of the Great Cities for School Improvement).

Diverse as their interests are, most Washington-based education groups perceive at least one common cause: to expand education's share of perennially scarce federal funds, with as few strings attached as possible. (Other claimants on federal funds are of course numerous—highway builders, defense contractors, urban renewers, health researchers, ad infinitum.)

To protect the interests of their respective clienteles, these interest groups monitor developments in the federal government, seeking to influence policy outcomes. To accomplish this, they must focus attention on the critical stages in the policy formulation process—when an education proposal is being drafted by the U.S. Office of Education or elsewhere in the executive branch or by an ad hoc presidential task force, when a congressional hearing is underway on an education bill or an appropriations measure, when a vote is about to be taken in an education subcommittee or full committee or on the floor of the House or Senate, or when the Office of Education or Department of Health, Education, and Welfare formulates guidelines for the implementation of newly enacted legislation.

The "education community" has experienced some moments of success in Washington, such as when a recently formed education coalition—the Emergency Committee for Full Funding of Education —influenced Congress in late 1970 to override President Nixon's veto of a major education appropriations bill. Observers have often concluded, though, that the educators, plagued by internal dissent and their ambivalence toward politics caused by their self-perception as professional educators, have been largely ineffective in their lobbying efforts at the national level.

The lack of cohesion stems, almost inevitably, from the very different education interests that the various associations represent. And at education's grass roots, most classroom teachers and university faculties have heretofore been reluctant to compromise their professionalism by becoming involved in partisan politics. This posture is eroding in the face of widespread collective bargaining among educators and growing bands of aggressive political activists within their ranks. But in 1968—at best a transition period with respect to these attitudes toward political involvement—it was not at all clear whether the Washington education lobby had the capability "to deliver," assuming it wanted to do so in the first place.

The "Education Congressman." Brademas's credentials as an education-minded legislator began with his assignment to the House Education and Labor Committee. (He tells the story of driving to Bonham, Texas, on his way back to Indiana from a trip to the West Coast following his election in 1958, in order personally to ask House Speaker Sam Rayburn that he be assigned to that committee. His request was subsequently granted.) As the 1968 election drew near, Brademas was nearing the completion of ten years on that House committee, the focal point of his legislative energies. At that time, he was eighth-ranking majority member (among eighteen Democrats) on the committee, and, more importantly, sat as the ranking majority member (that is, junior only to the chairman) on two key education subcommittees: the Special Subcommittee on Education (with jurisdiction for higher education legislation) and the General Subcommittee on Education (with jurisdiction for elementary and secondary education).

As a member of the full committee, Brademas had sponsored or cosponsored virtually every major education law enacted since 1959. In varying degrees, he contributed to the writing or passage of the Higher Education Facilities Act of 1963, the Technical Education Program of 1963, the Teacher Fellowship and Teacher Corps Program of 1965, the landmark Elementary and Secondary Education Act of 1965 and the 1967 amendments, the Higher Education Act of 1965 and the 1967 amendments, the International Education Act of 1966, and the Education Professions Development Act of 1967. Education and Labor Chairman Adam Clayton Powell had named Brademas in 1961 to chair an ad hoc advisory group on higher education and in 1966 to lead a special House task force on international education.

His support of education had earned him widespread recognition from education groups, including the Award for Distinguished Service in International Education from the Institute of International Education, and, during the course of the campaign, an award for distinguished service from the Legislative Commission of the National Education Association. By 1968 he had received honorary doctoral degrees from four universities; the citations usually emphasized his contributions to American education.

Another facet of Brademas's involvement with education was his active service on education boards and councils. He sat as a member of the Board of Visitors to Harvard University's John F. Kennedy School of Government and to its Department of Romance Languages and Literature. He was a member of Advisory Councils of the College of Liberal Arts, University of Notre Dame; the School of International Service, American University, Washington, D.C.; and the Institute of Urban Affairs, Boston College; and he was also a trustee of Saint Mary's College in Notre Dame, Indiana (where he had taught in 1957-58) and of the Educational Testing Service, Princeton, New Jersey.

By 1968, then, John Brademas's exceptional academic background and his immersion in education legislation for a decade had distinguished him above all but a few of his congressional colleagues as "an education congressman."

Education as a Campaign Issue. Brademas was aware that voters only infrequently are able to identify issues as the basis for voting *for* a congressman; a reliance on issues as grounds for voting *against* a candidate for Congress is somewhat more common. Moreover, it is rare, at least according to Brademas's judgment, that voters will cite "support of education" as a reason for voting for a congressman.

Why, then, were all the time and resources invested in reinforcing Brademas image as an "education congressman"? At the time and again in retrospect, Brademas recognized that his 1968 campaign for reelection may have siphoned off a disproportionately large amount of his resources for the purpose of wooing both the educators and, through his identification with education, the general electorate. Nevertheless, Brademas believed the strategy was sound, especially in light of his commitment, independent of the campaign, to promote public support for American education.

Further, many people other than educators find education to be one of their salient interests and recognize that education is a "good thing." More important, education is often a less controversial and hence less vulnerable issue than most, characteristics that are especially attractive to a liberal congressman representing a more conservative district. A legislator's strong identification with education is less likely to repel a conservatively disposed voter than is, say, a strong identification with the labor movement, with civil rights, or with foreign economic assistance.

True, a conservative voter can find fault with a congressman's preference for retaining significant federally centralized prerogatives which establish education priorities. But virtually no voter (excepting perhaps a few educators) makes sophisticated distinctions between federally determined categorical aid programs and more decentralized, state-oriented general aid programs. Indeed, a strong identification with "education" in general can deflect attention from a congressman's "liberal" record on such highly charged education issues as busing to achieve racial balance or opposition to the "student unrest amendments" that would suspend federal assistance to students who engage in illegal disruptive activities. Similarly, popular perceptions of a legislator as primarily pro-education can help to temper his larger record in issues unrelated to education. On balance, then, a congressman who develops a reputation as a promoter of education policy and interests may or may not win many committed friends, but he is not likely thereby to make many dedicated enemies.

Cultivating the Education Interest Groups. During his five terms in Congress, Brademas had developed a close working relationship with representatives of the most influential national education groups. To use the political vernacular, he had "delivered," that is, he had fought the educators' battles on Capitol Hill and unquestionably had contributed considerably to advancing the interests of education. Now, faced with a difficult reelection campaign in 1968, Brademas sought the support of some of these educational colleagues. The response was varied, given the wariness of education groups of becoming identified with partisan politics. Nevertheless, the Legislative Commission of the million-member National Educational Association (NEA) decided to award Brademas its Distinguished Service Award. John Lumley, NEA's assistant executive secretary for legislative and federal relations, wrote:

In recognition of your distinguished record in promoting educational legislation during the Ninetieth Congress, the Legislative Commission of the National Education Association has voted unanimously to award you their distinguished service plaque.

We will be pleased to make this presentation to you in your home district or at your Washington office as you prefer. I will appreciate hearing from you at your earliest convenience.

I want to express my personal appreciation to you for your dedication to improving the educational opportunities of the youth of this country. Best wishes for your continuing success.

A representative from the Legislative Commission office in Washington flew to South Bend to present this award. That the presentation ceremony, with appropriate fanfare, took place just five days prior to the election was hardly coincidental. For the occasion, Brademas's staff arranged a reception at the University of Notre Dame's Faculty Club. Numerous local school and university educators were invited and a top-ranking Department of Health, Education, and Welfare official was also on hand to make kind remarks about Brademas.

During the course of the event, a letter was read from Robert Wyatt, executive secretary of the Indiana State Teachers Association (the NEA affiliate). Wyatt had been national president of the NEA at the time the landmark Elementary and Secondary Education Act of 1965 was enacted and had developed a close working relationship with Brademas. Wyatt's timely letter of October 14 lavished praise on the congressman:

> As the 90th Congress adjourns, I want to take this opportunity to express to you, on behalf of the teachers of Indiana, our great appreciation for the outstanding contribution you have made to the progress of education in Indiana and throughout the Nation.
> Your role in the 90th Congress has been especially commendable in two respects: First, in your effort to prevent damaging cutbacks in appropriations for school aid programs authorized by earlier Congresses; second, in your sponsorship of new education laws sponsored by our organizations and enacted by the 90th Congress, including the Education Professions Development Act, the Elementary and Secondary Education Amendments of 1967, and the Vocational Education Amendments of 1968.
> We in Indiana take pride in your being the only member of Congress from our state on the House Committee on Education and Labor. Your leadership and hard work on these and other educational measures fully merit the description in *Look Magazine* as "Mr. Education in Congress."

The media was invited to attend, and considerable print and television coverage resulted—which was, of course, the point of the whole exercise.

The American Federation of Teachers (AFT), an AFL-CIO affiliate and the NEA's principal rival nationally, was quite helpful at the local level through the South Bend Federation of Teachers (SBFT), bargaining agent for South Bend classroom teachers and the local AFT affiliate. A telephone call from David Selden, national AFT president, to the president of the SBFT, Larry Bishop, helped stimulate the local organization's political activity. Bishop, with whom the Brademas staff had been in close contact, subsequently circulated a mimeographed memorandum entitled "Political Participation" to every AFT member in South Bend. It commented on Selden's call as follows:

> Dave pointed out that there isn't another congressman as dedicated to fur-thering the cause of education as Congressman Brademas and it would be a real tragedy to lose him. Since I received that call from Mr. Selden I have been in contact with Brademas Headquarters in South Bend to find out what we as teachers can do to help.
>
> There are several ways. First, they are in need of people to answer the phones in the afternoon. Second, on November 3rd from 1:30-5:30 they would like volunteers to knock on doors in different parts of the city to drum up support. Third, they would like to have an ad in the [South Bend] Tribune sponsored by teachers. Finally, they can always use people to stuff envelopes and similar tasks. . . . I hope you will give this request for help very careful consideration.

As a result of Bishop's recruiting, a small group of eighteen teach-ers, all SBFT members, volunteered to canvass for Brademas on the Sunday preceding the election. Brademas's staff briefed the group on two occasions, equipped them with badges prominently identifying them as "Teachers for Brademas," and dispatched them to crucial "swing" precincts. When they were "debriefed," the staff judged that their door-to-door salesmanship had met almost invariably with re-spect and, occasionally, enthusiasm, presumably reflecting the credi-bility generally accorded schoolteachers. Their apparent success could be contrasted with the somewhat less receptive attitudes often encountered by Brademas's student canvassers. In all, this small band of teacher-activists succeeded in blanketing fifteen key precincts two days prior to the election. Though the impact was not susceptible to measurement, it was thought to have been quite helpful.

Concurrently, a written appeal for support of Brademas was ini-tiated within the Department of Audiovisual Instruction (DAVI) in Washington, a highly autonomous division of the NEA. These indi-vidually addressed letters, written by DAVI's assistant executive sec-retary, but signed in her individual capacity, were sent from Washing-ton to all DAVI members in the South Bend area, i.e., to audiovisual specialists in the schools. Technically, the letters were sent neither by DAVI nor the parent NEA, but their impact likely was not too different than if they had been:

> I make this appeal to you as a private citizen, not as a staff member of your national organization nor even as a fellow I.U. [Indiana University] alumnus. I've never been active in politics but it seems to me it's time to become active and ask my colleagues to cross party lines, if necessary, to vote for a man who so ably represents our profession.

As an educator, how many times have you said to yourself: Why can't we get educated, intelligent men to run for office—thinking men who will bring *honesty* and *integrity* into politics! Well, you people in the Third Congressional District of Indiana gave Congress just such a man, a Rhodes scholar, a man who values education, who fights for your interests on the floor of Congress. He has supported our case; now let's support his.

Maybe you have never been active in politics either because it's been a forbidden area for teachers. Now that we have teacher power, let's use it. Let's do more than just cast a vote on election day. It's time to actively campaign for men like John Brademas. Urge everyone you meet to vote for him—if not for yourself, then for the kids. Keeping men like Brademas in Congress is our only hope for tomorrow.

The Federal Educators—Legislative-Executive Coordination. Several key HEW officials were quite helpful, although not in any highly organized or particularly visible way. Most notable was the assistance of two political scientists-turned-HEW-officials: the assistant secretary for legislation and his deputy for education legislation, both key figures in the federal education network. Brademas had fought their fights on Capitol Hill for a decade; they recognized that he now needed help, and they were responsive when he outlined his plight.

The assistant secretary, who was to be in the Midwest in late October, had volunteered to help in any way he could. He flew to South Bend for the NEA award presentation, where he made some highly flattering remarks about Brademas's contributions to American education. That evening he accompanied Brademas to a meeting of St. Joseph County Democratic candidates and party workers. Following remarks by the county chairman, the party's nominee for governor, and Brademas, he gave a short, spirited pep talk in which he sang hymns of praise for Brademas. He had also been very helpful some months earlier in suggesting the names of persons, within and outside the education community, who could be solicited by Brademas for contributions to his campaign fund.

The deputy assistant secretary, with whom Brademas had often collaborated in legislative matters, went one step further and personally wrote letters of solicitation to fifty or sixty potential contributors, many of whom worked within the federal education establishment. He did not, of course, write in his capacity as an HEW official.

Rallying the Local Educators. Brademas was hopeful that the local educators would rally to his banner. Indeed, he hoped that they could be tapped for campaign contributions and other support on the assumption, not unreasonable, that they would be willing to so express their appreciation of his efforts in Congress on their behalf.

Brademas's principal fund-raising device was a campaign kick-off banquet. Volunteers, frequently wives of Notre Dame professors, customarily compiled a list of persons to be invited and tended to the laborious task of sending out hundreds of letters. These affairs commanded the attention of the local press. For example, in April 1960 the principal speakers were presidential aspirant John F. Kennedy and Congressman Stewart L. Udall (D., Ariz.); in 1966 the featured speaker was Secretary of Labor Willard W. Wirtz. For the June 1968 affair Brademas achieved another coup. The speaker was John W. Gardner, who had very recently resigned as HEW secretary to become chairman of the newly organized Urban Coalition. Gardner was especially attractive for this occasion, for, in addition to being a political celebrity, he was a Republican, and every ounce of bipartisan identification that Brademas could muster was thought to be helpful. Banquet tickets were priced at $25 for "sponsors" and $100 for "patrons." The general response was enthusiastic; more persons bought tickets than ever before.

Ah, but the teachers. . . . Although a special letter of invitation had been mailed to each of the several thousand schoolteachers in the area, so few of them bought tickets that the idea of trying to rouse the education community seemed a dismal failure. Partly because of the disappointing turnout among teachers in June, some earlier plans to enlist the education community were abandoned, such as arranging fund-raising luncheons or teas for area teachers or running a newspaper advertisement to be sponsored and signed by schoolteachers.

One time-consuming project, however, was pursued. A special "Dear Educator" letter was mailed to each of the 9,000 school and college personnel in the Third District. In a brief cover letter, on congressional letterhead, Brademas underscored his intimate connection with education policy:

Because we have a common interest in education, I am taking the liberty of sending you a summary of the major education bills enacted into law by the ninetieth Congress.

As you may know, I have been a member of the House Committee on Education and Labor for the past ten years, and am presently ranking member of the two subcommittees that handle elementary and secondary school legislation and higher education bills.

The ninetieth Congress has built constructively on the education measures passed by the historic eighty-ninth Congress. Most of the measures we have approved in the last few years are already benefiting schools and colleges and universities, students and teachers and professors, throughout Indiana and the nation.

My own view is that we must maintain and strengthen American education at every level, from preschool through graduate school, in both public and private institutions, if our country is to be able to cope effectively with the challenges that history has thrust upon us.

I hope that you find this summary helpful and that you will feel free to send me any questions or suggestions you may have.

A four-page mimeographed enclosure enumerated the education accomplishments of the 90th Congress. Drafted over a period of many weeks, the enclosure described the Education Professions Development Act of 1967, the Elementary and Secondary Education Amendments of 1967, the Vocational Education Act amendments of 1968, the Higher Education Act of 1968, and five lesser bills.

Brademas's nonpartisan cover letter was sent as franked mail. The letters were mailed on October 24 and 25, less than two weeks before the election, triggering an outcry from the camp of his Republican opponent, Erwin, who alleged misuse of the congressional frank. But the issue, not pressed vigorously by the opposition, quickly faded from view; indeed, the practice of using the frank for such purposes is commonplace. So, for relatively little capital outlay, Brademas was able to remind 9,000 educators, in their homes, of their community of interest in a not-so-subtle preelection message.

Further efforts to energize the local higher education community centered around a project initiated during the last weeks of the campaign. Faculty wives from Notre Dame spent many hours contacting area college and university teachers to request from each the inclusion of his or her name and a contribution of a few dollars to run a newspaper advertisement in support of Brademas. On November 4, the day before the election, a nearly full-page ad, costing approximately $550, appeared in the *South Bend Tribune*. Its banner headline proclaimed:

350 COLLEGE AND UNIVERSITY EDUCATORS FROM
THE THIRD CONGRESSIONAL DISTRICT ENDORSE
CONGRESSMAN JOHN BRADEMAS' BID FOR REELECTION

The copy listed all 350 "Faculty Friends of John Brademas" and praised his support of education.

Despite the great time and energy directed at cultivating local educators to support and work for Brademas, the results, to the extent that they were tangible, were mixed at best. Little hard cash was raised. On the other hand, the assistance of the canvassing schoolteachers, and especially the help of the handful of Notre Dame wives, was valuable. Were votes changed by this special campaign within a campaign? No attempt was ever made to determine how this sizable number of local educators actually voted or whether they were influenced by Brademas's special attentiveness. Such a survey would have been revealing—but costly to conduct. In any event, it is clear that a mere handful of educators—perhaps forty at most—were actively involved in the campaign, investing, on the average, several hours of their time. A hard-nosed, cost-benefit analysis of this aspect of the campaign probably would yield disappointing conclusions.

Seeking an "Education Community-at-Large." Brademas had come to know well many university presidents and scholars. Through friendships formed at Harvard, Oxford, and Notre Dame, through contact with the Adlai Stevenson "braintrust," through persons he had met over a decade as a member of the House Education and Labor Committee and as an inveterate conference-goer, and through his membership on a number of education boards and councils, Brademas had become acquainted with a great many persons prominent in American education. In the 1968 election year, facing a close race, Brademas decided for the first time to try to harness this potential resource through an organized effort. Two endeavors are worth special mention: the National Friends of John Brademas fund-raising effort and a national education conference held at the University of Notre Dame. In early 1968, following the congressional redistricting, Brademas determined that he would have to spend substantially more money on his 1968 reelection than he had on any of his previous campaigns. The major fund-raising activity was the campaign banquet referred to previously. In addition, friends of Brademas ordinarily organized cocktail receptions in Washington, Chicago, and New York to help raise funds for him. But these smallish affairs could yield only a portion of the money needed for this campaign.

Now, for the first time in his eight campaigns for Congress, Brademas sought to make direct use of his national reputation in education circles by trying to tap an amorphous, elusive national education constituency. He reasoned that educators across the country and prominent persons sensitive to the needs of American education would be receptive because of his efforts for education during a decade in Congress. But did such a constituency in fact exist? And how might these fresh potential contributors be motivated to contribute to a relatively obscure political campaign in Indiana?

Over a period of months, the idea of organizing a special committee to solicit funds had been discussed. Brademas was in sporadic contact with friends to seek advice concerning potential contributors and how to reach them. However, with the press of other business, final decisions on how to organize this special appeal had been deferred. In May, Brademas met in New York with Francis Keppel and Peter H. Gillingham. Keppel, chairman of the board and president of the General Learning Corporation, was one of the most distinguished names in American education: youthful dean of Harvard's Graduate School of Education (1948-62) and U.S. commissioner of education (1962-65). Gillingham, an executive at the Education and World Affairs foundation in New York, had served as staff director of the Special House Committee Task Force on International Education which Brademas had chaired in 1966. They agreed on a general strategy: a dozen or so persons would be recruited as solicitors, who, in turn, would send personalized letters and a brochure to potential contributors whom they felt they could contact personally. Brademas lined up the solicitors, for the most part friends who were strongly identified with education policy. In addition to Keppel, they included, among others: Stephen K. Bailey, dean of the Maxwell School of Citizenship and Public Affairs, Syracuse University; Douglass Cater, special assistant to the president of the United States (specializing in education policy); Allan Cartter, chancellor and executive vice president, New York University; Charles U. Daly, vice president for development and public affairs, University of Chicago, a former Kennedy administration official; and Samuel Halperin, deputy assistant secretary for legislation, HEW.

Brademas and his advisers had discussed for some time how a national committee might be organized. Not until early August, however, was a name selected—"National Friends of John Brademas"— and membership on the executive committee decided upon. Two of the "solicitors" were designated as members of the Executive Committee: Francis Keppel, who served as chairman, and Stephen K. Bailey. In addition to those two, there were sixteen other committee members, including two prominent South Bend businessmen. Members of the Executive Committee and their positions at the time were: William Benton, chairman of the board, Encyclopaedia Britannica and former U.S. senator from Connecticut; Edward E. Booher, president, McGraw-Hill Book Company, Inc.; Paul H. Douglas, former U.S. senator from Illinois; J. Wayne Fredericks, a foundation executive and former Department of State official; J. Kenneth Galbraith, professor of economics, Harvard University, and former ambassador to India; Arthur J. Goldberg, U.S. representative to the United Nations, formerly secretary of labor and associate justice, U.S. Supreme Court; Richard G. Hatcher, mayor of Gary, Indiana; Walter W. Heller, professor of economics, University of Minnesota, former chairman, Council of Economic Advisers; Bert Liss, South Bend businessman and civic leader; George C. Lodge, lecturer, Harvard Business School, previously a federal official and in 1962 the Republican senatorial candidate from Massachusetts; Newton N. Minow, Chicago attorney (Adlai E. Stevenson's firm) and former chairman, Federal Communications Commission; Daniel P. Moynihan, director of the Harvard-M.I.T. Joint Center for Urban Studies, formerly a Labor Department official; George N. Shuster, assistant to the president, University of Notre Dame and former president of Hunter College, New York City; Adlai E. Stevenson III, Illinois state treasurer; Frank E. Sullivan, South Bend businessman and civic leader; and Marietta Tree, former U.S. representative to several United Nations agencies.

A special letterhead and brochure were designed for distribution exclusively outside the Third District; layout and copy emphasized that John Brademas was "A Congressman for the Nation." In September and October about 2,500 letters were sent to persons whose names had been suggested by solicitors or culled from various membership lists. The great bulk of these letters—about 1,800—were signed by Keppel; the remainder were signed by the various solicitors on the basis of their personal contacts. The appeal was cast chiefly in terms of Brademas's education ties:

For ten years, Congressman John Brademas of South Bend, Indiana, has been one of the ablest, most intelligent and effective members of the House of Representatives.

He has earned a reputation as a top authority in Congress on education. Indeed he has either sponsored or helped write nearly every major education bill enacted into law in the past several years.

You may know John Brademas because of his particular interest in higher education . . . .

Only a portion of these several thousand addresses were educators per se. However, most of the names were drawn from membership or board of director lists of elite organizations such as the Council on Foreign Relations, the Committee for Economic Development, the Institute for International Education, and numerous university and foundation boards. The assumption was that many of the persons solicited would at least recognize Brademas's name and, it was hoped, would be favorably impressed by the endorsement of the National Friends Committee.

A parallel endeavor was the mailing of a slightly different letter to Americans who had attended Oxford University. Brademas asked three friends, Rhodes Scholar classmates, to constitute "American Oxonians for Brademas." This committee consisted of John W. Dickey, attorney, Sullivan and Cromwell, New York City; James H. Billington, professor of history, Princeton University; and Lawrence C. McQuade, assistant secretary of commerce for domestic and international business. Because of poor training and the press of other campaign priorities, these letters were not mailed until October 23, a bare two weeks before the election.

Brademas's effort to raise money from a specialized constituency was not a unique congressional fund-raising technique; congressmen often receive campaign funds from trade associations, labor groups and other interests whose welfare is affected by the recipients' activity in Congress. But Brademas's attempt to mobilize an education constituency on a national basis was distinctive and perhaps unprecedented for a congressional campaign. As part of a total effort aimed at drawing support from educators and education-minded citizens, the National Friends campaign served reasonably well as a first effort, attracting contributions of about $5,000. More, doubtless, would have been raised if the National Friends' letters had been mailed earlier; nevertheless, the money constituted a helpful and welcome increment to the total campaign budget.

A Well-Timed Education Conference. Still another venture calculated to enhance Brademas's credentials as a public servant committed to education took the form of an education conference held at the University of Notre Dame on October 25-26, just days before the election. The conference was Brademas's idea: an event that would focus attention on policy questions in American education and, not coincidentally, on his own increasingly important role in federal education policy-making.

The conference, titled "Major Tensions in American Education: Shaping Policies for the '70's," was sponsored jointly by Brademas and the Department of Education at the University of Notre Dame. (His relationship with Notre Dame could best be described as symbiotic. As their "lobbyist" in Congress, he provided university scholars and administrators information about federal programs, helped to put federal agency officials in touch with university officials to facilitate grants, inserted in the *Congressional Record* an occasional article about the university or a speech by its dynamic president, the Reverend Theodore Hesburgh.) Several thousand invitations were mailed throughout northern Indiana to school administrators, teachers, university faculty and officials, guidance counselors, government and labor officials, and other community leaders. Brademas alone was responsible for securing commitments from the speakers, who included Francis Keppel, McGeorge Bundy (president of the Ford Foundation), Richard A. Graham (director of the teacher corps of the Office of Education), Paul W. Briggs (superintendent of the Cleveland schools), and Harold Howe II (U.S. commissioner of education).

With a line-up of national education luminaries, several hundred local educators and civic leaders were attracted to the conference. Brademas was careful not to use the conference as a partisan platform. He did not solicit kind remarks from the speakers, but each of them praised him warmly, some even extravagantly, in his opening remarks. (The speakers, after all, were political allies or personal friends of Brademas.) Ample coverage in Sunday's *South Bend Tribune* was given to the conference in general and, especially, to Brademas's key role in organizing it.

Recruiting Student Support in the Year of Disaffection. Early in the campaign, during the late spring and summer, it became clear to Brademas that he would need to mount the most extensive campaign of his career. A lot of manpower would be needed for anticipated projects: door-to-door canvassing, telephone "blitzes," stuffing envelopes, and so forth. Hence Brademas decided to harness as much student energy as possible for the campaign. The efforts of hundreds of student volunteers in the early McCarthy presidential primaries, especially New Hampshire, had dramatized the effectiveness of student campaigners. Student activism in the Indiana primary, both for McCarthy and Kennedy, dispelled any remaining skepticism regarding this potentially potent political resource.

But the Third District race was no glamour-filled, issue-packed presidential campaign. Could Brademas mobilize student support on his behalf? He was not a national figure (except perhaps among education's cognoscenti) and, though he related extremely well to students, he had neither the electrifying appeal of Robert Kennedy nor the White Knight image of Eugene McCarthy. And Brademas had opted against taking a strong, unequivocal position on the one issue that had galvanized student participation in the presidential race—the war in Vietnam. From opinion surveys of the Third District and discussions with his advisers and constituents, Brademas concluded that prudence required his avoidance of a "super-dove" label. Would his solid credentials as a liberal and his leadership role within the Democratic Study Group offset—for students—his "imperfect" position on the Vietnam War?

An extensive recruiting effort was launched during the summer months. Hundreds of letters were written to students who attended several of the colleges in the Third District—the University of Notre Dame, the South Bend Regional Campus of Indiana University, Saint Mary's College, Goshen College, and Bethel College. In some cases, the letter soliciting help was sent over the signature of Brademas himself, in others, over the signature of a student or student-faculty committee which Brademas had helped to establish. In some instances, the letter was sent to every student who attended a particular institution. In other cases, more selective appeals were mailed by Brademas to "probable sympathizers" identified from lists, where available, of Kennedy and McCarthy volunteers. For example:

Dear _____ :

I am taking the liberty of writing to you at the suggestion of a number of people who worked closely with Senator Robert F. Kennedy in the Indiana Presidential Primary. For the last week or so I have been getting in touch with leaders on college campuses in Northern Indiana who might be willing to help me this fall in what will probably be the toughest campaign I have ever faced.

To be specific, since early March of this year, my staff has been working on a registration and turnout strategy for the fall. I am pleased that Miss Gayle Stack, who was the office manager for the Kennedy Headquarters in the Primary, has joined this effort. The end product of this planning will be to define clearly the target population for the fall registration drive. . . .

As an example of a more generalized appeal, on August 22, 1968, several hundred letters were mailed from Washington to students who attended Indiana University at South Bend. In this letter, Brademas emphasized his connection with education, and concluded:

I am firmly convinced that the energies and abilities of college students in my campaign can be decisive in November. If you are willing to work for me this fall, please return the enclosed application to Professor James Conley, Department of Government, Indiana University Extension, South Bend, Indiana. Professor Conley is one of my campus organizers, and he will be responsible for organizing Indiana University Students for Brademas on the South Bend campus. We need to complete plans for a mass canvassing operation during the first few weeks of school.

Student leaders at the University of Notre Dame and Saint Mary's College, principally those who had been active in the McCarthy and Kennedy primary efforts in Indiana, signed letters similar to those sent by Brademas himself.

When students returned to their campuses in September, a series of organizational meetings were held to discuss techniques for recruiting students and to determine the most effective use of student help. Principal responsibility for recruiting was vested in one Brademas staffer, herself a very able graduate student on temporary leave from Princeton University's Woodrow Wilson School, and in several student contacts on each campus. Brademas headquarters provided mimeograph machines and telephones. Mimeographed notices and handouts distributed on campus underscored Brademas's role in education and entreated: "John Brademas needs your help."

In mid-September, an "All-Campus Rally" was organized to recruit a wider circle of college student support. The site was the South Bend Regional Campus of Indiana University. The featured speakers were Richard E. Neustadt—professor of government and director of the Institute of Politics, Harvard University, a man whose scholarship would be familiar to many college students—and Brademas himself. Professor Neusteadt flew from Boston to South Bend for this occasion. Following Neustadt's warm introductory remarks, Brademas spoke informally and then responded at length to student questions. The turnout of several hundred students was mildly disappointing, especially in view of the proliferation of publicity on the local campuses. Even so, if any significant proportion of these students could be enlisted as campaign volunteers, something very useful would have been accomplished.

The campaign seemed to be working; several highly favorable

columns appeared in the University of Notre Dame's daily paper, *The Observer*. Then, on October 16, that paper ran a long editorial entitled "The Essential Brademas," which concluded by urging students to "devote a few hours of your time in helping this man who symbolizes the hopes and aspirations of many of us. We urge that you vote for him and moreover that you work for him. He needs student help."

The recruiting campaign intensified. Meetings were held almost daily either at Brademas's headquarters or on the various campuses. Brademas's staffers worked hard to inspire hard-core enthusiasts to spread the word on their respective campuses. A recruiting campaign was mounted through the student press. Two advertisements underscoring Brademas's credentials as a liberal were placed in *The Observer*, both paid for by the contributions of Notre Dame Faculty Friends of John Brademas. The first, a full-page ad with 108 faculty names listed at the bottom of the page, borrowed for a headline the title of the *Look* article that had appeared three days before: "John Brademas: A Liberal Fights for Survival." Aimed at potential volunteers, the advertisements featured letters from Senator Eugene McCarthy and Senator Edward M. Kennedy (D., Mass.) urging support of Brademas. A subsequent, smaller advertisement featured one-sentence endorsements from the *New York Times*, the *New Republic*, McCarthy, Kennedy, and *Look*.

The results of these extensive efforts were less than overwhelming. College students did report to Brademas's headquarters in small clusters for stamp-licking and similar tasks. More often than not, though, the students who turned up at headquarters were more disposed to help formulate global strategies than to stuff envelopes. Ultimately, most of the necessary menial work was performed by women volunteers (especially the Notre Dame faculty wives), or, on occasion, by high school students.

The most effective potential use of college students, as seen by the Brademas staff, was door-to-door canvassing. A computer had been used to help identify key precincts. The staff's strategy was to mount "blitz" canvassing campaigns for as many as possible of the last six or seven weekends prior to the election. Unfortunately for the campaign, Notre Dame played three of its first four football games at home; on those Saturdays, any activity not involving the "Fighting Irish" was doomed. However, in the closing weeks of the campaign small groups of college students did cover a lot of territory. Whereas the staff at one time had hoped to recruit fifty to a hundred college students for an afternoon's canvassing activity, the actual turnout on any one weekend afternoon turned out to be closer to ten or fifteen students. As it developed, fifteen collegians, joined by an equal number of adults and high school students, could effectively cover a number of key precincts in an afternoon.

A final dividend of the recruiting efforts was student assistance in a telephone blitz operation. With seven days of the campaign to go, a bank of thirty telephones was installed in rented office space. Most of the telephones were operated by college students, some of them volunteers, others receiving a nominal hourly wage. A Notre Dame graduate student worked as a volunteer for five straight days and evenings overseeing and coordinating the operation. Calls were placed to all residents in high priority precincts and townships. Telephoning from 10:00 a.m. to 10:00 p.m., these workers dialed nearly 40,000 homes in the closing days of the campaign.

On balance, then, local students did make a significant contribution to the outcome of the campaign. The actual impact, of course, could not be measured. In one respect, perhaps the most important product of student activity was the image that their enthusiasm projected. In a national campaign notable for widespread student disaffection, residents of the Third District were made aware of student efforts on behalf of Brademas. Some adult voters may have appreciated the fact that, not unlike Senators Kennedy and McCarthy, Brademas had been able to inspire the confidence and support of at least some of America's young people.

National Mass Media Endorsements. In the closing days of the campaign, Brademas received an unusual degree of attention from the national press, typically focusing on his contribution as an education-minded legislator. The three-page article in *Look* cited previously—"Congressman John Brademas: A Liberal Fights for Survival"— hit the newsstands on October 15. The author, a *Look* senior editor, described Brademas as " 'Mr. Education' in the U.S. Congress." An editorial in the same issue of *Look* endorsed Brademas's bid for reelection: "The House of Representatives needs . . . more Democrats like John Brademas of Indiana. . . ." In a November 1 editorial, *Life,* which supported Nixon for president, singled out eight House incumbents and nine candidates for the Senate and encouraged its readers to vote for them. Brademas was one of three Democratic representatives so anointed:

In Indiana, the conservative trend, plus redistricting, threatens to unseat one of the House's most intelligent and effective Democrats, John Brademas, an experienced specialist in education. We hope Brademas makes it.

Brademas also received the endorsements of the *New York Times* (October 23, 1968) and the *New Republic* (October 26, 1968).

The Election Outcome

As election day, November 5, grew nearer, Brademas's campaign staff was wary. On the one hand, there was no solid evidence that Brademas was in fact trailing his opponent. On the other hand, there were a number of imponderables whose impact could not easily be measured. Nixon would carry Indiana big, that seemed certain. But how strong would his coattails be? George Wallace would siphon off a sizable number of votes. But how many Wallace-voting Democrats, disaffected with the Democratic presidential ticket, would split their ballot to vote for John Brademas? His opponent had campaigned vigorously for months, conducting a clean, aggressive campaign. Had he shaken enough hands and identified Brademas closely enough with "the mess in Washington" and East Coast liberalism to attract many swing votes? Brademas, thinking himself to be the front-runner with more to lose than to gain by appearing on the same platform as Erwin, had consistently refused to debate his opponent directly. Erwin had pounded away at Brademas for his reluctance to meet head-on. Had Brademas's strategy alienated the electorate?

The *South Bend Tribune* summed it up, somewhat melodramatically, two days before the election:

U.S. Rep. John Brademas ... will be struggling for his political life Tuesday. Despite enough woes to bring tears to a stone statue of Andrew Jackson or any other Democratic patriarch, Brademas appears to hold a precarious lead in his race for a sixth term in Congress.

A short while after the polls closed, the returns began to flow in. The first returns that night were from South Bend and St. Joseph County—Brademas's usual bastion of strength—and they were reassuring. He was off to an early lead. Significantly, Erwin's edge in key Republican precincts in South Bend was not cutting deeply into Brademas's big leads in predominantly Democratic precincts; it looked as though a lot of ticket-splitting had taken place, the sine qua non for a Brademas win. Indeed, Brademas's plurality in St. Joseph County kept mounting until it reached 20,000, a margin that simply could not be overcome by Erwin in the remaining three counties of the district. By ten o'clock that night the outcome was clear, and a weary, but beaming Brademas made the rounds of several of the television studios in the district to be interviewed, then returned to his campaign headquarters to the cheers of his supporters. Later results that evening and the next morning showed that Brademas had lost each of the other three counties; in one, Kosciusko, he barely managed 30 percent of the vote—a whopping net loss of almost 8,000 votes. Brademas held the loss in Elkhart County to a 3,600-vote deficit, and in much smaller Marshall County to 1,650 votes. In all, Brademas was reelected to a sixth term by a close vote of 94,452 to 86,354 (52.2 percent). In contrast to Brademas's 8,100 vote margin, Nixon carried the Third District handily—by 21,000 votes—and swept to a victory in Indiana with a 261,000 lead, his greatest plurality in any state. In the three-way presidential race, Nixon received 50.3 percent of the Indiana vote and Humphrey only 38.0 percent, with Wallace drawing 11.4 percent. (Nixon, it should be recalled, got but 43.4 percent of the national popular vote in 1968; Humphrey's share was 42.7 percent and Wallace's 13.5.) In the Third District, Nixon got 50.6 percent, Humphrey 39.2 percent—in contrast, as noted above to Brademas's 52.2 percent—and Wallace's 10.2 percent.

Indiana Democrats lost one of their five House seats. The Republicans regained the statehouse with a clean sweep of all state offices. Senator Birch Bayh barely survived a stiff challenge, receiving 51.8 percent of the vote.

Given these circumstances, Brademas's victory was clearly one he had in good part earned by his own strength. The *South Bend Tribune* was justified in terming his reelection "the most impressive win of his political career."

Concluding Observations

To what extent did Brademas's efforts to mobilize the "education community" on his behalf pay off? Although the answer will never be known with any precision, speculation about the "cost-effectiveness" of this particular dimension of the campaign is possible.

With respect to the national education interest groups, the award presented by the National Education Association attracted some favorable attention from the local media. Of greater importance, however, was the support of national AFT headquarters which prompted the canvassing activity of a score of South Bend teachers. This participation yielded over one hundred manhours of work in the field, ringing doorbells and talking to voters in "swing" precincts. Brademas's efforts to energize this particular interest group was minimal; the local impact of their efforts surely was helpful. Apart from the canvassing assistance provided by these activist members of the South Bend Federation of Teachers, the rather extensive efforts by Brademas to recruit volunteers and solicit contributions from among several thousand elementary and secondary school teachers in the Third District went virtually for naught.

Brademas did not expend much energy in contacting a handful of educator friends in the Executive branch. He placed telephone calls to several and hosted a few brief meetings. These efforts yielded the names of potential contributors, a few of whom he subsequently contacted personally. In addition, these friends sent out about a hundred letters soliciting contributions for Brademas. The payoff was minor in terms of money contributed to the campaign, but so, too, was the amount of time Brademas had to invest. On balance, then, a successful effort.

At the college level, a handful of faculty—and especially a few wives—contributed their time generously. In fact, campaign headquarters would have been substantially less productive without the consistent and effective work of three or four faculty wives. But, again, to the extent that Brademas's staff once envisioned squads of professors turning out the vote and "turning on" their students, the ultimate results were disappointing. Perhaps the staff should have concentrated in the beginning on trying to develop a small nucleus of enthusiasts on each college campus to function with more autonomy rather than trying to oversee the operation from headquarters. In sum, local college and university educators may well have voted for Brademas, and several hundred of them did contribute a few dollars each to sponsor several newspaper advertisements. Quite clearly, however, the education community in the Third District did not rise as one to demand that "Mr. Education in Congress" be returned to Washington.

The energies devoted to recruiting college students absorbed a great deal of staff time. The output was far from negligible. College volunteers rang many doorbells and dialed thousands of telephones throughout the district. But whether the staff time invested in recruiting and deploying college students was worth the results could be argued either way. A more modest effort was made to recruit high school students. Their assistance proved very valuable to the Brademas campaign. High school volunteers stamped and stuffed many an envelope and called at many a door. High school students had proven their value during the Kennedy and McCarthy primary races in Indiana. In retrospect, perhaps the Brademas staff should have given more attention to recruiting high school volunteers.

Finally, there was the effort to raise funds from a national educational constituency if, indeed, one existed. Many of the contributions raised through the National Friends of John Brademas were no doubt made in response to the interest in education demonstrated by Brademas and the National Friends Committee. The financial gleanings, at least in 1968, were rather thin.

On balance, then, the efforts made to harness educators at the local and national levels yielded visible but modest results. A cost-benefit analysis might well indicate that Brademas should have invested much of that campaign energy in ways other than those calculated to win minds, money, and manpower from within the education community. At the same time, the expected closeness of the election outcome would seem to have justified Brademas's every effort to mobilize his natural allies.

Postscript

John Brademas was returned to Congress in 1970 for his seventh term by 57.5 percent of the district vote; beset by fewer complications than had confronted him in 1968, he won by 23,000 votes. In 1972, he found his political career threatened for the third time in twelve years by a formidable Nixon presidential campaign in Indiana. Indeed, President Nixon swept the state by a two-to-one ratio (a 700,000 vote plurality), carrying the Third District by a whopping 48,000 votes (compared to 21,000 in 1968). Brademas campaigned with ferocious energy, bolstered this time by another, more favorable, redistricting, and won an eighth House term by 23,000 votes (55 percent). It was, according to the *South Bend Tribune,* a "remarkable personal triumph."

Meanwhile, the National Friends of John Brademas has expanded its fund-raising activities and has been more successful than the initial, hurried effort. Wilbur Cohen, dean of the School of Education at the University of Michigan and former HEW secretary, succeeded Francis Keppel as chairman for the 1972 campaign. Keppel, who invested a considerable amount of his time as chairman through two campaigns, remains as vice-chairman; other "glamor" names have been added to the committee.

John Brademas's congressional career has prospered. In 1969, he became chairman of the House Select Subcommittee on Education. Gradually expanding its jurisdiction, he has led the subcommittee to produce many bills that have been enacted into law, most notably the milestone legislation in 1972 to create a National Institute of Education. Also in 1972 he was appointed by the Speaker of the House to serve as a member of the President's National Commission on the Financing of Postsecondary Education. Of special importance, in January 1971 when the Democrats organized the 92nd Congress, Brademas was named to a new House leadership post as one of two deputy whips for the majority, the youngest member of the leadership team.

Following the 1972 election, Brademas's leadership responsibilities within the Democratic Party continued to expand. He was named chief deputy whip in the House and became a member of the newly-formed House Democratic Steering and Policy Committee.

Brademas's "extracurricular" education activities have grown apace. In 1969 he was elected to a six-year term on Harvard's Board of Overseers (its senior governing board) and was selected a Fellow of the prestigious American Academy of Arts and Sciences. Other honors and national education awards have accumulated, including election to the national Senate of Phi Beta Kappa.

Now a fifteen-year veteran of Congress and fifth most senior Democrat on the House Education and Labor Committee, John Brademas, a vigorous forty-six, will be an increasingly influential force in American education for years to come.

Some Larger Questions

John Brademas's 1968 campaign raises some basic questions about American national politics and education policy-making. In Brademas's political life, the challenge of serving two very different constituencies—Indiana's Third District and educators across the land—looms ever large, illustrating a debate in progress since the inception of the American nation: Should our national representatives function in Congress primarily as independent trustees (mindful of Edmund Burke's injunction to vote one's conscience), or should they assume more the role of their constituents' delegates, intent on reflecting as perfectly as possible their constituency's preferences? Of course, no simple answer exists; some balancing of these interests, when they clash, is inevitable. While John Brademas enjoys a great deal of latitude in Congress and increasing influence in shaping national policy, he knows that to secure that freedom—to be returned to Congress every two years—he and other congressmen from tough, marginal districts must pay incessant attention to the needs of their constituents. Brademas must never let up in the constant—and fatiguing—campaign for reelection. We must inquire: Do the continual pressures on marginal-district House members to campaign distort or enhance the democratic process? Would a four-year term for U.S. representatives make more sense? Would less pressure to campaign better serve the needs of American education?

The Brademas campaign raises a number of other questions concerning the relationship between politicians and interest groups. Was his interaction with his "special interest constituency" of education-minded citizens typical of the way other national legislators seek the assistance of interest groups? Was there any compromise of integrity by either politician or lobbyists? We must also note that the education lobby represents a predominantly nonprofit, service-oriented sector of society (with relatively little money available for lobbying purposes), while many other congressmen have similarly strong ties with more affluent profit-oriented constituencies (bankers, home-builders, defense suppliers, cotton growers, oil producers, bulk-rate mailers, and so forth). Is this distinction significant? Finally, does the pluralistic nature of American education preclude cohesive, effective lobbying efforts in Washington on behalf of education interests?

On reflection, the reader should find that the issues raised by these questions about political campaigning lie very close to the heart of the American democracy and impinge directly on the way in which education policy is formed in Washington.